ALL · IN · ONE

aPHR®

Associate Professional in Human Resources Certification

EXAM GUIDE

Second Edition

Christina Nishiyama, SPHR, SHRM-CP
Dory Willer, SPHR, SHRM-SCP
William H. Truesdell, SPHR, SHRM-SCP
William D. Kelly, SPHR-CA, SHRM-SCP

New York   Chicago   San Francisco
Athens   London   Madrid   Mexico City
Milan   New Delhi   Singapore   Sydney   Toronto

McGraw Hill books are available at special quantity discounts to use as premiums and sales promotions, or for use in corporate training programs. To contact a representative, please visit the Contact Us pages at www.mhprofessional.com.

aPHR® Associate Professional in Human Resources Certification All-in-One Exam Guide, Second Edition

1 2 3 4 5 6 7 8 9   LCR   26 25 24 23 22

Library of Congress Control Number: 2021951879

ISBN   978-1-264-28625-6
MHID   1-264-28625-2

Sponsoring Editor	**Technical Editor**	**Production Supervisor**
Wendy Rinaldi	Larry Bienati	Thomas Somers
Editorial Supervisor	**Copy Editor**	**Composition**
Patty Mon	Bart Reed	KnowledgeWorks Global Ltd.
Project Manager	**Proofreader**	**Illustration**
Tasneem Kauser,	Paul Tyler	KnowledgeWorks Global Ltd.
KnowledgeWorks Global Ltd.	**Indexer**	**Art Director, Cover**
Acquisitions Coordinator	Ted Laux	Jeff Weeks
Caitlin Cromley-Linn		

To all HR professionals who constantly strive to do better. This book is dedicated to all the new human resource management professionals who are entering our field of special skills. We need new talent. Whether you are in HR for your entire career or on a rotational assignment, we welcome you and want you to know how important your role is going to be for your organization.

—*The authors*

To Steve, Malea, and Siena for your love and encouragement. To my parents for being lifelong examples of what it means to have the "heart" of an HR person.

—*Christina Nishiyama*

I dedicate this book to my first HR boss, the late John Sharkey, who guided me to the career path of human resources, becoming my mentor and inspiring me to do well as an HR professional. He has left a great legacy for the profession.

—*Dory Willer*

My efforts are dedicated to the HR professionals who will find excitement and confidence in the process of gaining professional certification. Congratulations on your achievement.

—*Bill Truesdell*

I dedicate this book with love to my wife, Cheryl. Through days and nights, thick and thin, and months that have grown into years, you are always there—sometimes for support, sometimes for your knowledge and insights, sometimes to push, and sometimes just to be together. You are my rock. I love you!

—*Bill Kelly*

ABOUT THE AUTHORS

Christina Nishiyama has over 15 years of human resource and organizational development experience, as well as a history of leadership in project management, finance, and information technology. Christina received her bachelor's degree from the University of California, San Diego and her MBA from San Diego State University. She also holds her SPHR and SHRM-CP certifications and is currently pursuing her Ph.D. in learning sciences with a focus on group dynamics in technology settings. She has served on SHRM's National Young Professionals Advisory Board and as Board Chair of Southern Nevada SHRM Young Professionals. Christina is also the co-author of the *PHR/SPHR Professional in Human Resources Certification Exam Guide, Second Edition* and has published research in the academic journal *Innovations in Education and Teaching International*. Christina currently serves as vice president at Bienati Consulting Group, where she works with clients across the nation on human resource and organizational development projects. She also currently serves as an instructor in the Human Resource Certificate Program at the University of Nevada, Las Vegas. Prior to consulting and teaching, Christina served as director of human resources at MGM Resorts International where she managed the HR strategic plan and the project management office as well as ran HR operations at Vdara Hotel and Spa during her tenure. Prior to her role at MGM, she served as the director of human resources and finance for The Mob Museum, overseeing the human resources, finance, information technology, and volunteer operations.

Dory Willer is a certified executive coach with more than 30 years of experience as a senior HR executive, keynote speaker, and strategic planning facilitator. She has broad and diverse experience working for blue-chip and Fortune 100 companies, leaving her last corporate position as a vice president of HR to open Beacon Quest Coaching based in the San Francisco Bay Area. Willer coaches senior and C-suite executives in leadership enhancement, performance improvement, and career renewal, helping her clients to thrive in life and careers. Additionally, she facilitates strategic planning sessions that stretch paradigms, align behaviors with goals, and hold groups accountable to produce results. She was among the first graduating classes from Stanford's Executive HR Certification Program (Graduate School of Business 1994). Willer achieved the designation of SPHR more than 25 years ago. She holds a B.S. degree in behavioral science from the University of San Francisco and several advanced certifications in executive coaching.

William H. Truesdell is now retired. For 34 years he was president of The Management Advantage, Inc., a personnel management consulting firm. He spent more than 20 years in management with American Telephone and Telegraph, part of that in HR and operations. Truesdell is an expert on the subjects of personnel practices, employee handbooks, equal opportunity, and performance management programs. He is past president of the Northern California Employment Round Table and former HR course instructor at the University of California – Berkeley extension program. Truesdell holds the SPHR certification, the SHRM-SCP certification, and a B.S. in business administration from California State University – Fresno.

William D. Kelly is the owner of Kelly HR, an HR consulting services firm specializing in providing generalist HR consulting services and support for small business enterprises. Bill's experience includes more than 40 years of professional-level HR responsibilities, including 22 years at Bechtel in San Francisco and, later, at Brown and Caldwell Environmental Engineers in Pleasant Hill, California. His credentials include experience in employee relations, state and federal legal compliance, staffing and recruitment, equal employment opportunity and affirmative action, compensation, benefits, training and development, health and safety, and government contract management. Bill also has 20 years of experience in HR consulting that includes providing HR services, support, and advice to a wide range of Northern California clients. He has 17 years of experience as an instructor for the University of California extension program teaching such courses as Management of Human Resources; Recruiting, Selection, and Placement; California Employment Law; and Professional HR Certification Preparation. Bill has taught the Professional PHR/SPHR Certification Preparation Course for more than 17 years, SHRM's recently introduced SHRM-CP and SHRM-SCP Certification Preparation Course, and the California HR Certification Preparation Course for 8 years for the Society for Human Resource Management (SHRM) and the Northern California HR Association (NCHRA). He played a key role in the development of California's HR certification credential; he was also the project manager for the team of California HR professionals who developed SHRM's first California Learning System in support of California certification. Bill's professional leadership also includes roles on the board of directors and as national vice president for the SHRM, the board of directors and president for the HR Certification Institute (HRCI), state director for the California State Council of SHRM, the board of directors and president for the NCHRA, and commissioner and chair for the Marin County Personnel Commission. Bill received his B.S. in political science from Spring Hill College in Mobile, Alabama, and undertook post-graduate studies in organizational management at the College of William and Mary in Williamsburg, Virginia, and the University of Virginia in Richmond, Virginia. Prior to HR, Bill had a military career, achieving the rank of major in the United States Army with tours of duty in the United States, Germany, Thailand, and Vietnam.

About the Technical Editor

Dr. Larry Bienati has over 35 years of senior-level human resources experience in various organizational settings in the areas of retail, engineering, medical devices, and healthcare. As a consultant to management for over 30 years, he represents many well-known organizations in the public, private, and not-for-profit sectors. Among his many service offerings, his focus is in the areas of strategy, succession planning systems, leadership development, human resources mentoring, all process areas of HR-OD, and guiding organizations through transformational change efforts. Dr. Bienati holds a B.S. in industrial relations and personnel administration and an MBA in management sciences from California State University. He also holds a Ph.D. in business administration from Golden Gate University with an emphasis in the area of human resources management in his doctoral achievements. He has achieved lifetime certification as a Senior Professional in Human Resources (SPHR) for his early work in HR and teaching in various PHR/SPHR certification programs at UC Berkeley. He also is a Certified Compensation Professional (CCP), has the SHRM-SCP designation, and is a certified mediator handling complex employee/labor relations issues. He spent 15 years as core faculty for accelerated undergraduate and graduate degree programs at Saint Mary's College of California. Additionally, he taught many HR, OD, OB, and strategy courses in the EMBA programs at CSU, Sacramento and the MS in Engineering Management Program at CSU, Maritime Academy over the past 15 years. Currently, he is also an Associate Professor in the MHA and PsyD programs at California Northstate University.

CONTENTS AT A GLANCE

Part I   The Human Resource Profession

Chapter 1   Human Resource Certification 3

Chapter 2   U.S. Laws and Regulations 19

Part II   aPHR Body of Knowledge Functional Areas

Chapter 3   Talent Acquisition 79

Chapter 4   Learning and Development 121

Chapter 5   Compensation and Benefits 155

Chapter 6   Employee Relations 203

Chapter 7   Compliance and Risk Management 251

Chapter 8   Early HR Career–Level Tasks 281

Part III   Appendixes and Glossary

Appendix A   List of Common HR Acronyms 307

Appendix B   Case Laws by Chapter 329

Appendix C   For Additional Study 341

Appendix D   About the Online Content 345

   Glossary 349

   Index 391

CONTENTS

Acknowledgments xxi
Introduction xxiii

Part I The Human Resource Profession   1

Chapter 1 Human Resource Certification   3
Professional Certifications   3
HR Certification Organizations   3
   The HR Certification Institute (HRCI)   4
   The Society for Human Resource Management (SHRM) . . .   8
   The International Public Management Association
      for Human Resources (IPMA-HR)   9
Benefits of Certification 10
The aPHR Exam 11
   The Significance of the HR Body of Knowledge 11
   The Test Development Process 14
   The Exam Experience 15
   The aPHR Registration Process 15
   Preparing for the Exam 16
   Exam Readiness 17
Chapter Review 17
Endnotes 18

Chapter 2 U.S. Laws and Regulations 19
When You Have ONE or More Employees 19
   The Clayton Act (1914) 20
   The Consumer Credit Protection Act (1968) 20
   The Copeland "Anti-Kickback" Act (1934) 20
   The Copyright Act (1976) 20
   The Davis-Bacon Act (1931), as Amended in 2002 20
   The Dodd-Frank Wall Street Reform
      and Consumer Protection Act (2010) 21
   The Economic Growth and Tax Relief Reconciliation
      Act (EGTRRA) (2001) 21
   The Electronic Communications Privacy
      Act (ECPA) (1986) 21
   The Employee Polygraph Protection Act (1988) 22
   The Employee Retirement Income Security
      Act (ERISA) (1974) 22

The Equal Pay Act (an Amendment to the FLSA) (1963) ... 22
The FAA Modernization and Reform Act (2012) 22
The Fair and Accurate Credit Transactions
    Act (FACT) (2003) 23
The Fair Credit Reporting Act
    (FCRA) (1970), as Amended in 2011 23
The Fair Labor Standards Act (FLSA) (1938) 23
The Foreign Corrupt Practices Act (FCPA) (1977) 26
The Health Information Technology for Economic
    and Clinical Health (HITECH) Act (2009) 27
The Health Insurance Portability and Accountability
    Act (HIPAA) (1996) 27
The Immigration and Nationality Act (INA) (1952) 27
The Immigration Reform and Control Act (IRCA) (1986) ... 28
The IRS Intermediate Sanctions (2002) 28
The Labor-Management Relations Act
    (LMRA; Taft-Hartley Act) (1947) 28
The Labor-Management Reporting and Disclosure Act
    (Landrum-Griffin Act) (1959) 28
The Mine Safety and Health Act (1977) 29
The National Industrial Recovery Act (1933) 30
The National Labor Relations Act
    (NLRA; Wagner Act) (1935) 30
The Needlestick Safety and Prevention Act (2000) 30
The Norris-LaGuardia Act (NLRA) (1932) 31
The Occupational Safety and Health Act (OSHA) (1970) ... 31
The Omnibus Budget Reconciliation Act (OBRA) (1993) ... 34
The Pension Protection Act (PPA) (2006) 34
The Personal Responsibility and Work Opportunity
    Reconciliation Act (1996) 34
The Portal-to-Portal Act (1947) 35
The Railway Labor Act (1926) 35
The Rehabilitation Act (1973) 35
The Retirement Equity Act (REA) (1984) 36
The Revenue Act (1978) 36
The Sarbanes-Oxley Act (SOX) (2002) 36
The Securities and Exchange Act (1934) 37
The Service Contract Act (1965) 38
The Sherman Anti-Trust Act (1890) 38
The Small Business Job Protection Act (1996) 38
The Social Security Act (1935) 39
The Tax Reform Act (1986) 39
The Taxpayer Relief Act (1997) 40
The Trademark Act (1946) 40

The Unemployment Compensation Amendments
(UCA) (1992)   40
The Uniformed Services Employment
and Reemployment Rights Act (USERRA) (1994)   40
The Vietnam Era Veterans Readjustment Assistance Act (1974),
as Amended by the Jobs for Veterans Act (2002)   41
The Wagner-Peyser Act (1933), as Amended by
the Workforce Innovation and Opportunity Act (2014) . . .   41
The Walsh-Healey Act (Public Contracts Act) (1936)   42
The Work Opportunity Tax Credit (WOTC) (1996)   42
Whistleblowing   43
For FIFTEEN or More Employees   44
The Americans with Disabilities Act (ADA) (1990),
as Amended by the Americans with Disabilities Act
Amendments Act (ADAAA) (2008)   44
The Civil Rights Act (Title VII) (1964)   48
The Civil Rights Act (1991)   49
The Drug-Free Workplace Act (1988)   49
The Equal Employment Opportunity Act (EEOA) (1972) . . .   51
The Genetic Information Nondiscrimination
Act (GINA) (2008)   51
Guidelines on Discrimination Because of Sex (1980)   51
The Lilly Ledbetter Fair Pay Act (2009)   51
The Pregnancy Discrimination Act (1978)   52
The Uniform Guidelines on Employee
Selection Procedures (1978)   52
For TWENTY or More Employees   52
The Age Discrimination in Employment Act (ADEA) (1967),
as Amended   53
The American Recovery and Reinvestment
Act (ARRA) (2009)   53
The Consolidated Omnibus Budget Reconciliation
Act (COBRA) (1986)   53
The Older Workers Benefit Protection
Act (OWBPA) (1990)   54
For FIFTY or More Employees   54
Executive Order 11246: Affirmative Action (1965)   54
The Family and Medical Leave Act (FMLA) (1993),
Expanded 2008, 2010   55
The Mental Health Parity Act (MHPA) (1996)   56
The Mental Health Parity and Addiction Equity
Act (MHPAEA) (2008)   56
The National Defense Authorization
Act (2008), Expanded in 2010   56

The Patient Protection and Affordable Care
Act (PPACA) (2010) 57
Executive Order 13706: Paid Sick Leave
for Federal Contractors (2015) 57
For ONE HUNDRED or More Employees 57
The Worker Adjustment and Retraining Notification
(WARN) Act (1988) 57
For Federal Government Employees 59
The Civil Service Reform Act (1978) 59
The Congressional Accountability Act (1995) 59
The False Claims Act (1863) 60
The Homeland Security Act (2002) 60
The Privacy Act (1974) 60
The USA PATRIOT Act (2001) 61
Employment Visas for Foreign Nationals 61
E Nonimmigrant Visas 61
H Visas 62
L-1 Intracompany Transferee 63
O-1 Alien of Extraordinary Ability in Arts, Science,
Education, Business, Athletics 63
P Visa Categories 63
EB Employment-Based Visas 64
Chapter Review 64
Questions 65
Answers 72
Endnotes 75

Part II   aPHR Body of Knowledge Functional Areas

Chapter 3   Talent Acquisition 79
Knowledge of 79
Laws and Regulations 80
Federal Laws 80
Workforce Planning 81
Forecasting Staffing Needs 81
Job Analysis 82
Job Descriptions and Job Specifications 83
Alternative Staffing Practices 85
Phased Retirement 86
Contractor Payrolling 87
Employee Leasing and Professional
Employer Organizations (PEOs) 87
Outsourcing and Managed Service Providers (MSPs) 87
Temp-to-Lease Programs 87
Rehires and Transfers 88

Talent Sourcing 88
  Internal Recruitment 88
  External Recruitment 89
  Applicant Databases 94
  Records Retention 95
  Résumés vs. Job Applications 97
  Self-Identification 99
  Pre-employment Skill Testing 101
Interviewing Techniques 101
  Types of Interviews 101
  Interviewing Skills and Techniques 103
  Interviewing Bias 105
After the Interview 106
  Job Offers 106
  Background Checks 107
  Medical Examinations 108
Onboarding 109
  Administrative Paperwork 109
  Onboarding for Retention 111
Return on Investment 112
  Some Ways to Measure Hiring 112
Chapter Review 113
  Questions 113
  Answers 118
Endnotes 119

Chapter 4   Learning and Development 121
  Knowledge of 121
Laws and Regulations 122
HR's Role in Training and Development 123
  Organizational Values 123
  Setting Expectations in Orientation 124
Instructional Design 125
  Learning Objectives 125
  ADDIE Model 127
  Teacher-Centered Approaches 128
  Learner-Centered Approaches 128
  Chunking 129
  Learning Curves 129
Training Delivery Format 131
  Classroom 132
  E-Learning 133
  On-the-Job Training (OJT) 135
Techniques to Evaluate Training Programs 136
  Participant Surveys and Questionnaires 138
  Pre- and Post-Testing 138

Measuring Behavior: After-Action Review 138
Return on Investment 139
Tracking and Reporting 140
Career Development Practices 140
Succession Planning 141
Career Pathing 143
Dual-Ladder Careers 143
Career Counseling 144
Change Management 145
Popular Theories 145
Chapter Review 147
Questions 147
Answers 152
Endnotes 153

Chapter 5 Compensation and Benefits 155
Knowledge of 155
Laws and Regulations 156
The Employee Retirement Income Security Act (ERISA) . . . 157
Fair Labor Standards Act (FLSA) (1938), as Amended 157
Health Insurance Portability and Accountability
Act (HIPAA) 157
Social Security Act 158
The Uniformed Services Employment
and Reemployment Rights Act (USERRA) 158
Consolidated Omnibus Budget Reconciliation
Act (COBRA) 158
Family and Medical Leave Act (FMLA) 158
Patient Protection and Affordable Care Act (PPACA) 158
Total Rewards 159
Secrecy or Transparency? 160
Job Evaluation 160
Job Evaluation Methods 161
Pricing and Pay Rates 165
Pay Grades and Ranges 166
Variations in Pay: Red and Green Circle Rates 168
Base Pay Systems 168
Single or Flat-Rate System 169
Time-Based Step Rate Systems 169
Performance-Based Merit Pay System 170
Productivity-Based Systems 170
Straight Piece-Rate System 171
Differential Piece-Rate System 171

Person-Based Systems 171
   Knowledge-Based System 171
   Skill-Based System 171
   Competency-Based System 171
Financial Incentives 171
   Differential Pay 172
   Overtime Pay 172
   Hazard Pay 172
   Shift Pay 172
   Reporting Time Pay 172
   On-Call Pay 173
   Callback Pay 173
   Geographic Differentials 173
   Weekend and Holiday Pay 173
   Team and Group Incentives 173
Organization-Based Pay 174
   Profit Sharing 174
   Gainsharing 174
Payroll 174
   Payroll Administration 175
   Payroll Systems 176
   Wage Statements 176
Employee Benefits 177
   Government-Mandated Benefits 177
Healthcare Benefits 179
   Health Benefits Eligibility 179
   Health Benefits Enrollment 179
   Healthcare Plan Designs 180
   Prescription Drug Plans 183
   Dental Plans 184
   Vision Care Plans 184
   Healthcare Costs 184
Common Benefits Provided to Employees 185
   Disability Benefits 185
   Life Insurance 185
   Long-Term Care (LTC) Insurance 186
   Employee Assistance Programs (EAPs) 186
   Retirement Plans 186
   Supplemental Unemployment Benefits (SUBs) 187
   Paid Leaves 187
Supplemental Benefits 190
   Tuition Reimbursement 190
   Paid Volunteer Time 190
   Workplace Amenities 190

Employee Recognition Programs	. . . .	190
Childcare Services	. . . .	191
Elder Care	. . . .	191
Commuter Assistance	. . . .	191
Prepaid Legal Insurance	. . . .	191
Gym Membership	. . . .	192
Housing or Relocation Assistance	. . . .	192
Travel Stipends	. . . .	192
Legal Compliance	. . . .	192
Taxable and Nontaxable Benefits	. . . .	192
Communication Required by Law	. . . .	193
Benefits Communication	. . . .	194
Total Rewards Statements	. . . .	194
Communicating Through Employee Self-Service		
(ESS) Technologies	. . . .	194
Chapter Review	. . . .	195
Questions	. . . .	196
Answers	. . . .	199
Endnotes	. . . .	202
Chapter 6	Employee Relations	203
	Knowledge of	203
	Laws and Regulations	204
	State Laws	204
	Federal Regulations	204
	Rights and Responsibilities	205
	Employer	206
	Employee	206
	Organizational Strategy	206
	Mission	207
	Vision	207
	Values	207
	Goals and Objectives	207
	Strategic Planning	207
	Organizational Structure	208
	Organizational Communication	209
	Human Resource Information Systems (HRISs)	210
	Human Resource Policies	211
	Employee Handbook	211
	Employee Engagement Programs	213
	Recognition	213
	Work/Life Balance	214
	Alternative Work Arrangements	215
	Special Events	215

Employee Feedback 216
    Employee Surveys 216
    Processes for Obtaining Feedback 217
Diversity and Inclusion Programs 218
    Cultural Sensitivity and Acceptance 219
    Social Responsibility 219
    Measuring Diversity 222
Performance Management 222
    Performance Standards 223
    Performance Appraisal Methods 223
    Shortcomings of Performance Appraisals 226
    Performance Improvement Plan (PIP) 227
Workplace Behavior 227
    Attendance and Absenteeism 227
    Violation of Code of Conduct 228
    Employee Conflicts 230
    Workplace Harassment 230
Complaints and Grievances 233
    Methods of Investigation 233
Progressive Discipline 235
    Identifying Steps of Discipline 236
    Documenting Progressive Discipline 237
    When to Escalate Corrective Action 238
    Termination 239
Off-Boarding 240
    Payroll Processing: Final Paycheck 240
    Benefit Processing 241
    Documenting Reason for Separation 241
Chapter Review 242
    Questions 242
    Answers 247
Endnotes 249

Chapter 7   Compliance and Risk Management 251
    Knowledge of 251
Laws and Regulations 252
    Employment-at-Will 255
    Equal Employment Opportunity Commission (EEOC) 255
    Department of Labor (DOL) 255
Labor Unions 256
    NLRB Procedures for Recognizing a Union 256
    Collective Bargaining 257
    Contract Negotiation 257
    Establishing Contract Costs 257

Administering Union Contracts (MoU or CBA) 258
Unfair Labor Practices 258
Complaint/Grievance Handling 259
Mediation and Arbitration
    (Alternative Dispute Resolution, or ADR) 260
Risk Mitigation 260
Injury and Illness Prevention Plan (IIPP) 260
Health and Safety Monitoring 263
Handling Workplace Violence 263
Handling Emergencies 264
Business Continuity 264
Workforce Restructuring 264
Security Risks 267
Data Security/Cyber-Crimes 267
Inventory and Supply Security 268
Equipment Security 268
Theft Prevention/Loss Prevention 269
Preventing Equipment Damage 269
Securing Passwords 270
Terrorism 270
Workers' Compensation Compliance 270
Reporting Requirements 270
Return-to-Work Policies 271
OSHA Compliance 272
Workplace Safety Inspections 272
Accident Reporting 272
Chapter Review 274
Questions 274
Answers 278
Endnotes 280

Chapter 8 Early HR Career–Level Tasks 281
Task #1: Access, Collect, and Provide Information
    and Data to Support HR-Related Decisions 283
Task #2: Comply with All Applicable Laws and Regulations 284
Task #3: Coordinate and Communicate with External Providers
    of HR Services 285
Task #4: Maintain Employee Data in HRIS or System of Record 285
Task #5: Maintain, File, and Process HR Forms 286
Task #6: Prepare HR-Related Documents 286
Task #7: Provide Internal Customer Service by Answering
    or Referring HR-Related Questions from Employees
    as the First Level of Support 287
Task #8: Communicate Information about HR Policies
    and Procedures 288

Task #9: Communicate the Organization's Core Values,
Vision, Mission, Culture, and Ethical Behaviors 289
Task #10: Identify Risk in the Workplace 290
Task #11: Minimize Risk by Conducting Audits 291
Task #12: Document and Update Essential Job Functions
with Support of Managers 292
Task #13: Post Job Listings 293
Task #14: Manage Applicant Databases 294
Task #15: Screen Applicants for Managers to Interview 294
Task #16: Answer Questions from Job Applicants 295
Task #17: Coordinate Interview Logistics 296
Task #18: Interview Job Candidates 296
Task #19: Arrange for Tests and Assessments of Applicants 296
Task #20: Coordinate the Employment Offer 297
Task #21: Administer Post-Offer Employment Activities 298
Task #22: Communicate Compensation and Benefits Programs
and Systems 298
Task #23: Coordinate Activities to Support Employee
Benefits Programs 298
Task #24: Coordinate Payroll-Related Information 299
Task #25: Process Claims from Employees 300
Task #26: Resolve Routine Employee Compensation
and Benefits Issues 300
Task #27: Conduct Orientation and Onboarding
for New Hires, Rehires, and Transfers 300
Task #28: Coordinate Training Sessions 301
Task #29: Conduct Employee Training Programs 302
Task #30: Coordinate the Logistics for Employee Relations
Programs 303
Task #31: Monitor Completion of Performance Reviews
and Development Plans 303
Chapter Review 304
Endnote 304

Part III Appendixes and Glossary

Appendix A List of Common HR Acronyms 307

Appendix B Case Laws by Chapter 329
Chapter 3: Talent Acquisition 329
Chapter 4: Learning and Development 331
Chapter 5: Compensation and Benefits 331
Chapter 6: Employee Relations 333
Chapter 7: Compliance and Risk Management 340
Chapter 8: Early HR Career–Level Tasks 340

Appendix C For Additional Study 341

Appendix D About the Online Content 345

System Requirements 345
Your Total Seminars Training Hub Account 345
Privacy Notice 345
Single User License Terms and Conditions 345
TotalTester Online 347
Technical Support 347

Glossary 349

Index 391

ACKNOWLEDGMENTS

First, we'd like to thank all the highly skilled staff at McGraw Hill for their help getting this book to print so quickly. Special thanks goes to our editor, Wendy Rinaldi, for her endless kindness, support, and unrivaled expertise. It is always a joy working with you!

Additionally, a special note of acknowledgment comes from Christina to her coauthors, Dory Willer, Bill Truesdell, and Bill Kelly. You are truly HR legends. I am so appreciative for the opportunity to work on the second edition of this book. Dory, Bill, and Bill, the wealth of knowledge you put into the first edition has been such an incredible asset to early-career HR professionals everywhere. You have supported so many people in achieving their career goals from all walks of life, including me. For that, I will be forever grateful to you.

Finally, to Larry Bienati, better known as Led Poppi and technical editor extraordinaire. You never cease to amaze me. Thank you for always supporting me and taking the time to share your valuable thoughts and insights on every chapter of this book. You have inspired so many HR professionals in your career, and I am thrilled for this book to inspire a new generation of HR professionals.

INTRODUCTION

Allow us to be the first to congratulate you on making the decision to sit for the HR Certification Institute (HRCI) certification exam and to strive to obtain your Associate Professional in Human Resources (aPHR) certification! Professional certifications are a mark of distinction that sets you apart in the profession and speaks volumes about your commitment to your career. More than 500,000 of your colleagues around the globe have obtained the HRCI certifications, including us.

Human resources is most likely part of our DNA makeup; we've lived it and breathed it for many decades. Our purpose is to share with you some strategies and experience that will assist you when you sit for the certification exam. It is our intention that this book will provide the knowledge and concepts you are expected to have mastered as an aPHR candidate. It is our pleasure to share those things with you. You also bring your own professional experience to the process. As you combine your experience with the information included in this book, you will be better able to answer the situational-based and competency-based questions about human resource situations you will find on the exam.

We want you to be successful. It is our belief that the HRCI professional certifications are important because the certifications endorse your knowledge and expertise to employers and clients. Having a professional certification has become increasingly important. It may be a requirement of your next job assignment or the promotion you are pining for within your organization. You may decide that these certifications are necessary qualifications for future HR professionals that you may hire in your future. In any event, we wish you the best professional regards and success in passing your exam and earning the prestigious designation of aPHR.

HRCI Certification vs. SHRM Certification

Over the past few years, there has been a great deal of buzz from both the Society of Human Resource Management (SHRM) and the HRCI regarding the two accredited institutes certifying HR professionals. Both certifications have their merits and result in a professional level of recognized achievement in HR. HRCI will continue to confer its industry-recognized certifications for professional levels of achievement in the application of knowledge and competencies expected of HR professionals.

How to Use This Book

This book has been completely updated for the 2022 aPHR exam release. Each chapter describes the new aPHR Body of Knowledge (BOK) as it has been divided into functional topic areas of human resources. Our ordering of the functional areas is as follows:

1. HR certifications
2. U.S. laws and regulations
3. Talent acquisition
4. Learning and development
5. Compensation and benefits
6. Employee relations
7. Compliance and risk management
8. Early human resource career-level tasks

Additionally, within each functional area, we have organized the presentation of topics to follow this same logic. As you progress through the material, we hope you will do so with a feeling of accomplishment associated with mastering the information presented and thereby increase your drive and motivation to continue.

The following is a brief overview of the organization of this book and how we feel this organization will benefit you.

Chapter 1: Human Resource Certification

In Chapter 1, we explain everything you need to know about the aPHR exam and also discuss the different types of HR certifications available. Additionally, you'll find information about the process of registering for the exams, the actual exam experience, and what the style and format of questions are on the exams.

Chapter 2: U.S. Laws and Regulations

Chapter 2 provides a list of all the U.S. laws and regulations you will need to know. We placed this information in a chapter rather than an appendix to emphasize the importance of reviewing these laws and regulations prior to diving into the functional areas. Understanding these laws should make it easier for you to grasp the reasoning behind the material presented in Chapters 3–7. You will find some questions on the certification exams that are directly related to these laws. While it is true that you don't have to be a lawyer to function as an HR professional, it is critical that you have a grasp on the essential requirements of each federal law so you can guide your internal organization clients toward legal compliance.

Chapter 3: Talent Acquisition

In this chapter, you'll find information about how to identify recruiting sources, management of applicant databases, methods of recruiting, and alternative staffing practices. It also covers interviewing techniques and post-offer activities (medical exams, background checks, employee onboarding, and so on).

Chapter 4: Learning and Development

In this chapter, you'll find information about how to deliver and evaluate training programs, what career development programs mean to your organization, and how to manage change in your organization.

Chapter 5: Compensation and Benefits

Compensation and benefits are topics held dear by every employee. This chapter includes how to determine base pay, incentives, differentials, and job evaluation programs. Employee benefits are always receiving attention in the news. In this chapter, you will find information about determining which benefit programs might be best for your organization and how to support them with enrollment and training efforts.

Chapter 6: Employee Relations

Employee relations includes information about methods for gaining employee feedback, establishing and implementing expectations for employee behavior, handling complaints and grievances, and progressive discipline approaches. If you ever wondered about employee engagement and diversity programs, you will find what you need here. This chapter also covers performance evaluation methods for employees.

Chapter 7: Compliance and Risk Management

Many legal compliance issues are associated with health and safety programs. As a new HR professional, you will be involved in some or all of them. Risk management and processing safety reports are components you will discover are critical to the success of HR programs.

Chapter 8: Early HR Career–Level Tasks

In this final chapter, you will find a series of 31 HR tasks that will occupy your time as a new HR professional. While the tasks will not appear on the aPHR exam, they all derive from the knowledge areas in preceding chapters. Additionally, you will find special sections in this chapter, titled "In the Trenches," that contain valuable insight and advice about several of the HR tasks from an early-career HR perspective.

Exam Tips

Sprinkled throughout the book are "Exam Tips" designed to give you a bit of a head start over those who don't have the advantage of seeing them; they point out areas to pay attention to that will help you on the exam.

Questions and Answers

At the end of Chapters 2 through 7, you will find a set of review questions and answers to help you test your knowledge and comprehension. Practice, practice, practice—it will pay off on exam day.

Appendixes

We have also included four appendixes to supplement the information you need to know.

Appendix A

Appendix A is a list of acronyms. The HR field is notorious for abbreviations creating the jargon in HR language, and these abbreviations have flowed into the everyday business language of employers, employees, and the public at large. It is likely you will see questions on the exams that include and reference these acronyms, so be sure to familiarize yourself with this list.

Appendix B

In Appendix B, we have listed all the associated legal cases you should know and review prior to sitting for the exams. The cases are organized by functional area and include a brief synopsis of what each case addressed. A URL is provided so that you can review each case in more detail, and we recommend that you spend time reviewing these cases.

Appendix C

Here are additional reading materials you will find helpful if you choose to extend your study.

Appendix D

This appendix includes directions on how to access the 250 practice exam questions that are available online in the TotalTester customizable test engine. You can test yourself in both Practice and Exam modes, and narrow your preparation by domain or chapter.

Glossary

A glossary of terms has been created for your ease of reference. Using the glossary will help you review the key terms covered in this book and for the HR profession in general.

Index

In the very back of the book is an index that will guide you to the appropriate pages where a term is mentioned or discussed.

The Examination

The aPHR exam is not a simple true/false or memory-recall exam. You will be sitting for a 2-hour and 15-minute, 100-question multiple-choice (plus 25 pretest questions) exam that will test your knowledge of the HR profession. The knowledge-based questions will require you to know your facts. These questions test your knowledge of different HR laws. Sometimes you will be asked to identify an example chart or graph, so pay attention to the figures included in the chapters.

 EXAM TIP It usually takes roughly a year (or more) for the HRCI exam to reflect new laws, executive orders, and regulations. Don't be fooled, though. You may still see questions related to changes that have been recently introduced by the U.S. president or Congress. It is your responsibility to follow these updates and master the new requirements.

Preparing Is the Key

Preparing for any type of certification exam is not about memorizing information. The aPHR exam requires that new HR professionals are capable of understanding the laws and concepts in which HR management is based.

 EXAM TIP You may have already invested in an education for your career; investing in serious study time and preparation will pay off so that you can pass your exam.

For those with more limited experience or the minimal experience qualifications, we suggest you begin preparation and study 6 months prior to your exam date. For those with significantly more experience and time on the job as an HR professional, 3 months should be your yardstick. If you decide not to study the material outlined in this book, your chances of passing the aPHR exam will likely be low, even if you have been in an HR exempt position for a few months or years. We aren't saying that it can't be done, but your chances of passing the exam are much better if you study the information in this book and the accompanying practice exam questions to prepare for the time when you will sit in that room with only a computer screen. Guessing strategies are not foolproof and not a good substitute for solid study habits in preparation for an exam. The best preparation strategy is one that is focused on committed preparation with study time spent in a productive manner.

 NOTE If you are interested in working through even more practice exam questions as you prepare for the exam, we recommend *aPHR Associate Professional in Human Resources Certification Practice Exam, Second Edition*.

Final Thoughts

In the past few years, we've battled a worldwide pandemic, and HR professionals have been the "glue" holding organizations together. There have been new federal and state laws, executive orders, and EEOC guidance. How these changes affect your organization and HR long-term is yet to be seen. Your responsibility as an HR professional is to monitor what is happening and guide your employer through the changing compliance requirements as laid out by the U.S. president or Congress. There will also be many related policy choices to be made. If you have a labor-management attorney, getting updates from that person would be helpful.

This book has been designed not only to assist you, the HRCI exam candidate, in studying for the aPHR exam, but also to serve as a reliable reference book to be placed on the shelf in your office. There is a lot for a human resource professional to remember. It is our hope that this book becomes a convenient resource that guides you when something pops up for which you need a refresher. At a minimum, we hope it gives you direction in your effort to improve your HR circumstance.

Finally, thank you for selecting this book. We sincerely hope your aPHR exam goes well and wish you the absolute best on exam day!

PART I

The Human Resource Profession

■ **Chapter 1**   Human Resource Certification
■ **Chapter 2**   U.S. Laws and Regulations

Human Resource Certification

As you begin a career in human resources (HR), the skills and abilities you will use to produce your desired results as an HR professional require a mastery of sorts. Mastery of any profession will involve a continuous career-long commitment to learning, and that is a foundational truth within the HR profession. HR has been, and continues to be, an evolving component of an organization because its basic focus is on people. The constant changes and outside influences on an organization's workforce increase the demands on HR professionals. HR professionals today must master the art of staying two steps ahead while having one foot firmly planted in the present.

Professional Certifications

Certifications demonstrate to your employer and colleagues that you are educated in your profession and committed to a higher standard. When you achieve your first HR credential, it signals your mastery of core knowledge in human resources, raising the confidence of an employer and your peers in your knowledge and abilities. Because the HR profession is constantly evolving, it is important for HR professionals to regularly update their HR competencies and knowledge. Achieving certification and recertification is a good method to do this.

A professional certification should not be confused with a certificate program. Professional certifications are based on work experience and education, along with recertification requirements. Certificate programs do not require work experience or an educational component, and they do not require recertification. Professional certifications address a critical need in the global marketplace because employers expect more today from their internal experts, and the HR profession must be ready to meet those expectations.

HR Certification Organizations

As of 2021, three certifying organizations offer HR professionals the opportunity to become professionally certified: the HR Certification Institute (HRCI), the Society for Human Resource Management (SHRM), and the International Public Management Association for Human Resources (IPMA-HR). As of this writing, only HRCI offers a certification for entry-level career HR professionals with the Associate Professional in Human Resources® (aPHR) exam. All three organizations' certifications test knowledge required of HR professionals, as well as the application of that knowledge.

The HR Certification Institute (HRCI)

The HR Certification Institute (www.hrci.org) was established in 1976 as an internationally recognized certifying organization for the human resource profession. Its mission is to develop and deliver the highest-quality certification programs that validate mastery in the field of human resource management and contribute to the continued improvement of individual and organizational performance. Nearly 140,000 HR professionals in more than 100 countries are certified. Until 2015, HRCI was the only certifying organization for the HR profession.

HRCI exists to enhance the professionalism of the HR profession with its various certification processes. HRCI certifications demonstrate relevance, competence, experience, credibility, and dedication to human resources. The institute is designated a 501(c)(3)[1] nonprofit organization by the Internal Revenue Service (IRS). The Society of Human Resource Management is a 501(c)(6)[2] organization. HRCI was accredited by the National Commission for Certifying Agencies (NCCA) in 2008.

HRCI's Body of Knowledge (BoK) is a complete set of knowledge and responsibilities statements required to successfully understand and perform generalist HR-related duties associated with each of HRCI's credentials, which are Associate Professional in Human Resources® (aPHR), Professional in Human Resources® (PHR), Senior Professional in Human Resources® (SPHR), Global Professional in Human Resources® (GPHR), Professional in Human Resources – California® (PHRca), Associate Professional in Human Resources™ – International (aPHRi), Professional in Human Resources – International™ (PHRi), and Senior Professional in Human Resources – International™ (SPHRi). The BoK is periodically updated, typically every 5 to 7 years, to ensure it is consistent with and reflects current practices in the HR field. Our book *PHR/SPHR Professional in Human Resources Certification All-in-One Exam Guide, Second Edition*[3] provides in-depth preparation for the PHR and SPHR exams.

aPHR

HRCI's Associate Professional in Human Resources is the first-ever HR certification designed for professionals who are just beginning their HR career journey. It certifies that a person has the knowledge of foundational human resources.

Eligibility Requirements   To sit for the aPHR exam, no prior education or experience is required since the aPHR credential is a knowledge-based credential.

PHR

The Professional in Human Resources (PHR) certification demonstrates mastery of the operational aspects of HR practices and U.S. laws and regulations at the professional level.

The PHR is appropriate for HR professionals who focus on program implementation with a tactical orientation, who report to another HR professional within the organization, and have responsibilities that focus on the HR department rather than the whole organization.

Eligibility Requirements   To sit for the PHR exam, you must have one of the following:

- A minimum of 1 year of experience in a professional-level HR position and a master's degree or higher
- A minimum of 2 years of experience in a professional-level HR position and a bachelor's degree
- A minimum of 4 years of experience in a professional-level HR position with less than a high-school diploma or equivalent

SPHR

The Senior Professional in Human Resources certification demonstrates that a person has mastered the strategic and policy-making aspects of HR management as practiced in the United States. The credential is designed for the HR professional who plans rather than implements HR policy, focuses on the "big picture," has ultimate accountability in the HR department, has breadth and depth of knowledge in all HR disciplines, understands the business beyond the HR function, and influences the overall organization.

Eligibility Requirements   To sit for the SPHR exam, you must have one of the following:

- A minimum of 4 years of experience in a professional-level HR position and a master's degree or higher
- A minimum of 5 years of experience in a professional-level HR position and a bachelor's degree
- A minimum of 7 years of experience in a professional-level HR position with less than a high-school diploma or equivalent

GPHR

The Global Professional in Human Resources is a global, competency-based credential that is designed to validate the skills and knowledge of an HR professional who operates in a global marketplace. The credential demonstrates a mastery of cross-border HR responsibilities that include strategies of globalization, development of HR policies and initiatives that support organizational global growth and employer retention, and creation of organizational programs, processes, and tools that achieve worldwide business goals.

Eligibility Requirements   To sit for the GPHR exam, you must have one of the following:

- A minimum of 2 years of experience in a global professional-level HR position and a master's degree or higher
- A minimum of 3 years of experience in a professional-level HR position (at least 2 in global HR) and a bachelor's degree
- A minimum of 4 years of experience in a professional-level HR position (at least 2 in global HR) with less than a high-school diploma or equivalent

Global HR experience is defined as having direct, cross-border HR responsibilities for two or more countries or regions.

PHRca

The Professional in Human Resources – California demonstrates mastery of the laws, regulations, and HR management practices specific to the state of California. The PHRca is for HR or business professionals who are responsible for human resources in California. You do not have to be located in California to earn a PHRca.

Eligibility Requirements   To sit for the PHRca exam, you must have one of the following:

- A minimum of 1 year of experience in a professional-level HR position and a master's degree or higher
- A minimum of 2 years of experience in a professional-level HR position and a bachelor's degree
- A minimum of 4 years of experience in a professional-level HR position with less than a high-school diploma or equivalent

aPHRi

The Associate Professional in Human Resources – International is a global, competency-based credential that is designed to validate foundational HR knowledge and skills. The credential is best suited for entry-level HR or business professionals located outside of the United States.

Eligibility Requirements   To sit for the aPHRi exam, no prior education or experience is required since the aPHRi credential is a knowledge-based credential.

PHRi

The Professional in Human Resources – International is a global, competency-based credential that is designed to validate professional-level HR knowledge and skills. The credential demonstrates a mastery of generally accepted technical and operational

HR principles. Through demonstrated knowledge, the credential enhances the credibility of HR professionals outside of the United States and the organizations they serve.

Eligibility Requirements To sit for the PHRi exam, you must have one of the following:

- A minimum of 1 year of experience in a professional-level HR position and a master's degree or global equivalent
- A minimum of 2 years of experience in a professional-level HR position and a bachelor's degree or global equivalent
- A minimum of 4 years of experience in a professional-level HR position with less than a secondary education or global equivalent

SPHRi

The Senior Professional in Human Resources – International is a global, competency-based credential that is designed to validate professional-level core HR knowledge and skills. This credential demonstrates a mastery of generally accepted HR principles in strategy, policy development, and service delivery. Independent of geographic region, this credential complements local HR practices. Through demonstrated knowledge, this credential enhances the credibility of HR professionals outside of the United States and the organizations they serve.

Eligibility Requirements To sit for the SPHRi exam, you must have one of the following:

- A minimum of 4 years of experience in a professional-level HR position and a master's degree or global equivalent
- A minimum of 5 years of experience in a professional-level HR position and a bachelor's degree or global equivalent
- A minimum of 7 years of experience in a professional-level HR position with less than a secondary education or global equivalent

Recertification

Recertification is the process of renewing one's certification. To maintain certification, a certification holder must be prepared to show that they are building their knowledge, growing as a professional, and increasing their experience. HRCI recertification is required every 3 years through demonstrated professional development and professional achievements (the preferred method) or retaking the exam.

Here are some examples of ways to earn recertification credit. A complete list can be found at www.hrci.org:

- Continuing education
- Instruction
- On-the-job experience

- Research/publishing
- Leadership
- Professional membership

Recertification requires much more than attending conferences and workshops. Most certified HR professionals earn their recertification credits through the activities they do daily for their organizations. Effective 2021, all HRCI certifications require that one recertification credit in each 3-year cycle is focused on ethical practices and behaviors in the workplace.

The Society for Human Resource Management (SHRM)

For more than 70 years, the Society for Human Resource Management (www.shrm.org) has served the human resource profession and HR professionals worldwide. Founded in 1948, SHRM is the world's largest HR membership organization devoted to human resource management. Representing more than 300,000 members in more than 165 countries, SHRM is the leading provider of resources to serve the needs of HR professionals and advance the professional practice of human resource management. SHRM has more than 575 affiliated chapters within the United States and subsidiary offices in China, India, and the United Arab Emirates.

SHRM began offering its own certifications in 2015, the SHRM Certified Professional® (SHRM-CP) and the SHRM Senior Certified Professional® (SHRM-SCP) certifications, which are associated with its defined Body of Competency and Knowledge (BoCK). Accreditation was received in late 2016.

SHRM-CP

The SHRM-Certified Professional exam is for HR professionals who implement policies and strategies, serve as a point of contact for staff and stakeholders, deliver HR services, and perform operational HR functions.

Eligibility Requirements The following are the SHRM-CP eligibility requirements to sit for the exam:

Less Than a Bachelor's Degree*	**HR-Related Program** Three years in HR role	**Non-HR Program** Four years in HR role
Bachelor's Degree	**HR-Related Degree** One year in HR role	**Non-HR Degree** Two years in HR role
Graduate Degree	**HR-Related Degree** Currently in HR role	**Non-HR Degree** One year in HR role

*Less than a bachelor's degree includes the following: working toward a bachelor's degree, associate's degree, some college qualifying HR certificate program, high-school diploma, or general educational development (GED).

SHRM-SCP

The SHRM-Senior Certified Professional exam is for HR professionals who develop strategies, lead the HR function, foster influence in the community, analyze performance metrics, and align HR strategies to organizational goals.

Eligibility Requirements The following are the SHRM-SCP eligibility requirements to sit for the exam:

Less Than a Bachelor's Degree*	**HR-Related Program** Six years in HR role	**Non-HR Program** Seven years in HR role
Bachelor's Degree	**HR-Related Degree** Four years in HR role	**Non-HR Degree** Five years in HR role
Graduate Degree	**HR-Related Degree** Three years in HR role	**Non-HR Degree** Four years in HR role

*Less than a bachelor's degree includes the following: working toward a bachelor's degree, associate's degree, some college qualifying HR certificate program, high-school diploma, or GED.

Recertification

Recertification is how you will continue to grow and adapt to meet the evolving needs of the profession. SHRM-CP or SHRM-SCP credential holders must do one of the following for recertification:

- Earn 60 professional development credits (PDCs) within a 3-year recertification period
- Retake the certification exam at the end of the 3-year recertification period

The International Public Management Association for Human Resources (IPMA-HR)

Whereas HRCI and SHRM offer certifications covering all employment sectors (private, public, international, and federal government), IPMA-HR focuses solely on public sector human resource professionals. It is international in scope.

IPMA-CP

This designation is for entry- to mid-level public sector HR professionals. It requires that candidates participate in a fee-based Public Sector HR Essentials training course, which is currently offered three times a year. You may then sit for the exam. Once you have passed the exam, you will be certified.

IPMA-SCP

This designation is for public sector human resources professionals who have reached the manager, director, senior management, or executive level in their profession. Regardless of the educational level achieved, all candidates for this certification must have a minimum of 1 year of work experience in the public sector. Eight years of HR work experience are required if there is no degree beyond high school. Those with an associate degree must have 6 years of HR work experience. Bachelor degree holders must have 4 years of HR work experience, and graduate degree holders must have a minimum of 2 years of HR work experience. All IPMA-SCP candidates must be in jobs that are classified as exempt under the Fair Labor Standards Act (FLSA) at the time an application is submitted for testing.

Benefits of Certification

Earning an HR credential adds a level of recognition as an expert in the HR profession. This certification is a distinction that sets you apart in the profession, indicating you have a high level of knowledge and skills. It adds to your career value and to the organization you work in. Your HR certification could mean the difference between you and your competition. In fact, according to research by PayScale, HR professionals who hold certifications make more money and progress more quickly in their careers than their peers who do not.[4] HR certification is becoming an important means for employers to recognize HR expertise and for HR professionals to increase their value and worth.

Earning an HR credential can help you do the following:

- Boost your confidence
- Create recognition for you as an HR professional
- Master the expertise needed in the HR profession
- Protect your organization from risk by knowing regulatory compliance
- Stand out from other HR candidates in job searches and promotions
- Broaden your perspective in the HR field
- Keep up with HR innovations, developments, and legislative changes
- Demonstrate your commitment to the HR profession

Many organizations, including a number of Fortune 500 organizations, now require or prefer HR certification for their new HR hires or for internal promotions. A study from Software Advice, Inc., called "Study: What Employers Are Looking For in HR Positions,"[5] revealed that employers increasingly demand certification for job candidates. Table 1-1 lists the HR certification preferences, broken down by job title, published by the study.

Job Title Classification	Certification Required	Certification Preferred	Total
HR Business Partner	70%	30%	100%
Associate HR Director	35%	30%	65%
Senior HR Manager	10%	45%	55%
HR Director	10%	45%	55%
HR Manager	5%	40%	45%
Senior HR Generalist		55%	55%
Senior HR Business Partner		45%	45%
Employee Relations Manager		30%	30%
HR Generalist		15%	15%
Other		30%	30%

Table 1-1   HR Certification Specifications by Job Title

This survey suggests that certification is essential for any professional-level HR job candidate. If an individual wants to be considered for a senior-level HR position, then certification is nearly an absolute requirement. Those expectations will be further solidified as time goes on.

The aPHR Exam

The aPHR exam is a computer-based test (CBT) that is 2 hours and 15 minutes long. It includes 100 multiple-choice questions plus 25 pretest questions. The multiple-choice questions consist of a statement, known as a *stem,* and three or four choices. The choices consist of one correct or best choice that is the correct answer as well as incorrect or inferior choices knowns as *distractors.* The pretest questions are non-scored questions that are included to develop a statistical history that serves as a basis for validating the questions for future use as scored questions. Pretest questions are randomly placed throughout the test. New exams are produced annually.

The aPHR exam covers the identified BoK for the level of HR experience required of an aPHR professional and the federal laws applicable to the employment relationship, which are covered in detail in Chapter 2. HRCI realizes that employment laws change constantly. As such, exam candidates are responsible for knowing the HR laws and regulations that are in effect as of the start of their exam period.

The Significance of the HR Body of Knowledge

The Associate Professional in Human Resources (aPHR) exam was created using the aPHR Exam Content Outline, which details the BoK needed by those performing early HR career roles. HR subject-matter experts created the outline through a rigorous practice analysis study, which was then validated by HR professionals working in the field through an extensive survey instrument. It is updated periodically to ensure it is consistent with current practices in the HR field.

The BoK is broken down into five functional areas. These functional areas, with their respective exam weighting noted, are covered in the following sections.

Functional Area 1: Talent Acquisition (19%)

Fundamental understanding of all aspects related to the talent acquisition process, including planning, sourcing, recruiting, screening, selection, hiring, and onboarding of a new hire.

Knowledge of:

1. Methods to identify staffing needs and guide talent acquisition efforts; for example, forecasting, job analysis, the creation and structure of job descriptions, and alternative staffing approaches

2. Talent sourcing tools and techniques to identify and engage prospective candidates; for example, employer branding, social media, candidate pipelines, resume mining, job postings, job fairs, and employee referrals

3. Recruiting procedures and strategies for screening and selecting qualified applicants; for example, recruitment firms/staffing agencies, skills assessments, interview techniques and best practices, and biases

4. The lifecycle of hiring and onboarding a selected applicant; for example, reference and background checks, offer letters and counteroffers, employment contracts, and the distribution and collection of company-mandated documents such as employee handbook and policy acknowledgments, non-disclosure or other agreements, and benefits paperwork

5. The use of technology for collecting, storing, reviewing, and analyzing candidate/applicant information and recruiting data; for example, applicant tracking systems, human resource information systems (HRIS), return on investment (ROI), cost-per-hire, and time-to-fill

Functional Area 2: Learning and Development (15%)

Assessing the needs of the organization and understanding the techniques and methods for delivering training programs in order to provide employees with the tools, skills, and knowledge to align with current and future organizational goals.

Knowledge of:

1. The overall purpose and desired outcomes of employee orientation for new hires and/or internal hires; for example, setting expectations, building relationships, and acclimation

2. The concept of instructional design and components of commonly used models and methods for developing an organizational learning strategy; for example, knowledge, skills, and abilities (KSAs), ADDIE model, needs analysis, goals/objectives, available training resources, and intended audience

3. Elements and suitable applications for various training formats and delivery techniques; for example, blended, virtual, self-paced, instructor-led, on-the-job, role play, facilitation, and in-house vs. external training services

4. The concept, purpose, and key/desired outcomes of a change management process; for example, assessing readiness, communication plans, identifying needs, and providing resources and training

5. Methods and tools used to track employee development and measure the effectiveness of the training; for example, learning management systems (LMSs), reporting, post-training evaluation, and metrics

Functional Area 3: Compensation and Benefits (17%)

Understanding elements of the total rewards package, including compensation, benefits programs, retirement planning, and how they support organizational competitiveness.

Knowledge of:

1. The elements involved in developing and administering an organization's compensation strategy, such as pay structures, pay adjustments, and incentive programs; for example, external service providers, market analysis, job evaluation/classifications, merit increases, pay scales/grades, cost of living adjustments, and service awards

2. Health benefit and insurance programs, including eligibility requirements, enrollment periods, and various designs; for example, high deductible plans, health savings accounts, flexible spending accounts, preferred provider organizations, and short- or long-term disability

3. Supplemental wellness and fringe benefit programs commonly offered by organizations; for example, employee assistance programs (EAPs), gym membership, online therapy, housing or relocation assistance, and travel/transportation stipends

4. Employee eligibility for and enrollment in retirement plans as well as rules regarding contributions and withdrawals; for example, 401(k), 457(b), catch-up contributions, and hardship withdrawals

5. Components of wage statements and payroll processing; for example, taxation, deductions, differentials, garnishments, leave reporting and final pay, and total reward statements

Functional Area 4: Employee Relations (24%)

Understanding the methods organizations use to monitor and address morale, performance, and retention. Balancing the operational needs of the organization with the well-being of the individual employee.

Knowledge of:

1. The purpose and difference between mission, vision, and value statements and how they influence an organization's culture and employees

2. How HR supports organizational goals and objectives through HR policies, procedures, and operations; for example, functions of human resource information systems (HRISs), organizational structures, preparing HR-related documents, basic communication flows and methods, SWOT analysis, and strategic planning

3. Techniques used to engage employees, collect feedback, and improve employee satisfaction; for example, employee recognition programs, stay interviews, engagement surveys, work/life balance initiatives, and alternative work arrangements

4. Workforce management throughout the employee lifecycle, including performance management and employee behavior issues; for example, goal setting, benchmarking, performance appraisal methods and biases, ranking/rating scales, progressive discipline, termination/separation, offboarding, absenteeism, and turnover/retention

PART I

5. Policies and procedures to handle employee complaints, facilitate investigations, and support conflict resolution; for example, confidentiality, escalation, retaliation, and documentation

6. The elements of diversity and inclusion initiatives and the impact on organizational effectiveness and productivity; for example, social responsibility initiatives, cultural sensitivity and acceptance, unconscious bias, and stereotypes

Functional Area 5: Compliance and Risk Management (25%)

Complying with laws, regulations, and policies as well as educating stakeholders in order to identify, mitigate, and respond to organizational risk. Awareness of records management, storage, and retention regulations and reporting requirements.

Knowledge of:

1. Applicable laws and regulations related to talent acquisition, training, and employee/employer rights and responsibilities, such as nondiscrimination, accommodation, and work authorization; for example, EEOC, DOL, I-9 form completion, employment-at-will, Title VII, ADA, Immigration Reform and Control Act, and Title 17 (copyright law)

2. Applicable laws, regulations, and legal processes affecting employment in union environments; for example, WARN Act, NLRA, collective bargaining, and alternative dispute resolution methods

3. Applicable laws and regulations related to compensation and benefits, such as monetary and non-monetary entitlement, wages, and hours; for example, ERISA, COBRA, FLSA, USERRA, PPACA, and tax treatment

4. Applicable laws and regulations related to workplace health, safety, security, and privacy; for example, OSHA, Drug-Free Workplace Act, ADA, HIPAA, Sarbanes-Oxley Act, WARN Act, and sexual harassment

5. Risk assessment and mitigation techniques to promote a safe, secure, and compliant workplace; for example, emergency evacuation procedures, violence, business continuity plan, intellectual and employee data protection, and theft

6. Organizational restructuring initiatives and their risks to business continuity; for example, mergers, acquisitions, divestitures, integration, offshoring, downsizing, and furloughs

The Test Development Process

HRCI follows certification-industry best practices to create and update all of its exams. Practicing HR professionals are involved in every step of the exam development process, which is overseen by the Pearson Vue testing organization. The following are the steps taken to develop all of HRCI's exams:

1. HRCI exams are based on Exam Content Outlines developed for each exam. These outlines are created by a small group of practicing HR professionals and then validated by a much larger group through a practice analysis study.

2. Certified HR professionals write the exam questions (also known as *items*), based on the Exam Content Outline.

3. The questions go to another group, the Item-Review Panel, which checks for accuracy and proper coding.

4. Approved questions are then "pretested" for reliability.

5. Multiple exam forms are created and reviewed by a panel of subject-matter experts.

6. A passing score for each exam is determined.

The Exam Experience

Applicants must meet both HR work experience and education requirements, if required, to qualify for each exam. Applicants should complete the application process early to increase the chance of getting their first choice for test date and location. As of this writing, the current exam fee is $300 plus a $100 nonrefundable application fee. Testing for the aPHR exam is year-round, subject only to space availability at a Pearson Vue testing center of your choice.

The aPHR Registration Process

HRCI describes the application process[6] in steps:

1. Create an online account with HRCI.

2. Choose the exam that's right for you (aPHR, PHR, SPHR, and so on). We will presume that your background and qualifications indicate that the aPHR exam is right for you.

3. Build your own bundle. Decide whether you would like to purchase preparation materials through HRCI's "Build Your Own Bundle" option. We feel that this study guide would be sufficient for your studying efforts.

4. Affirm that all the information submitted on the application is complete and true and that you have read the HRCI Certification Handbook (available online through the HRCI web site at https://www.hrci.org/).

5. Submit the application with payment.

6. Schedule your exam date with Pearson Vue and plan your preparation.

7. Take the exam. Make sure to bring an official, valid, government-issued identification with you to the exam.

8. Receive your preliminary results at the testing center and an official score report 24 to 48 hours after testing.

Preparing for the Exam

From our years of experience helping HR professionals achieve their certifications, we have compiled a list of tips for exam takers. First, let's begin with studying. The following tips will help you get the most benefit from your preparation efforts:

- Before studying, go for a brief walk to take in some air and clear your mind in preparation for the focused time to study. Put all your other thoughts and projects of the day on a back burner and give your mind a clean slate, setting the intention that this specific amount of time is exclusively for HRCI studying.

- Make sure your "do not disturb" sign is on your door if you are at home or in the office and that others clearly know that nothing is to disturb you for the next hour. Speaking of an hour, that's plenty of time to devote on a regular schedule to study. Most people find that 4 or 5 hours a week is sufficient for this type of material.

- Clear your study area. It should be void of anything that might distract you from studying. Keep the focus on your studying and be sure to create a bit of visual incentive for yourself—such as a letter mock-up stating that you have successfully passed your exam. Spoof a letter from HRCI, print it, put it in a nice picture frame, and place it in front of you every time you begin studying. What the mind can conceive, you can achieve!

- Select a time of day that is optimal for you to study. Are you best in the wee hours of the early morning with a cup of coffee prior to work, or perhaps you're more focused at the noon hour? Maybe you're a person whose rhythm kicks in just after dinner. Find that sweet hour and make the appointment on your calendar, listing it as "VIP-HRCI." *You* are the very important person, and this appointment will cause you to think twice before allowing another activity to muscle in on your time slot.

- The old adage that practice makes perfect is not quite right. "Perfect practice makes perfect" is a better way to state the intention. As you make your study time perfect and practice saying "no thank you" to others and things that interrupt your study time, you are practicing the perfect combination that will allow you to stay focused and produce the results you want.

- Two days prior to the exam, be sure to get a full night's sleep each night, which is typically 7 to 9 hours for most people.

- Hydrate, hydrate, hydrate the day before and the day of the exam. Try to avoid massive amounts of caffeine because it will lead to dehydration.

The following are some suggestions to keep in mind as you take your exam:

- Trust your gut, or your first impression. Your first impression of the correct answer is many times the best choice. This should not be confused with guessing. This refers to topics you know that you know.

- Watch out for basing your answer on what your current organization's policy is. Keep focused on generally accepted HR practices for correct answers.

- There will be no patterns, so don't even try to look for them. The psychometric exam process used for the HRCI exam prevents questions from falling into patterns.

- Only federal laws apply—don't mix your state laws with your federal laws.

- The most common weakness of HR test-takers is overanalyzing the options. Be thorough, but be reasonable in your analysis and selection of the options.

- When stumped, try to eliminate the obviously incorrect answers and then just focus on what remains.

- Read all answer options—it may be that you need to select the best answer and yet all answers are correct.

- Resist the urge to change your answers. This goes hand in hand with trusting your instincts. If you are absolutely, positively sure that you have an incorrect answer, go ahead. But for the most part, resist the urge to change answers.

- Don't rush. Manage your time. You will have a little over a minute for each question. A clock is visible on your monitor screen counting down the amount of time left.

Exam Readiness

HRCI's aPHR Exam Content Outline is one of your most important documents leading to a successful exam experience. Each exam question has a specific corresponding functional knowledge area that is identified in the applicable Exam Content Outline. As such, this valuable information will enable you to use the Exam Content Outline as an exam readiness checklist to indicate the knowledge topics you need to know and comprehend in order to pass this exam. Additionally, we recommend you use our practice exams to determine which functional areas you may need to study more. The following is the exam weighting given to each functional area:

- Talent Acquisition (19%)
- Learning and Development (15%)
- Compensation and Benefits (17%)
- Employee Relations (24%)
- Compliance and Risk Management (25%)

Chapter Review

The number of HR professionals needed in the coming years to manage the human capital in organizations will continue to expand. The U.S. Bureau of Labor Statistics anticipates that the number of HR manager positions will grow 9 percent and will grow 10 percent for HR specialist positions by the year 2030.[7] In addition, employer-selection systems will increasingly use certification as an employment-screening element. The value of certification is being recognized in all levels of the organization and throughout the HR profession. We're confident that beginning your professional career in human resources by adding the aPHR certification to your résumé will draw special attention to your achievement and to the commitment of growing your abilities in the profession.

Endnotes

1. To be tax exempt under section 501(c)(3) of the Internal Revenue Code, an organization must be organized and operated exclusively for exempt purposes set forth in section 501(c)(3), and none of its earnings may inure to any private shareholder or individual. In addition, it may not be an action organization; i.e., it may not attempt to influence legislation as a substantial part of its activities, and it may not participate in any campaign activity for or against political candidates. Organizations described in section 501(c)(3) are commonly referred to as charitable organizations. Organizations described in section 501(c)(3), other than testing for public safety organizations, are eligible to receive tax-deductible contributions in accordance with Section 170. (IRS Code, https://www.irs.gov/charities-non-profits/charitable-organizations/exemption-requirements-section-501-c-3-organizations)

2. IRC 501(c)(6) provides for exemption of business leagues, chambers of commerce, real estate boards, boards of trade, and professional football leagues (whether or not administering a pension fund for football players), which are not organized for profit and no part of the net earnings of which ensures to the benefit of any private shareholder or individual. (IRS Code, https://www.irs.gov/pub/irs-tege/eotopick03.pdf)

3. William H. Truesdell, Christina Nishiyama, and Dory Willer, *PHR/SPHR Professional in Human Resources Certification All-in-One Exam Guide, Second Edition* (McGraw Hill, 2019)

4. PayScale Human Capital research report, "HR Certifications: How They Impact Pay and Career Trajectory, 2018 U.S. Edition," https://www.payscale.com/data/hr-certifications-pay

5. Brian Westfall, "Study: What Employers Are Looking For in HR Positions," *Software Advice* (July 18, 2017), https://www.softwareadvice.com/resources/what-employers-look-for-hr-jobs/

6. https://hrci.org/aphr

7. Bureau of Labor Statistics, U.S. Department of Labor, *Occupational Outlook Handbook, 2020 Edition,* https://www.bls.gov/ooh/

U.S. Laws and Regulations

This chapter introduces the federal laws and legislation that all human resource (HR) professionals must know and understand. Federal laws apply to every state in the United States (U.S.) and will be covered on the Associate Professional in Human Resources (aPHR) exam. There are also many laws that apply only to the U.S. state(s) in which your employer operates. State laws will not be covered on the aPHR exam or in this chapter, but it is important to know your state's laws to be successful in your HR position.

When you thoroughly read these laws and regulations, you will better understand the material in Part II of this book. Knowing these laws can sometimes make the difference in selecting the right answer on the Associate Professional in Human Resources (aPHR) exam. After studying this chapter and completing the practice questions, you should have a better understanding of the relevance of these laws in the employment relationship. HR professionals in both small and large companies play an important role in dealing with day-to-day employment issues relating to recruiting, hiring, managing, and training employees. Also, HR systems must be guided by legal requirements.

Many times, as you read this chapter, you will discover the phrase "engaged in interstate commerce." This is a term used by Congress to identify which employers will be subject to a law's requirements. Interstate commerce includes shipping a Maine lobster to a New Mexico restaurant for tonight's dinner, for example. Also included are selling products on Amazon, eBay, or a similar Internet site to customers in states other than the one you are in and purchasing products from a supplier in a state other than the one you are in. As you can tell, it is a broad statement that applies to many employers, both large and small. The following sections cover what you need to know concerning federal laws and regulations that govern employment.

When You Have ONE or More Employees

Employers sometimes forget that the moment they hire their first employee, they become subject to a host of legal requirements. Here are 52 laws that will impact an employer with one or more employees on the payroll.

The Clayton Act (1914)

This legislation modified the Sherman Anti-Trust Act by prohibiting mergers and acquisitions that would lessen competition. It also prohibited a single person from being a director of two or more competing corporations. The law also allowed for more union activity, such as labor strikes, picketing, and boycotts, by restricting the use of injunctions against these activities. An injunction is a court order requiring a person or an organization to stop doing something. For more information, see 15 U.S.C. Sec. 12 at www.law.cornell.edu/uscode/text/15/12 or perform an Internet search for the law by name.

The Consumer Credit Protection Act (1968)

Congress expressed limits to the amount of wages that can be garnished or withheld in any one week by an employer to satisfy creditors. This law also prohibits employee dismissal because of garnishment for any one indebtedness.

For more information, see https://www.dol.gov/agencies/whd/wage-garnishment or perform an Internet search for the law by name.

The Copeland "Anti-Kickback" Act (1934)

This act prevents a federal contractor or subcontractor from encouraging an employee to give up any part of their wages to the employer for the benefit of having a job. For more information, see https://webapps.dol.gov/elaws/elg/kickback.htm or perform an Internet search for the law by name.

The Copyright Act (1976)

The Copyright Act offers protection of "original works" for authors so others may not print, duplicate, distribute, or sell their work. In 1998, the Copyright Term Extension Act further extended copyright protection to the duration of the author's life plus 70 years for general copyrights and to 95 years for works made for hire and works copyrighted before 1978. If anyone in the organization writes technical instructions, policies and procedures, manuals, or even e-mail responses to customer inquiries, it would be a good idea to speak with your attorney and arrange some copyright agreements to clarify whether the employer or the employee who authored those documents will be designated the copyright owner. Written agreements can be helpful in clearing up any possible misunderstandings. For more information, see www.copyright.gov/title17/92appa.pdf or perform an Internet search for the law by name.

The Davis-Bacon Act (1931), as Amended in 2002

This law requires contractors and subcontractors on certain federally funded or assisted construction projects worth more than $2,000 in the United States to pay wages and fringe benefits at least equal to those prevailing in the local area where the work is performed. This law applies only to laborers and mechanics. It also allows trainees and apprentices to be paid less than the predetermined rates under certain circumstances. For more information, see www.dol.gov/whd/regs/statutes/dbra.htm or perform an Internet search for the law by name.

The Dodd-Frank Wall Street Reform and Consumer Protection Act (2010)

This law offers a wide range of mandates affecting all federal financial regulatory agencies and almost every part of the nation's financial services industry. It includes a nonbinding vote for shareholders on executive compensation, golden parachutes, and return of executive compensation based on inaccurate financial statements. A golden parachute is an agreement with an employee that they will receive significant benefits if their employment is terminated. Also included are requirements to report chief executive officer (CEO) pay compared to the average employee compensation and provision of financial rewards for whistleblowers. In 2018, the Economic Growth, Regulatory Relief, and Consumer Protection Act made some banks exempt from these requirements. For more information, see www.sec.gov/about/laws/wallstreetreform-cpa.pdf or perform an Internet search for the law by name.

The Economic Growth and Tax Relief Reconciliation Act (EGTRRA) (2001)

This law introduced modifications to the Internal Revenue Code that adjust pension vesting schedules, increasing retirement plan limits, permitting pretax catch-up contributions by participants older than 50 in certain plans (which are not tested for discrimination when made available to the entire workforce), and modifying distribution and rollover rules. For more information, see www.irs.gov/pub/irs-tege/epchd104.pdf or perform an Internet search for the law by name.

The Electronic Communications Privacy Act (ECPA) (1986)

This is a unique law composed of two pieces of legislation: the Wiretap Act and the Stored Communications Act. Combined, they provide rules for access, use, disclosure, interpretation, and privacy protections of electronic communications, and they provide the possibility of both civil and criminal penalties for violations. They prohibit interception of e-mails in transmission and access to e-mails in storage. The implications for HR have to do with recording employee conversations. Warnings such as "This call may be monitored or recorded for quality purposes" are intended to provide the notice required by this legislation. Having cameras in the workplace to record employee or visitor activities is also covered, and notices must be given to anyone subject to observation or recording. Recording without such a notice can be a violation of this act. If employers make observations of employee activities and/or record telephone and other conversations between employees and others and proper notice is given to employees, employees will have no expectation of privacy during the time they are in the workplace.

For more information, see www.justice.gov/jmd/ls/legislative_histories/pl99-508/pl99-508.html or perform an Internet search for the law by name.

The Employee Polygraph Protection Act (1988)

Before 1988, it was common for employers to use "lie detectors" as tools in investigations of inappropriate employee behavior. That changed when this act prohibited the use of lie detector tests for job applicants and employees of companies engaged in interstate commerce. Exceptions are made for certain situations, including law enforcement and national security. There is a federal poster requirement. Note: Many state laws also prohibit the use of lie detector tests. Be sure you understand state laws where you have work locations.

For more information, see https://www.dol.gov/agencies/whd/polygraph or perform an Internet search for the law by name.

The Employee Retirement Income Security Act (ERISA) (1974)

This law doesn't require employers to establish pension plans but governs how those plans are managed once they have been established. It establishes uniform minimum standards to ensure that employee benefit plans are established and maintained in a fair and financially sound manner; protects employees covered by a pension plan from losses in benefits due to job changes, plant closings, bankruptcies, or mismanagement; and protects plan beneficiaries. It covers most employers engaged in interstate commerce. Public-sector employees and many churches are not subject to ERISA. Some charities, schools, and volunteer organizations are also not subject to ERISA due to the Cooperative and Small Employer Charity Pension Flexibility Act, which became a law in 2014. Employers that offer retirement plans must also conform to the Internal Revenue Service (IRS) code in order to receive tax advantages. For more information, see https://www.dol.gov/general/topic/health-plans/erisa or perform an Internet search for the law by name.

The Equal Pay Act (an Amendment to the FLSA) (1963)

Equal pay requirements apply to all employers. The act is an amendment to the Fair Labor Standards Act (FLSA) and is enforced by the Equal Employment Opportunity Commission (EEOC). It prohibits employers from discriminating on the basis of sex by paying wages to employees at a rate less than the rate paid to employees of the opposite sex for equal work on jobs requiring equal skill, effort, and responsibility and which are performed under similar working conditions. It does not address the concept of comparable worth. For more information, see https://www.eeoc.gov/statutes/equal-pay-act-1963 or perform an Internet search for the law by name.

The FAA Modernization and Reform Act (2012)

Congress took action in 2012 to amend the Railway Labor Act to change union certification election processes in the railroad and airline industries and impose greater oversight of the regulatory activities of the National Mediation Board (NMB). This law requires the Government Accountability Office (GAO) initially to evaluate the NMB's certification procedures and then audit the NMB's operations every 2 years. For more information, see https://www.congress.gov/bill/112th-congress/house-bill/658/text or perform an Internet search for the law by name.

The Fair and Accurate Credit Transactions Act (FACT) (2003)

The financial privacy of employees and job applicants was enhanced in 2003 with these amendments to the Fair Credit Reporting Act, providing for certain requirements in third-party investigations of employee misconduct charges. Employers are released from obligations to disclose requirements and obtain employee consent if the investigation involves suspected misconduct, a violation of the law or regulations, or a violation of preexisting written employer policies. A written plan to prevent identity theft is required. For more information, see www.gpo.gov/fdsys/pkg/PLAW-108publ159/pdf/PLAW-108publ159.pdf or perform an Internet search for the law by name.

The Fair Credit Reporting Act (FCRA) (1970), as Amended in 2011

This was the first major legislation to regulate the collection, dissemination, and use of consumer information, including consumer credit information. It requires employers to notify any individual in writing if a credit report may be used in making an employment decision. Employers must also get a written authorization from an individual before asking a credit bureau for a credit report. The Fair Credit Reporting Act also protects the privacy of background investigation information and provides methods for ensuring that information is accurate. Employers who take adverse action against a job applicant or current employee based on information contained in the prospective or current employee's consumer report will have additional disclosures to make to that individual. For more information, see https://www.ftc.gov/enforcement/statutes/fair-credit-reporting-act or perform an Internet search for the law by name.

The Fair Labor Standards Act (FLSA) (1938)

The FLSA is one of a handful of federal laws that establish the foundation for employee treatment. It is a major influence in how people are paid, in employment of young people, and in how records are to be kept on employment issues such as hours of work. The law established a national minimum wage, guaranteed "time-and-a-half" for overtime in certain jobs, and prohibited most employment of minors in "oppressive child labor," a term that is defined in the statute. It applies to employees engaged in interstate commerce or employed by an enterprise engaged in commerce or in the production of goods for commerce, unless the employer can claim an exemption from coverage. It is interesting to note that the FLSA, rather than the Civil Rights Act of 1964, is the first federal law to require employers to maintain records on employee race and sex identification.

Provisions and Protections

Employers covered under the "enterprise" provisions of this law include public agencies; private employers whose annual gross sales exceed $500,000; those operating a hospital or a school for mentally or physically disabled or gifted children; and a preschool, an elementary or secondary school, or an institution of higher education (profit or nonprofit). Individuals can still be covered even if they don't fit into one of the enterprises listed. If the employees' work regularly involves them in commerce between the states, they would be covered. These include employees who work in communications or transportation;

regularly use the mail, telephone, or telegraph for interstate communication or keep records of interstate transactions; handle shipping and receiving goods moving in interstate commerce; regularly cross state lines in the course of employment; or work for independent employers who contract to do clerical, custodial, maintenance, or other work for firms engaged in interstate commerce or in the production of goods for interstate commerce. The FLSA establishes a federal minimum wage that has been raised from time to time since the law was originally passed. The FLSA prohibits shipment of goods in interstate commerce that were produced in violation of the minimum wage, overtime pay, child labor, or special minimum wage provisions of the law.

Recordkeeping Requirements

The FLSA prescribes methods for determining whether a job is exempt or nonexempt from the overtime pay requirements of the act. If a job is exempt from those requirements, incumbents can work as many hours of overtime as the job requires without being paid for their overtime. On the other hand, people who work in nonexempt jobs must be paid overtime according to the rate computation methods provided for in the act. Exempt versus nonexempt status attaches to the job, not the incumbent. So, someone with an advanced degree who is working in a clerical job may be nonexempt because of the job requirements, not their personal qualifications. Employers are permitted to have a policy that calls for paying exempt employees when they work overtime. That is a voluntary provision of a benefit in excess of federal requirements. State laws may have additional requirements. Usually, this is a requirement for overtime after 40 hours of regular time worked during a single workweek. The act also describes how a workweek is to be determined.

Each employer covered by the FLSA must keep records for each covered, nonexempt worker. Those records must include the following:

- Employee's full name and Social Security number
- Address, including ZIP code
- Birth date, if younger than 19
- Sex
- Occupation
- Time and day of week when employee's workweek begins
- Hours worked each day and total hours worked each workweek. (This includes a record of the time work began at the start of the day, when the employee left for a meal break, the time the employee returned to work from the meal break, and the time work ended for the day.)
- Basis on which employee's wages are paid (hourly, weekly, piecework)
- Regular hourly pay rate
- Total daily or weekly straight-time earnings
- Total overtime earnings for the workweek

- All additions or deductions from the employee's wages
- Total wages paid each pay period
- Date of payment and the pay period covered by the payment

There is no limit in the FLSA to the number of hours employees age 16 and older may work in any workweek. There is a provision for employers to retain all payroll records, collective bargaining agreements, sales, and purchase records for at least 3 years. Any time card, piecework record, wage rate tables, and work and time schedules should be retained for at least 2 years. A workplace poster is required to notify employees of the federal minimum wage.

The federal child labor provisions of the FLSA, also known as the child labor laws, were enacted to ensure that when young people work, the work is safe and does not jeopardize their health, well-being, or educational opportunities. These provisions also provide limited exemptions. Workers younger than 14 are restricted to jobs such as newspaper delivery to local customers, babysitting on a casual basis, or acting in movies, TV, radio, or theater. Under no circumstances, even if the business is family owned, may a person under 18 work in any of the 17 most hazardous jobs. See Figure 2-1 for a list of the 17 most hazardous jobs.

• Manufacturing or storing of explosives	• Using power-driven meat-processing machines, slaughtering, meat and poultry packing, processing or rendering
• Driving a motor vehicle or working as an outside helper on motor vehicles	• Using power-driven bakery machines
• Coal mining	• Using balers, compactors, and power-driven paper-products machines
• Forest fire fighting and forest fire prevention, timber tract, forestry service, and occupations in logging and sawmilling	• Manufacturing brick, tile, and related products
• Using power-driven woodworking machines	• Using power-driven circular saws, band saws, guillotine shears, chain saws, reciprocating saws, wood chippers, and abrasive cutting discs
• Exposure to radioactive substances	• Working in wrecking, demolition, and ship-breaking operations
• Using power-driven hoisting apparatuses	• Roofing and work performed on or about a roof
• Using power-driven metal-forming, punching, and shearing machines	• Trenching or excavating
• Mining, other than coal	

Source: "U.S. Department of Labor, eLaws Fair Labor Standards Act Advisor" on September 15, 2021, https://webapps.dol.gov/elaws/whd/flsa/docs/haznonag.asp

Figure 2-1 The 17 most dangerous jobs that may not be performed by workers younger than 18

For workers aged 14 and 15, all work must be performed outside school hours, and these workers may not work:

- More than 3 hours on a school day, including Friday
- More than 18 hours per week when school is in session
- More than 8 hours per day when school is not in session
- More than 40 hours per week when school is not in session
- Before 7 A.M. or after 7 P.M. on any day, except from June 1 through Labor Day, when nighttime work hours are extended to 9 P.M.

For workers aged 16 through 17, there are no restrictions on the number of hours that can be worked per week. There continues to be a ban on working any job among the 17 most hazardous positions. All of these conditions must be met or the employer will be subject to penalties from the U.S. Department of Labor.

Overtime Computation

Overtime is required at a rate of 1.5 times the normal pay rate for all hours worked over 40 in a single workweek. An employer may designate that their workweek begins at a given day and hour and continues until that same day and hour 7 days later. Once selected, that same workweek definition must be maintained consistently until there is a legitimate business reason for making a change. That change must be clearly communicated in advance to all employees who will be affected by the change. No pay may be forfeited because the employer changes its workweek definition. Compensating time off is permitted under the FLSA if it is given at the same rates required for overtime pay.

Enforcement

Provisions of the FLSA are enforced by the U.S. Department of Labor's Wage and Hour Division. With offices around the country, this agency is able to interact with employees on complaints and follow up with employers by making an on-site visit if necessary. If violations are found during an investigation, the agency has the authority to make recommendations for changes that would bring the employer into compliance. Retaliation against any employee for filing a complaint under the FLSA is subject to additional penalties. Willful violations may bring criminal prosecution and fines up to $10,000. Employers who are convicted a second time for willfully violating the FLSA can find themselves in prison.

The Wage and Hour Division may, if it finds products produced during violations of the act, prevent an employer from shipping any of those goods. It may also "freeze" shipments of any product manufactured while overtime payment requirements were violated. A 2-year limit applies to recovery of back pay unless there was a willful violation, which triggers a 3-year liability. For more information, see www.dol.gov/whd/regs/statutes/FairLaborStandAct.pdf or perform an Internet search for the law by name.

The Foreign Corrupt Practices Act (FCPA) (1977)

The FCPA prohibits American companies from making bribery payments to foreign officials for the purpose of obtaining or keeping business. Training for employees who are involved with international negotiations should include a warning to avoid anything even looking like a bribery payment to a foreign company or its employees. For more information, see www.justice.gov/criminal/fraud/fcpa/ or perform an Internet search for the law by name.

The Health Information Technology for Economic and Clinical Health (HITECH) Act (2009)

The HITECH Act requires that anyone with custody of personal health records send notification to affected individuals if their personal health records have been disclosed, or the employer believes they have been disclosed, to any unauthorized person. Enacted as part of the American Recovery and Reinvestment Act (ARRA), this law made several changes to the Health Insurance Portability and Accountability Act, including the establishment of a federal standard for security breach notifications that requires covered entities, in the event of a breach of any personal health information (PHI), to notify each individual whose PHI has been disclosed without authorization. For more information, see www.hhs.gov/ocr/privacy/hipaa/administrative/enforcementrule/hitechenforcementifr.html or perform an Internet search for the law by name.

The Health Insurance Portability and Accountability Act (HIPAA) (1996)

This law provides privacy requirements related to medical records for individuals as young as 12. It also ensures that individuals who leave or lose their jobs can obtain health coverage even if they or someone in their family has a preexisting health condition. It also restricts the ability of employers to impose actively-at-work requirements as preconditions for health plan eligibility, as well as a number of other benefits. For more information, see www.hhs.gov/ocr/privacy or perform an Internet search for the law by name.

The Immigration and Nationality Act (INA) (1952)

The INA is the first law that pulled together all of the issues associated with immigration and is considered the foundation on which all subsequent immigration laws have been built. It addresses employment eligibility and employment verification. It defines the conditions for the temporary and permanent employment of aliens in the United States.

The INA defines an *alien* as any person lacking citizenship or status as a national of the United States. The INA differentiates aliens as follows:

- Resident or nonresident
- Immigrant or nonimmigrant
- Documented and undocumented

The need to curtail illegal immigration led to the enactment of the Immigration Reform and Control Act (IRCA). For more information, see https://www.uscis.gov/laws-and-policy/legislation/immigration-and-nationality-act or perform an Internet search for the law by name.

The Immigration Reform and Control Act (IRCA) (1986)

This is the first law to require new employees to prove both their identity and their right to work in this country. Regulations implementing this law created Form I-9,[1] which must be completed by each new employee and the employer. Form I-9 has been updated many times since 1986. Be sure you are using the most current version of the form. There are document retention requirements. The law prohibits discrimination against job applicants on the basis of national origin or citizenship. It also establishes penalties for employers who hire illegal aliens. For more information, see https://www.congress.gov/bill/99th-congress/senate-bill/1200 or perform an Internet search for the law by name.

The IRS Intermediate Sanctions (2002)

Here we find guidelines enacted by the IRS for determining reasonable compensation for executives of nonprofit organizations. These rules allow the IRS to impose penalties when it determines that top officials have received excessive compensation from their organizations. Intermediate sanctions may be imposed either in addition to or instead of revocation of the exempt state of the organization. For more information, see www.irs.gov/pub/irs-tege/eotopice03.pdf or perform an Internet search for the law by name.

The Labor-Management Relations Act (LMRA; Taft-Hartley Act) (1947)

Also called the Taft-Hartley Act, this is the first national legislation that placed controls on unions. It prohibits unfair labor practices by unions and outlaws closed shops, where union membership is required in order to get and keep a job. Employers may not form closed-shop agreements with unions. It requires both parties to bargain in good faith and covers non-management employees in private industry who are not covered by the Railway Labor Act. For more information, see https://www.nlrb.gov/about-nlrb/who-we-are/our-history/1947-taft-hartley-substantive-provisions or search the Internet for the law by name.

The Labor-Management Reporting and Disclosure Act (Landrum-Griffin Act) (1959)

Also called the Landrum-Griffin Act, this law outlines procedures for remedying internal union problems, protects the rights of union members from corrupt or discriminatory labor unions, and applies to all labor organizations. Specific requirements include the following:

- Unions must conduct secret elections, the results of which can be reviewed by the U.S. Department of Labor.
- A Bill of Rights guarantees union members certain rights, including free speech.
- Convicted felons and members of the Communist Party cannot hold office in unions.
- Annual financial reporting from unions to the Department of Labor is required.
- All union officials have a fiduciary responsibility in managing union assets and conducting the business of the union.

- Union power to place subordinate organizations in trusteeship is limited.
- Minimum standards for union disciplinary action against its members are provided.

For more information, see https://www.nlrb.gov/about-nlrb/who-we-are/our-history/ 1959-landrum-griffin-act or perform an Internet search for the law by name.

The Mine Safety and Health Act (1977)

Following a series of deadly mining disasters, the American people demanded that Congress take action to prevent similar events in the future. This law converted the existing Mine Enforcement Safety Administration (MESA) to the Mine Safety and Health Administration (MSHA). For the first time, it brought all coal, metal, and nonmetal mining operations under the same Department of Labor jurisdiction. Regulations and safety procedures for the coal mining industry were not altered, just carried into the new agency for oversight. For more information, see https://www.dol.gov/general/topic/ safety-health/mining or perform an Internet search for the law by name.

Provisions and Protections

This law requires the secretaries of Labor and Health, Education, and Welfare to create regulations governing the country's mines. All mines are covered if they are involved in commerce, which any active mining operation would be. Regulations that implement this law specify that employees must be provided with certain protective equipment while working in a mine. These devices relate to respiration and fire prevention, among other protections. Protecting against "black lung disease" is a key concern, even today, in the coal mining industry.

Recordkeeping Requirements

Employers engaged in mining operations must inspect their worksites and document the results, reflecting hazards and actions taken to reduce or eliminate the hazards. Employees are to be given access to information related to accident prevention, fatal accident statistics for the year, and instructions on specific hazards they will face while working in the mine. Requirements detail the content of written emergency response plans, emergency mapping, and rescue procedures. Individual employee exposure records must be maintained. Each mine operator is required to conduct surveys of mine exposures and hazards, have a plan to deal with those problems, and record the results. This information must be made available to MSHA inspectors if they request it.

MSHA Standards

The agency enforces mine safety standards that involve ventilation, chemical exposure, noise, forklifts and other mining equipment, mine shoring, and more. Material Safety Data Sheets (MSDSs) must be available to employees in mining as they are in other industries overseen by the Occupational Safety and Health Administration (OSHA) agency.

MSHA Enforcement

MSHA has a team of federal inspectors that conduct on-site audits of mining operations. MSHA has the authority to cite mine operators for violations of its regulations, and as of the time of this writing, citations can reach up to $274,000 in some circumstances.[2]

The National Industrial Recovery Act (1933)

This was an attempt to help the country get out from the Great Depression. It proposed the creation of "Codes of Fair Competition" for each of several different industries. Essentially, every business would have to identify with and belong to a trade association. The association would then be required to create a Code of Fair Competition for the industry. Antitrust laws would be suspended in favor of the code. Of course, the code would have to be approved by the president of the United States, and the administration would issue federal licenses to every business in the country. If a business refused to participate in the code, its license could be suspended, and that would be the signal for that business to end all operations. There were financial penalties as well. This law didn't fare very well. It was declared unconstitutional by the U.S. Supreme Court in 1935 and was replaced by the National Labor Relations Act later that same year.

For more information, see https://guides.loc.gov/national-recovery-administration or perform an Internet search for the law by name.

The National Labor Relations Act (NLRA; Wagner Act) (1935)

This is the "granddaddy" of all labor relations laws in the United States. It initially provided that employees have a right to form unions and negotiate wage and hour issues with employers on behalf of the union membership. Specifically, the NLRA grants to employees the right to organize, join unions, and engage in collective bargaining and other "concerted activities." It also protects against unfair labor practices by employers.

Following on the heels of the National Industrial Recovery Act's failures, this law stepped into the void and addressed both union and employer obligations in labor relations issues. It established the National Labor Relations Board (NLRB), which would help define fair labor practices in the following decades. The NLRB has the power to accept and investigate complaints of unfair labor practices by either management or labor unions. It plays a judicial role within an administrative setting. This law is sometimes called the Wagner Act. The following are some key provisions:

- The right of workers to organize into unions for collective bargaining
- The requirement of employers to bargain in good faith when employees have voted in favor of a union to represent them
- Requirement that unions represent all members equally
- Covers non-management employees in private industry who are not already covered by the Railway Labor Act

For more information, see https://www.nlrb.gov/about-nlrb/rights-we-protect/the-law or perform an Internet search for the law by name.

The Needlestick Safety and Prevention Act (2000)

This law modifies the Occupational Safety and Health Act by introducing a new group of requirements in the medical community. *Sharps,* as they are called, are needles, puncture devices, knives, scalpels, and other tools that can harm either the person using them or someone else. The law and its regulations provide rules related to handling these devices, disposing of them, and encouraging invention of new devices that will reduce or eliminate the risk associated with injury due to sharps. Injuries due to sharps are to be recorded on the OSHA 300 log with "privacy case" listed and not the employee's name. Blood-borne pathogens and transmission of human blood-borne illnesses such as AIDS/HIV and hepatitis are key targets of this law. Reducing the amount of injury and subsequent illness due to puncture, stab, or cut wounds is a primary objective. There are communication requirements, including employment poster content requirements.

For more information, see https://www.congress.gov/bill/106th-congress/house-bill/5178 or perform an Internet search for the law by name.

The Norris-LaGuardia Act (NLRA) (1932)

Remember that this was still 3 years before the NLRA came to pass. When unions tried to use strikes and boycotts, employers would trot into court and ask for an injunction to prevent such activity. More often than not, they were successful, and judges provided the injunctions. Congress had been pressured by organized labor to restore their primary tools that could force employers to bargain over issues unions saw as important. The following are key provisions of this law:

- It prohibited "yellow-dog" contracts, which were agreements in which employees promised employers that they would not join unions. This new law declared such contracts to be unenforceable in any federal court.

- It prohibited federal courts from issuing injunctions of any kind against peaceful strikes, boycotts, or picketing when used by a union in connection with a labor dispute.

- It defined "labor dispute" to include any disagreement about working conditions.

For more information, see https://www.law.cornell.edu/uscode/text/29/chapter-6 or perform an Internet search for the law by name.

The Occupational Safety and Health Act (OSHA) (1970)

Signed into law by President Richard M. Nixon on December 29, 1970, the Occupational Safety and Health Act created an administrative agency within the U.S. Department of Labor called the Occupational Safety and Health Administration (OSHA). It also created the National Institute of Occupational Safety and Health (NIOSH), which resides inside the Centers for Disease Control (CDC).

Provisions and Protections

Regulations implementing this legislation have grown over time. They are complex and detailed. It is important that HR professionals understand the basics and how to obtain additional detailed information that applies to their particular employer circumstance.

There are many standards that specify what employers must do to comply with their legal obligations. Overall, however, the law holds employers accountable for providing a safe and healthy working environment. The "General Duty Clause" in OSHA's regulations says employers shall furnish each employee with a place of employment free from recognized hazards that are likely to cause death or serious injury. It also holds employees responsible for abiding by all safety rules and regulations in the workplace. Some provisions require notices be posted in the workplace covering some of the OSHA requirements. Posters are available for download from the OSHA web site at no charge. The law applies to all employers regardless of the employee population size.

Recordkeeping Requirements

OSHA regulations require that records be kept for many purposes. It is necessary to conduct and document inspections of the workplace, looking for safety and health hazards. It is necessary to document and make available to employees records about hazardous materials and how they must be properly handled. Employers with ten or more people on the payroll must summarize all injury and illness instances and post that summary in a conspicuous place within the workplace. That report must remain posted from February 1 to April 30 each year. Certain employers are exempt from some OSHA recordkeeping requirements. They generally are classified by industry Standard Industrial Classification (SIC) Code. A list is available on OSHA's web site at www.OSHA.gov. Any time there is a serious or fatal accident, a full incident report must be prepared by the employer and maintained in the safety file. These records must be maintained for a minimum of 5 years from the date of the incident. Known as a log of occupational injury or illness, it must include a record of each incident resulting in medical treatment (other than first aid), loss of consciousness, restriction of work or motion, or transfer or termination of employment. If you are in the medical industry, construction industry, or manufacturing industry, or if you use nuclear materials of any kind, there are other requirements you must meet. The key to compliance with OSHA rules is communication with employees. Training is often provided by employers to meet this hazard communication requirement. In summary, then, OSHA recordkeeping involves the following:

- Periodic safety inspections of the workplace
- Injury or illness incident reports
- Annual summary of incidents during the previous calendar year
- Injury and Illness Prevention Program (if required by rules governing your industry)
- Employee training on safety procedures and expectations
- Records of training participation
- Material Safety Data Sheets for each chemical used in the workplace (made available to all employees in a well-marked file or binder that can be accessed at any time during work hours)

Occupational Safety and Health Act Enforcement

OSHA inspections may include the following:

- **On-site visits that are conducted without advance notice**   Inspectors can just walk into a place of employment and request that you permit an inspection. You don't have to agree unless the inspector has a search warrant. In the absence of the warrant, you can delay the inspection until your attorney is present.

- **On-site inspections or phone/fax investigations**   Depending on the urgency of the hazard and agreement of the person filing the complaint, inspectors may telephone or fax inquiries to employers. The employer has 5 working days to respond with a detailed description of inspection findings, corrective action taken, and additional action planned.

- **Highly trained compliance officers**   OSHA Training Institute provides training for OSHA's compliance officers, state compliance officers, state consultants, other federal agency personnel, and the private sector.

Inspection priorities include the following:

- **Imminent danger**   Situations where death or serious injury are highly likely. Compliance officers will ask employers to correct the conditions immediately or remove employees from danger.

- **Fatalities and catastrophes**   Incidents that involve a death or the hospitalization of three or more employees. Employers must report these incidents to OSHA within 8 hours.

- **Worker complaints**   Allegations of workplace hazards or OSHA violations. Employees may request anonymity when they file complaints with OSHA.

- **Referrals**   Other federal, state, or local agencies, individuals, organizations, or the media can make referrals to OSHA so the agency may consider making an inspection.

- **Follow-ups**   Checks for abatement of violations cited during previous inspections. These are also conducted by OSHA personnel in certain circumstances.

- **Planned or programmed investigations**   OSHA can conduct inspections aimed at specific high-hazard industries or individual workplaces that have experienced high rates of injuries and illnesses. These are sometimes called *targeted investigations*.

Two Types of Standards

The law provides for two types of safety and health standards. The agency has therefore developed its regulations and standards in those two categories.

Normal Standards   If OSHA determines that a specific standard is needed, any of several advisory committees may be called upon to develop specific recommendations.

There are two standing committees, and ad hoc committees may be appointed to examine special areas of concern to OSHA. All advisory committees, standing or ad hoc, must have members representing management, labor, and state agencies, as well as one or more designees of the Secretary of Health and Human Services (HHS). The occupational safety and health professions and the general public also may be represented.[3]

Emergency Temporary Standards   OSHA is also authorized to set emergency temporary standards that take effect immediately. Examples of situations that call for an emergency temporary standard are exposure to toxic substances that present a serious danger to workers or a new hazard. You might recall that the COVID-19 pandemic resulted in emergency temporary standards. Within 6 months, the temporary standard can be made permanent, and it can be challenged in the U.S. Court of Appeals. For more information, see https://www.osha.gov/laws-regs/oshact/completeoshact or perform an Internet search for the law by name.

The Omnibus Budget Reconciliation Act (OBRA) (1993)

Signed into law by President Bill Clinton on August 10, 1993, this legislation reduces compensation limits in qualified retirement programs and triggers increased activity in nonqualified retirement programs. It also calls for termination of some plans. For more information, see https://www.congress.gov/bill/103rd-congress/house-bill/2264 or perform an Internet search for the law by name.

The Pension Protection Act (PPA) (2006)

Focused solely on pensions, this law requires employers that have underfunded pension plans to pay a higher premium to the Pension Benefit Guarantee Corporation (PBGC). It also requires employers that terminate pension plans to provide additional funding to those plans. This legislation impacted nearly all aspects of retirement planning, including changes to rules about individual retirement accounts (IRAs). For more information, see https://www.dol.gov/agencies/ebsa/laws-and-regulations/laws/pension-protection-act or perform an Internet search for the law by name.

The Personal Responsibility and Work Opportunity Reconciliation Act (1996)

This law requires all states to establish and maintain a new hire reporting system designed to enhance enforcement of child support payments. It requires welfare recipients to begin working after 2 years of receiving benefits. States may exempt parents with children younger than 1 from the work requirements. Parents with children younger than 1 may use this exemption only once; they cannot use it again for subsequent children. These parents also are still subject to the 5-year time limit for cash assistance. HR professionals will need to establish and maintain reporting systems to meet these tracking requirements. For more information, see www.acf.hhs.gov/programs/css/resource/the-personal-responsibility-and-work-opportunity-reconcilliation-act or perform an Internet search for the law by name.

The Portal-to-Portal Act (1947)

By amending the FLSA, this law defines "hours worked" and establishes rules about payment of wages to employees who travel before and/or after their scheduled work shift. The provisions of the act are fairly complicated, and remote work hours continue to be addressed.[4] Commuting time and before-or-after work activities are not compensable under the act, but activities that are critical to job performance such as changing uniforms are compensable. The use of technology such as smart phones and laptops has added additional complexity because the lines between work and personal time have become blurred. At the time of this writing, this continues to be an area of increased litigation. As an HR professional, it is important to set an internal policy to manage hours worked to avoid potential legal pitfalls. For more information, see 29 U.S.C. Chapter 9 at http://uscode.house.gov/ or perform an Internet search for the law by name.

The Railway Labor Act (1926)

Originally, this law was created to allow railway employees to organize into labor unions. Over the years, it has been expanded in coverage to include airline employees. Covered employers are encouraged to use the Board of Mediation, which has since morphed into the National Mediation Board, a permanent independent agency. For more information, see 45 U.S.C. Chapter 8 at https://uscode.house.gov/ or perform an Internet search for the law by name.

The Rehabilitation Act (1973)

This replaced the Vocational Rehabilitation Act and created support for states to create vocational rehabilitation programs. It helped address the notion of equal access for individuals with disabilities and has been updated several times since its inception. The term originally used in this legislation was *handicapped*. The law was later modified to replace that term with *disabled*.

For more information, see https://www.congress.gov/bill/93rd-congress/senate-bill/7 or perform an Internet search for the law by name. Table 2-1 notes some of the most important sections of the Rehabilitation Act.

Section	Requirement
Section 501	Requires nondiscrimination and affirmative action in hiring disabled workers by federal agencies within the executive branch
Section 503	Requires nondiscrimination and affirmative action by federal contractors and subcontractors with contracts valued at $10,000 or more
Section 504	Requires employers subject to the law to provide reasonable accommodation for disabled individuals who can perform the major job duties with or without accommodation
Section 508	Requires that federal agencies' electronic and information technology is accessible to people with disabilities

Table 2-1 Key Employment Provisions of the Rehabilitation Act of 1973

The Retirement Equity Act (REA) (1984)

Signed into law by President Ronald Reagan on August 23, 1984, the REA provides certain legal protections for spousal beneficiaries of qualified retirement programs. It prohibits changes to retirement plan elections, spousal beneficiary designations, or in-service withdrawals without the consent of a spouse. Changing withdrawal options does not require spousal consent. It permits plan administrators to presume spousal survivors annuity and reduce primary pension amounts accordingly. Specific written waivers are required to avoid spousal annuity. For more information, see https://www.congress.gov/bill/98th-congress/house-bill/4280 or perform an Internet search for the law by name.

The Revenue Act (1978)

This law added two important sections to the Internal Revenue Tax Code relevant to employee benefits: Section 125, Cafeteria Benefit Plans, and Section 401(k), originally a pretax savings program for private-sector employees known as Individual Retirement Accounts (IRAs), subsequently expanded to a second plan opportunity known as "Roth IRAs" that permitted funding with after-tax savings. For more information, see https://www.congress.gov/bill/95th-congress/house-bill/13511 or perform an Internet search for the law by name.

The Sarbanes-Oxley Act (SOX) (2002)

In response to many corrupt practices in the financial industry and the economic disasters they created, Congress passed the Sarbanes-Oxley Act to address the need for oversight and disclosure of information by publicly traded companies.

Provisions and Protections

This law brought some strict oversight to corporate governance and financial reporting for publicly held companies. It holds corporate officers accountable for proper record-keeping and reporting of financial information, including internal control systems to ensure they are working properly. There are also requirements for reporting any unexpected changes in financial condition, including potential new liabilities such as lawsuits. Those lawsuits can involve, for example, employee complaints of illegal employment discrimination. It requires administrators of defined contribution plans to provide notice of covered blackout periods and provides whistleblower protection for employees.

This law protects anyone who reports wrongdoing to a supervisor, an appointed company official who handles these matters, a federal regulatory or law enforcement agency, or a member or committee of Congress. It even extends to claims that prove to be false as long as the employee reasonably believed the conduct was a violation of Security Exchange Commission (SEC) rules or a federal law involving fraud against shareholders.

On March 4, 2014, the U.S. Supreme Court issued its opinion in the case of *Lawson v. FMR LLC*. (No. 12–3).[5] The 6–3 decision held that all contractors and subcontractors of publicly held companies are subject to the Sarbanes-Oxley Act, even if they are not publicly held. The takeaway from this ruling is that nearly everyone is now subject to the whistleblower provisions of the Sarbanes-Oxley Act. As Justice Sotomayor suggested in her dissenting opinion:

> For example, public companies often hire "independent contractors," of whom there are more than 10 million, and contract workers, of whom there are more than 11 million. And, they employ outside lawyers, accountants, and auditors as well. While not every person who works for a public company in these nonemployee capacities may be positioned to threaten or harass employees of the public company, many are.

> Under [the majority opinion] a babysitter can bring a … retaliation suit against his employer if his employer is a checkout clerk for the local PetSmart (a public company) but not if she is a checkout clerk for the local Petco (a private company). Likewise the day laborer who works for a construction business can avail himself of [this ruling] if her company has been hired to remodel the local Dick's Sporting Goods store (a public company), but not if it is remodeling a nearby Sports Authority (a private company).

Recordkeeping Requirements

Internal control systems are required to ensure that public disclosure of financial information is done as required. The registered accounting firm responsible for reviewing the company's financial reports must attest to the proper implementation of internal control systems and procedures for financial reporting.

SOX Enforcement

Enforcement of the law is done by private-firm audits overseen by the Public Company Accounting Oversight Board (PCAOB). The PCAOB is a nonprofit corporation created by the act to oversee accounting professionals who provide independent audit reports for publicly traded companies. It essentially audits the auditors.

Companies and corporate officers in violation of the act can find themselves subject to fines and/or up to 20 years imprisonment for altering, destroying, mutilating, concealing, or falsifying records, documents, or tangible objects with the intent to obstruct, impede, or influence a legal investigation. For more information, see https://www.congress.gov/bill/107th-congress/house-bill/3763 or perform an Internet search for the law by name.

The Securities and Exchange Act (1934)

When companies "go public" by issuing common stock for trade, it is done on the "primary market." This law provides for governance in the "secondary market," which is all trading after the initial public offering. It created the Securities and Exchange Commission (SEC), which has oversight authority for the trading of stocks in the U.S. The SEC also monitors the financial reports that publicly traded companies are required to disclose and oversees the conduct of financial professionals, including brokers and investment advisors. For more information, see https://www.fdic.gov/regulations/laws/rules/8000-6300.html or perform an Internet search for the law by name.

The Service Contract Act (1965)

Also known as the McNamara-O'Hara Service Contract Act, this law applies to federal contractors (and subcontractors) offering goods and services to the government. It calls for payment of prevailing wages and benefit requirements to all employees providing service under the agreement. All contractors and subcontractors, other than construction services, with contract values in excess of $2,500 are covered. Safety and health standards also apply to such contracts.

The compensation requirements of this law are enforced by the Wage and Hour Division in the U.S. Department of Labor (DOL). The Service Contract Act safety and health requirements are enforced by the Occupational Safety and Health Administration, also an agency within DOL. For more information, see https://www.dol.gov/agencies/whd/government-contracts/service-contracts or perform an Internet search for the law by name.

The Sherman Anti-Trust Act (1890)

If you were to travel back in time to the latter part of the nineteenth century, you would find that big business dominated the landscape, including Standard Oil, Morgan Bank, U.S. Steel, and a handful of railroads. They were huge by comparison with other similar enterprises at the time, and people were concerned that they were monopolizing the marketplace and holding prices high just because they could. John Sherman, a Republican senator from Ohio and chairman of the Senate Finance Committee, suggested that the country needed some protections against monopolies and cartels. Thus, this law was created and subsequently used by federal prosecutors to break up the Standard Oil Company into smaller units. Over the years, case law has developed that concludes that attempting to restrict competition, or fix prices, can be seen as a violation of this law. Restraint of trade is also prohibited. For more information, see https://www.justice.gov/atr/file/761131/download or perform an Internet search for the law by name.

The Small Business Job Protection Act (1996)

This law increased federal minimum wage levels and provided some tax incentives to small business owners to protect jobs and increase take-home pay. It also amended the Portal-to-Portal Act for employees who use employer-owned vehicles. It created the SIMPLE 401(k) retirement plan to make pension plans easier for small businesses. Other tax incentives created by this law include the following:

- Employee education incentive—allowed small business owners to exclude up to $5,250 from an employee's taxable income for educational assistance provided by the employer
- Increased the maximum amount of capital expense allowed for a small business to $7,000 per year
- Replaced the Targeted Jobs Tax Credit with the Work Opportunity Tax Credit
- Provided a tax credit to individuals who adopted a child (up to $5,000 per child) and a tax credit of up to $6,000 for adoption of a child with special needs

For more information, see https://www.congress.gov/bill/104th-congress/house-bill/ 3448 or perform an Internet search for the law by name.

The Social Security Act (1935)

The Social Security program began in 1935 in the heart of the Great Depression. It was initially designed to help senior citizens when that group was suffering a poverty rate of 50 percent. It currently includes social welfare and social insurance programs that can help support disabled workers who are no longer able to earn their wages.

The Social Security program is supported through payroll taxes with contributions from both the employee and the employer. Those payroll tax rates are set by the Federal Insurance Contributions Act (FICA) and have been adjusted many times over the years. There are many programs currently under the control of the Social Security Act and its amendments. These include the following:

- Federal old-age benefits (retirement)
- Survivors benefits (spouse benefits, dependent children, and widow/widower benefits)
- Disability insurance for workers no longer able to work
- Temporary Assistance for Needy Families
- Medicare Health Insurance for Aged and Disabled
- Medicaid Grants to States for Medical Assistance Programs
- Supplemental Security Income (SSI)
- State Children's Health Insurance Program (SCHIP)
- Patient Protection and Affordable Care Act

There is currently a separate payroll deduction for Medicare Health Insurance, which is also funded by both the employee and employer. Also, the Patient Protection and Affordable Care Act provided medical insurance coverage to a greater number of people. A personal Social Security number is used as a tax identification number for federal income tax, including bank records, and to prove work authorization in this country. For more information, see www.ssa.gov/history/35act.html or perform an Internet search for the law by name.

The Tax Reform Act (1986)

This law made extensive changes to the Internal Revenue Service tax code, including a reduction in tax brackets and all tax rates for individuals. Payroll withholdings were affected, many passive losses and tax shelters were eliminated, and changes were made to the alternative minimum tax computation. This is the law that required all dependent children to have Social Security numbers. That provision reduced the number of fraudulent dependent children claimed on income tax returns by 4.2 million[6] in its first year.

For HR professionals, answers to employee questions about the number of exemptions to claim on their Form W-4 are greatly influenced by this requirement for dependent Social Security numbers. For more information, see https://www.congress.gov/bill/99th-congress/house-bill/3838 or perform an Internet search for the law by name.

The Taxpayer Relief Act (1997)

Congress wanted to give taxpayers a couple of ways to lower their tax payments during retirement, so the Taxpayer Relief Act was passed to create new savings programs called Roth IRAs, Education IRAs, and the child tax credit. Many individuals were able to achieve a better tax position through these tools. For more information, see https://www.congress .gov/bill/105th-congress/house-bill/2014 or perform an Internet search for the law by name.

The Trademark Act (1946)

This is the legislation that created federal protections for trademarks and service marks. Officially it was called the Lanham (Trademark) Act, and it set forth the requirements for registering a trademark or service mark to obtain those legal protections. HR people may have a role to play in training employees how to properly handle organizational trademarks and the policies that govern those uses. For more information, see www.uspto.gov/trademarks/law/tmlaw.pdf or perform an Internet search for the law by name.

The Unemployment Compensation Amendments (UCA) (1992)

This law established 20 percent as the amount to be withheld from payment of employee savings accounts when leaving an employer and not placing the funds (rolling over) into another tax-approved IRA or 401(k). For more information, see https://www.congress.gov/bill/102nd-congress/house-bill/5260 or perform an Internet search for the law by name.

The Uniformed Services Employment and Reemployment Rights Act (USERRA) (1994)

USERRA provides instructions for handling employees who are in the reserves and receive orders to report for active duty. The law protects the employment, reemployment, and retention rights of anyone who voluntarily or involuntarily serves or has served in the uniformed services. It requires that employers continue paying for the employee's benefits to the extent they paid for those benefits before the call to duty. It also requires that employers continue giving credit for length of service as though the military service was equivalent to company service. There are specific detailed parameters for how long an employee may wait to engage the employer in return-to-work conversations after being released from active military duty.

This law and its provisions cover all eight U.S. military services and other uniformed services:

- Army
- Navy
- Air Force

- Marines
- Public Health Service Commissioned Corps
- National Oceanic and Atmospheric Administration Commissioned Corps
- Coast Guard
- National Guard groups that have been called into active duty

For more information, see https://webapps.dol.gov/elaws/elg/userra.htm or perform an Internet search for the law by name.

The Vietnam Era Veterans Readjustment Assistance Act (1974), as Amended by the Jobs for Veterans Act (2002)

Current covered veterans include the following:

- Disabled veterans
- Veterans who served on active duty in the U.S. military during a war or campaign or expedition for which a campaign badge was awarded
- Veterans who, while serving on active duty in the Armed Forces, participated in a U.S. military operation for which an Armed Forces service medal was awarded pursuant to Executive Order 12985
- Recently separated veterans (veterans within 36 months from discharge or release from active duty)

These requirements apply to all federal contractors with a contract valued at $150,000 or more, regardless of the number of total employees.

This veteran support legislation requires all employers subject to the law to post their job openings with their local state employment service. These are the three exceptions to that requirement:

- Jobs that will last 3 days or less
- Jobs that will be filled by an internal candidate
- Jobs that are senior executive positions

Affirmative action outreach and recruiting of veterans are required for federal contractors meeting the contract value threshold. For more information, see https://webapps .dol.gov/elaws/elg/vietvets.htm or perform an Internet search for the law by name.

The Wagner-Peyser Act (1933), as Amended by the Workforce Innovation and Opportunity Act (2014)

The Wagner-Peyser Act created a nationwide system of employment offices known as Employment Service Offices. They were run by the U.S. Department of Labor's Employment and Training Administration (ETA). These offices provided job seekers with assistance in their job search, assistance in searching jobs for unemployment insurance recipients, and recruitment services for employers.

The Workforce Investment Act, which was replaced by the Workforce Innovation and Opportunity Act, created the "One Stop" centers within Employment Service Offices. The federal government contracts with states to run the Employment Service Offices and One Stop centers. Funds are allocated to states based on a complicated formula. The Workforce Innovation and Opportunity Act established local workforce boards and updated board requirements to better help workers find employment and help employers find qualified employees. Education and training program goals focus on adults, workers who have lost their jobs, and youth. For more information, see https://www.dol.gov/agencies/eta/american-job-centers/wagner-peyser or perform an Internet search for the law by name.

The Walsh-Healey Act (Public Contracts Act) (1936)

President Franklin Roosevelt signed this into law during the Great Depression. It was designed to ensure the government paid a fair wage to manufacturers and suppliers of goods for federal government contracts in excess of $10,000 each. The provisions of the law included the following:

- Overtime pay requirements for work done over 8 hours in a day or 40 hours in a week. The Defense Authorization Act (1968) later excluded federal contractors from overtime payments in excess of 8 hours in a day.
- A minimum wage equal to the prevailing wage.
- Prohibition on employing anyone under 16 years of age or a current convict.

For more information, see https://www.dol.gov/agencies/whd/government-contracts/pca or perform an Internet search for the law by name.

The Work Opportunity Tax Credit (WOTC) (1996)

Finally, this law provides federal income tax credits to employers who hire from certain targeted groups of job seekers who face employment barriers. The amount of tax credit is adjusted from time to time and currently stands at $9,600 per employee.

Targeted groups include the following:

- Qualified recipients of Temporary Assistance to Needy Families (TANF).
- Qualified veterans receiving food stamps (referred to as Supplemental Nutrition Assistance Program [SNAP] today) or qualified veterans with a service-connected disability who:
    - Have a hiring date that is not more than 1 year after having been discharged or released from active duty, or
    - Have aggregate periods of unemployment during the 1-year period ending on the hiring date that equals or exceeds 6 months.

- WOTC also includes family members of a veteran who received food stamps (SNAP) for at least a 3-month period during the 15-month period ending on the hiring date or a disabled veteran entitled to compensation for a service-related disability hired within a year of discharge or unemployed for a period totaling at least 6 months of the year ending on the hiring date.

- Ex-felons hired no later than 1 year after conviction or release from prison.

- Designated Community Resident—an individual who is between the ages of 18 and 40 on the hiring date and who resides in an Empowerment Zone, Renewal Community, or Rural Renewal County.

- Vocational rehabilitation referrals, including Ticket Holders with an individual work plan developed and implemented by an Employment Network.

- Qualified summer youth ages 16 through 17 who reside in an Empowerment Zone, Enterprise Community, or Renewal Community.

- Qualified SNAP recipients between the ages of 18 and 40 on the hiring date.

- Qualified recipients of Supplemental Security Income (SSI).

- Long-term family assistance recipients.

- Qualified long-term unemployment recipients who have been unemployed for at least 27 consecutive weeks.

 NOTE   These categories change from time to time.

In addition to these specific federal laws, there are laws dealing with payroll that HR professionals need to understand. While it is true that accounting people normally handle the payroll function in an employer's organization, occasionally HR professionals get involved and have to work with accounting people to explain deductions and provide input about open enrollment for healthcare benefit programs, among other things. Those things can include garnishments, wage liens, savings programs, benefit premium contributions, and income tax, FICA, and Medicare withholdings.

For more information, see https://www.irs.gov/businesses/small-businesses-self-employed/work-opportunity-tax-credit or perform an Internet search for the law by name.

Whistleblowing

It is important to highlight the issue of whistleblowing. Protections against retaliation are embedded in various laws we cover in this chapter. Laws with those provisions and protections include the Civil Rights Acts, OSHA, MSHA, the Sarbanes-Oxley Act, ADA, and more.

Whistleblower laws usually apply to public-sector employees and employees of organizations contracting with the federal government or state governments. They are designed to protect individuals who publicly disclose information about corrupt practices or illegal activities within their employer's organization. Often, such events occur when someone is mishandling money, contracts, or other assets. Construction projects not being built to specifications can result in whistleblowing by governmental employees. Employees of financial services companies (banks, credit unions, stock brokerages, and investment firms) have been in the headlines during recent years. They uncovered and disclosed misbehavior among people in their companies and were protected under whistleblower provisions of various laws. Whistleblowers are protected from disciplinary action, termination, or other penalty. For more information, see https://osc.gov/ or perform an Internet search for the law by name.

For FIFTEEN or More Employees

Once employers have added 15 or more employees to their payroll, it becomes necessary to comply with an additional 10 major federal laws.

The Americans with Disabilities Act (ADA) (1990), as Amended by the Americans with Disabilities Act Amendments Act (ADAAA) (2008)

Prior to this legislation, the only employees who were protected against employment discrimination were the ones working for the federal, state, or local government and federal government contractors. They were captured by the Rehabilitation Act. As a matter of fact, it was the Rehabilitation Act that was used as a model for developing the ADA. Five years after the Rehabilitation Act, the Developmental Disabilities Act of 1978 spoke specifically to people with developmental disabilities. It provided for federally funded state programs to assist people in that category of the population. The ADA had been first proposed in 1988, and it was backed by thousands of individuals around the country who had been fighting for rights of their family members, friends, and co-workers. They thought it was only appropriate for those people to have equal access to community services, jobs, training, and promotions. It was signed into law by President George H. W. Bush on July 26, 1990. It became fully effective for all employers with 15 or more workers on July 26, 1992.

Provisions and Protections

Title 1 of the act applies to employers with 15 or more workers on the payroll. These employers may not discriminate against a physically or mentally disabled individual in recruitment, hiring, promotions, training, pay, social activities, and other privileges of employment. Qualified individuals with a disability are to be treated as other job applicants and employees are treated. If a job accommodation is required for a qualified individual to perform the assigned job, employers are required to provide that accommodation or recommend an alternative that would be equally effective. The interactive process between employers and employees should result in an accommodation or explanation about why making the accommodation would provide an undue hardship on the employer. Title 1 is enforced by the Equal Employment Opportunity Commission (EEOC). Part of the interactive discussion about accommodation requests involves the employer investigating other accommodations that may be equally effective yet lower in cost or other resource requirements. Employers are not obligated to accept the employee's request without alteration.

U.S. Supreme Court Interpretation of the ADA

There were several U.S. Supreme Court cases that interpreted the ADA very narrowly. They limited the number of people who could qualify as disabled under the Court's interpretation of Congress's initial intent. Reacting to those cases, Congress enacted the ADA Amendment Act in September 2008. It became effective on January 1, 2009.

ADA Amendments Act of 2008

Following the U.S. Supreme Court decisions in *Sutton v. United Airlines*[7] and in *Toyota Motor Manufacturing, Kentucky, Inc., v. William,*[8] Congress felt that the Court had been too restrictive in its interpretation of who qualifies as disabled. It was the intent of Congress to be broader in that definition. Consequently, Congress passed the ADA Amendments Act to capture a wider range of people in the disabled classification. An individual with a disability is now defined as "a person who has a physical or mental impairment that substantially limits one or more major life activities, a person who has a history or record of such an impairment, or a person who is perceived by others as having such an impairment."[9]

When determining whether someone is disabled, there may be no consideration of *mitigating circumstances*. In the past, we used to say people who had a disability under control were not disabled. An employee with a prosthetic limb did everything a whole-bodied person could do. An employee with migraines that disappeared with medication wasn't considered disabled. Under the old law, epilepsy and diabetes were not considered disabilities if they were controlled with medication. Now, because the law prohibits a consideration of either medication or prosthesis, they are considered disabilities. You can see that a great many more people are captured within the definition of disabled as a result of these more recent changes. The only specifically excluded condition is the one involving eyeglasses and contact lenses. Congress specifically said having a corrected vision problem if eyeglasses or contact lenses are worn may not constitute a disability under the law.

An individual can be officially disabled but quite able to do his or her job without an accommodation of any sort. Having more people defined as disabled doesn't necessarily mean there will be more people asking for job accommodations. For more information, see www.eeoc.gov/laws/statutes/adaaa.cfm or perform an Internet search for the law by name.

"Substantially Limits"

Employers are required to consider as disabled anyone with a condition that "substantially limits," but does not "significantly restrict," a major life activity. Even though the limitation might be reduced or eliminated with medication or other alleviation, the treatment may not be considered when determining the limitations. So, people who use shoe inserts to correct a back problem or who take prescription sleeping pills may now be classified as disabled. The same might be said of people who are allergic to peanuts or bee stings. Yet there may be no need for any of them to request a job accommodation.

"Major Life Activities"

Caring for oneself, seeing, hearing, touching, eating, sleeping, walking, standing, sitting, reaching, lifting, bending, speaking, breathing, learning, reading, concentrating, thinking, communicating, interacting with others, and working all are considered "major life activities." Also included are major bodily functions such as normal cell growth, reproduction, immune system, blood circulation, and the like. Some conditions are specifically designated as disabilities by the EEOC. They include diabetes, cancer, human immunodeficiency virus and acquired immunodeficiency syndrome (HIV/AIDS), multiple sclerosis (MS), cerebral palsy (CP), and cystic fibrosis (CF) because they interfere with one or more of our major life activities.

"Essential Job Function"

Essential job functions are portions of a job that employees must be able to perform, with or without reasonable accommodation. Defining the essential functions of a job helps interpret employee rights under the ADA. For example, if a job requires an incumbent to drive a delivery truck, driving would be an essential function of that job. A disability that prevented the incumbent from driving the delivery truck would likely block that employee from working—unless an accommodation could be found that would permit the incumbent to drive in spite of the disability.

There is nothing in the Americans with Disabilities Act of 1990, or its amendments, that requires employers to create job descriptions. However, smart employers are doing that in order to identify physical and mental requirements of each job. Job descriptions also make it easy to identify essential job functions that any qualified individual would have to perform, with or without job accommodation. It is easier to administer job accommodation request procedures and to defend against false claims of discrimination when an employer has job descriptions that clearly list all of the job's requirements. It also makes screening job applicants easier because it shows in writing what the job will entail. Then, recruiters may ask, "Is there anything in this list of essential job functions that you can't do with or without a job accommodation?"

People are sometimes confused about temporary suspension of job duty being a permanent job accommodation. It is not necessary for an employer to redesign job content to make a job accommodation, but it can be done by the employer voluntarily as a way to retain an employee. Those situations are not job accommodations, however. They are job reassignments.

"Job Accommodation"

Someone with a disability doesn't necessarily need a job accommodation. Remember that we select people and place them in jobs if they are qualified for the performance of the essential functions, with or without a job accommodation. Someone with diabetes may have the disease under control with medication and proper diet. No accommodation would be required. However, if it were essential that the employee had food intake at certain times of the day, there could be a legitimate request for accommodating that need. The employer might be asked to consistently permit the employee to have meal breaks at specific times each day.

Job accommodations are situationally dependent. First, there must be a disability and an ability to do the essential functions of the job. Next, there must be a request for accommodation from the employee or the employer must be aware of a potential disability. Being aware of a potential disability is where the law gets a little tricky. As a good rule of thumb, when you are aware of a physical or mental impairment that is impacting an employee's job duties, even if they have not said this directly, the interactive process should be triggered by the employer. It is perfectly acceptable for an employer to request supporting documentation from medical experts identifying the disability. There might even be recommendations for specific accommodations, including those requested by the employee.

Once an accommodation is requested, the employer is obliged to enter into an interactive discussion with the employee. For example, an employee might ask for something specific, perhaps a new piece of equipment (a special ergonomic chair) that will eliminate the impact of disability on their job performance. The employer must consider that specific request. Employers are obligated to search for alternatives that could satisfy the accommodation request only when the specific request cannot be reasonably accommodated. This is the point where the Job Accommodation Network (JAN)[10] can become a resource. It can often provide help for even questionable and unusual situations.

The employer must consider if making that accommodation would be an "undue hardship" considering all it would involve. You should note that most job accommodations carry a very low cost. Often they cost nothing. The larger an employer's payroll headcount, the more difficult it is to fully justify using "undue hardship" as a reason for not agreeing to provide an accommodation. Very large corporations or governments have vast resources, and the cost of one job accommodation, even if it does cost some large dollar amount, won't likely cause an undue hardship on that employer.

Recordkeeping Requirements

The ADA requires that employers store information about disability-related inquiries, the interactive process, or associated medical examinations in a separate, confidential medical file. Additionally, if job descriptions are kept, an annual review of job description content is required under EEOC guidelines. It is important to maintain accurate listings of essential job functions and physical and mental job requirements. An annual review will help ensure that you always have current information in your job descriptions. It is also a good practice to obtain an employee's signature on their job description at the time of hire and proactively ask if there are any needs for accommodation to perform the essential functions of the job. This is an easier way to stay compliant with the ADA and give employees the opportunity for this conversation early in employment.

EEOC procedures prohibit employers from inviting job applicants to identify their disability status prior to receiving a job offer. Federal regulations related to affirmative action requirements for disabled workers require contractors to invite job applicants to identify their status as disabled and then provide the same invitation to identify themselves as disabled once they have been hired. Federal contractors are also required to conduct a general survey of the entire employee population every 5 years (at a minimum) with an invitation to self-identify as disabled. At any time, employees are permitted to identify themselves as disabled to their employer.

ADA Enforcement

The EEOC enforces Title 1 of the ADA. That agency will accept complaints of illegal discrimination based on mental or physical disability. Once an employee has established that they are disabled and claims that they have been prohibited from some employment benefit because of the disability (for example, hiring, promotion, access to training, or inappropriate termination), there is a *prima facie* case (meaning it is true on its surface).

Then the EEOC notifies the employer of the complaint and asks for the employer's response. This process can work back and forth from employer response to employee response for several cycles. Ultimately, the agency will determine that the case has cause (is a valid claim of discrimination), the case has no cause (the claim cannot be substantiated), or the case should be closed for administrative purposes (the employee asks for the case to be closed, or the time for an investigation has expired). Each of those three outcomes is followed by a "Right to Sue" letter, allowing the employee to get an attorney and file a lawsuit in federal court seeking remedies under the law.[11]

Once a complaint (called a *charge of illegal discrimination*) is filed with the EEOC, employers are instructed to cease talking about that issue directly with their employee. All conversation about the complaint must be directed through the EEOC. Unfortunately, that complicates the communication process, and it provides a strong incentive for employers to resolve complaints internally before they reach the formal external complaint stage. Working directly with an employee on the subject of accommodation, or any other personnel issue, is preferable to working through an agent such as the EEOC. For more information, see www.ada.gov or perform an Internet search for the law by name.

The Civil Rights Act (Title VII) (1964)

Although this was not the first federal civil rights act in the country,[12] it came to us through a great deal of controversy. It was signed into law by President Lyndon Johnson on July 2, 1964. Following the assassination of President John F. Kennedy the previous November, President Johnson took it upon himself to carry the civil rights banner and urge Congress to pass the law.

Employment Protections

Title VII of the act speaks to employment discrimination and cites five protected classes of people. Before the final days when Congress was discussing the issues, there were only four protected classes listed: race, color, religion, and national origin. There was a great deal of opposition in the Senate from Southern states. They decided that they would strategically add another protected category to the list. They thought that if "sex" was added to the list, the bill would surely fail because no one would vote for having women protected in the workplace. Well, it passed…with all five protected categories in place. From that time forward, when making employment decisions, it has been illegal to take into account any employee's membership in any of the protected classifications.

Penalties for Violations

Penalties can be assessed by a federal court. Protocol requires a complaint be filed with the Equal Employment Opportunity Commission, the administrative agency tasked with the duty to investigate claims of illegal employment discrimination. Regardless of the outcome of that administrative review, a "Right to Sue" letter is given to the complaining employee so the case can move forward to federal court if that is what the employee wants to do next.

Penalties that can be assessed if an employer is found to have illegally discriminated include the following:

- **Actual damages**   Costs for medical bills, travel to medical appointments, equipment loss reimbursement, lost wages (back pay), lost promotional increase, lost future earnings (front pay). The limitation is usually 2 years into the past and unlimited number of years into the future.

- **Compensatory damages**   Dollars to reimburse the victim for "pain and suffering" caused by this illegal discrimination.

- **Punitive damages**   Dollars assessed by the court to "punish" the employer for treatment of the employee that was egregious in its nature. This is usually thought of as "making an example" of one case so as to send a message to other employers that doing such things to an employee or job applicant will be severely punished.

For more information, see www.eeoc.gov/laws/statutes/titlevii.cfm or perform an Internet search for the law by name.

The Civil Rights Act (1991)

This act modified the 1964 Civil Rights Act in several ways:

- It provided for employees to receive a jury trial if they wanted. Up to this point, judges always heard cases and decided them from the bench.

- It established requirements for any employer defense.

- It placed a limitation on punitive damage awards by using a sliding scale, depending on the size of the employer organization (payroll headcount):

  - For employers with 15 to 100 employees, damages are capped at $50,000.

  - For employers with 100 to 200 employees, damages are capped at $100,000.

  - For employers with 201 to 500 employees, damages are capped at $200,000.

  - For employers with more than 500 employees, damages are capped at $300,000.

For more information, see https://www.eeoc.gov/statutes/civil-rights-act-1991 or perform an Internet search for the law by name.

The Drug-Free Workplace Act (1988)

This legislation requires some employers to maintain a drug-free workplace. Employee compliance must be ensured by subject employers.

Provisions and Protections

This law applies to organizations receiving federal contracts of $100,000 or more and all organizations receiving grants from the federal government. If you are covered, you are required to ensure that all the employees working on the contract or grant are in compliance with its drug-free requirements. Covered employers are required to have a drug-free policy that applies to its employees. To determine that an employer is in compliance with the requirements, drug testing is usually performed on employees and applicants who have received a job offer. Random drug testing is also used in some organizations to ensure employees subject to the law or policy are continuing to comply with the requirements. Any federal contractor under the jurisdiction of the Office of Federal Contract Compliance Programs (OFCCP) in the Department of Labor must comply with this legislation.

Employee notification about the policy must include information about the consequences of failing a drug test. Whenever an employee has been convicted of a criminal drug violation in the workplace, the employer must notify the contracting or granting agency within 10 days.

Recordkeeping Requirements

Covered employers are required to publish a written policy statement that clearly covers all employees or just those employees who are associated with the federal contract or grant. Each covered employee must be given a copy of the policy statement, and it is a good idea, although it is not required, to have employees sign for receipt of that policy statement. The statement must contain a list of prohibited substances. At a minimum it must cite controlled substances.[13]

Some employers choose to include in the policy prohibition of alcohol and prescription drug misuse, although that is not a requirement. Subject employers must also establish a drug-free awareness training program to make employees aware of the dangers of drug abuse in the workplace; the policy of maintaining a drug-free workplace; any available drug counseling, rehabilitation, and employee assistance programs; and the penalties that may be imposed on employees for drug abuse violations. Records should be maintained showing each employee who received the training and the date it occurred.

Drug-Free Workplace Act Enforcement

Federal contractors under the jurisdiction of the OFCCP will find that the agency requires proof of compliance when it conducts a general compliance evaluation of affirmative action plans. Any employee who fails a drug test must be referred to a treatment program or given appropriate disciplinary action. Care should be given to treating similar cases in the same way. It is fairly easy to be challenged under Title VII for unequal treatment based on one of the Title VII protected groups.

Each federal agency responsible for contracting or providing grants is also responsible for enforcing the Drug-Free Workplace Act requirements. These responsibilities are spelled out in the Federal Acquisition Regulation (FAR). Failing to comply with the act may result in penalties, including suspension of payment or termination of a grant of contract, and being barred from applying for future government funding.

For more information, see https://www.congress.gov/bill/100th-congress/house-bill/4719 or perform an Internet search for the law by name.

The Equal Employment Opportunity Act (EEOA) (1972)

The EEOA amended the Civil Rights Act of 1964 by giving the EEOC litigation authority and changing some terminology. It also required a new employment poster for all covered work locations explaining that "EEO is the Law."

For more information, see https://www.govtrack.us/congress/bills/92/hr1746/text or perform an Internet search for the name of the law.

The Genetic Information Nondiscrimination Act (GINA) (2008)

In general terms, GINA prohibits employers from using genetic information to make employment decisions. This legislation was brought about by insurance companies using genetic information to determine who would likely have expensive diseases in the future. That information allowed decisions to exclude them from hiring or enrollment in medical insurance programs. With the implementation of this law, those considerations are no longer legal.

For more information, see www.eeoc.gov/laws/statutes/gina.cfm or perform an Internet search for the law by name.

Guidelines on Discrimination Because of Sex (1980)

Although not technically a law, the Equal Employment Opportunity Commission (EEOC) took an important step in addressing sexual harassment by publishing these guidelines to help employers understand what constituted unwanted behavior and harassment. They were issued long before the U.S. Supreme Court considered the leading cases on sexual harassment. This is about the only thing at the time that employers were able to turn to for help in managing the problem of sexual harassment in the workplace.

For more information, see https://www.eeoc.gov/laws/guidance/policy-guidance-current-issues-sexual-harassment or perform an Internet search for the guidelines by name.

The Lilly Ledbetter Fair Pay Act (2009)

This was the first piece of legislation signed by President Barack Obama after he was inaugurated the 44th president of the United States. It was passed in reaction to the U.S. Supreme Court decision in *Ledbetter v. Goodyear Tire & Rubber Co., Inc.,* 550 U.S. 618 (2007).

This law amends the Civil Rights Act of 1964 and states that the clock will begin running anew each time an illegal act of discrimination is experienced by an employee. In Lilly Ledbetter's situation, her pay was less than that for men doing the same job. The old law didn't permit her to succeed in her complaint of discrimination because she failed to file 20 years earlier on the first occasion of her receiving a paycheck for less than her male counterparts. Under the new law, the 180-day statute of limitations for filing an equal-pay lawsuit regarding pay discrimination resets with each new paycheck affected by that discriminatory action. For more information, see www.eeoc.gov/laws/statutes/epa_ledbetter.cfm or perform an Internet search for the law by name.

The Pregnancy Discrimination Act (1978)

This law modified the Civil Rights Act of 1964. It defined pregnancy as protected within the definition of "sex" for the purpose of coverage under the Civil Rights Act. It also specifically said that no employer shall illegally discriminate against an employee because of pregnancy. It defines pregnancy as a temporary disability and requires accommodation on the job if it is necessary. It guarantees the employee rights to return to work to the same or similar job with the same pay following her pregnancy disability. For more information, see www.eeoc.gov/laws/types/pregnancy.cfm or perform an Internet search for the law by name.

The Uniform Guidelines on Employee Selection Procedures (1978)

This set of regulations is often overlooked by employers and HR professionals alike. Details can be found in 41 C.F.R. 60-3. For covered employers with 15 or more people on the payroll, this set of requirements is essential in preventing claims of discrimination.

There are two types of illegal employment discrimination: adverse or disparate treatment and adverse or disparate impact. The latter almost always results from seemingly neutral policies having a statistically adverse impact on a specific group of people. To avoid illegal discrimination, the guidelines require that all steps in a hiring decision be validated for the job being filled. Validity of a selection device can be determined through a validity study or by applying a job analysis to demonstrate the specific relationship between the selection device and the job requirements. Selection devices include things such as a written test, an oral test, an interview, a requirement to write something for consideration, and a physical ability test.

Employers can get into trouble when they use selection tools that have not been validated for their specific applications. For example, buying a clerical test battery of written tests and using it to make selection decisions for administrative assistants as well as general office clerks may not be supportable. Only a validity analysis will tell for sure. What specific validation studies have been done for the test battery by the publisher? Any publisher should be able to provide you with a copy of the validation study showing how the test is supposed to be used and the specific skills, knowledge, or abilities that are analyzed when using it. If you can't prove the test measures things required by your job content, don't use the test. According to the Uniform Guidelines, "While publishers of selection procedures have a professional obligation to provide evidence of validity which meets generally accepted professional standards, users are cautioned that they are responsible for compliance with these guidelines."[14] That means the employer, not the test publisher, is liable for the results.

For more information, see https://www.eeoc.gov/laws/guidance/employment-tests-and-selection-procedures or perform an Internet search for the law by name.

For TWENTY or More Employees

The next threshold for employers occurs when they reach a headcount of 20 employees. At that point, another four major federal laws begin their influence on the organization.

The Age Discrimination in Employment Act (ADEA) (1967), as Amended

When this law was first passed, it specified the protected age range of 40 to 70. Anyone younger than 40 or older than 70 was not covered for age discrimination in the workplace. Amendments were made a few years later that removed the upper limit. Today, the law bans employment discrimination based on age if the employee is 40 years old or older. Remedies under this law are the same as under the Civil Rights Act. They include reinstatement, back pay, front pay, and payment for benefits in arrears. Some exceptions to the "unlimited" upper age exist. One example is the rule that airline pilots may not fly commercial airplanes after the age of 65.[15] For more information, see www.eeoc.gov/laws/statutes/adea.cfm or perform an Internet search for the law by name.

The American Recovery and Reinvestment Act (ARRA) (2009)

The thrust of this legislation was to create government infrastructure projects such as highways, buildings, dams, and such. It was an attempt to find ways to re-employ many of the workers who had become unemployed since the great recession began in 2007. There was a temporary provision that provided partial payment of COBRA premiums (see the Consolidated Omnibus Budget Reconciliation Act, covered next) for people who still had not found permanent job placement.

ARRA also modified HIPAA privacy rules. It applies HIPAA's security and privacy requirements to business associates. Business associates are defined under ARRA as individuals or organizations that transmit protected medical data, store that data, process that data, or in any other way have contact with that private medical information. All parties are responsible for proper handling and compliance with the HIPAA rules. For more information, see https://www.congress.gov/bill/111th-congress/house-bill/1/titles or perform an Internet search for the law by name.

The Consolidated Omnibus Budget Reconciliation Act (COBRA) (1986)

This law requires employers with group health insurance programs to offer employees the opportunity to continue their health plan coverage after they are no longer on the payroll or no longer qualify for benefits coverage because of a change in employment status, such as a reduction in hours. The cost must be at group rates, and the employer can add a small administrative service charge. It turns out that many employers turn these programs over to vendors who administer the COBRA benefits for former employees. They send out billing statements and provide collection services. Two percent is the maximum administrative overhead fee that can be added. The total cost of COBRA premiums and administrative fees is paid by employees participating in COBRA. The duration of coverage is dependent on some variables, so it may be different from one person to another. For more information, see www.dol.gov/dol/topic/health-plans/cobra.htm or perform an Internet search for the law by name.

The Older Workers Benefit Protection Act (OWBPA) (1990)

In the 1980s, it was common for employers, particularly large employers, to implement staff reduction programs as a means of addressing expenses. Often those programs were targeted at more senior workers because, generally speaking, their compensation was greater than that of new employees. Reducing one senior worker could save more money than the reduction of a more recently hired worker. Congress took action to prevent such treatment based on age when it passed this law.

The key purposes of the Older Workers Benefit Protection Act (OWBPA) are to prohibit an employer from the following:

- Using an employee's age as the basis for discrimination in benefits
- Targeting older workers during staff reductions or downsizing
- Requiring older workers to waive their rights without the opportunity for review with their legal advisor

This law is particularly important when offering a severance agreement to an employee, which is a contract an employer may ask an employee being terminated from a job to sign in exchange for a payment to the employee. Any employee 40 years or older must be offered more time to review the severance agreement: 21 days, with a 7-day period after signing where the agreement can be revoked.

For more information, see https://www.congress.gov/bill/101st-congress/senate-bill/1511 or perform an Internet search for the law by name.

For FIFTY or More Employees

Once the employee headcount reaches these higher levels, additional legal obligations become effective for employers. Some of them apply only if the employer is subject to affirmative action requirements as a federal contractor.

Executive Order 11246: Affirmative Action (1965)

This is the presidential order that created what we now know as employment-based affirmative action. In 1965, President Lyndon B. Johnson was past the days when he approved the Civil Rights Act, and he was in the process of examining how it was being implemented around the country by employers. He concluded that the law was pretty much being ignored. He needed something to stimulate implementation of the employment provisions in the Civil Rights Act, Title VII. His staff suggested they require affirmative action programs from federal contractors, and thus a new program was born. President Johnson said that if a company wanted to receive revenue by contracting with the federal government, it would have to implement equal employment opportunity and establish outreach programs for minorities and women. At the time, minorities and women were being excluded from candidate selection pools. If they couldn't get into the selection pools, there was no way for them to be selected. Therefore, affirmative action programs were created. Outreach and recruiting were the main parts of these programs.

Analysis of the incumbent workforce, the available pool of qualified job candidates, and the training of managers involved in the employment selection process all contributed to a slow movement toward full equality for minorities and women.

The Office of Federal Contract Compliance Programs (OFCCP) is the law enforcement agency that currently has responsibility for enforcing the executive order along with other laws. Federal contractors must meet several conditions in return for the contracting privilege. One is the requirement to abide by a set of rules known as the Federal Acquisition Regulation (FAR). In addition, there is affirmative action for the disabled and veterans. Any business that doesn't want to abide by these requirements can make the business decision to abandon federal revenues and contracts. If you want the contracts, you also have to agree to the affirmative action requirements.[16] For more information, see www.dol.gov/ofccp/regs/statutes/eo11246.htm or perform an Internet search for the executive order by name.

The Family and Medical Leave Act (FMLA) (1993), Expanded 2008, 2010

In general, the Family and Medical Leave Act sets in place new benefits for some employees in the country. If their employer has 50 or more people on the payroll, then they are required to permit FMLA leave of absence for their workers. FMLA provides for leaves lasting up to 12 weeks in a 12-month period, and it is unpaid unless the employer has a policy to pay for the leave time. The 12-month period begins on the first day of leave. A new leave availability will occur 12 months from the date the first leave began. During the leave, it is an obligation of the employer to continue paying any benefit plan premiums that the employer would have paid if the employee had remained on the job. If there is a portion of the premium for health insurance that is normally paid by the employee, that obligation for co-payment continues during the employee's leave time. The 12 weeks of leave may be taken in increments of 1 day or less.

To qualify, employees must have more than 1 year of service and must have worked at least 1,250 hours in the past year. The amount of hours you need to work to qualify is different for the airline industry due to the Airline Flight Crew Technical Corrections Act (2009). The leave is authorized to cover childbirth, adoption, or foster care; to care for a seriously ill child, spouse, or parent; in case of the employee's own serious illness; or needs related to a child, spouse, or parent on active military duty. The employee is guaranteed return to work to the same job or an equivalent job, at the same pay, under the same conditions prior to the leave of absence.

There are provisions for "Military Caregiver Leave" lasting up to 26 weeks of unpaid leave of absence for employees with family members needing care due to a military duty–related injury or illness. The 26-week limit renews every 12 months. The law provides for "National Guard and Military Reserve Family Leave." Employees who are family members of National Guard or Military Reservists who are called to active duty may take FMLA leave to assist with preparing financial and legal arrangements and other family issues associated with rapid deployment or post-deployment activities. An employer may agree to any non-listed condition as a qualifier for FMLA leave as well.

FMLA provides for "Light Duty Assignments." It clarifies that "light duty" work does not count against an employee's FMLA leave entitlement. It also provides that an employee's right to job restoration is held in abeyance during the light duty period. An employee voluntarily doing light duty work is not on FMLA leave.

There is an employment poster requirement. The notice must be posted at each work location where employees can see it without trouble. A "Medical Certification Process" is part of the newer provisions. DOL regulations have specified who may contact the employee's medical advisor for information, written or otherwise, and specifically prohibits the employee's supervisor from making contact with the employee's medical advisor.

Specific prohibitions are made against illegal discrimination for an employee taking advantage of the benefits offered under this law. These provisions are enforced by the EEOC. For more information, see https://www.dol.gov/agencies/whd/fmla or perform an Internet search for the law by name.

The Mental Health Parity Act (MHPA) (1996)

This legislation requires health insurance issuers and group health plans to adopt the same annual and lifetime dollar limits for mental health benefits as for other medical benefits. For more information, see https://www.congress.gov/bill/104th-congress/house-bill/4058/text or perform an Internet search for the law by name.

The Mental Health Parity and Addiction Equity Act (MHPAEA) (2008)

This is an amendment of the Mental Health Parity Act of 1996. It requires that plans that offer both medical/surgical benefits and mental health and/or substance abuse treatment benefits provide parity between both types of benefits. All financial requirements (for example, deductibles, copayments, coinsurance, out-of-pocket expenses, and annual limits) and treatment requirements (for example, frequency of treatment, number of visits, and days of coverage) must be the same for treatment of both mental and physical medical problems. For more information, see https://www.congress.gov/bill/110th-congress/house-bill/6983 or perform an Internet search for the law by name.

The National Defense Authorization Act (2008), Expanded in 2010

This is the origin of benefit provisions under FMLA for leaves of absence due to military and military family reasons. Qualifying events for individuals include notice of deployment, return from deployment, and treatment for an injury sustained while on deployment. The provision is for up to 26 weeks, which can be taken in increments of a day or less if, for example, treatment is required for a service-related injury. The 2010 amendments expanded leave for family needs related to a covered family member being on, or called to, active duty. For more information, see https://www.dol.gov/agencies/whd/fmla/military-families or perform an Internet search for the law by name.

The Patient Protection and Affordable Care Act (PPACA) (2010)

Signed into law by President Barack Obama on March 23, 2010, this law is commonly referred to as the Affordable Care Act. It has created health insurance trading centers in each state where employees and those who are unemployed can shop for health insurance coverage. These trading centers are the American Health Benefit Exchanges and Small Business Health Options Program (SHOP). Individuals and business owners of organizations with fewer than 100 workers can purchase insurance through these exchanges.

It applies to all employers with 50 or more full-time workers on the payroll. Employers with fewer than 50 full-time workers are exempt from coverage under the law. Effective January 1, 2014, the original law required employers to either provide minimum health insurance coverage to their full-time employees or face a fine of $2,000 per employee, excluding the first 30 from the assessment. Employers with fewer than 25 employees receive a tax credit if they provide health insurance to their workers. In 2018, changes in the Affordable Care Act included elimination of the financial penalties for individuals who did not sign up for health insurance. Consequently, the number of people who are underinsured has increased. Cost of coverage has been increasing steadily through all of the insurance companies. Congress, however, has failed to pass new legislation that would either replace or repeal the act. For more information, see https://www.dol .gov/agencies/ebsa/laws-and-regulations/laws/affordable-care-act or perform an Internet search for the law by name.

Executive Order 13706: Paid Sick Leave for Federal Contractors (2015)

Federal contractors are directed to provide up to 56 hours of paid sick leave annually. The leave is accrued at the rate of an hour for every 30 hours worked. It may be carried over from year to year. For more information, see https://www.gpo.gov/fdsys/pkg/ FR-2015-09-10/pdf/2015-22998.pdf or perform an Internet search for the executive order by number.

For ONE HUNDRED or More Employees

The final major threshold for employers is reached when the payroll reaches 100 employees. At that time, employers become subject to the WARN Act and are required to submit annual reports to the government summarizing their race and sex demographics.

The Worker Adjustment and Retraining Notification (WARN) Act (1988)

This was the first attempt by Congress to involve local communities early in the private sector's downsizing process. It also prevented employers from just shutting the door and walking away without any worker benefits. It applies to all employers with 100 or more full-time workers at a single facility. The law specifies a qualifying employer to be one that has 100 or more employees who in the aggregate work at least 4,000 hours per week (exclusive of hours of overtime).

Definitions

The term *plant closing* refers to the permanent or temporary shutdown of a single site of employment, or one or more facilities or operating units within a single site of employment, if the shutdown results in an employment loss at the single site of employment during any 30-day period for 50 or more employees, excluding any part-time employees.

The term *mass layoff* refers to a reduction in force that is not the result of a plant closing. It results in an employment loss at the single site of employment during any 30-day period for (1) at least 500 full-time employees *or* (2) when at least 33 percent of the workforce (excluding any part-time employees) are going to be removed from the payroll in a layoff where there are a total of 50 to 499 workers before the layoff.

Required Actions

The law requires 60 days' advance notice to employees of plant closing or mass layoffs. Any employment loss of 50 or more people, excluding part-time workers, is considered a trigger event to activate the requirements. Notification of public officials in the surrounding community in addition to notification of employees are requirements. The local community leaders must be informed and invited to participate in the process of finding new jobs for laid-off workers. There is a provision that says an employer can pay 60 days' separation allowance if it gives no notice to workers who will be terminated.

Exemptions to Notice Requirement

Notice is not required, regardless of the size of layoff, if the layoff, downsizing, or terminations result from the completion of a contract or project that employees understood would constitute their term of employment. It is not uncommon for workers to be hired in a "term" classification that designates them as employees for the life of a project. If they understand that from the beginning of their employment, their termination would not trigger the WARN Act.

WARN is not triggered in the following cases:

- In the event of strikes or lockouts that are not intended to evade the requirements of this law.

- In the event the layoff will be for less than 6 months.

- If state and local governments are downsizing. They are exempt from the notice requirement.

- In the event that fewer than 50 people will be laid off or terminated from a single site.

- If 50 to 499 workers lose their jobs and that number is less than 33 percent of the active workforce at the single site.

For more information, see https://www.dol.gov/agencies/eta/layoffs/warn or perform an Internet search for the law by name.

For Federal Government Employees

The federal government is subject to some of the same laws as the private-sector employers. Yet, there are additional obligations that government employers have. Some of those obligations stem from the United States Constitution. Others come from the following laws.

The Civil Service Reform Act (1978)

This legislation eliminated the U.S. Civil Service Commission and created three new agencies to take its place:

- **The Office of Personnel Management (OPM)**   This is the executive branch's human resource department. It handles all HR issues for agencies reporting to the U.S. president.

- **The Merit Systems Protection Board (MSPB)**   This part of the law prohibits consideration of marital status, political activity, or political affiliation in dealing with federal civilian employees. It also created the Office of Special Counsel, which accepts employee complaints and investigates and resolves them.

- **The Federal Labor Relations Authority (FLRA)**   This is the agency that enforces federal civilian employee rights to form unions and bargain with their agencies. It establishes standards of behavior for union officers, and these standards are enforced by the Office of Labor-Management Standards in the U.S. Department of Labor.

For more information, see https://www.congress.gov/bill/95th-congress/senate-bill/2640 or perform an Internet search for the law by name.

The Congressional Accountability Act (1995)

Until this law was implemented, the legislative branch of the government was exempt from nearly all employment-related requirements that applied to other federal agencies and private employers. This law requires Congress and its affiliated agencies to abide by 12 specific laws that already applied to other employers, in and out of government:

- Americans with Disabilities Act
- Age Discrimination in Employment Act
- Employee Polygraph Protection Act
- Federal Service Relations Statute
- Genetic Information Nondiscrimination Act
- Rehabilitation Act

- Civil Rights Act (Title VII)
- Fair Labor Standards Act
- Family and Medical Leave Act
- Veterans Employment Opportunities Act
- Worker Adjustment and Retraining Notification Act
- Occupational Safety and Health Act

For more information, see https://www.ocwr.gov/sites/default/files/CAA_508v2.pdf or perform an Internet search for the law by name.

The False Claims Act (1863)

During the Civil War, people were selling defective food and arms to the Union military. This law, sometimes referred to as the Lincoln Law, prohibits such dishonest transactions. It prohibits making and using false records to get those claims paid. It also prohibits selling the government goods that are known to be defective. For HR professionals today, it is wise to train all employees about the need to avoid creating records that are inaccurate or, even worse, fictitious. Doing things that are illegal, just because the boss says you should, will still be illegal. Employees need to understand that concept.

For more information, see www.justice.gov/civil/docs_forms/C-FRAUDS_FCA_Primer.pdf or perform an Internet search for the law by name.

The Homeland Security Act (2002)

This cabinet-level organization (Department of Homeland Security) was created by Congress and President George W. Bush to consolidate security efforts related to protecting U.S. geography. Immigration and Customs Enforcement (ICE) is part of this department. The E-Verify system resides here. Used by federal contractors as part of their affirmative action obligations and other private employers on a voluntary basis, the system is intended to assist in rapid verification of Social Security numbers (SSNs) and confirm that the individual attached to the SSN has a valid right to work in this country. For more information, see https://www.dhs.gov/homeland-security-act-2002 or perform an Internet search for the law by name.

The Privacy Act (1974)

This law provides that governmental agencies must make known to the public their data collection and storage activities and must provide copies of pertinent records to the individual citizen when requested—with some specific exemptions. Those exemptions include law enforcement, congressional investigations, census use, "archival purposes," and other administrative purposes. In all, there are 12 statutory exemptions from disclosure requirements. If employees are concerned about employers using their Social Security numbers in records sent to the government, this act ensures privacy. Although such private information is required by the government, the government is prohibited from releasing it to third parties without proper authorization or court order. For more information, see www.justice.gov/opcl/privstat.htm or perform an Internet search for the law by name.

The USA PATRIOT Act (2001)

The Uniting and Strengthening America by Providing Appropriate Tools Required to Intercept and Obstruct Terrorism (USA PATRIOT) Act was passed immediately following the September 11, 2001, terrorist attacks in New York City and at the Pentagon in Virginia. It gives the government authority to intercept wire, oral, and electronic communications relating to terrorism, computer fraud, and abuse offenses. It also provides the authorization for collecting agencies to share the information they collect in the interest of law enforcement. This law can have an impact on private-sector employers in the communications industry. It can also have an impact on any employer when the government asks for support to identify and track "lone wolves" suspected of terrorism without being affiliated with known terrorist organizations. HR professionals may find themselves involved in handling the collection and release of personal, confidential information about one or more employees. When legal documents such as subpoenas and court orders are involved, it is always a good idea to have the organization's attorney review them before taking any other action. For more information, see www.justice.gov/archive/ll/highlights.htm or perform an Internet search for the law by name.

Employment Visas for Foreign Nationals

Under some circumstances, it is possible for people from other countries to come work in the United States. There are several classifications of workers that can be used depending on the type of work to be done and the level of responsibilities.

E Nonimmigrant Visas

There are three types of E Nonimmigrant Visas: E-1 Treaty Traders, E-2 Treaty Investors, and E-3 Specialty Occupation Professionals from Australia. For more information on E Nonimmigrant Visas, see https://www.uscis.gov/forms/explore-my-options/e-visas-e-1-e-2-and-e-3-for-temporary-workers.

E-1 Treaty Traders

The individual must be a citizen of the treaty country; there must be substantial trade; the trade must be principally with the treaty country; the individual must have executive, supervisory, or essential skills; and the individual must intend to depart the United States when the trading is completed.

E-2 Treaty Investors

The individual must be a citizen of the treaty country and be invested personally in the enterprise. The business must be a bona fide enterprise and not marginal, and the investment must be substantial. E-2 employees must have executive, supervisory, or essential skills, and E-2 investors must direct and develop the enterprise. The E-2 investor must depart the United States when the investment is concluded.

E-3 Specialty Occupation Professionals from Australia

The individual must be an Australian national with a job offer for a specialty job occupation in the United States and possess the educational or qualifying credentials for that job. This visa allows a stay in the United States for 2 years, with no limit on additional 2-year extensions.

H Visas

These are visas available to employers and employees for specialized talent or educational requirements. For more information, see https://travel.state.gov/content/travel/en/us-visas/employment/temporary-worker-visas.html.

H1-B Special Occupations and Fashion Models

These visas require a bachelor's or higher degree or its equivalent. The job must be so complex that it can be performed only by a person with the degree. Fashion models also fall into this category.

H1-B1 Free Trade Agreement Professional

These visas apply to citizens of Chile and Singapore in a specialized occupation. The individual must have a post-secondary degree involving at least 4 years of study in the field of specialty.

H-2A Temporary Agricultural Workers

The employer must be able to demonstrate that there are not sufficient U.S. workers who are able, willing, qualified, and available to do the temporary seasonal work. The employer must also show that the employment of H-2A workers will not adversely affect the wages and working conditions of similarly employed U.S. workers.

H-2B Temporary Non-Agricultural Workers

The employer must show that there are not enough U.S. workers who are able, willing, qualified, and available to do the temporary work and that the employment of H-2B workers will not adversely affect the wages and working conditions of similarly employed U.S. workers. The employer must also show that the need for the prospective worker's services is temporary, regardless of whether the underlying job can be described as temporary.

H-3 Nonimmigrant Trainee

To qualify, employees must be trainees receiving training in any field of endeavor, other than graduate medical education or academia that is not available in their home country. Alternatively, they must be a Special Education Exchange Visitor who will participate in a special education training program focused on the education of children with physical, mental, or emotional disabilities.

L-1 Intracompany Transferee

This allows a qualifying organization to move an employee from another qualifying country into the United States for a temporary assignment either that is managerial in nature or that requires specialized knowledge.

L1-A Managers and Executives

These are intracompany transferees coming to the United States to work in a managerial or executive capacity. The maximum stay in the United States allowed under this visa is 7 years.

L1-B Specialized Knowledge

This is someone with specialized knowledge of the employer's product, service, research, equipment, techniques, management, or other interests and its application in international markets, or with an advanced level of knowledge or expertise in the organization's processes and procedures. An L1-B visa holder may stay in the United States for only 5 years.

O-1 Alien of Extraordinary Ability in Arts, Science, Education, Business, Athletics

These people have a level of expertise indicating that they are among the small percentage who have risen to the top of their field of endeavor. Alternatively, they represent extraordinary achievement in motion-picture and television productions, or they have extraordinary ability and distinction in the arts.

P Visa Categories

There are seven variations of athletics-based or art-based visas:

- P1-A Individual Athletes or Athletic Teams
- P1-B Entertainment Groups
- P1-S Essential Support needed for P1-A or P1-B
- P2 Artist or Entertainer Under a Reciprocal Exchange Program
- P2-S Essential Support for P2
- P3 Artist or Entertainer Under a Culturally Unique Program
- P3-S Essential Support for P3

EB Employment-Based Visas

There are five levels of employment-based visas. They are prioritized so that once the first-level immigrant applicants are processed, the next level of priority will be considered. That continues until the maximum allotment of visas is reached. In recent years, about 140,000 employment-based visas were permitted each year.[17]

EB-1 Alien of Extraordinary Ability

The employer must demonstrate that the alien has extraordinary ability in the sciences, arts, education, business, or athletics, which has been demonstrated by sustained national or international acclaim and whose achievements have been recognized in the field through extensive documentation. It must also be shown that the work to be done in the United States will continue in the individual's area of extraordinary ability. It shall also be shown how the alien's entry into this country will benefit the United States.

EB-2 Alien of Extraordinary Ability

This is a classification that applies to any job that requires advanced degrees and persons of exceptional ability.

EB-3 Skilled Workers

This category applies to professionals and even unskilled workers who are sponsored by employers in the United States.

EB-4 Certain Special Immigrants

Included here are some broadcasters, ministers of religion, employees or former employees of the United States government, Iraqi or Afghan interpreters and translators, and other similar workers.

EB-5 Immigrant Investors

These are people who will create new commercial enterprises in the United States that will provide job creation.

Chapter Review

While this chapter is not meant to be a comprehensive statement of each law, studying and learning these laws will help you understand the basics as you perform your professional human resource responsibilities. As you read through the other chapters in this book, it's important to remember that one or more of these laws will be the underlying basis for the HR Certification Institute's (HRCI's) subject matter. Additionally, while using this chapter as a reference guide in your day-to-day application as an HR professional, ensure you also consult the statutes and regulations themselves via the URLs we have provided or perform an Internet search for the topic by name. A thorough understanding of the various laws and regulations that impact the employment relationship will enhance your ability to protect your organization in matters involving employment and employee relations.

Questions

The following are all questions about U.S. laws and regulations concerning employee management.

1. John, a new employee, has just arrived at the orientation program where everyone completes their payroll forms and signs up for healthcare benefits. He brings his W-4 form to you and says he isn't subject to payroll withholding because he pays his taxes directly each quarter. What is your response?

   A. "That's okay. We won't process a W-4 form for you. We will give you a Form 1099."

   B. "I'll check with the accounting department to find out whether you can do that."

   C. "Unfortunately, all employees are subject to payroll tax withholding."

   D. "If you can show me a W-10 form you have submitted to the IRS, we can block your paycheck withholding."

2. The Wagner-Peyser Act protects employees who are:

   A. Unemployed

   B. Injured on the job

   C. Unable to work because of pregnancy

   D. Have two or more jobs

3. Pete is sensitive about the security of his personal identity information since his credit card has been stolen twice in the past year. He is trying to clear up his credit rating because of the problems with the stolen cards. Now, he has approached the HR manager at his organization and requested that his Social Security number be removed from all of the company records. He thinks that a mistake could cause him more grief if the Social Security number were to be obtained by thieves. As the HR professional, what should you do?

   A. Delete the Social Security number from the company's records to protect Pete.

   B. Keep the Social Security number for tax reporting.

   C. Keep the Social Security number for census reporting.

   D. Although the company has no need for the Social Security number, you should keep it regardless.

4. Pat is talking with her colleagues about illegal discrimination at work. Someone mentions that the company is going to be sending out a request for updated race and sex information. Pat says that isn't legal. The company isn't supposed to track any of that information. Which of the following statements is true in this case?

   A. Pat has not understood the FLSA requirements that employers keep race and sex data on employees.

   B. The EEOC has issued guidelines that agree with Pat's belief that it is illegal to maintain that information in company records.

   C. Only federal contractors are required to maintain the race and sex identification for employees.

   D. It is only the public-sector employees who are exempt from providing their race and sex identification to employers.

5. The Tractor and Belt Company (TBC) handles conveyor belt installations for many small firms. Each of the customer projects begins on a day that is most convenient for the customer. Sometimes, that's Monday; sometimes it's Thursday or some other day. The HR manager says that the company will adjust its workweek to begin when the customer's project starts. That way, each installation team has a separate workweek, and those workweeks can shift several times a month. What is your advice about this strategy?

   A. The HR manager is simply taking advantage of the FLSA's provisions for flexible workweeks that support small business. No change is required.

   B. Once the workweek has been designated to begin on a certain day of the week, it should not be changed by the HR manager.

   C. It depends on state laws and regulations whether the workweek begins on any specific day of the week.

   D. The FLSA says a workweek should always begin on Sunday.

6. Sandy is 15 years old and a sophomore at Central High School. She gets a job at the local hamburger drive-in. Her boss says he needs her to work the following schedule during the Spring Break week: 4 hours at lunch time every day, 9 hours on Saturday, and 6 hours on Sunday. Is that schedule acceptable for Sandy given that she has a work permit from the school?

   A. Because it is a school vacation week, there are no restrictions on the hours that Sandy can work.

   B. Only state laws impact what hours Sandy can work because it happens during a vacation week.

   C. Federal law says Sandy cannot work more than 8 hours a day when it is a vacation week.

   D. Because Sandy won't be working more than 40 hours for the week, there is no problem.

7. Gary is a junior at Southpark High School. He is 17 years old. The school needs some help in its warehouse during the summer, and Gary needs a job so he can save money for college. His boss is the facilities manager. Gary is assigned to work 9 hours every day during the week because one of the other employees is on disability leave. And because the other employee was the forklift driver, Gary has been given training in how to drive that equipment around the warehouse and loading dock. He likes that duty because he has been driving a car for only a few months. The forklift is cool. Is there any difficulty with the facilities manager's requirements of Gary?

   A. Everything the facilities manager has required Gary to do is permissible under federal laws.

   B. Since there is no restriction to the number of hours Gary can work, everything should be okay.

   C. Whatever the facilities manager wants Gary to do is okay because it's only a summer job.

   D. Even though Gary can work unlimited hours, he cannot be assigned to drive the forklift.

8. Hank puts in the following hours at work: Sunday, 0; Monday, 8; Tuesday, 8; Wednesday, 9; Thursday, 8; Friday, 8; Saturday, 7. His boss says he will give Hank compensating time off for every hour of overtime Hank works. How many compensating hours off should Hank receive for this work time according to federal requirements?

   A. One day of compensating time off.

   B. One-and-a-half days of compensating time off.

   C. Seven hours of compensating time off.

   D. Compensating time off is not permitted under the FLSA.

9. The Tractor and Belt Company (TBC) doesn't have an HR manager. HR is handled by the payroll clerk. When a new employee is assigned to the production department as an assembler, the payroll clerk raises a question. Should the new person be paid the same as all the other employees, all women, in the department, or is it okay to pay her more because she made more at her former job?

   A. There are no restrictions on the amount a new employee can be paid. It is market driven.

   B. The Fair and Decent Treatment Act requires all people doing the same work be paid the same amount.

   C. There is no restriction on the amount paid because all the incumbents are women.

   D. Once a valid market survey has been done, it can be used to determine starting pay for new people.

10. Finding a life insurance company to provide benefits to its workforce has been difficult for Aisha, the HR manager. She decides to recommend that her company offer a self-insured plan. What controls might Aisha have to consider in her planning?

    A. There are no federal restrictions on a company providing its own life insurance plan to employees.

    B. The Employee Retirement Income Security Act regulates welfare benefit plans, including life insurance.

    C. The Life Insurance Benefit Plans Act has control over what Aisha is able to do with her idea.

    D. Only state laws will have an influence on Aisha's development of a self-insured benefit plan.

11. Simone has just been hired and is asked to complete a Form I-9. She offers her driver's license as proof of her identity. What else is required for her to complete the document?

    A. She may offer any document authorized on the Form I-9 instructions as proof of her authorization to work in this country.

    B. She must have a Social Security number to submit on the form.

    C. Simone has a U.S. passport but is told that she can't use it for her Form I-9.

    D. As long as Simone offers to get a Social Security number in the next 30 days, she can submit her Form I-9.

12. Steve is the HR director for a crane operations company. He just got a phone call from one of his field supervisors with tragic news. One of their units has collapsed, and their operator is in the hospital with serious injuries. What should Steve do with that information?

    A. Steve should immediately call the hospital to be sure all the insurance information is on file for their employee.

    B. He should notify the Occupational Safety and Health Administration about the accident and the injuries.

    C. He should notify the Crane Safety Institute of America to be sure they are able to add this accident to its database.

    D. Steve should call the crane operator's spouse to let her know about the tragedy.

13. Every year Donna has to attend training on the use of the company vehicles she drives. She thinks this is a silly waste of time. Donna knows how to drive, and she knows the company vehicles. Why should she attend training every year?

    A. There is no federal requirement for Donna to take yearly training.

    B. OSHA requires training be done only once for vehicle operation.

C. Only state safety provisions govern how frequently training must be done in Donna's situation.

D. Safety programs must be developed that provide for refresher training on all equipment operating procedures.

14. Jerry just arrived at work and found a sinkhole in the parking lot. He is early enough that other people have not yet begun arriving for work. Because the hole is about 10 feet across at the moment, what should Jerry be doing about the problem?

    A. If Jerry is a management employee, he should take charge of the situation and begin the process of alerting others to the danger posed by the sinkhole.

    B. If Jerry is a non-management employee, he should give his boss a call and leave a voice mail message, if necessary, about the sinkhole.

    C. If the sinkhole poses an immediate danger of death or serious injury, Jerry should call 911 and report it. He should barricade the perimeter of the sinkhole with tape or something else to prevent people from falling in.

    D. Jerry should first test the edges of the sinkhole to see whether it could grow in size. Then he should barricade the perimeter of the sinkhole so no one will fall in.

15. Theresa attended a seminar recently that pointed out the need to post a yearly summary of injury and illness cases. Her boss doesn't want to do that, saying he doesn't want to publicize the problems the organization has had. What should Theresa tell him?

    A. Posting requirements call for display of the report in a prominent location if there are 10 or more people on the payroll.

    B. Posting requirements can be met by putting a report on the back of the closet door in the employee lounge.

    C. Posting requirements can be met by making the report available in a binder in the HR manager's office.

    D. Posting requirements are optional, but good employers are using the report as a "best practice" in safety programs.

16. An employer routinely works with hazardous chemicals, trucking them for delivery to various customer locations. After each load, the truck must be cleaned before being loaded with a different chemical. Cleaning has to be done by someone inside the tanker using special absorbent materials. What else should be considered?

    A. Personal protective equipment should be provided by the employer, including breathing apparatuses and hazmat suits.

    B. Standard coveralls and boot covers should be provided for employees to use if they want.

    C. Workers should never be sent into a tanker truck for any reason.

    D. Breathing equipment is absolutely a requirement if someone will be in the tanker truck for longer than 30 minutes.

17. Shelly has worked for the same dentist for more than 10 years. In all that time, there has been no mention of any special requirements for handling syringes. She arranges the doctor's equipment trays every day and cleans them up after they have been used. She just tosses the used equipment into the autoclave or into the trash if it won't be used again. If you were advising Shelly about the practices used in her dental office, what would you say?

A. Needles should be broken off before they are thrown into the trash can.

B. Sharps should be triple wrapped in a stiff paper to protect from sticking someone handling the trash.

C. Any possible harm can be prevented if used syringes are placed into an approved sharps container.

D. Putting used syringes into any solid container that is wrapped in red paper is sufficient to meet requirements.

18. The price of gold is climbing, and folks at the Golden Nugget Mine are planning to reopen their operation. They know that safety is an important consideration. But what about federal regulations for gold mines? Are there such things?

A. There are only OSHA regulations in general. All of those rules still apply.

B. There are MSHA regulations to be considered, but because they are not in the coal mining business, the Golden Nugget Mine won't have to worry about them.

C. MSHA rules apply to all mining operations in the United States. The Golden Nugget Mine will have to study those rules and get ready for inspections by the government.

D. MSHA can tell the mine what to do, but it has no authority to conduct inspections because the Golden Nugget is not a coal mine.

19. Olivia suspects her payroll clerk of embezzlement. She has inspected the records for the past 3 months, and the pattern is clear. But to be sure it is the payroll clerk and not the accounts payable clerk, Olivia wants to confront her and demand she take a lie detector test.

A. Good going, Olivia. You caught her. Sure enough, demanding that she take a lie detector test is a good way to confirm your suspicions.

B. While lie detector tests can be used for some employees, accounting employees are exempt. You can't test her.

C. Lie detector tests are not permitted for any use by any employer. You can't test her.

D. Lie detector tests can be required only in limited circumstances, and this isn't one of them. You can't test her.

20. For the past 6 years, Sandeep's company has been a federal contractor working on equipment for the Department of Defense. The company has additional contract opportunities coming up, and Sandeep isn't sure if there will be an extra burden related to disabled workers because they are subject to both the Americans with Disabilities Act and the Rehabilitation Act.

    A. Sandeep should rest easy. The ADA and the Rehabilitation Act are identical in their content and requirements.

    B. Sandeep's company has already met its recruiting obligations and now only has to worry about meeting ADA requirements.

    C. Handling job accommodation requests is a requirement of the ADA but not the Rehabilitation Act. Things should be easier.

    D. Whatever Sandeep thinks, the ADA and Rehabilitation Act requirements have applied to his company for 6 years already. Adding more contracts won't change his current obligations.

21. Arthur has applied for a job with the AB Trucking Company. He is told he must take and pass a urine drug test. If he fails the test and any subsequent random drug test after he is hired, he will be dismissed from the company. Arthur reacts loudly and says, "That's an invasion of my privacy! I won't do it." What happens now?

    A. Arthur can call his lawyer and have the drug test waived since he doesn't want to take it.

    B. Arthur can discontinue his participation in the AB Transit Company's employment process.

    C. Arthur can take the test now and still refuse to participate in random tests later.

    D. Arthur can have his friend take the test for him.

22. Cynthia works for a large multistate manufacturing company and approaches her boss one morning and tells him that her husband has just received orders from the Coast Guard to report for deployment to the Middle East. They have a week to get everything ready for his departure. She wants to know if she can have excused time off during the coming week. If you were her boss, what would you tell her?

    A. She can have the time off, but it will be logged as unpaid and charged as FMLA leave.

    B. She can take the time off, but it will be unexcused because she didn't give more than a week's notice.

    C. If she wants the time off, she will have to use her paid vacation time for the week.

    D. Jennifer has already requested the week off for vacation, but only one person can be off at any one time or else the unit won't be able to function. Cynthia's request is denied with regrets.

23. Roberto works for a congressional representative and suffers a disabling injury in an automobile accident. Roberto cannot work more than 3 hours per day according to his doctor. Weeks later, when he returns to work, he asks for a job accommodation and is told that it can't be done. When he presses the point, his supervisor says the reason is:

   A. Congressional staff people aren't covered by the ADA, so they don't have to even discuss his request.

   B. The request he has made would exempt him from several of his job's key responsibilities.

   C. The request he has made would set a precedent that other representatives' offices would have to follow.

   D. Because congressional staff members have to meet the public every day, they can't have people seeing disabled workers in the office. It doesn't look good.

24. Jaime has been told he can get healthcare coverage from his company because of the Affordable Care Act. His company employs only 10 people, but Jaime is excited that he will finally get some insurance. He hasn't been feeling very good lately. Which of the following statements is true in this case?

   A. Jaime might have to wait until he can arrange for insurance through one of the exchanges.

   B. Jaime should get an enrollment form from his boss because all employees will be covered by the requirement that employers provide healthcare coverage to workers.

   C. Jaime is out of luck. The new law only covers employers with 50 or more people, and there is no way Jaime will be getting health insurance under the new law.

   D. Jaime's boss just ran out of forms, but he will get some more from HR and then have Jaime sign up for his coverage.

Answers

   1. **C.** If the new worker is classified as an employee, on the payroll, the IRS demands that income tax, Social Security tax, and Medicare tax be withheld. People are not allowed to opt out because they want to file their own tax payments each quarter.

   2. **A.** The Wagner-Peyser Act of 1933 provides for federal unemployment insurance and sets guidelines for state unemployment insurance programs.

   3. **B.** Both the FLSA and the IRS regulations require employers to obtain and report Social Security numbers from all employees. A Social Security number is required for completion of Form I-9 to prove authorization to work in this country. The company may not remove it from its records, regardless of how concerned Pete may be.

4. **A.** Race and sex data is specifically required by the FLSA. For employers with 15 or more people on the payroll that are engaged in interstate commerce, EEOC regulations also require maintenance of those data records.

5. **B.** The FLSA requires employers to designate a day as the beginning of the workweek. To change that designation, there should be a significant business reason. Moving the workweek to begin based on projects is not acceptable. The FLSA requires consistency because of the need to pay overtime for hours in excess of 40 in a workweek. Constantly moving a workweek could deprive employees of earned overtime.

6. **C.** The FLSA prohibits people aged 14 and 15 from working more than 8 hours in a day even when school is not in session.

7. **D.** Operating a "power-driven hoisting apparatus" is one of the 17 most dangerous jobs that may not be performed by workers younger than 18. At Gary's age, the FLSA has no restriction on the hours he may work in a week.

8. **B.** The FLSA requires all hours of work in excess of 40 in a week be paid overtime at the rate of 1.5 times the normal hourly pay rate. Compensating time off, in lieu of overtime pay, must be given at the rate of 1.5 hours for every overtime hour. So, a day of overtime (8 hours) should be compensated for with 1.5 days of compensating time off.

9. **C.** The Equal Pay Act requires men and women doing the same work to be paid the same rate. If there are no men in the job, only women, there is no Equal Pay Act issue. If all the incumbents are women, there is no employment discrimination based on sex because there is only one sex represented. So, with those conditions, there is no barrier to paying the new employee more based on her previous job's compensation.

10. **B.** ERISA specifically regulates welfare benefit plans such as health insurance and life insurance. That is in addition to regulation of pension and retirement plans offered by employers. It makes no difference who underwrites the life insurance—the employer or a vendor. ERISA will still provide requirements.

11. **A.** The deadline for completing a Form I-9 is 3 days after hire. Any documents listed on the form are acceptable. The employer may not designate certain documents as requirements. A Social Security number is one way to demonstrate authorization to work in this country. A valid U.S. passport is also a way to demonstrate both identity and work authorization.

12. **B.** The company has 8 hours after the accident to file its report of serious injury with OSHA. We don't know how long ago the accident happened, but it was long enough that the operator is now in the hospital. Steve should gather all the information needed for the report and get it called in to the OSHA office.

13. **D.** Injury and Illness Prevention Programs are required by OSHA. Part of the identification and remediation of workplace hazards is employee training. Even if employees have been trained on equipment operation, periodic refresher programs can help overcome bad habits that might have developed. Refresher programs conducted on a yearly basis represent a reasonable interval for Donna's situation.

14. **C.** It doesn't matter if Jerry is a manager or not. All employees should be trained to react to imminent dangers by taking immediate action to prevent anyone from serious injury. Also, walking up to the edge to see if the sinkhole is going to collapse is not safe.

15. **A.** Theresa should show her boss the requirement in OSHA regulations. A prominent display location excludes places such as the back of a closet door or inside a binder somewhere in the manager's office.

16. **A.** Working inside an enclosed space with dangerous fumes calls for hazmat equipment and adequate breathing equipment. OSHA regulations specify the personal protective equipment (PPE) necessary in this and other working conditions.

17. **C.** The Needlestick Safety and Prevention Act requires all sharps be disposed of in approved sharps containers. It also requires posting of warnings and information about blood-borne pathogens.

18. **C.** The Mine Safety and Health Administration has jurisdiction over all mining operations, not just coal mines. It handles safety complaints and conducts inspections of both aboveground and underground mining operations. All mine operators are required to conduct their internal safety inspections and maintain records of those inspections.

19. **D.** Except for law enforcement, security officers, and people who handle controlled substances, lie detectors are no longer permitted in the workplace. They were commonly used prior to 1988's Employee Polygraph Protection Act.

20. **D.** Sandeep's company will not incur any additional obligations for disabled workers if they seek additional government contracts. They have been obligated under both laws for 6 years.

21. **B.** Arthur has to decide whether he wants to continue seeking employment with the AB Transit Company. If so, he must participate in its drug testing program. If he wants to avoid testing, he must drop out of the job application process and seek employment elsewhere.

22. **A.** Under the FMLA, Cynthia is entitled to unpaid leave of absence as a spouse of a covered military service worker. It will be logged as unpaid time off, unless she wants to use some of her accrued paid time off. It will also be logged in her record as FMLA leave.

23. **B.** Even the congressional offices are subject to the ADA's requirement to consider and discuss requests for job accommodation. Job accommodations must be made to make it easier for an employee to perform one of the job's essential functions. If he can't do that, even with an accommodation, he is not eligible for assignment to that job. If there is no other job available, the employer can't return him to work until his status changes.

24. **A.** Employers are required to provide health insurance coverage only if they have 50 or more full-time workers. With only 10 employees, Jaime's employer is not obligated to provide health insurance coverage. Jaime may purchase it for himself through one of the exchanges set up for that purpose.

Endnotes

1. "Instructions for Employment Eligibility Verification," U.S. Department of Homeland Security, U.S. Citizenship and Immigration Services, accessed September 15, 2021, https://www.uscis.gov/sites/default/files/document/forms/i-9instr.pdf

2. "FAQs: Mine Safety and Health Administration – Inflation Adjustment Act," U.S. Department of Labor, Mine Safety and Health Administration, accessed September 15, 2021, https://www.msha.gov/regulations/rulemaking/department-labor-federal-civil-penalties-inflation-adjustment-act-catch-0

3. "OSHA Standards Development," U.S. Department of Labor, Occupational Safety and Health Administration, accessed September 15, 2021, https://www.osha.gov/laws-regs/standards-development

4. "FLSA Opinion Letter 2020-19," U.S. Department of Labor, Wage and Hour Division, accessed September 15, 2021, https://www.dol.gov/sites/dolgov/files/WHD/opinion-letters/FLSA/2020_12_31_19_FLSA.pdf

5. *Lawson v. FMR LLC,* U.S. No. 12-3, accessed on September 15, 2021, http://www.supremecourt.gov/opinions/13pdf/12-3_4f57.pdf

6. Sara LaLumia and James M. Sallee, "The Value of Honesty: Empirical Estimates from the Case of the Missing Children," *International Tax and Public Finance, 20*(2), 192–224 (2012), https://doi.org/10.1007/s10797-012-9221-4

7. *Sutton v. United Air Lines, Inc.,* 527 U.S. 471 (1999)

8. *Toyota Motor Manufacturing, Kentucky, Inc. v. Williams*, 534 U.S. 184 (2002)

9. "A Guide to Disability Rights Laws," U.S. Department of Justice, Civil Rights Division, accessed September 16, 2021, https://www.ada.gov/cguide.htm

10. The Job Accommodation Network (JAN), 800-526-7234, or www.askjan.org (accessed on September 16, 2021), is a free resource for employers. It is a service provided by the U.S. Department of Labor's Office of Disability Employment Policy (ODEP). JAN has been providing services for more than 35 years.

11. "Disability Discrimination," U.S. Equal Employment Opportunity Commission, accessed on September 16, 2021, https://www.eeoc.gov/laws/types/disability.cfm

12. The first was the Civil Rights Act of 1866, which protected the right to enter into contracts regardless of race.

13. A list of controlled substances can be found in Schedules I through V of Section 202 of the Controlled Substances Act (21 U.S.C. 812) and as further defined in Regulation 21 C.F.R. 1308.11–1308.15.

14. 41 C.F.R. 60-3.7

15. Fair Treatment of Experienced Pilots Act (December 13, 2007), Public Law 110-135

16. 41 C.F.R. 60

17. "Employment-Based Visa Categories in the United States," American Immigration Council, accessed on September 20, 2021, https://www.americanimmigrationcouncil.org/research/employment-based-visa-categories-united-states

PART II

aPHR Body of Knowledge Functional Areas

- **Chapter 3**   Talent Acquisition
- **Chapter 4**   Learning and Development
- **Chapter 5**   Compensation and Benefits
- **Chapter 6**   Employee Relations
- **Chapter 7**   Compliance and Risk Management
- **Chapter 8**   Early HR Career-Level Tasks

Talent Acquisition

The functional area Talent Acquisition is 19 percent of the Associate Professional in Human Resources (aPHR) exam weighting. Understanding the hiring process, including planning for staffing needs, sourcing of applicants, formal interview and selection processes, and onboarding of a new hire, are responsibilities that are guided by laws. This includes federal laws, which are discussed in this book, as well as the laws in the state where your organization operates. You must be able to apply the laws in practical terms so managers can select and hire the best applicants.

Additionally, advancements in technology have changed the hiring process in many ways. Many hiring processes are now managed almost entirely on the Internet and social media—a far cry from the methods used in HR just a handful of years ago. Technological systems for storing applicant information have removed some of the administrative hurdles associated with legal requirements and offer useful metrics for evaluating talent acquisition processes. It will be useful to apply these best practices using technology to help your organization develop a strong employer brand and seamlessly manage important data.

The Body of Knowledge statements outlined by the HR Certification Institute (HRCI) for the Talent Acquisition functional area for those performing early HR career roles are as follows:

Knowledge of

- **01** Methods to identify staffing needs and guide talent acquisition efforts; for example, forecasting, job analysis, the creation and structure of job descriptions, and alternative staffing approaches

- **02** Talent sourcing tools and techniques to identify and engage prospective candidates; for example, employer branding, social media, candidate pipelines, résumé mining, job postings, job fairs, and employee referrals

- **03** Recruiting procedures and strategies for screening and selecting qualified applicants; for example, recruitment firms/staffing agencies, skills assessments, interview techniques and best practices, and biases

- **04** The lifecycle of hiring and onboarding a selected applicant; for example, reference and background checks, offer letters and counteroffers, employment contracts, and the distribution and collection of company-mandated documents, such as employee handbook and policy acknowledgments, non-disclosure or other agreements, and benefits paperwork

- **05** The use of technology for collecting, storing, reviewing, and analyzing candidate/applicant information and recruiting data; for example, applicant tracking systems, human resource information systems (HRISs), return on investment (ROI), cost-per-hire, and time-to-fill

Laws and Regulations

Many federal laws impact the Talent Acquisition functional area. Be sure to refer to Chapter 2 for in-depth information about each of these crucial laws impacting hiring activities. HR professionals must be able to apply these laws and guide hiring managers to do the same. You may expect that any or all of these laws will be subjects on the aPHR certification exam.

 EXAM TIP You can expect that the exam will have several questions about the interviewing and applicant processes, along with their legal compliance issues.

Federal Laws

Here is a list of all the federal laws you will need to understand when you have job responsibilities associated with talent acquisition. Only federal laws will be on the aPHR exam, but as an HR professional, you should consult the laws in your employer's state as well.

- The Employee Polygraph Protection Act (EPPA) (1988)
- The Fair and Accurate Credit Transactions Act (FACT) (2003)
- The Fair Credit Reporting Act (FCRA) (1970)
- The Fair Labor Standards Act (FLSA) (1938)
- The Immigration and Nationality Act (INA) (1952)
- The Immigration Reform and Control Act (IRCA) (1986)
- The Personal Responsibility and Work Opportunity Reconciliation Act (1996)
- The Service Contract Act (SCA) (1965)
- The Vietnam Era Veterans Readjustment Assistance Act (VEVRAA) (1974), as amended by the Jobs for Veterans Act (JVA) (2008)
- The Wagner-Peyser Act (1933), as amended by the Workforce Innovation and Opportunity Act (2014)

- The Work Opportunity Tax Credit (WOTC) (1996)
- Americans with Disabilities Act (ADA) (1990), as amended by the Americans with Disabilities Act Amendments Act (ADAAA) (2008)
- The Civil Rights Act (Title VII) (1964, 1991)
- The Drug-Free Workplace Act (1988)
- The Equal Employment Opportunity Act (EEOA) (1972)
- The Genetic Information Nondiscrimination Act (GINA) (2008)
- The Uniform Guidelines on Employee Selection Procedures (1978)
- The Age Discrimination in Employment Act (ADEA) (1967)
- Executive Order 11246 – Affirmation Action (1965)
- The Congressional Accountability Act (1995)
- The False Claims Act (1863)
- The Homeland Security Act (2002)
- All the various employment visas for foreign nationals

Workforce Planning

We will approach this chapter by following the lifecycle of the hiring process. Although activities like recruiting and interviewing often get the bulk of attention in talent acquisition, workforce planning is an important first step. In simple terms, planning allows your organization to be proactive in finding great talent, and not reactive, leaving you racing to find a suitable replacement.

Forecasting Staffing Needs

Identifying job openings before they exist is an activity known as *forecasting*. It is best performed with the aid of operations managers who will be supervising the new positions. Given what is anticipated for growth (or workforce reduction), you can convert workload into staffing requirements.

Determining the portion of jobs that will be part time versus full time is another contribution of the forecasting process. Forecasting staffing needs is usually done in terms of the number of full-time-equivalent people. You will likely hear this term a lot because it is also used for budgeting purposes. Full-time employees usually work 40 hours per week, but sometimes organizations define full-time somewhere between 30 and 40 hours per week.

 NOTE Here is the formula for determining how many people you need to work in a department: Full-Time-Equivalent (FTE) People Required = Total Department Workload / Workload Handled by One Person.

Forecasting may also be required for temporary changes in business needs. For example, a toy manufacturer has more demand for product over the holidays and therefore needs more staff members during that time. In this example, forecasting how much the workload will increase during the holidays will help the organization determine the right number of staff members needed to get the work completed.

Job Analysis

Job analysis is a process where data is collected on a job. That data is examined to determine the job's duties and requirements. A job analysis also considers the job's relationship to other positions in the organization and the conditions under which work should be performed. Put simply, job analysis is a process where judgments are made about data collected on a job.

Legal Aspects of Job Analysis

An important concept of job analysis is that the analysis is conducted of the job, not the person working in that job. While job analysis data may be collected from incumbents through interviews or job analysis questionnaires, the product of the analysis is a description or specification of the job, not a description of the person.

Job analysis can be used in selection procedures to legally identify or develop the following:

- Job duties that should be included in advertisements of vacant positions
- Appropriate salary level for the position to help determine what salary should be offered to a candidate
- Minimum requirements (education and/or experience) for screening applicants
- Interview questions
- Selection tests/instruments (for example, written tests, oral tests, and job simulations)
- Applicant appraisal/evaluation forms
- Orientation materials for applicants/new hires

Job Analysis and the ADA

With the passage of the Americans with Disabilities Act (1990), job analysis has taken on an increasing importance. To comply with the ADA, employers must not discriminate against an individual with a disability in regard to job application procedures, hiring, advancement, discharge, compensation, training, and other terms of employment. The ADA requires that individuals with a disability be given "reasonable accommodation" in the workplace so that they will not be unreasonably excluded from employment. Job analysis is a process to identify the tasks and duties performed on the job as well as the equipment used. This information may be helpful in determining what "reasonable accommodations" could be made for an individual to perform the job.

Job Analysis and the FLSA

The Fair Labor Standards Act (FLSA) requires that most employees in the United States be paid at least the federal minimum wage for all hours worked and be paid overtime at 1.5 times the regular rate of pay for all hours worked more than 40 hours in a workweek. The FLSA provides an exemption, or exclusion, from both minimum wage and overtime pay for employees employed in certain types of positions. These are known as "exempt" jobs. There are requirements that must be met for a job to be exempt. The job must meet the conditions of one of the following major categories: executive, administrative, professional, computer professional, or outside sales employee. Through a job analysis, it is possible to determine whether the job duties of a position require overtime pay or fall in to an exempt category that does not require overtime pay. You can find a wealth of information on exempt jobs at the Department of Labor's website (https://www.dol.gov/agencies/whd/flsa).

Job Analysis and Affirmative Action

On August 27, 2013, the Office of Federal Contract Compliance Programs (OFCCP) announced rules outlining how federal contractors should handle their affirmative action and nondiscrimination obligations for protected veterans and for individuals with disabilities. Several of these requirements require a job analysis to stay compliant. The requirements include the following:

- Applying the "Internet applicant" rule to the new rules so that electronic applications and inquiries will be handled the same way they are handled for other groups covered by affirmative action (race, color, religion, sex, or national origin)

- Changing the 2-year recordkeeping requirement to 3 years

- Removing the requirement in the disabilities rule to review all physical and mental job qualification standards on an annual basis and replacing it with a requirement for contractors to establish their own schedule for reviewing job qualifications

- Requiring employers to achieve specific numeric goals to document compliance

- Requiring that contractors compare the number of individuals with disabilities (IWDs) who apply to the number of IWDs who are hired and keep those records for 3 years for auditing purposes

- Maintaining an applicant flow log showing the name, race, sex, date of application, job title, interview status, and the action taken for all individuals applying for job opportunities

- Maintaining records pertaining to the company's compensation design and system

- Filing EEO-1 and VETS 4212 reports annually

Job Descriptions and Job Specifications

Job descriptions outline a specific job based on the findings of a job analysis. Job descriptions generally include duties, purpose, responsibilities, scope, and working conditions of a job along with the job's title and the name or designation of the person to whom the employee reports. A job specification is different and is usually found at the end of a job description. It is a statement of the essential components of a job class, including the minimum qualifications and requirements necessary to perform the essential functions of the job.

Job Description Components

A job description need not account for every task that might ever be done. Here are the most critical components of a good job description:

- **Heading information** This should include job title, pay grade or range, reporting relationship (by position, not individual), hours or shifts, and the likelihood of overtime or weekend work.

- **Summary objective of the job** This should list the general responsibilities and descriptions of key tasks and their purpose; the relationships with customers, co-workers, and others; and the results expected of incumbent employees.

- **Job duties and responsibilities** It's more important to list what must be performed and accomplished than how, if there is more than one way to do it. Being too specific on how to accomplish a duty could lead to ADA issues when an employee asks for an accommodation.

- **Knowledge and qualifications** State the education, experience, training, and technical skills necessary for entry into this job.

- **Special demands** This should include any extraordinary conditions applicable to the job (for example, heavy lifting, exposure to temperature extremes, prolonged standing, or travel).

Why Use Job Descriptions

The following are reasons job descriptions are important:

- They ensure you're hiring the right people to fill the right position.

- Well-written and effectively developed job descriptions are communication tools that allow both employees and candidates to clearly understand the expectations of the role, its essential duties and responsibilities, and the required educational credentials and experience. They also define what "success looks like" for the alignment of expectations for both the employee and supervisor.

- As individual roles change over time, job descriptions should change with them. There are few positions that do not evolve; most change. Systems and processes also evolve. The job descriptions should be continually updated as the duties change over time.

- Writing concise and effective job descriptions can help you attract the best candidates. Poorly worded or incomplete job descriptions can be a turn off to applicants, making an organization seem disorganized and unprofessional.

Alternative Staffing Practices

These days, there are many alternatives to hiring full-time employees. At times, hiring employees in traditional, full-time positions can be challenging based on the labor market. It may also not be the most effective approach for the organization, depending on the work required of a position. Using creative staffing approaches might better suit the needs of your workforce and the organization. It may also set you apart from the competition.

Temporary Employees

One change to full-time employment is the use of temporary employees. It is not necessary to hire people by placing them on the payroll. Employers can expand their workforce quickly and easily by contracting with temporary talent agencies to satisfy their need for additional people. Temporary workers can be used on production lines, in accounting departments, or in any other portion of an organization experiencing a workload that cannot be handled by the permanent staff. Agencies pay their employees, take care of payroll withholding and tax reporting, add a profit margin, and then pass the final rate to the employer contracting for that help.

Job Sharing

Job sharing is an employment technique that you hear about more and more these days. It offers two or more workers the opportunity to collectively constitute one full-time-equivalent employee. One person works the job in the morning, and another works the same job in the afternoon. Considerations involve briefing the "job-sharing partner" on the current issues to be dealt with during the next portion of work time. There are some financial considerations, too. Each employee will require the employer's full contribution toward Social Security and Medicare. That may cost the employer more than if one person were to occupy the position.

Part Time vs. Full Time

Sometimes it may make more sense to hire part-time versus full-time workers. A good example is for positions where college students are a great fit but are unable to work full time due to class schedules. Or parents who also have caregiving roles at home but still want to remain in the workforce in some capacity. In cases such as these, it can be helpful to consider part-time positions.

It is important to note that there are financial considerations associated with part-time employees. Two part-time workers will likely cost you more than one full-time worker. There are contributions toward Social Security and Medicare for both workers. Also, where local employment taxes are based on head count, part-time employees will add to your expenses.

Under the Affordable Care Act, employers can escape paying for benefit coverage of some workers if those workers maintain a part-time status. By policy, other benefit programs may or may not be available to part-time workers. It is not uncommon to have access to an IRA or other retirement program based on the number of hours worked each week. The amount of supervision available can also impact the ratio of full-time to part-time workers.

Project Hires/Contract Labor/Gig Employees/Floaters

Using project hires and contract labor is another alternative to full-time employment. *Project hires* are people who are recruited and placed on the payroll with the understanding that their employment will be terminated once the project is completed. This is common in organizations that seek out projects from client organizations. A staff is hired for the project and then let go when the project comes to an end.

Contract labor refers to people who are hired for a specific period of time. An organization may believe that the workload will last until this time next year; therefore, it contracts with people to handle that workload for the year. At the end of the contract, those people will come off the payroll, whether or not the project has concluded. They could be "extended" (payroll status maintained) for a designated period of time if the workload has not diminished.

Gig employees are contracted employees who are utilized for a specific project and then not again until that type of project occurs again. An example would be a concierge type of skilled worker who is employed for only new store openings. Gig employees have grown increasingly in recent years with the rise of ride-sharing services like Uber and Lyft. This is an area to keep an eye on for legislation updates, as there has been growing concern about the lack of benefits provided to gig employees and the need for a better definition of what constitutes an employee and what doesn't.

Floaters are employees who are on the organization's payroll and work on a temporary basis for a specific period of time, such as vacation relief, and may rotate among several positions or departments. A floater is helpful to have available on an on-call basis, is able to fill in for temporary assignments (for example, due to illness, vacation, or a leave of absence), and is an ideal position for former employees such as early retirees.

Retiree Annuitant

A resource who is already trained, has organizational knowledge, and is experienced in job requirements should not be overlooked. It may be cheaper in the short run to bring back a retired worker to "fill in" temporarily than to hire another type of temporary worker.

Retiree annuitants are folks who have retired from the organization but are called back to work because of emergencies, unexpected workload, or another unforeseen need. They are defined by the Internal Revenue Service (IRS)[1] as people who are entitled to draw benefits from their retirement program while earning compensation from their employer for continuing employment, whether or not they are continuing to pay into the retirement program.

Phased Retirement

As opposed to instant full-time retirement, phased retirement is another alternative to full-time employment. It allows an individual to take partial retirement while continuing to work a reduced schedule. This can take the form of job sharing or part-time, seasonal, temporary, or project work. A major advantage of phased retirement is that it allows employees to get used to working less and having more time to themselves. It prevents the sudden shock of not having a work routine that comes with traditional retirement.

Contractor Payrolling

When a job needs to be done and the organization does not want to hire someone onto its own payroll to do that job, an alternative is to contract with a vendor who will hire someone to do the job at the client organization. Contractor payrolling is used when you need to adjust to seasonal fluctuations, fill a vacancy while searching for a permanent replacement, bridge the gap in personnel when there is unexpected growth, or use interns for a set period of time. It has many applications, but the greatest benefit is in protecting against legal charges, in that the person hired is not an independent contractor but an employee—a problem that cost Microsoft just under $100 million in payroll taxes, penalties, fines, and legal fees.[2] This is usually a process used for less than an entire workforce. When single employees or small groups of employees are needed, payrolling services can solve the need.

Employee Leasing and Professional Employer Organizations (PEOs)

Similar to payrolling, employee leasing is a process of moving employees to another company's payroll as a service for a client organization. Typically, professional employer organizations will take over the entire workforce in a client company. PEOs provide payroll services, tax tracking and depositing, retirement program management, healthcare benefit program management, and even employee counseling and support services. In essence, employee leasing is the outsourcing of the human resource department and the payroll function together. Employees usually become employees of both organizations: the client where they perform their work and the vendor (PEO) that handles the payroll and HR functions for the client. It means both employers are liable for legal compliance. This is called a co-employment relationship.

Outsourcing and Managed Service Providers (MSPs)

Another alternative is outsourcing. This is shifting a workload out of the organization through a contract with another employer organization, either here in the U.S. or somewhere else in the world. Managed service providers manage functions as part of a strategic decision to move certain departments out of an employment organization to a vendor that can perform them less expensively. Customer service departments are a common example of this. Such a decision is designed to allow the client company to focus on key activities within its core business while a vendor handles support activities for the client.

Temp-to-Lease Programs

When a need exists for employees on a seasonal basis or for jobs that will last longer than a few days or weeks, it is possible for employers to lease their workers from a vendor organization. The vendor provides the underlying employment relationship with the worker. When temporary needs stretch into longer-term needs, it still may not be wise to increase payroll in the client organization. That's when contracting for temporary agency workers can be converted into long-term employee leases. These workers often have no benefits provided to them. The client organization pays an employment agency a fee in addition to the pay received by the worker assigned to the client. All payroll operations are maintained by the temporary service agency.

Rehires and Transfers

When workloads rise unexpectedly, it is sometimes difficult to bring in new hires quickly enough to respond to that increased demand. Rehiring laid-off workers and bringing in transfers from other portions of the organization can sometimes be good solutions. Rehired workers are already trained and can be productive immediately. Transfers from other portions of the organization have the advantage of already knowing the culture and, if coming from a similar or identical type of work, can also be productive rather quickly.

Talent Sourcing

There are a variety of methods to find the right person to fill a position. Often, employers search both inside and outside their organization for someone who can fill a job opening.

Internal Recruitment

Some organizations overlook their own workforce as a legitimate source of qualified candidates when job openings occur. Internal recruiting can be handled either formally or informally. In union-represented organizations, a procedure for internal job postings is usually specified in the memorandum of understanding (MOU) or union contract (collective bargaining agreement). Details within collective bargaining agreements (CBAs) might specify what information should be included in job postings and how long job openings will remain posted. Sometimes internal recruiting must happen for a specified number of days prior to any external recruiting efforts being made. In the absence of unions, the employer will have the opportunity to develop its own policies and procedures in this staffing area.

Often, internal resources can fill the needs of the job opening in question. Current employees are constantly changing, through education or temporary job assignments. They may be working on certifications that would better qualify them for a different job. It is important to consider these resources because they represent less expensive candidate pools than those built with external candidates. Most importantly, hiring from within shows employees that their professional development is valued by the company and it pays off! It begs the question of whether it is necessary to have a database that tracks current employee skills and certifications. Training accomplishments, new educational achievements, and demonstrated skill performance should all be identified periodically (annually or more often).

One tool that can assist the internal recruiting process is an employee skills database. Information tracked in this database will be confidential to a large extent. Yet, it can help you identify qualified candidates for internal placement when the need arises. Your list of data content will likely be different from that created by other HR professionals in different types of organizations. Table 3-1 lists some of the basics that could be included.

Sample Employee Skills Database Content	
Advanced degree (MBA, functional specialty)	Languages (specific language fluency)
Certifications (CPA, SHRM-CP, SPHR, surveyor, architect)	Licenses (attorney, physician, pharmacist, private investigation, nursing)
Computer programming (languages)	Specific software application skills (Microsoft Office, accounting programs)
CPR/first aid certification	Task force leadership
Craft specialty (welding, plumbing, electrician, carpentry)	Teaching credentials (teaching specialty)
Driving (automobiles, trucks, forklifts)	Training programs attended
Executive or leadership training	Typing (rate and accuracy)

Table 3-1   Employee Skills Database Content

Internal recruiting can contribute substantially to your overall placement needs. When people are already on the payroll, transferring them to a new job assignment reduces the costs associated with recruiting, hiring, and even sometimes Social Security and Medicare tax. This practice also can help with retention efforts to keep high-performing employees within your organization, instead of them developing these skills and looking for jobs elsewhere.

Job Posting

Internal job posting is an internal job announcement, typically posted on an organization's web site that is accessed only by employees. A basic job description and duties are included along with a deadline for applications. Usually, morale is positively affected when workers see the employer is making opportunities available to the existing workforce before searching outside for job candidates. The job posting might also encourage employee referrals.

Former Employees

Former employees can be a good source for recruitment, especially those who previously held the position. Inviting former employees to apply for re-employment is a viable option, especially with former employees who may have left the workforce because of family care needs or even those who may have had their jobs eliminated because of downturns in the organization's financial picture. If the employee was a top contributor and exited the organization on good terms, inviting a former employee to reapply for an opening can send a positive message to the current workforce and lessen the time required to learn the nuances of the job and company.

External Recruitment

In contrast to internal recruiting is external recruiting, which is just as it sounds: you source candidates from outside the organization. External recruitment best begins with a strategy and putting on a marketing and sales hat. You must know your applicant base, and that requires research. You must figure out how to reach candidates using the marketing tools and methods available, all at a cost that is within your recruitment budget.

PART II

While for some, posting job openings at state employment agencies is a requirement, it is nonetheless a recruitment strategy. Recruitment strategies can take many forms. Generally speaking, there are four key components of recruiting strategies that every organization should employ:

- **Identifying your brand** If you are the leading company in a specific arena, let people know that.

- **Targeting specific candidate sources** Identify the most likely sources for the type of candidates you seek. If you want professional engineers, look in engineering associations and college institutions. If you want electricians, look at the union organizations in the locations where your need exists. Target the specific sources you know will give you the qualified candidates you need.

- **Working with your key sources** When you find organizations that have job candidates that can fill your needs, cultivate relationships with the people in those organizations. Give them tours of your facilities and stress how it is possible for you to work together to reach mutually dependent goals. Federal contractors have obligations to foster these types of relationships with sources of veterans and disabled job candidates in addition to those serving female and minority job seekers.

- **Preparing your sales pitch** Be prepared to sell your best job candidate on the benefits of working for your organization. Explain the environment, the working conditions, the side benefits, and the culture in a way that entices the job candidate to want to accept your job offer. This is also called *employee value proposition*, which is the value employees gain by working in your organization.

Branding and Marketing the Organization

Branding is a key recruiting strategy but it differs from marketing. Branding is a strategic exercise, whereas marketing is a tactical process. Branding is a method of conveying what the organization values, whereas marketing is a process of encouraging people to purchase the organization's products or services. They are often confused simply because they are so closely related.

HR professionals can help the organization advance its brand when discussing the organization with job candidates and employees. "Here are the things we value as an employer." "Here is the way we do things around here." "Here we have a culture that values _____." All of these are statements about the organization's brand. When we hear things like, "We can provide that solution for you with our product/service," we know we are hearing a marketing statement. It says "buy me." It is more direct and pointed than a branding statement.

Traditional Media

Newspaper and magazine print advertising can take the form of classified ads or display ads. These days, magazines and newspapers have companion editions online. Buying advertising in one format can also provide the same advertising in the other format.

Radio and television are other forms of traditional media advertising and can be highly effective when trying to fill a number of positions, such as seasonal labor or a new facility opening. Ads can be created and used at a theater during the previews, on grocery carts, on metro buses, and even on the local sports arena billboards. The creativity is never-ending—where do your desired applicants go, what do they do, and where would you reach them?

Internet and Social Media

The Internet offers several avenues for recruiting, ranging from entry-level and hourly job posting vacancies to professional and management-level openings. HR staff members are integral to managing online recruiting tools. As an early-career HR professional, you will most likely be managing the company's job opportunity section of the web site, which will be a totally separate platform devoted to careers and job opportunities. You'll be intimately involved and have knowledge of all the various generic job boards and sites such as Indeed.com, CareerBuilder.com, Monster.com, ZipRecruiter.com, and others. You'll be browsing how other organizations are posting their vacancies.

Today, many white-collar jobs are being filled through LinkedIn. LinkedIn.com is a paid resource for employers. Posting job openings on LinkedIn, as of this writing, requires payment of a fee, and that is typically true of the other Internet job boards. Social media is growing new tentacles and reaching far and wide, as it is quickly becoming a cost-effective and fast method to recruit for a variety of staffing positions. Today, companies are investing dollars into creating mobile applications to make recruiting easier for prospective applicants to apply via smart phones. Your organization will likely have a presence on Instagram and Facebook as well as use a Twitter account to announce its job vacancies. At the same time, you can request your current workforce retweet a job posting or announce it on their own social media accounts. It's no longer the Wild West, yet it's still a frontier to be expanded and creatively used to broaden your outreach and quest in attracting applicants.

Résumé Mining

Another great way to make use of the Internet to recruit candidates is by doing résumé mining. On many job boards like Indeed and LinkedIn, people can keep their résumés in the web site's database. Then, recruiters can type the search criteria for the job they are hiring for in the database, such as the job title or certifications needed for the position. It is wise to try your search with a number of different criteria that may qualify someone for the job so you don't miss out on any great candidates. The database will show the results of any résumés matching those criteria. This allows employers to reach out to people with a strong résumé in the database, even if these people are not actively looking for a position at the time. Résumé mining is a more proactive method of recruitment. Oftentimes, good candidates are comfortable with their present job but could be interested in a new opportunity if the right one arises.

Public Employment Services

Many public employment services have been created specifically to help employers hire skilled workers and help workers find suitable employment. The following are all types of public employment services:

- **State employment services**   Each state has an agency dedicated to providing job search services to job seekers, which includes free posting for job openings of all types of jobs. Many include job search centers where formerly employed workers can have a one-stop place to view openings, obtain assistance with their interviewing skills, and get help with résumés.

- **Veterans' organizations**   Most state employment agencies have linkages to veterans' organizations and often have veteran coordinators on their staff to maintain those relationships. Get to know these people and how they can help with your recruiting efforts.

- **Organizations for the disabled**   Many qualified job seekers are classified as disabled for one reason or another. In many cases, the disability will have no impact on that person's ability to perform the essential job functions. Don't overlook a valuable resource.

- **Local educational institutions**   High schools, community colleges, and universities will usually be glad to post job opening information so their graduating students can find employment in their chosen field of work.

Employment Agencies

Employment agencies recruit and perform as matchmakers for applicants and employers. Many agencies focus on a specific field, such as finance, executive-level positions, or drivers. Generally, the employer pays a contractual fee to the agency when a successful hire is made. For recruiting of executives and senior levels of management, these agencies are often known as *headhunters*. They often source executives who are currently working at another job but are interested in a job change.

Outplacement firms also provide a level of assistance, generally for management-type employees, but not always. When there is a large layoff or facility closure, an outplacement firm may open up a job search center at the organization to assist displaced workers with seeking new employment. This source of potential employees can make recruitment efforts highly cost effective in having a pool of qualified candidates that may know your industry and simply need to be instructed on the nuances of how your organization does business. Several outplacement firms may also provide retraining for different jobs.

Employee Referral

Potential applicants can be referred by current employees, which are great resources. Recommendations from existing employees can result in long-term hires because studies have shown that employees will remain longer with a company where they have established a strong bond of friendship and are usually better performers.[3] Moreover, a referral program that provides a monetary cash incentive to employees encourages such referrals. It can also reduce costs per hire for the employer.

College and University Recruiting

A good source of entry-level hires is college and university recruiting. Large organizations often have an entire HR group devoted to college recruiting. This type of recruitment can be highly effective when capitalizing on school ties, using existing employee alumni to join recruiters on campus during recruitment fairs. Delivering presentations and talking about the culture of your organization and the career path opportunities are going to be highly valued with this resource. With today's technology, many recruitment activities include virtual information webinars and videos that showcase the organization—very much like the colleges and universities themselves use when attracting students to their school.

Professional and Trade Associations

If the employer is a member of an industrial association, there are frequently job posting services offered by such associations, and they are usually free. Also, if the employer sponsors its professional employees with membership in their professional trade associations, here again is another source of posting a job vacancy. These can also include alumni associations.

Diversity Groups

Diversity groups are sometimes called employee affinity groups. They typically are organized along race, gender, disability, or veteran status (for example, African-American Employees Association, Women Engineers Club, and AB Trucking Veterans Association). Sometimes they are sponsored by employers, sometimes they are not. Often, employers provide meeting space and refreshments in exchange for conversations with the groups on topics of diversity management, employee relations, employee development, and so on. Such groups can be a valuable resource for employer human resource management. Diversity groups should be included in external recruiting efforts, encouraging further referrals of job candidates from minority, female, disabled, and veteran populations.

Supplies and Vendors

Although it's often an overlooked source, your organization's vendors and suppliers can "spread the word" about your vacancies. A word of caution, though, if you use a monetary referral incentive—you don't want to necessarily be known as a poacher or a client that hires away the vendor's/supplier's own employees. That might cause you a greater headache.

Candidate Pipelines

This is where the value of an applicant tracking system (discussed later in this chapter) comes into play. Having a database coded with prospective applicants who may have interviewed for other positions, or perhaps have already been interviewed and determined to be qualified for the current vacant position and a candidate for cultural fit, can be very useful. Perhaps they were not selected for a previous position because there was only one position and they came in a close second. Previous applicants represent a pool of talent that your organization can quickly and easily identify and contact when a new opening occurs. Courting this group of applicants, in a manner similar to how marketing would court prospective customers and clients, will have a big payoff in cost-effectiveness, not to mention the goodwill it leaves with applicants.

Labor Unions

Labor unions, especially those related to your industry, are a source of applicants. Members will have access to announcements at their local union web site and hiring hall. This source can be a great place to attract talent and skills to cross over to other industries. Of course, if your organization is unionized, pay special attention to the requirements and restrictions the union contract may have related to hiring for vacancies, particularly the notification to union members first before going externally to the public at large.

Job Fairs and Open Houses

Job fairs are designed to bring a number of employers and job seekers alike into a large hall for quick meet-and-greet interviews, exchanging of résumés, and first impressions. This format provides employers a chance to meet a number of potential candidates in a short period of time. These job fairs can be for entry- to mid-level positions. Open houses are where the employer invites job applicants to visit its facilities and do the same meet-and-greet as at a job fair. This provides a noncompetitive atmosphere for the employer and a chance to offer a tour of the working environment. Both job fairs and open houses are cost-effective methods for seasonal hiring, filling positions that have high turnover, such as sales, and hiring for new plant/facility openings.

Walk-Ins

This used to be a reliable method for attracting applicants. Nowadays, if a prospective applicant were to walk in to give their résumé for future openings, they are most likely met with the receptionist advising them that the company only accepts résumés via its online platform and to please visit the company web site. Most walk-ins occur at small mom-and-pop businesses or other retail-associated establishments that are service oriented, such as restaurants and non-chain retail stores. This method is not to be completely discounted, though, because hanging a big sign on your organization's building stating "Now Hiring" still has a big impact, especially for frontline vacancies and seasonal labor. However, you could provide a kiosk in your lobby for the walk-ins to complete their application online rather than using a pencil-and-paper application process.

Applicant Databases

Applicant databases track applicants' information for job openings and are standard for the type of recordkeeping needed in both small and large organizations. Applicant tracking systems (ATSs) provide an automated method for monitoring and tracking the information on applicants from the time they first apply to selection (or non-selection) and beyond (such as when a future opening occurs). These systems range from simple Excel spreadsheets to elaborate and sophisticated modules of the human resource information system (HRIS). They provide reports that can be used for EEO-1 reporting and affirmation action plans (AAPs). Federal contractors and organizations with 100 or more employees are required to maintain records of job applicants.

ATSs are helpful for the enormity of the administrative tasks and communications associated with hiring. A hiring management system (HMS) takes the technology up a notch. An HMS integrates with recruiting web sites by moving the candidate's

Information Element	Element Content
Applicant name	Applicant name.
Address	Applicant's current mailing address.
Telephone number	Applicant's current telephone number (home, cell, work).
E-mail or other method of contact	Applicant's e-mail address.
Self-identification of race and sex	This information should not be passed on to the selecting manager (or managers).
Self-identification of protected veteran and disabled status	This information should not be passed on to the selecting manager (or managers).
Source	How did this person get information about your job opening?
Position applied for	Always insist on applicants identifying the specific job opening they are interested in. This might be a job requisition number or a job title.
Job location	If more than one location is available, ask for a preference.
Qualifications for the job	This could be satisfied by a résumé or CV. Alternatively, you can require every applicant to complete your specific job application form.
Availability	How soon will the candidate be available to start work?
Compensation desired	While many people won't answer this question, it is good to ask it anyway. If someone replies with a number significantly above your budget range, you do not need to waste more time on their candidacy.
References	Be sure to track references provided by the job applicant, including educational institutions (and degrees), former employers (with job titles and compensation amounts), and personal references.

Table 3-2   Applicant Tracking Data

information directly from input into a database. This reduces errors and allows for faster communication responses via the prescreening capabilities of the HMS. An HMS also provides additional recruitment support by using templates, auto-responders, and standardization of communications. Most HMSs will have advanced report-writing capabilities that can be customized. Table 3-2 provides the typical information that an ATS will track.

Records Retention

The management of employment-related records concerning the legal requirements for retention can be daunting and confusing. The confusion is often a result of the complexity and variety of restrictions imposed by the many laws. Some requirements apply to most employers hiring; others apply to just government contractors and subcontractors. Same or similar records are often required by more than one law, but the periods of retention may vary. Some requirements depend on the industry or the location, and federal as well as state laws in which an employer exists apply. Table 3-3 provides a reference for HR professionals to use when considering documentation that is associated with the recruitment and selection function. A wise approach in considering which documents to retain is to answer the following three questions:

- What records must be kept under each federal law?
- What is the retention period for those records?
- What is the applicability for each federal law?

Type of Record	Relevant Law	Years to Be Kept	Records Covered
Selection, hiring, and employment records	Age Discrimination in Employment Act (20 or more employees) Americans with Disabilities Act (15 or more employees) Civil Rights Act of 1964 (Title VII) (15 or more employees) Section 503 of the Rehabilitation Act of 1973 (federal contractors) Vietnam Era Veterans Readjustment Assistance Act (federal contractors) Executive Order 11246 (applies to federal contractors) Service Contract Act, Davis-Bacon Act, Walsh-Healey Act (apply to federal contractors)	1 year after creation of the document or the hire/no-hire decision, whichever is later (3 years for federal contractors)	Job applications, résumés, job ads, screen tools/tests, interview notes, and other records related to hire/no-hire decisions Records related to promotions, demotions, transfers, performance appraisals, terminations, reasonable accommodations, and/or requests, training records, incentive plans, merit systems, and seniority systems AAP records relating to hiring benchmarks and utilization goal analyses, hiring metrics analyses, and self-identification records for veterans and individuals with disabilities Copy of EEO-1 survey and intake forms if applicable
Form I-9	Immigration Reform and Control Act (one or more employees)	3 years after date of hire or 1 year after date of termination, whichever is later	
Polygraph test records	Employee Polygraph Protection Act (one or more employees)	3 years	Polygraph test result(s) and the reason for administering

Table 3-3 Federal Record Retention for Recruitment and Selection Records (*continued*)

Type of Record	Relevant Law	Years to Be Kept	Records Covered
Affirmative action plan/data	Executive Order 11246 (applies to federal contractors) The Uniform Guidelines on Employee Selection Procedure (15 or more employees)	2 years	
Credit reports	Fair and Accurate Credit Transactions (one or more employees)	No retention requirement; law requires shredding of all documents containing information derived from a credit report; however, don't discard for at least 1 year (see "Selection, hiring, and employment records" in this table)	
Drug test records	Department of Transportation (DOT)–covered safety-sensitive transportation positions; aviation, trucking, railroads, mass transit, and pipelines	1 year from test date (up to 5 years for records relating to drug testing for DOT positions; see https://www.fmcsa.dot.gov/regulations/title49/section/382.401 for specific DOT retention requirements)	

Source: U.S. Department of Labor and the EEOC

Table 3-3 Federal Record Retention for Recruitment and Selection Records

 EXAM TIP Recordkeeping is a usual responsibility of the early-career HR professional. Expect to see a question on the aPHR exam about record retention in both the pre- and post-employment phases.

Résumés vs. Job Applications

So far, no federal law or regulation requires employers to use job applications or résumé forms in their employment process. That means employers are left to their own devices about how to process job applicants. Evaluating differences among job applicants is the primary task. Carefully crafted job application forms can help HR professionals in that evaluation process.

What is required by federal law is that employers meet the requirements of equal employment opportunity laws and are able to demonstrate that they made their employment decisions without regard to any of the protected categories. Some organizations prefer to use résumés rather than job applications, and in some companies neither is a requirement.

If a job application is used, it can be designed by the employer to contain requests for information the employer deems to be necessary in making the employment decision. Obviously, information categories should not include things such as birth date, race, sex, marital status, or other reference to protected categories.

There are countless ways to write a résumé, and not all of them will contain the same data elements. Further, résumés almost never provide written authorization for employers to gather information from previous employers. Job application forms can be designed with those authorizations and liability release statements to facilitate background checking.

Advantages of Job Application Forms

While there is no requirement for employers to use job application forms, they can be enormously helpful. As an employer, you might expect to gain some or all of these benefits:

- Consistently gather the same data in the same format from each prospective employee. With an employment application, employers gain standardization of the information requested.

- Gather information about the applicant's previous experience that candidates would not usually include in a résumé or cover letter. Examples include reasons why the applicant left a prior employer as well as the names of and contact information for immediate supervisors.

- Obtain the applicant's signature attesting that all statements on the employment application are true.

- Obtain the applicant's signature enabling a potential employer to check the accuracy of all data provided on the employment application, including employment history, education history, degrees earned, and so forth. Fraudulent claims and information on application materials, including fake degrees, exaggerated claims about former job responsibilities or compensation, fake dates of employment, and other falsehoods, are a significant problem.

- Get the applicant's signature to attest that the applicant has read and understands certain employer policies and procedures that are spelled out on the employment application. These typically include the fact that the employer is an at-will employer; that the employer is an equal opportunity, nondiscriminating employer; and any other facts that the employer wants the applicant to read and understand on the employment application. When applicable, this may include the requirement that the applicant must pass a drug test prior to being hired.

- Obtain the applicant's signature agreeing to a background check, including criminal history, creditworthiness (for certain jobs), driving record (for certain jobs), and anything else required by the job.

- Obtain voluntary self-identification data about race, sex, disability, and veteran status to enable proper reporting to government organizations as required and analysis of employment data by the employer.

Online vs. Hard Copy

Many people today prefer to dispense with paper copies of documents, and there are legitimate environmental reasons for moving to electronic copies. There are advantages to each approach.

Hard-Copy Records   Job applications and résumés can provide an insight into the candidate's organization and language skills. Sloppiness and misspellings can be readily detected on paper records. Asking applicants to fill out a form can offer some insights into their reading skill, handwriting, and written articulation. When such records are converted to electronic format, the same types of information may not be as obvious.

Online Records   The most obvious advantage of electronic records is that they can be shared by multiple people at the same time. In the case of group interviews, this can be particularly nice. Many years ago there were problems with the legality of electronic signatures on e-documents. The Uniform Electronic Transactions Act of 1999[4] remedied that problem for the most part.

Self-Identification

Invitations to self-identify as part of the application process should be treated as confidential, just as all other HR data is considered confidential. We know from the Fair Labor Standards Act (see Chapter 2) and the EEOC requirement for annual filing of the EEO-1 report that many employers are required to establish and maintain records of employee demographics. The categories of information are for race, gender/sex, veteran, and disabled status.

Race and Gender/Sex

All employers with 100 or more employees and all federal contractors with 50 or more employees and contracts of $50,000 or more (or a construction contract valued at $10,000 or more) must maintain sex and ethnic identification of each employee.

There are seven race/ethnic categories on the EEO-1 form. So, an invitation to self-identify given to employees and job applicants should contain all seven categories. They are as follows:

- Hispanic or Latino
- White
- Black or African-American
- Native Hawaiian or other Pacific Islander
- Asian
- American Indian or Alaska Native
- Two or more races

 EXAM TIP Be sure to note the category names. The exam's multiple-choice selection may include a question about EEO-1 category names with an answer selection that seems apparent in today's world, such as transgender; however, that is not one of EEO-1 categories.

When an employee fails to self-identify, the employer is responsible for making an observation and best guess as to the race category in which the employee should be reported. If the employee later decides to report their race/ethnicity, that information should be accepted and recorded by the employer. The invitation to self-identify should also ask for identification of gender/sex, either male or female. Again, if the individual refuses to self-identify, the employer is obligated to make a selection based on observation.

Veteran and Disabled Status

Federal contractors with $25,000 or more in contract value must abide by regulations related to affirmative action requirements for the disabled and veterans. As of 2014, all federal contractors are required to invite self-identification as disabled and veteran from both applicants and employees. When talking about veterans, we mean U.S. veterans. Someone who has served in the armed forces of a foreign country is not included in the government's definition.

The EEOC has determined that it is acceptable to request identification of disability prior to an employment offer being extended as long as the invitation form is the one specified by the Office of Federal Contract Compliance Programs (OFCCP) and it is in an effort to comply with affirmative action obligations. Of course, any request for accommodation during the application process should be handled as required by the Americans with Disabilities Act.

Each of the four categories of veteran should be clearly identified on the self-ID request form. The four categories are: disabled veteran, recently separated veteran, active duty wartime or campaign badge veteran, and armed forces service medal veteran. The applicant or employee should be able to choose from that list. Also, a brief explanation of each category should be given so the form user can understand what they mean.

The disability identification should be available as a selection, along with an opportunity to request any job accommodation or applicant accommodation that might be desired.

Pre-employment Skill Testing

Some companies test their applicants before in-depth interviews; others do this afterward. It all depends on the nature of the job. As an example, a job vacancy in IT may have applicants taking a coding test to determine whether they possess the coding skill.

Because of EEO concerns, many organizations ceased testing in the 1970s. You might remember from Chapter 2 that the passing of the Uniform Guidelines on Employee Selection Procedures in 1978 addressed these specific concerns. Pre-employment testing may involve the risk of litigation on the grounds that the tests discriminate against minorities, the disabled, or other classes of protection if improperly conducted. However, if property conducted, nondiscriminatory formal tests can be of great benefit in identifying and screening good candidates.

A general guideline that is followed for pre-employment testing is like that of any other phase in the hiring processes: the test must be a valid, reliable, job-related predictor. Care must be taken to comply with the Civil Rights Acts of 1964 and 1991 as well as the ADA and any state laws that may apply and be restrictive to pre-employment testing.

EXAM TIP   Monitoring of all required pre-employment testing and making every effort to avoid tests that have adverse impact on minority applicants is a major responsibility of HR. You can expect questions on the aPHR to address the Civil Rights Act.

Interviewing Techniques

Interviewing is an important part of the selection process. A large portion of the workforce is hired only after one or more interviews with the prospective employer. Some organizations conduct a series of interviews, ranging from short prescreening interviews to long and in-depth interviews that might last an entire day. The key is to spend sufficient time with the applicant to be able to not only judge their skills and behaviors but also assess whether a "fit" is apparent for the candidate and your company.

Types of Interviews

Employers can select from several primary types of interviews. The types of interviewing styles you will be using, or the hiring managers who you will be coordinating for, will depend on the preference of the interviewer (or interviewers), the situation, and the required consistency that must be kept for legality purposes.

EXAM TIP   The various types of interviews is more than likely going to be a question on the aPHR exam.

Prescreening

Prescreening interviews are helpful when there is a high volume of candidates for a job vacancy. HR usually conducts the prescreening interview, which puts them in the role of "gatekeeper." A series of prequalification questions is selected to screen out candidates who do not have the minimum qualifications or whose salary expectations do not fit the organization's salary range.

Structured

An interviewer asks every applicant the same questions along with follow-up probes that may be different depending on the initial response. Structured interviews make it possible to gather similar information from all candidates.

Patterned

In the patterned interview, sometimes called a targeted interview, an interviewer asks each applicant questions that are from the same knowledge, skill, or ability (KSA) area; however, the questions are not necessarily the same. They differ depending on the candidate's background. For example, questions asked of a recent college graduate may differ from those asked of a candidate with years of related experience.

Directive

In this type of interview, an interviewer poses specific questions to the candidate, maintaining tight control; it is a highly structured interview. Every candidate is asked the same questions.

Nondirective

In this type of interview, the interviewer asks open-ended questions and provides only general direction; the interviewer allows the candidate to guide the process. A response to one question dictates what the next question will be.

Behavioral

In a behavioral interview, an interviewer focuses on how the applicant previously handled actual situations (real, not hypothetical). The interviewer probes specific situations looking for past behaviors and how the applicant handled those experiences. For example, "give me an example of a time when you held steadfast to your ethical values even though it was unpopular to do so." The questions probe the knowledge, skills, abilities, and other personal characteristics identified as essential to success on the job. The interviewer looks for three things: a description of an actual situation or task, the action taken, and the result or outcome. The principle behind behavioral interviewing is that past performance is the best predictor of future performance.

Stress

In this type of interview, an interviewer creates an aggressive posture—in other words, deliberately creating some type of stress to see how the candidate reacts to stressful situations. For example, using a room where the candidate has to face an open window with the sun in their eyes can put the candidate under stress. This type of interview is used more often in law enforcement, air traffic control, and similar high-stress occupations. The stress interview was more common in the 1970s and 1980s. Today, it is not recommended because of the likelihood that it will be interpreted as personal bias.

Situational

In a situational interview, the interviewer elicits stories and examples that illustrate the applicant's skills and qualifications for the job. Situational interviewing is similar to behavioral interviewing; the only difference is that in a behavioral interview, the interviewer is probing for actual past experiences, whereas in a situational interview, the interviewer develops hypothetical situations and asks the applicant how they would handle them.

Group/Panels

Group interviews happen when multiple job candidates are seen by one or more interviewers at the same time. Group interviews are used in specific situations where a number of candidates are being considered for the same job in which the duties are limited and clearly defined, such as a merry-go-round operator. A *fishbowl interview* brings multiple candidates together to work with each other in an actual group activity or exercise. A *team interview* typically involves a group of interviewers, each with a different perspective of the actual interactions associated with the job. This might include supervisors, subordinates, peers, customers, and so on. It is like a 360-degree exercise. Finally, in a *panel interview,* questions are distributed among a group of interviewers, typically those most qualified in a particular area. At the conclusion of the panel interview, the panel caucuses with the purpose of coming to a group consensus regarding the result.

Panels can be structured or unstructured. In the public sector, consistency is often a key factor in selection decisions, so structured interviews are conducted by panels. Panel members will sometimes ask the same question of each candidate, and sometimes the panel members will alternate their selection of questions to be asked. Panel size also varies from two to something more. It is common to see panels composed of three to four individuals. Because this is an expensive approach to interviewing (it requires multiple people to spend time in the interview), it is usually reserved for professional and managerial job selections.

Interviewing Skills and Techniques

Conducting effective interviews requires a range of abilities and skills. The following sections cover guidelines that are known to be effective.

Plan Ahead

Be clear on what the job requirements are by reviewing the job and its description with the hiring manager. Observe the job or interview an incumbent. Ask hiring managers what they plan to change about the job from what the predecessor was doing. This provides an opportunity to help plan the standardization of questions.

Create Rapport

Creating rapport early in the interview process allows applicants to feel more at ease and allows them to open up with dialogue. Remember, the interview is a two-way street—the applicant is also interviewing your organization. This is especially important for interviews conducted over the Internet, as this setting can be more difficult to develop a personal connection.

Listen

Reflective listening is a technique that comes in handy in interviewing. Paraphrase or summarize what the candidate said to ensure you have the correct impression. Be sure you are asking open-ended questions so that the interview offers a 70/30 split—by that we mean the candidate is speaking 70 percent of the time and you are speaking 30 percent of the time.

Nonverbal Behavior

Gestures, expressions, eye movement, and body positions are all helpful in the interview. You should be looking for inconsistencies between applicants' verbal and nonverbal cues. Of course, any nonverbal behavior is going to have the filter of your subjective interpretation, and this can be especially difficult in videoconferencing settings. Yet, it should be noted if they have difficulty in coming up with examples when asked or appear uneasy about certain inquiries.

Be Inquisitive

Ask questions. The more open-ended questions you can ask, the better the information will be in helping you determine whether you have a viable candidate. From your open-ended questions, you can ask more targeted questions and "peel back the onion" to learn more about the candidate.

You should also plan your questions; this is not the time to wing it. Also, for legal reasons, be sure to follow the list of questions with all the candidates you interview. Start off with questions such as "Tell me about a time when you _____" and "Describe a time when you were required to _____."

Paint a Realistic Picture

As mentioned earlier, the interview is a two-way dialogue where the candidate will also be interviewing the organization, determining whether this is the job they would like to accept if it is offered. To that end, be sure to provide realistic information about the job, the company, and what the applicant can expect if employed. Culture and values would be ideal to discuss. Be honest and forthright in answering the candidate's questions, yet avoid making promises or making predictions.

Take Notes

It's perfectly fine to jot down notes using an electronic device, computer, or good old pen and paper. Avoid writing on the applicant's résumé/application, and never make a note that would be construed as discriminatory in some fashion. Notes will help you document the qualifications and the responses when comparing all the applicants being interviewed.

Be Courteous

Be prepared, be on time, be professional, minimize any disruptions, and be sure you've reviewed the applicant's résumé *before* they sit in the chair across from you. You are providing an impression about your organization, and having respect for the applicant and their time to interview should be a lasting impression you'll want to make for your organization.

Interviewing Bias

Hiring managers who interview may inadvertently create EEO problems or make ill-fated selection choices without the proper training and guidance from HR. Hiring is typically not a frequent responsibility of a line manager; it may have been several years since they had to hire an employee. A discussion of some common factors that may create problems in interviewing would be helpful from HR. They include the following:

- **Stereotyping**   This involves forming a generalized opinion about how candidates of a particular gender, religion, or race may think, act, feel, or respond. An example would be presuming a woman would prefer to work indoors rather than outdoors.

- **Inconsistency in questioning**   This involves asking different questions of different candidates. An example would be asking only the male candidates to describe a time when they used critical-thinking skills in their last job.

- **First-impression error**   This is when the interviewer makes a snap judgment and lets their first impression (be it positive or negative) cloud the entire interview. An example is where credence is given to a candidate because the person graduated from an Ivy League college.

- **Negative emphasis**   This involves rejecting a candidate on the basis of a small amount of negative information. An example is when a candidate is wearing a large earring plug and in the interviewer's judgment this is inappropriate. Yet, the job that the candidate is interviewing for is a phone customer service position—there is no customer visual contact.

- **Halo/horn effect**   This is when the interviewer allows one strong point that they value to overshadow all other information. Halo is in the candidate's favor, and horn is in the opposite direction.

- **Nonverbal bias**   An undue emphasis is placed on nonverbal cues that are unrelated to potential job performance. An example is a distracting mannerism such as biting nails.

- **Contrast effect**   This is when a strong candidate has interviewed after a weak candidate and it makes them appear more qualified than they actually are—only because of the contrast.

- **Similar-to-me error**   The interviewer selects candidates based on personal characteristics that they share, rather than job-related criteria. An example would be that both interviewer and candidate attend the same local NFL team's home games.

- **Cultural noise**   This is when a candidate is masking their response, providing what is considered as "politically correct," and not revealing anything or being factual.

EXAM TIP   Cultural noise is not associated with a particular geographical location's culture—be sure to not be fooled by the word *cultural*.

After the Interview

Once you have a candidate that is a good fit for the job and they have accepted all the job conditions you have explained, you can proceed with the last few steps of the hiring process. Often, employers add a few more steps to the screening process. Some state laws require that these activities be completed after a job offer has already been provided to a candidate, so be sure to review your state's laws on these activities.

Job Offers

Once the candidate has accepted all the job conditions you have explained, it is time to put the offer in writing. The offer letter will detail the compensation, start date, job title, organization, and immediate supervisor. You should have a signature block at the bottom of the letter for the candidate to sign and date as acceptance of the terms. One copy should be returned to you with the signature.

 NOTE   It is wise to attach a copy of the job description to the offer letter.

Counteroffers

Sometimes candidates don't agree with the initial job offer, usually with respect to compensation or benefits. So, you may have a candidate who makes a *counteroffer* that includes a request for something like more vacation time or a higher amount of pay. It is up to the employer to decide if they want to accept a counteroffer from a candidate. It is important to consider whether the requests in the counteroffer will create any inequity between the candidate and other employees in the same position. This may violate legal requirements such as the Fair Pay Act.

Employment Contracts

An employment contract is an agreement between an employee and the company. It is often reserved for executives or management-level employees. It clearly outlines the obligations of both parties in the employment relationship. In addition to including the information in an offer letter, it may also include a requirement for the employee to stay in the position for a certain amount of time, details on a bonus plan, or a requirement that the employee does not work for a competitor for a certain amount of time after leaving the organization. This is called a *noncompete agreement* and is common for sales employees. It is wise to consult a legal representative before drafting an employment contract to ensure it is crafted according to state and federal laws.

Background Checks

Job offers are often conditioned upon successful completion of a background check, a reference check, and sometimes even a credit check. In some instances, a job offer could be conditioned on passing a medical evaluation or a drug screening.

Before conducting background or credit checks, review the current legal limitations on their use. The EEOC has issued guidelines on consideration of conviction records because the population of convicted felons includes more members of minority groups. Considering conviction records has a disparate impact on those racial groups. Thus, only if the conviction has a direct relationship to the job content will considering it in the hiring decision be permitted by the EEOC.[5]

References

There may be several types of references your organization requires. They may include the following:

- **Employment references**   Information you ascertain from previous employment of the applicant to verify dates of employment, job titles, and type of work performed. Many employers are reluctant to provide more information than name, job title, and dates of employment for privacy reasons, but as long as the information is factual and provided in good faith, most states consider it "qualified privileged," which protects the reporting employer.

- **Educational references**   Used to verify the applicant's degrees or educational attainment, including years of attendance and requests for transcripts.

- **Financial references**   Generally used only when candidates will be handling financial transactions, cash, or other financial resources. Financial references are obtained through one of the three credit reporting bureaus and are subject to requirements of the federal FCRA.

Credential Verification

As with educational references, credential verification may be necessary when a job requires a credential, such as a license or certification. Negligent hiring could occur if an employer did not verify professional or technical certification. Such would be the case if a physician whose license has expired or was revoked performs a procedure that was unsuccessful on a patient.

Public Records

Public records, such as criminal records, can uncover information about violent behavior, substance abuse, and property crimes, such as theft or embezzlement. It can be difficult to extract this level of information if your organization is a private employer, so many times you'll need to employ an investigative third party that does have the ability and credentials to obtain a public record. Criminal record checks must comply with related FCRA requirements.

Social Media Searches

Not so long ago the idea of checking a candidate's social media as part of the hiring process was not even considered. Doing so was thought of little value to understanding an applicant's professional viability. However, that has vastly changed, and checking has since become a much more common screening strategy. How a candidate acts on social media isn't just a reflection of their professionalism and personality. Their online behavior can also be a sign of how they will represent your business as an employee.

Popularity aside, social media screening can lead to some expensive legal pitfalls. For example, social media accounts often contain a lot of personal information about a person that may alter the decision to hire them, thus violating the FCRA, Title VII of the Civil Rights Act, or EEOC standards. Thankfully, social media screening is now performed by many background check vendors in compliance with federal laws. Adding this service to your background check package is a wise idea. A hefty discrimination claim will cost you much more than the additional vendor fee.

Legal and Privacy Issues

There are privacy issues related to background check information. Keep the data confidential. Only those people having a need to access the content of the results should be allowed access. Records should be secured at all times, so passersby cannot pull open a file drawer and remove documents.

Medical Examinations

Under the Americans with Disabilities Act, employers may require medical examinations only if they are job related and consistent with business necessity and only after an offer of employment has been made to the candidate. The purpose of the exam is so it can be used to determine whether the candidate can perform the essential job functions and/or whether a reasonable accommodation is necessary.

Medical examinations can be completed by a physician specified by the company or, in the case of large employers, in their on-site medical centers. Employers have a right to conduct a medical exam, and it is normally limited to "fitness for duty" situations. Examples are an operator of heavy equipment, an air traffic controller, and a first responder. In some organizations, a particular level of management is required to take a physical exam.

Drug Testing

Employers risk the torts of negligent hiring if they knowingly hire a drug or alcohol abuser who causes harm to someone while on the job. That, along with federal mandates for some employers and/or occupations, is the purpose behind pre-employment drug testing. Validated studies by OSHA have proven that drug-screening pre-employment tests reduce job-related accidents. Drug-screening tests are specifically excluded from the ADA's medical exam requirement. The successful passing of a drug test may be required prior to extending an offer of employment.

Legal and Privacy Issues

Access to information about applicants should be strictly limited to those people in your organization with a need to know the information. Many states are aggressive protectors of employee and applicant privacy; there are severe penalties for a lack of privacy. Make sure you store an applicant's medical exam results and drug testing results in a secure location and that they are not left unattended on your computer screen. Only those people with a need to access the content of the files should be allowed access.

Onboarding

Once a job candidate has completed all of the necessary screening requirements, it is time to officially make that person an employee of the organization. In good onboarding, there is an administrative component to help abide by state and federal laws, and there is an employee retention component. We will discuss both in this section.

Administrative Paperwork

Federal laws require a few important forms to be completed when a new employee starts at your organization. In addition, many employers also use this time to review important company documents to help the new employee start on the right foot. It is best to review this paperwork with the employee on their first day of work to ensure any required deadlines are met. Here are some examples of paperwork you should prepare for a new employee:

- **Form W-4**   This form collects personal information such as the employee's number of dependents and marital status to calculate federal income tax withholdings. You will need this information for payroll purposes. Employees may update their W-4 as frequently as they would like, and the employer must keep track of these changes.

- **Enrollment in benefit programs**   Benefits enrollment options should be reviewed at the time of hire. Depending on your employer's benefits plan, employees may be eligible for benefits a few weeks from their hire date.

- **Personal information**   Data on race, sex, disability, and veteran status likely needs to be collected for federal requirements, and it is useful to keep an employee's emergency contact information on file.

- **Confidentiality and non-disclosure agreements**   During the course of their jobs, many employees have access to confidential information. Confidential information could range from data in a laboratory testing a new vaccine to customer contact information. It is a good practice to ask employees to sign a legal agreement outlining the employer's expectations for keeping this information confidential.

- **Employee handbook**   Many organizations have a handbook or policy manual that outlines organizational rules, internal processes for abiding by state and federal laws, and benefits such as vacation, sick, and holiday time. Reviewing this document with new employees is a good way to set clear expectations and clarify any questions or concerns early in the employment journey.

Employment Authorization – Form I-9

The Immigration Reform and Control Act of 1986 (see Chapter 2) introduced the requirement for all employees in the United States to provide proof of identity and proof that they have the legal right to work in this country. That law brought us the Form I-9. Every person hired after November 30, 1986 must furnish information on a Form I-9, and the employer must complete the document citing the specific identification presented by the new worker. The employer must also cite the document used to prove the new employee has authorization to work in this country. This form changes from time to time, so employers should visit www.uscis.gov/files/form/i-9.pdf to be sure they are using the most current version of the form.

Form 1-9 includes two components:

- **Proof of identity**   Also required for employment is a photo identification of some variety, issued by a governmental agency that contains the individual's name as well as a current or recent image. This can be a U.S. passport (Passport Book or Passport Card), or in most cases, a driver's license issued by the state in which the person lives. All states will issue a non-driver identification card if requested to do so. A list of acceptable documents is included on the instructions for Form I-9. The employer must accept any document listed on Form I-9.

- **Proof of work authorization**   A Social Security Card number is the usual form of authorization offered by new employees. It does not provide proof of identity because it does not have a photo of the card owner, but it does offer proof that the owner is authorized to work in this country. Documents accepted for work authorization include visas of various types and any other form specified on the instructions for Form I-9. Refer to Chapter 2 for a detailed outline of visa types related to employment.

Employers have 3 workdays from the time of hire to complete Form I-9 and have it ready for inspection by any authorized federal investigator. If, at the end of 3 days, the newly hired employee has not provided the required documentation, the employer is instructed to remove the worker from the payroll. Retaining someone who is not properly documented will represent a violation of the federal law. There are fines per error on Form I-9 and court-imposed fines for retaining illegal aliens on the payroll.

E-Verify System

E-Verify began life as a voluntary program offered by the government as a way for employers to get online verification of new employees' Social Security numbers. It has evolved into a combination voluntary/involuntary program as federal and state governments mandate portions of the employer community to participate. The program was intended to reduce the number of false positives received when the Social Security Administration was checking new hire reports for invalid Social Security number matches.

The Department of Labor now requires federal contractors who are subject to the affirmative action regulations to participate in E-Verify. And, as time has passed, the accuracy of the Social Security number database has improved.

As of September 2021, eight states require all or most employers to participate in the E-Verify program. An additional 16 states require public employers or contractors to participate, and some local jurisdictions have their own requirements. The message here is that HR professionals should check their local and state requirements frequently so they remain in compliance.

Onboarding for Retention

Employee retention is a practice focused on keeping good employees on the payroll. Many of the HR topics we discuss in later chapters are an important part of the function for this very reason. Starting a new job is stressful, and first impressions are important. It is a common belief that the first 90 days of a worker's experience on a new job will determine how the relationship goes for the balance of their employment. One way to get off on the right foot is to provide a quality orientation program (also referred to as *onboarding*) to every new employee.

A strong orientation program will include items such as the following:

- **Welcome by the CEO/senior executive**   Providing evidence that senior management cares about employees can begin during orientation. Senior executives who believe it isn't worth their time convey a strong message also.

- **Discussion about culture**   This is an opportunity to discuss the values within the organization. These shared values have a strong influence on the people in the organization and inform how they dress, act, and perform their jobs. What gets rewarded in the organization? What type of image does the employer want to project to the world? What are expectations of ethics?

- **Tour of employee common areas**   This can include the cafeteria or break room, the location for labor law compliance posters, and restrooms.

- **Safety equipment and emergency exits**   This is often overlooked when it should be on the orientation agenda. If there are emergency breathing apparatuses, eye-wash stations, emergency shutdown switches, first-aid stations, or other important safety points of interest, this is the time to show each new worker where they are.

- **Introduction to co-workers and supervisors**   Guide the employees to their new work locations and introduce them to their new co-workers and supervisors, even if they may have met some of them during the interviewing process. Have someone designated to explain where to get office supplies, how to access computer terminals, and who to ask when questions come up. These things are just common employment courtesy.

- **Buddy or mentor**   Sometimes the best way for a new employee to understand an organization's culture is to pair them up with someone who is established in the organization. Having someone a new employee feels safe seeking advice from or asking questions of can allow for a more seamless transition.

Return on Investment

One final aspect to consider for the talent acquisition function is how well it's working. Return on investment (ROI) is a way of measuring what you put in to a process, divided by the cost of doing it. You want your ROI to be positive, meaning that you get back more than you invest in a process.

There are different ways to measure ROI in recruiting, depending on what factors you are looking at. Measuring recruiting is valuable because it can tell you the cost of each step in the process as well as the overall cost of a new hire, and knowing costs associated with recruiting can help with budgeting for future staffing requirements. We share a few examples next.

Some Ways to Measure Hiring

Valuable recruitment measurements that can be undertaken include the following:

- **Time to fill** How long it takes from the time you advertise a job until someone is actually on the payroll. This can be monitored separately for various candidate sources (social media, employer web site, professional associations, or other sources). The goal is to ultimately shorten the time to fill.

- **Quality of hire** Considerations include the job performance rating of new hires, the percentage of new hires promoted within a year, the percentage of new hires retained after a year, and any number of other possibilities.

- **Employee retention** Grasps the percentage of new hires that are retained for a year (or any other designated period of time) after they have been hired.

- **Turnover cost** The opposite of retention, turnover measures the rate of employee loss. It can include unemployment insurance expense, workers' compensation expense, the cost of training a replacement, the cost of recruiting and hiring a new employee, and other factors.

- **Cost per hire** This formula looks at the number of hires in a given time period and the costs to obtain them. It enables you to derive expenses for each new hire stated as an average.

Cost Per Hire Example

Here is an example of how to calculate cost per hire. This formula is likely to end up on the aPHR exam. Cost per hire begins with considering the external and internal costs of hiring someone.

$$\text{Cost Per Hire} = \frac{(\text{Sum of External Costs} + \text{Sum of Internal Costs})}{(\text{Total Number of Hires in a Time Period})}$$

External costs are those expenses such as external agency fees, advertising costs, job fair costs, travel costs, and other similar expenses for the time period being analyzed. Internal costs are expenses that can include fully loaded salaries and benefits of the recruiting team as well as the extra costs of overtime for employees working in the understaffed department waiting for the new hire.

Here is a worked example of the formula:

$$\text{Cost Per Hire} = \frac{(\text{External Costs} = \$100,000 + \text{Internal Costs} = \$100,000)}{(\text{Total Number of Hires in a Time Period} = 50)}$$

Cost Per Hire = $4,000

Chapter Review

The talent acquisition process covers a wide range of knowledge and responsibility. Many laws impact this area of HR responsibility that the early HR career professional will need to follow. Also, a great deal of skill will need to be developed. It takes some time for HR professionals to acquire the skills for effective interviewing. Just as important is the level of creativity needed for the functions of sourcing viable candidates for job vacancies.

From job postings to reference checks and from illegal employment discrimination to legal hiring practices, HR professionals have extensive responsibilities and knowledge requirements. The laws impacting this function area will be an important foundation to understanding the methods and techniques utilized in recruitment and selection.

Questions

1. Lebron serves as the HR director for a startup company, and his bosses want him to hire people quickly, so they have given him some tests to use in the screening process. He was told to hire the applicants with the best scores. Are these tests something Lebron should use?

   A. It is okay to use tests if they are job specific in their measurement.

   B. No way. He should not use any tests that he hasn't bought from a legitimate test publisher.

   C. Tests are just fine. He should be sure the passing scores are set so they can get the best people.

   D. If the boss says to use the tests, he has little choice. He just has to be sure to score them properly.

2. AB Trucking has had a policy that nobody will be hired unless they complete the company's job application. Now, all of the job applications are being processed online, and some applicants want to submit their résumés instead of a job application form. What can AB Trucking do about the résumé vs. application controversy?

   A. It is entirely up to the company how it wants to handle the policy. Application forms are not a legal requirement, but using them is generally considered a best practice in the employment arena. Job candidates can be forced to go through the company's process of completing an application form, online or offline.

   B. The government has set up regulations that say employers have to accept résumés if they are submitted in a job search. The company doesn't really have any choice but to accept them.

   C. Job applications are old-school. Almost no employer uses them these days. The company should change its policy and use only résumés in the future.

   D. Résumés don't have all the information that can be gathered on a job application, and people lie on résumés anyway. That alone is reason for the company to continue using its job application forms.

3. An employee in Cortez's organization came to him and suggested that she and her co-worker could consolidate their duties into one job and each work part-time. What is this arrangement known as?

   A. Part-time jobbers

   B. Job sharing

   C. Impossible

   D. Double-duty

4. Abel has been having trouble selecting quality accounting people. Everyone claims to be able to use Excel spreadsheets, but few actually can once they get on the job. In the end, he has had to terminate people because of poor performance. He is thinking he will use a test he saw at the local office-supply warehouse. As Abel's HR recruiting liaison, what advice would you give him about his plans for testing?

   A. It sounds like a good idea. It certainly could control the cost of turnover. We should try it.

   B. It sounds like a good idea. Will he be able to show that the test actually predicts success on the jobs he wants to use it for? If not, he should find a different screening tool.

   C. It doesn't sound like a good idea. With everyone talking about the liability of written tests these days, we can't take that risk for any job.

   D. It doesn't sound like a good idea. It is going to create more paperwork for HR, and we can't stand any workload increase.

5. Which of the following is an in-person recruiting method?

   A. Job board

   B. Job bidding

   C. Job fair

   D. Posting on company web site

6. What should your organization do if the retention requirements for the same record differ between three laws?

   A. Keep duplicates of each record in different files according to the differing requirements.

   B. Make a judgment about the maximum retention based on the law that has the most importance.

   C. Retain the information for the longest period of time required.

   D. Keep the records for the shortest time required unless it involves a federal contractor.

7. Which of the following statements is *true* about medical examinations?

   A. Temporary employees can be required to submit to a medical exam before employment.

   B. Pre-employment health checklists can be requested before an employment offer is made.

   C. Exams must be job related and can be required only after an employment offer is made.

   D. The exam must be completed by the company's medical staff.

8. As the employment coordinator for your organization, you have been requested to arrange interviews with three of the top qualified candidates for a customer service position. The interviewers will be a select group of employees from the customer service department who would be the candidate's co-workers. This is an example of what type of interview?

   A. Stress interview

   B. Group/panel interview

   C. Situational interview

   D. Rapport interview

9. A job offer letter should be sent to a selected candidate immediately after:

   A. The hiring decision is made.

   B. All contingencies are addressed.

   C. Both parties review the employment contract.

   D. Both parties verbally agree to any relocation expenses.

10. Leslie is reviewing the list of interview questions the hiring manager has submitted. Which interview question on the hiring manager's list has the potential to be discriminatory under federal law?

  A. "Are you legally blind?"

  B. "Do you have any relatives who work for our headquarters?"

  C. "The job requires you to lift a 30-pound package once a month and place it on a shelf in the supply closet. Can you do that?"

  D. "Are you older than 18?"

11. Leslie notices another question on the hiring manager's list. Which additional question is not allowed because of its discriminatory manner under federal law?

  A. "Did you graduate from high school?"

  B. "Have you ever filed a workers' compensation claim?"

  C. "Do you have proper documentation to work in the United States?"

  D. "Did you receive any training in the military?"

12. Which of the following statements indicates a nondirective interview?

  A. The hiring manager asks all applicants the same questions.

  B. The hiring manager purposefully creates a high level of stress.

  C. Each candidate interviewed is asked different questions about the same skill and ability.

  D. The hiring manager's next question is formulated by the candidate's response to the previous open-ended question.

13. Under which of the flexible staffing options would a professional employer organization (PEO) be most likely to provide temporary workers with benefits?

  A. Payrolling

  B. Master vendor contract

  C. Outsourced or managed services

  D. Temp-to-lease arrangement

14. "Floater" employees are:

  A. Scheduled to work less than a regular workweek on an ongoing basis

  B. Self-employed independent contractors hired on a contract basis for specific functions

  C. People who are employed by the organization, receive a W-2, and fill in on a short-term basis for a temporary period of time and may rotate among several positions or functions

  D. Long-term contracted temporary employees assigned to one department

15. A benefit of job posting within an organization first is that it:

    A. Provides a cost-effective manner to target a desired pool of applicants at one time

    B. Provides an easy way to create a database for job vacancies

    C. Allows individuals to maximize their career opportunities within a company

    D. Allows existing employees to indicate interest in an opening

16. Deidre was disappointed in the lack of qualified responses to a recent print media advertisement, causing several of her open vacancies to exist for longer than anticipated. To expand her recruiting efforts, Deidre should utilize all of the following *except* which one?

    A. College/universities and job fairs

    B. The state employment agency

    C. Employee referrals

    D. Job bidding

17. Which federal agency is used to investigate charges of discrimination in hiring practices under Title VII?

    A. NLRB

    B. EEOC

    C. Pre-employment hiring board

    D. ADA board

18. What type of interviewing bias is being applied when the hiring manager is making a judgment about the applicant based on the manner in which they are dressed?

    A. Stereotyping

    B. Negative emphasis

    C. Contrast effect

    D. Cultural noise

19. When can the Trustworthy Bookkeeping and Tax Preparation organization require a polygraph test of a new employee?

    A. When a candidate is applying for an HR recruiting position

    B. When a candidate is applying for a clerical position

    C. When an accountant candidate is applying for a job in a function that has embezzlement potential

    D. When a candidate is recovering from substance abuse

20. The hiring manager states the following to an applicant in an interview: "I notice that you are applying for our job and yet you have a lot more knowledge, experience, and skill than is required for the job. How do you feel about working in a job that is lower than your experience indicates you can perform?" The candidate responds with the following statement: "I have always admired and wanted to work at your organization." What interviewing bias is the candidate portraying?

   A. Halo/horn effect

   B. Underachiever effect

   C. Cultural noise

   D. Similar-to-me error

Answers

1. **A.** Remember that it is the user of a test that holds the liability, not the publisher of the test. If a test has been validated to properly predict success in specific jobs with specific knowledge and skill requirements, it can be used for those jobs. Using it for *all* jobs is not a good idea. If the boss insists, he needs to be told what the consequences can be.

2. **A.** The company is not constrained by the government on how it designs its job application process. If it wants to have a certain form completed, it can establish that policy. A decision should be made about what documents it will accept from job applicants. Consistency in how the process is applied is critical in avoiding complaints of bias.

3. **B.** Job sharing is where two or more workers collectively work a job on a part-time basis to constitute one full-time equivalent employee.

4. **B.** The test should measure Excel skills because those are the predictors of success for Abel's accounting positions.

5. **C.** Job fairs are designed to bring in a number of employers and job seekers alike into a large hall for quick meet-and-greet interviews.

6. **C.** When the same or similar records are required by more than one law but the period of retention varies, retain the record for the longer period of time.

7. **C.** Only after a job offer is made can an employer require a job candidate to have a medical exam to determine fitness for duty. Only the medical examiner's conclusions about job fitness may go to the employer, not the actual test results.

8. **B.** Group and panel interviews happen when multiple job candidates are interviewed by one or more interviewers at the same time.

9. **A.** Time is of the essence. Put it in writing so the candidate has assurance and understanding of what the job offer parameters are and so they can give notice to their current employer when necessary.

10. **A.** You may ask questions associated with the applicant's ability to perform the identified functions of the job. You cannot ask about the nature or severity of a disability or recent or past surgeries.

11. **B.** Asking about previous workers' compensation claims is considered potentially discriminatory and is not relevant to the job. A high school diploma may be required for the position, and eligibility to work in the U.S. is required under the IRCA.

12. **D.** With nondirective interviews, the hiring manager will ask open-ended questions and provide only general direction. A response to one question by the candidate dictates what the next question will be.

13. **D.** An organization contracts with a temp service assigning a long-term temporary worker who, after a period of time of working for the employer, transfers to the employer's payroll.

14. **C.** Employees who are on the organization's payroll and fill in for temporary short-term assignments among several positions or departments are known as *floaters*. They provide continuity of knowledge and experience.

15. **C.** It is a morale booster and retention method to offer the existing workforce the opportunity to apply for job vacancies before an employer seeks candidates externally.

16. **D.** Job bidding is only for internal existing candidates from the current workforce.

17. **B.** The EEOC is the agency responsible for investigating all charges of discrimination under Title VII, rather than pre-employment hiring practices or post-employment activities.

18. **B.** Negative emphasis often happens when subjective factors such as dress or nonverbal communication taint the hiring manger's judgment.

19. **C.** Although the Employee Polygraph Protection Act prohibits employers from requiring or requesting pre-employment polygraph exams under most circumstances, if the position has been identified as a high risk for possible embezzlement, this test can be administered as long as all candidates for the same function are examined.

20. **C.** Cultural noise is when the candidate skirts the question and is reluctant to tell the interviewer unacceptable facts about themselves.

Endnotes

1. Internal Revenue Service, "Retiree Annuitants," accessed on September 21, 2021, https://www.irs.gov/government-entities/federal-state-local-governments/rehired-annuitants

2. Reuters, "Don't Treat Contractors Like Employees," accessed on September 21, 2021, https://www.reuters.com/article/businesspropicks-us-findlaw-dont-treat-c/dont-treat-contractors-like-employees-idUSTRE53063S20090401

3. SHRM, "Designing and Managing Successful Employee Referral Programs," accessed on September 27, 2021, https://www.shrm.org/resourcesandtools/tools-and-samples/toolkits/pages/tk-designingandmanagingsuccessfulemployeereferralprograms.aspx

4. U.S. Congress, "H.R. 1714," accessed on September 24, 2021, https://www.congress.gov/bill/106th-congress/house-bill/1714/text

5. U.S. Equal Employment Opportunity Commission, "Pre-Employment Inquiries and Arrest & Conviction," accessed on September 24, 2021, https://www.eeoc.gov/pre-employment-inquiries-and-arrest-conviction

Learning and Development

The Learning and Development functional area encompasses 15 percent of the Associate Professional in Human Resources (aPHR) exam. This functional area has an important bottom-line impact on any employer organization. Keeping employees' skills and knowledge current is necessary for maintaining the effectiveness of the organization. Further developing high-performing employees can be vital to organizational growth, helping these employees learn to lead through difficult periods of change. Understanding the techniques and methods for delivering training programs and developing individual employees is what the aPHR will address.

The Body of Knowledge (BoK) statements outlined by the HR Certification Institute (HRCI) for the Learning and Development functional area by those performing early HR career roles are as follows:

Knowledge of

- **01** The overall purpose and desired outcomes of employee orientation for new hires and/or internal hires; for example, setting expectations, building relationships, and acclimation

- **02** The concept of instructional design and components of commonly used models and methods for developing an organizational learning strategy; for example, knowledge, skills and, abilities (KSAs), ADDIE model, needs analysis, goals/objectives, available training resources, and intended audience

- **03** Elements and suitable applications for various training formats and delivery techniques; for example, blended, virtual, self-paced, instructor-led, on-the-job, role play, facilitation, and in-house vs. external training services

- **04** The concept, purpose, and key/desired outcomes of a change management process; for example, assessing readiness, communication plans, identifying needs, and providing resources and training

- **05** Methods and tools used to track employee development and measure the effectiveness of the training; for example, learning management systems (LMSs), reporting, post-training evaluation, and metrics

Laws and Regulations

The following eight federal laws have an impact on the Learning and Development functional area. Be sure to refer to Chapter 2 for more information about each of these laws. Understanding them is critical to serving as an effective HR professional. You may expect that any or all of these laws will be subjects on the aPHR certification exam.

- **The Copyright Act (1976)** The Copyright Act offers protection of "original works" for authors so others may not print, duplicate, distribute, or sell their work. This becomes important when you are developing training programs and using content from another source. Permission from the original author may be required.

- **The Trademark Act (1946)** The Trademark Act sets forth the requirements for registering a trademark or service mark. HR usually has a role to play in training employees on how to properly handle organizational trademarks and the policies that govern those uses.

- **The Uniform Guidelines on Employee Selection Procedures (1978)** This law provides guidelines to avoid illegal discrimination in employment decisions, including selection devices, such as written or oral tests, and performance evaluation, which often go hand in hand with training and development.

- **The Age Discrimination in Employment Act (1967)** This law bans employment discrimination, including training and other conditions of employment, based on age for those 40 years or older.

- **The U.S. Patent Act (1953)** This law was established to protect inventions for 20 years. U.S. law grants the inventor the right to exclude others from making, using, or selling the invention. This law may apply when developing training, or educating employees on the law.

- **Title VII of the Civil Rights Act (1964)** Title VII of the Civil Rights Act speaks to employment discrimination and cites five protected classes of people: race, color, sex, religion, and national origin. HR is responsible for providing training to all employees on employment discrimination.

- **The Americans with Disabilities Act (1990)** This act prohibits discrimination in employment, public services, public accommodations, and telecommunications for people with disabilities. Training programs must consider accommodations for employees with disabilities, such as effective delivery for someone who is hearing impaired.

- **The Uniformed Services Employment and Reemployment Rights Act (1994)** This act provides instructions for handling employees who are in the reserves and receive orders to report for active duty. The law also protects the employment, reemployment, and retention rights of anyone who voluntarily or involuntarily serves or has served in the uniformed services, which includes training and development.

HR's Role in Training and Development

From an employee's first day on the job through their entire employment journey, HR is responsible for managing the training and development function. *Training* is the process of teaching new employees the skills they need to perform their jobs. *Development* is the act of encouraging employees to acquire new or advanced skills, knowledge, and viewpoints by providing learning opportunities and avenues where such new ideas can be applied. Great HR teams also develop a culture that supports *organizational learning*. Put simply, this means an organization not only invests in learning but sees the benefit it has to business growth.

Here are some characteristics of a culture that supports organizational learning:

- Learning is part of the organization's values.
- The organization has invested in effective learning delivery systems, such as an e-learning platform or a classroom training facility.
- Knowledge sharing and creative ideas are encouraged in meetings or other group settings, and employees have access to materials they need to contribute, such as the strategic plan.
- Employees have personalized learning plans to help them reach their career goals.
- Employees receive personalized coaching to achieve the career goals they establish.
- Leaders also set learning goals and are open to feedback from others, including employees who report to them, about their own career development.
- Learning achievements and creativity are rewarded.
- Core competencies are well defined in job descriptions.

Organizational Values

Values represent what is important to the organization and the principles that the organization will abide by, no matter what. It is an important role of both management and the HR group to consistently and clearly communicate the organization's values. Training and development programs should be aligned with organizational values and are also a great vehicle to communicate them. When this happens, employees gain a sense of purpose. They have a better idea of what the expectations of the organization are and what they should strive to accomplish.

Values can be positive drivers of behavior, such as treating everyone with respect. Values can also describe behaviors that are less than desirable. For example, if work/life balance is an organizational value, being tethered to your smart phone 24/7 to respond to work e-mails is a good example of a behavior that is not aligned with organizational values.

Setting Expectations in Orientation

Training and development should begin on an employee's first day of work. The new hire orientation program is often a responsibility of early career HR professionals. An employee's first day of work is an important time to start communicating organizational values. If respecting others is a core value of the organization, training a new hire how to respond to someone respectfully during conflict is a good example of how to communicate this value.

Also, it's important that employees understand what specific performance and behaviors are expected of them in their jobs. For example, if "putting the customer first" is expected as a standard of behavior, each employee's job description needs to have clear examples of what represents "putting the customer first." For example, this should include behaviors such as trusting a customer's point of view in a disagreement no matter what. It should also include results, such as "every customer should leave happy." To achieve this result, some sort of concession may need to be made to the customer, such as a future discount for their inconvenience.

Acclimation

It goes without saying that no two organizations are alike. Even if ten different restaurant chains share the same organizational values, they don't all operate in the exact same way. There are different people employed at each location, different facilities, and different resources allocated to each facility. So, when a new employee starts work or transfers from a different location, they need to become acclimated to these conditions.

Acclimation requires new employees to first understand how they contribute to the big picture. Employees need to know the requirements of their job and what results are expected of them. Second, employees need to know what they can expect back from the organization to help them make this contribution. Organizational resources like on-the-job training, mentorship programs, management support, and how employees will be evaluated on their performance review are helpful ways to describe this organizational support.

Building Relationships

Effective orientation programs should also allow employees to build relationships that will help them meet the expectations of their job and desire to stay with the organization long-term. This can be done in the following ways:

- Introducing the new employee in an e-mail to staff prior to them starting work. Rather than a new hire wandering the grounds of the facility aimlessly on the first day, this can help current staff welcome the employee and direct them to the right place.

- Select a peer, sponsor, or buddy of the new hire to help with the acclimation process. By selecting someone who is a good role model, you give the new hire an excellent prototype to follow and a valuable resource to ask questions.

- Supervisors should be heavily involved in onboarding new employees. A supervisor is responsible for overseeing an employee's work on a day-to-day basis; the bond between an employee and their supervisor can make or break the employment relationship. Research has shown that having a poor relationship with a supervisor is the leading factor in employee dissatisfaction.[1] Onboarding is a great time to start this relationship off on the right foot.

- Set up a few group lunches early in employment as a way for the new employee to socialize and get to know other coworkers.

Instructional Design

In addition to onboarding, developing and delivering training programs is another important HR responsibility. There is not one perfect teaching method for every situation. As a matter of fact, the method that should be used will depend on several factors, including the material being covered and the group of people being trained. An important first step in instructional design is considering your audience. In general terms, good instructional design starts with understanding what learners already know, what they need to know, and what intervention will move them from point A to point B.

There are various theories about the best way to learn new material. Instructional design is rooted in cognitive and behavioral psychology, and it has developed over time to apply to distinct social environments and cultures as well as online delivery methods. In 1956, Benjamin Bloom first crafted Bloom's taxonomy,[2] which is still commonly used to structure learning objectives, activities, and assessments. Bloom's taxonomy includes three classifications, each of which addresses a specific learning goal: knowledge-based, skills-based, and affective-based. These terms can be loosely described as "knowing/head," "doing/hands," and "feeling/heart" and are closely aligned with the knowledge, skills, and abilities you see in job descriptions. Table 4-1 outlines the three classifications within Bloom's taxonomy.

As you may have noticed, the three different classifications apply to different situations. Knowledge-based learning is typically what you see in HR programs. However, skills-based learning often applies to new hires, where a job requires the development of new skills such as how to drive a forklift. Lastly, affective-based learning can be particularly important for training that addresses values such as diversity and inclusion. In order for the training to be effective, learners must be willing to learn the values and able to incorporate the content into their daily lives.

 EXAM TIP   Exam questions will likely address how to teach employees various knowledge, skills, and abilities. Bloom's taxonomy can help you think through these questions.

Learning Objectives

Objectives provide a means to measure what was learned and are an important aspect in designing any training program. When you're designing training objectives, employing the use of the SMART outline is helpful. SMART stands for *specific, measurable,*

Classification	Level of Expertise
Knowledge-based	• **Knowledge** This level of cognitive learning is where the learner recalls specific facts and instruction. • **Comprehension** This level of learning allows the learner to interpret information. • **Application** This is the ability to use the learned information in new experiences and situations. • **Analysis** This is being able to see how information connects and fits together with other information. • **Synthesis** This is where the learner is able to respond to new experiences, dissect problems, and consider appropriate tactics for solutions. • **Evaluation** This is the highest level of cognitive learning, wherein the learner will make judgments.
Skills-based	• **Perception** This level of learning allows the learner to use observations to guide actions. • **Set** This level of learning describes when the learner is ready to perform a task. • **Guided response** This is the ability to know the steps required to complete a task. • **Mechanism** This is being able to perform a task confidently and proficiently. • **Complex overt response** This is where the learner is able to modify the actions in a task to adapt to new or problematic situations. • **Organization** This involves incorporating new tasks or objectives into the ones the learner already knows.
Affective-based	• **Receiving** This level of learning is a willingness to participate in the activity. • **Responding** This is when a learner shows interest in the learning activity. • **Valuing** This is the ability to show appreciation for the value of the learning activity. • **Organization** This is being able to compare different values and resolve any conflicts between them. • **Characterization by a value** This where the learner is able to adopt a value that is consistent and predictable.

Table 4-1 The Three Classifications of Bloom's Taxonomy

achievable, relevant, and *timed.* Composing objectives with the SMART outline and the use of action verbs such as "identify," "describe," and "define," will be a helpful guide. An example of an objective might be something like this: "With the knowledge and techniques taught in this three-day training course on operating the new widget processor, the participant will be able to operate the widget processor at 100 percent production capacity."

When writing objectives, keep in mind that action is needed. Saying that an objective is for participants in a training program "to understand..." is not an action statement. How will you know if they understand? It is better to say something like, "to demonstrate," "to explain," "to answer 80 percent of the test questions correctly," or "to teach someone else to successfully...."

ADDIE Model

The ADDIE model is a commonly used instructional design approach. Each letter in ADDIE stands for one of the model's components:

- **A**nalysis
- **D**esign
- **D**evelopment
- **I**mplementation
- **E**valuation

The analysis phase of the model clarifies the *needs analysis,* which is the gap between what the learner already knows and what they need to learn from the training. Some questions instructional designers ask during this phase are, Who are the learners? What is the desired new knowledge, skill, or behavior? What constraints are there, such as time or resources? What are our options for delivering this training material?

The design phase begins with understanding the learning objectives and the content that meets those objectives. For example, if a learning objective is applying the definition of harassment to different situations, learning content should address what harassment is as well as offer some practice exercises to help an employee think through whether or not a situation constitutes harassment. The design phase also considers what resources you have available to teach the content. This might include what multimedia should be used (videos, PowerPoint presentation, and so on), the best way to deliver the content (in person, online, and so on), and how your budget might impact these resources.

The development phase goes hand in hand with the design phase. This is when the learning content is actually developed. This might include developing a presentation, creating handouts, or testing e-learning platforms to be sure that they operate effectively.

Implementation is when training actually occurs. It also involves training the facilitators to actually deliver the training, preparing the training environment, such as the classroom or e-learning platform, and preparing the learners for the training. Oftentimes, asking learners to do a bit of pre-work can help make the training more effective. This might involve reading about the learning material or receiving training on how to use the e-learning platform.

The last phase is evaluation. It includes formative and summative evaluation. *Formative evaluation* occurs while a training program is forming or occurring and seeks to understand whether the training is clear, useful, and relevant to participants. It might include such things as pilot-testing and focus group feedback. *Summative evaluation* occurs when the training program is completed. It addresses whether the training was effective and participants actually learned the content outlined in the learning objectives. It also addresses how future training could be improved.

Teacher-Centered Approaches

Training delivery usually occurs in some combination of two approaches: teacher-centered and learner-centered. Teacher-centered learning is viewed as a traditional style of teaching. It typically comes in the form of lecture-based training where participants are more passively involved in the learning process, but it can be helpful when training a large group of people at once. Elements of a teacher-centered approach include the following:

- **Demonstration** Showing participants how something is done.
- **Direct instruction** Conveying concepts and skills.
- **Lecture** Instructing on a topic while participants passively listen and take notes.
- **Lecture-discussions** Questions are added to the lecture.

Learner-Centered Approaches

Learner-centered approaches have become more common as research has shown the benefits of activities like group work, reflection, and learning through problem-solving.[3] Considering your audience is an important part of the training design phase. Although training is typically delivered in a group setting, no two learners are alike. Everyone will process the information differently. By using a combination of learner-centered teaching approaches, you provide individuals with ample opportunity to process the training content in a way that works best for them and to transfer it to new settings.

The following are elements of a learner-centered approach:

- **Case studies** Require application of knowledge to respond to a "real" problem.
- **Collaborative learning** Small group working on solving a problem or completing a task.
- **Discussion** Classroom or online interaction among participants and with the teacher.
- **Discovery** Using prior knowledge and experience to discover new things.
- **Graphic organizers** Diagrams, maps, and webs as illustrations of material.
- **Journals/blogs** Recordings of reflections and ideas.
- **K-W-L** Structured table showing columns with what participants know (K), what they want to know (W), and what they learned in the end (L).
- **Learning centers** Independent or small group work aimed at completing a task.
- **Role play** Solving problems through action or performance.

- **Scaffolding**   Teacher modeling skills and thinking for participants, allowing participants to take over those expressions based on the initial structure provided by the teacher.

- **Problem-based learning (inquiry learning)**   The teacher provides a problem where inquiry must be utilized to reach a solution.

- **Simulations**   Situations designed to be as realistic as possible without the risk of a real-life circumstance.

- **Storytelling**   Use of multimedia technology (for example, PowerPoint) to present interactive opportunities involving any subject.

 EXAM TIP   Although teacher-centered approaches such as lectures are still very common for training, adding some learner-centered activities to your training content usually makes training more effective.

Chunking

In both teacher- and learner-centered approaches, content chunking is an important concept to be aware of. *Content chunking* is the technique of breaking up content into shorter, bite-size pieces that are more manageable and easier to remember. No matter your audience, chunking content will allow learners to more easily move information from short-term to long-term memory.

In 1956, Harvard professor George A. Miller said that short-term memory could only hold five to nine chunks of information at a time.[4] Since then, scientists have argued about the exact number of knowledge chunks people can hold, but the concept of breaking training into chunks remains an established part of information-processing theory.

Chunking as a technique has been applied quite successfully to online training programs. Actually, any self-paced training program can benefit from the chunking design technique. Teaching materials in small chunks has been demonstrated to offer greater success with participants than a constant flow of information in one large stream.

Learning Curves

When you're designing instruction, it is important to remember that adults learn at different rates. This is referred to as a *learning curve,* which is a graphical representation of the increase of learning (vertical axis) with experience (horizontal axis). The factors that determine how quickly an adult will learn are as follows:

- The person's motivation for learning
- The person's prior knowledge or experience
- The specific knowledge or task that is to be learned
- The person's aptitude and attitude about the knowledge or skill to learn

The following are the four most common types of learning curve:

- **Increasing returns**   This is the pattern that comes into play when a person is learning something new. The start of the curve is slow while the basics are being learned. The learning increases and takes off as knowledge or skills are acquired. This curve assumes that the individual will continue to learn as time progresses. An example would be when an IT programmer needs to learn a new coding language. Learning will be slow at first, until they grasp the new coding protocol, and after mastering the basics, the learning becomes easier and/or quicker as they acquire more knowledge about the particular language.

- **Decreasing returns**   This pattern is when the amount of learning increases rapidly in the beginning and then the rate of learning slows down. The assumption with this learning curve is that once the learning is achieved, the learning then stops. This occurs with routine tasks and is the most common type of learning curve. An example is when a data entry clerk learns how to enter a sales order—the learning is complete.

- **S-shaped curve**   This learning curve is a blend of the increasing and decreasing returns curves. The assumption with this learning curve is that the person is learning something difficult, such as problem-solving or critical thinking. Learning may be slow at the beginning, until the person learning becomes familiar with the learning material, and at that point, learning takes off. The cycle continues with a slow-to-faster progression as new material is presented. An example of this is when a production lead is trained on new equipment, yet this equipment has not been utilized in the production of the product before. There might be trial and error for adjustments until the new production equipment is working as expected and is adjusted to the new product. Then, when another product is introduced, the equipment and process needs adjust again until everything works smoothly.

- **Plateau curve**   Just as the name suggests, learning on this curve is quick in the beginning and then flattens, or *plateaus*. The assumption is that the plateau is not permanent and that, with additional coaching, training, and support, the person's learning can ramp up again. With this curve, it can be frustrating to the learner if they are not getting the support and additional training needed to master the task. An example of the plateau curve is a salesperson who has met quotas in the past, and when a new line of equipment is introduced into the product line, the salesperson is provided a minimal level of training/knowledge about it, but not enough to answer all the questions of the prospective customers. The anticipation of additional sales with the new product is not being achieved because the salesperson requires more training in order to pitch the new product and convince the customer to purchase it.

The four most common learning curves are illustrated in Figure 4-1.

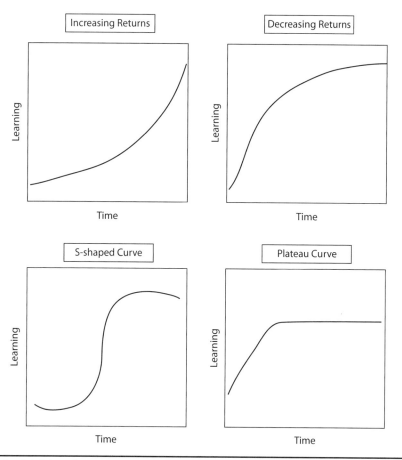

Figure 4-1   Adult learning curves

Training Delivery Format

Regardless of the type of training to be conducted, there are a number of methods and approaches that an organization can use to deliver the training. With today's rapid pace of growth in technology, the available choices are expanding exponentially. Whatever the selected approach, there are a variety of considerations when deciding on the methods:

- The subject matter
- Team versus individual training
- Offering the training in-house or using an external service
- Self-guided versus guided
- Number of trainees

- Geographical restrictions
- Resources and costs
- Time frame for the training
- Traditional or e-learning
- Conditions and parameters set by recertification requirements
- Legal issues with the selection of individuals for inclusion in training

Many of these decisions are guided by the organization's budget for the training program, who the attendees are, and what content needs to be learned. For example, your budget will often guide the method of training (e-learning versus traditional) and whether you use an in-house trainer or need to pay for an external service due to the complexity of the material. Who your attendees are will determine geographical restrictions and accommodations that may need to be made for disabilities or cultural differences. Lastly, if content is complex and needs to be applied to the job immediately, the mode of delivery will likely need to include more social interaction through problem-based learning, case study activities, or instructor scaffolding.

Classroom

Instructor-led classroom training continues to be the most commonly used approach to training. This traditional mode usually happens internally through the organization with in-house instructors, vendors, or through a professional organization. This face-to-face classroom setting permits the use of several learning methods: presentation, case study, reading, role-playing, exercises, group discussion, and demonstration. Table 4-2 explains when to use each method.

Classroom Facilitation Method	When to Use
Presentation	When information needs to be delivered to a group, especially large groups and perhaps at different locations
Case study	When trainees need to apply the knowledge to different situations on the job
Reading	When independent study is needed to process the information being disseminated
Role-playing	When trainees need to practice the information or skills being taught and learn skills quickly
Exercises	When practice is necessary to fully develop the new skills or learning
Group discussion	When trainees need to have an exchange of experience and information sharing with other trainees
Demonstration	When new information or skills are being presented

Table 4-2 Classroom Learning Methods

Virtual Classroom

With current technology, remote instruction has become a regular system of delivery for training materials. Today, organizations reach out to their employee groups efficiently and effectively via the virtual classroom. It is common to use a learning management system such as Canvas or Blackboard to allow the trainer and the trainees to have real-time chats and electronic file exchanges. Live streaming video allows a trainer in one geographical location to see and respond to a group class in a number of other locations.

As with any delivery of training modality, the coordination of creating the virtual classroom, the materials, the instructor, the intended trainees, *and* the technology (especially the technology) usually involves a number of important elements that will influence the success of the training program. This is the most visible stage of the ADDIE process because success is to be measured by the learning that takes place during the delivery of the training. It would benefit trainers to create checklists to ensure participants have PDF files of handouts and to set up automatic e-mail reminders for participants with time zone information and web links or phone numbers for questions or technical issues.

Corporate Universities

Corporate universities have been a growing trend in corporations since the 1990s. Large organizations such as Boeing, Walt Disney, and Yahoo! have developed their in-house universities to assist their organizations in fostering individual and organizational learning and knowledge.[5] McDonald's Corporation has a well-known corporate university, Hamburger University, in Chicago.

For the most part, corporate universities are not universities per se in the strict sense of the term. Not to be confused with accredited universities that may be hosted at an organization's facility, the corporate university does not provide accredited undergraduate and postgraduate degrees. A corporate university limits its scope to providing job and organization-specific training. They are set up for a variety of reasons, yet most organizations will have the same basic needs:

- To support a common culture, loyalty, and belonging to a company
- To organize training as part of the curricula for employees
- To remain competitive in their industry
- To retain employees
- To start and support change in the organization
- To offer training and development to fit the career goals of employees

These types of in-house universities offer value-added training and education to employees, but they also help organizations retain and promote key employees.

E-Learning

Only a few years ago, e-learning was not an option in the workplace. Learning was accomplished by attending a classroom session lasting from a few hours to several days, weeks, or months. Today, employees are able to log on to a computer and participate in training programs at their own pace, on their own schedule.

These e-learning systems provide materials, review, and testing to ensure the employee has accomplished specific learning objectives before moving to the next training step. They also offer an audit trail to report on who has participated in each program. That is handy when you have to be sure everyone has gone through specific training programs. There is no need for an instructor. Each individual works with the materials presented, and perhaps some reference materials, to meet the training objectives.

E-learning is usually asynchronous. This means that training participants access information at different times and maybe even in different places. When there are synchronous components to e-learning, which is when training participants interact together in real time, this is usually a blended e-learning program, which will be reviewed in the next section.

There are also important considerations in the e-learning classroom. Without an instructor to keep tabs on learning progress and questions, the design of content in e-learning becomes extremely important. If developed poorly, it may be difficult to achieve learning objectives. The following are some pointers to keep in mind when designing e-learning training:

- The design of the content should be simple. Having too much information on the screen to attend to can detract attention from the important concepts that need to be learned.

- Trainees need to have familiarity with the software and computer equipment being used for the training.

- Ensure models, simulations, online notepads, tests, and games are created to keep the trainee's attention span and offer the ability to learn using different forms of multimedia.

- Font size, colors, and graphics should be consistent and allow for easy navigation through the program. Too much rapid movement can cause distraction for the trainee.

- Online and telephone support for the trainee should be made available.

- Language barriers, cultural considerations, and accommodations for disabilities need to be considered.

EXAM TIP   E-learning is evolving at a rapid pace and becoming the norm for cost-effective delivery for employers. Expect the exam to have questions related to the pros and cons of e-learning.

Blended

Blended training is an e-learning approach that includes synchronous time with an instructor. This may be in the form of a live webinar or an in-person group session. The benefit of blended delivery is that participants can learn at their own pace, but also receive more support from the instructor and interact with other participants.

Combining individualized learning with social interaction helps provide a more comprehensive understanding of the material, especially for those students who need some scaffolding, or support from the instructor.[6]

On-the-Job Training (OJT)

On-the-job training is specific training provided to existing employees at the actual job site or desk. It utilizes the actual performance of the task or skill of the job function to be accomplished. Some advantages for OJT include a "just-in-time" demonstration of expectations in the real environment where the employee would be expected to perform. It also provides an opportunity for immediate feedback. OJT training can also be done in groups or one-on-one. A major disadvantage to OJT training can be potential safety issues (for example, with the use of machinery), and it can be distracting to other coworkers.

Skills Training

Skills training generally encompasses specific skill sets associated with jobs as identified in job descriptions. Skill development is a constantly moving target because of the nature of changing workplace requirements. With the added complexity of technology and rules/regulations, most jobs will have changing skill-set requirements throughout their existence in the organization. Categories of skills training will normally include the following:

- Sales training
- Technology training
- Equipment training
- Quality training
- Communication skills training
- Emotional intelligence
- Basic on-the-job training

Other skills training may be specifically targeted to supervisory-level positions such as leadership/supervisory skills training, discrimination/harassment prevention training, and diversity and ethics training.

Apprenticeships   Apprenticeships relate to a technical skills type of training for a specific position or function. Unions and employer groups will have apprenticeship programs with a set of standards that include an on-the-job training period, some form of learning curriculum that may include classroom instruction, and specific operating procedures with timelines. The U.S. apprenticeship system is regulated by the Bureau of Apprenticeship and Training (BAT) of the U.S. Department of Labor. Apprentices are not exempt from the FLSA's minimum wage and overtime rules and regulations or their particular states. Federal rules on apprentices can be located at the Code of Federal Regulations (https://www.gpo.gov; search for *29 CFR 520*).

Internships   Internships are programs that are normally designed to give students who are in a course of professional studies an opportunity to gain real-time experience in their chosen professional career prior to earning their degree or certification. By having a learning experience in a real work environment, the student gains valuable exposure to the profession, the industry, and the organization that the internship is at. Organizations benefit by developing low-cost access to potential new graduates and the opportunity to observe the intern's performance and "fit" for potential job openings. They also provide a mode of alternative staffing for the employer.

Job Rotation   Job rotation is the shifting of an employee between different jobs. An example would be an employee working one day in the emergency room (ER) of a hospital and then the next day working in the urgent-care unit of that same hospital. In the case of a manufacturing plant, the employee may work on an assembly line one day and the next day in the quality control inspection station. This not only provides a lot of flexibility for staffing needs for the employer but also enriches employees' skills, which has been proven to increase engagement in their work.[7]

Today, a new form of job rotation has emerged that is related to "gig assignments." Gig workers can be employed for a defined short-term engagement and then rotated to another short-term engagement, such as an employee with several different skill sets that may be assigned to project teams. This is becoming more frequent in technology jobs.

   EXAM TIP   You may not use trending terms such as *gig assignments* and *gig workers* in your organization, but you should know what they mean for the exam.

Cross-Training   Cross-training happens when employees are trained to do more than one job—sometimes several jobs. As an example, a payroll specialist may know how to process accounts payable and accounts receivables. The advantages of cross-training for the organization are flexibility with coverage, such as for vacation relief or job vacancy. Advantages for the employee would be professional development and career growth. It's not uncommon to see employees seeking out cross-training opportunities to prepare them for a potential promotion. Unions have been known to not be in favor of cross-training, as it threatens job jurisdiction and could broaden the job descriptions.

Techniques to Evaluate Training Programs

The final phase of the ADDIE model involves evaluating, which means measuring the effectiveness of the training program. Having training objectives identified before the training is conducted is necessary for measuring the outcome of a training program.

Having a basic understanding of how to evaluate training and HR programs is helpful for early HR career professionals to make meaningful contributions to the processes. The most widely known model is Donald Kirkpatrick's four levels. Kirkpatrick's model focuses primarily on evaluating the effectiveness of the training presented.[8] Figure 4-2 illustrates the four levels.

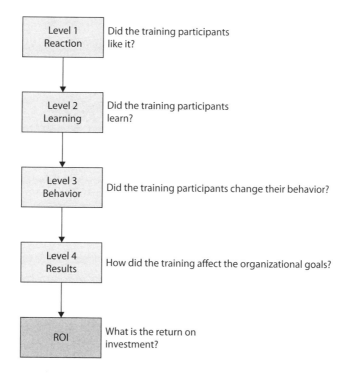

Figure 4-2
Kirkpatrick's four levels of evaluating training

The first level measures the reaction of the participant. A survey given at the conclusion of the training is the most common method. Participants detail how they liked the training and their thoughts as to its applicability. This measures the immediate reaction about the training delivery and its environment rather than their level of learning.

The second level measures how well participants in the training learned facts, concepts, theories, and behaviors. Using this measure normally requires HR professionals or consultants who are trained in statistics to interpret the results. Use of a learning management system can also do the job for you. For example, by comparing results from a test conducted before the training to the same test after the training, you will see what employees learned.

The third level deals with the measurement of behavior and is more difficult to assess than the previous two levels because it can be difficult to determine whether behavior changed solely because of the training program; other outside influences could be involved. In level three measurement, observations, interviews, 360-degree feedback instruments, and simulations can be used.

The fourth level deals with the measurement of results to determine whether the planned effectiveness of the training delivered the desired results. The difficulty with this measurement is determining whether the training was the sole factor affecting the results. This is typically done by examining the organization's return on investment (ROI), or comparing the overall costs of the training to the benefits received.

When you're evaluating the training program's effectiveness, it is important to achieve an objective viewpoint. Choose techniques that will solicit information from all affected sources—not just the training participants and presenter but also the sources affected by the training, which could be other departments, management, and even customers.

Participant Surveys and Questionnaires

One technique to measure the reaction level of the trainees is to administer participant-written surveys or questionnaires immediately after the conclusion of training. Another method would be an oral interview with the trainees. Use caution, though, because the immediate reaction typically measures only how people like the training and the environment that was used rather than their level of learning and application. It is the easiest method to administer and thus is used the most frequently. This is referred to as level one in Kirkpatrick's model.

Pre- and Post-Testing

Level two of Kirkpatrick's model measures how well trainees learned facts, concepts, theories, ideas, and skills or behavior. Pre- and post-testing would fall into level two. A pre-test of what the trainee's knowledge is and then a post-test of what their knowledge level is after the training would establish the measurement. This technique determines how much the trainee's knowledge, or skill level, has changed because of the training.

Measuring Behavior: After-Action Review

An after-action review involves measuring behavior, and behavior is more difficult to measure than reaction and learning because it involves the circumstances of the trainee. It's difficult to determine whether a behavior change is related solely to the attendance at a training program. For example, if a supervisor has improved relationships with subordinates, was it through a management training program the supervisor attended or from a recent 360-degree feedback instrument that pointed out a deficiency in that area?

Changes in behavior can be evaluated using a variety of techniques and apply to level three of Kirkpatrick's model. Combining several techniques may provide a truer evaluation of the behavior change. The techniques are performance tests, critical incidents, 360-degree feedback, observations, and simulations.

Performance Tests

A performance test is administered to training participants and contains actual samples of content that was taught in the training. This type of technique measures behavior changes desired for the work environment. An example of a performance test would be conducting an oral scenario interview after an ethics training course and having the trainee role-play the suggested behavior response.

Critical Incidents

With the critical incidents method, a record of both positive and negative incidents is scored to measure the training's outcomes. Normally this would be completed by the trainee's direct supervisor. An example of this method might be after a salesperson concluded their negotiation tactics training, and during an actual new client meeting, the salesperson's manager is present and noting the behaviors that were effective, and least effective, in the negotiation.

360-Degree Feedback

The 360-degree appraisal is where trainees, their peers, their direct reports, internal (or even external) customers and suppliers, and other relevant people whose perspectives "count" give feedback about effective behaviors and ineffective behaviors. Perceptions may be right or wrong; what matters is that perceptions count! Which perceptions does the trainee need to change? This type of feedback focuses in on what specific behavior the trainee would benefit from changing and, over time, measures how well they changed it. This is a popular technique used in management and supervisory training in organizations and is an administratively intense process that HR is normally intimately involved with.

Observations

Observation can be a helpful method to evaluate changed behavior, that is, if the behavior has been observed both pre- and post-training. The difficulty is in determining whether the other conditions before and after the observation are the same, and whether the observer is biased in any way. Observations can assess complex performance that is difficult to measure or evaluate by the other techniques. External executive coaches are often hired by organizations for senior management and observe their coachee to assess where improvement has occurred (for example, facilitation of meetings) or behavior has changed (for example, body language in meetings).

Simulations

With this training evaluation technique, the training participant performs a simulation of what was learned and applies it in real time on the job. This is an experiential bridge between the training and its actual application in the world of the trainee's work. How well the trainee performs the simulation can be a measurement of the training's effectiveness on the trainee. Simulations that accurately reflect the work conditions and environment can be costly to construct by way of resources and time.

Return on Investment

Another important item to consider in training evaluation is whether the benefits of training are greater than the costs. There is usually a budget for training, and management likes to see a return on their investment (ROI). In combination with the evaluation metrics noted previously that can demonstrate reaction to the program, and learning of actual skills and behaviors, Kirkpatrick's fourth level is concerned with ROI.

To measure ROI, you must first determine the costs of training. This includes the costs of developing training, hiring or training an instructor, and costs related to the actual training environment such as an e-learning platform or conference room fees. You also need to consider the cost of staff time to design, develop, and implement the training program.

Next, the harder part is developing a value for the benefit of training. As an example, imagine you train your customer service team on a new computer-based chat system that will increase the number of customer service inquiries each team member can handle per day. Before the training, you would measure how many inquiries each employee handled per day. The additional number of inquiries per day each employee manages after the new chat system is in place shows the benefit of training. Each member of the customer service team is more efficient at helping customers because of the training. The point is that somehow you need to put a value on the benefit of training.

Tracking and Reporting

For early career HR professionals, tracking and reporting training will likely be a responsibility. There are many training programs where attendance is mandatory for participants, especially for programs geared toward state or federal laws with training requirements. HR is responsible for tracking attendance of participants and ensuring training is completed in a timely fashion. This can often be easily done through a learning management system or HRIS system, which will create training reports for you. Otherwise, good old-fashioned Excel can be a helpful tracking and reporting tool.

Career Development Practices

Although training and development go hand in hand, they are different. Career development is a lifelong individual process that involves planning, managing, learning, and transitions at all ages and stages of work life. In organizations, it is an approach used to match employee goals with the business's current and future needs. An individual's work-related preferences and needs continuously evolve throughout life's phases. At the same time, organizations are also continuously adapting to economic, political, and societal changes.

It is not just the individual employee and HR involved in career development. The direct line of management and the organization's leaders have roles to play, too.

Today, individuals are required to be proactive in planning their career progressions and not rely on an organization to direct their career paths. Organizations typically have the structures in place to support this process, but individual employees should be aware of their needs for increased knowledge, skills, and experience associated with their career ambitions. Figure 4-3 illustrates the stages of an individual's career development.

An employee's direct supervisor normally serves a support role in helping an individual assess their current effectiveness and potential. Supervisors will often wear many hats in this process, including coach, appraiser, and guidance counselor. Because supervisors usually have better visibility into career paths at the organization, they can also refer other resources to the employee, such as HR or mentors from another department.

HR professionals are involved in the development of career pathing, personal development programs, and skill development training in order to help employees achieve their career goals. Creating a skill inventory database is needed to assess the current workforce's talents. Additionally, HR professionals monitor training and development needs and create programs to meet those needs, along with communicating job progression opportunities.

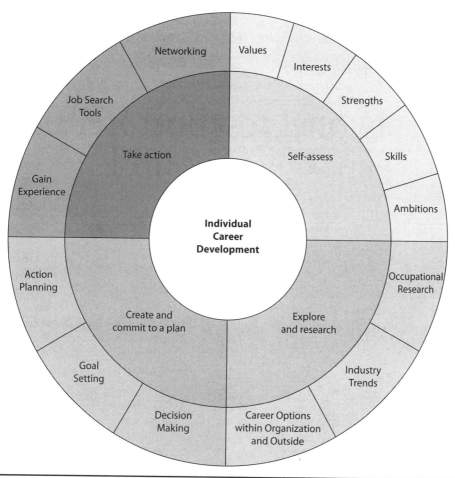

Figure 4-3 Individual career development

The organizational leader's role in career development includes communicating the organization's mission and vision to the workforce. This helps link the organization's goals with the anticipated talent needs. Fostering a culture of support for career development is another important function of the organizational leader's role.

In the role of early-career HR, the HR professional will most likely have responsibilities associated with tracking, monitoring, and providing resources with regard to the organization's career development practices.

Succession Planning

Succession planning identifies, assesses, and develops talent to drive business success. It is an ongoing process that enables an organization to plan for or recover from losing critical employees. An effective succession plan includes a focus on identifying, developing, and preparing the placement of high-potential employees for future opportunities.

Succession planning should be developed to anticipate managerial staffing needs or key employee positions that would interrupt the business process if an incumbent were to vacate.

It is an important process because organizations often make the mistake of assuming that critical employees can be quickly replaced. Even when they provide notice, replacing a key employee takes time. The time to train a new employee must also be considered. So, having internal talent ready to take on a new challenge is extremely valuable.

A succession plan contains an identification of high-risk positions along with those positions with known or potentially known vacancy dates (as with retirements). Competencies for those positions are identified, and a gap analysis is performed using the current workforce to review potential candidates. High-potential internal employees are identified, also considering those who have interest in the future job opening. After all, not every individual may be interested in moving into a position with more responsibility. Tentative plans are created for shortages, which may include seeking outside candidates.

HR is typically responsible for maintaining a candidate database of skills and career development plans, along with the monitoring of development activities. This function is generally one that is handled by early-career HR professionals. Additionally, HR is responsible for the sourcing or creation of training needs for candidates and monitoring their continued interest. Figure 4-4 provides a typical progression of steps in succession planning.

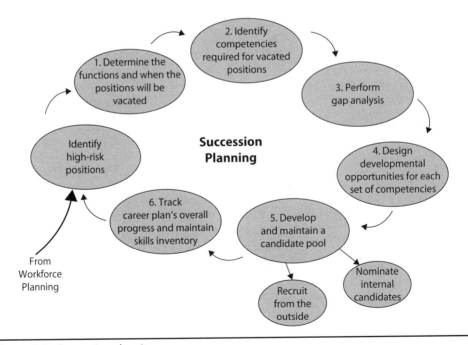

Figure 4-4 Succession planning

Career Pathing

Career pathing is a practice in which an employee charts a course within their organization for their career development. Using HR as an example, an early-career HR employee, who may have started out in the organization as an HR intern during their college studies, may have decided that the area of HR that most interests them and aligns with their talents is compensation. The HR employee will research the responsibilities and requirements for the different positions within the HR compensation function. They may plan to attend an outside course to attain a certification in compensation, or they may observe a union salary negotiation.

Additionally, with career pathing, a formalized employee self-assessment tool may be used to assist employees in understanding their strengths and where to focus their development. Self-assessments will identify where the employee is now in their career, where they intend to grow, and, more importantly, what gaps they need to fill. Creating a plan that gains the employee the exposure, experience, and knowledge to move through their various career goals is career pathing.

 EXAM TIP In career pathing, employees design and drive their chosen career progression with input from others. It varies significantly by individual. Also, it is vastly different from formal company career development programs where selected individuals may be fast tracked in a career progression such as management training.

Dual-Ladder Careers

Dual-ladder career development programs allow mobility for employees without requiring that they be placed into a management position. Mostly associated with technical, medical, engineering, and scientific occupations, this type of program is a way to advance employees who are not interested in pursuing a management track. These individuals usually exhibit one or more of the following characteristics:

- Have technical or professional expertise beyond the basic levels
- Have licensure or required credentials
- Are known for innovation
- May or may not be well suited for management or leadership roles

An objective within a dual-ladder development program is to increase the employee's complexity and value to the organization. This allows you to increase the employee's salary as well as improve satisfaction and retention without a management job title. Lateral movement may occur within a dual-ladder program such as team membership, internal consultative roles, mentorships, or larger facility rotation. Figure 4-5 shows an example of a dual-ladder career path.

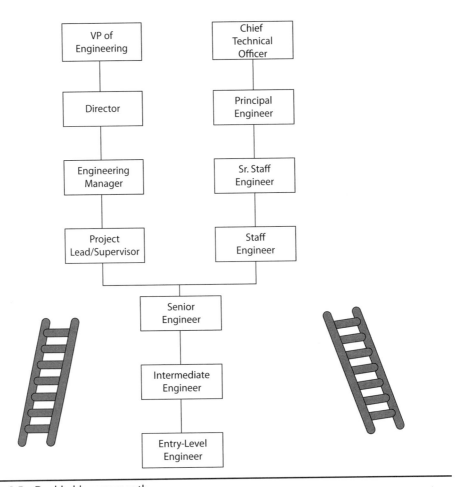

Figure 4-5 Dual-ladder career path

Career Counseling

Whether in a large or small organization, HR will generally receive a knock on the door from employees who are seeking guidance regarding their careers within the organization. With career counseling, there must be a balance between HR support, management engagement, and employee ownership of their chosen area of growth. Individual counseling and coaching involve one-on-one discussions about specific direction and needs between an aspiring employee and experienced individuals within the organization who are normally in the career path the employee is intending to pursue. This can be a supervisor, a mentor, a retiree, or a hired career consultant. HR's role is to help the employee sort out their options and engage the resources available to them.

Change Management

Of all the many competencies required for the HR professional, being a masterful change agent is probably the most important. Change is constant. Sometimes change comes internally from an organization. It may be planned to improve a process or react to a problem that occurred. Change can also arise from external sources like a new employment law that regulates behavior in the workplace.

Regardless of the source, change can be challenging for both employees and managers to accept. Helping both employees and management in an organized process through the rollercoaster ride of change, as identified by Elisabeth Kubler-Ross in her book *On Death and Dying*,[9] is an emotionally intelligent (EQ) competency skill for HR professionals and leaders. First, shock and denial about the change is awakened within people. Anger is the next response. Depression eventually sets in about the "loss" of status quo resulting from the change. Then movement toward bargaining and dialogue occur related to the change. Finally, the rollercoaster ride ends as employees reach a level of acceptance about the change. The key knowledge is in understanding the change and the management of the anticipated reactions.

Early-career HR professionals are usually not responsible for leading change management processes, but they will be assigned various responsibilities to help with deployment. For example, employee communication about the reason for the change and how it will impact internal processes is a common responsibility. Also, employee training is often needed to help employees learn new knowledge or skills as a result of a change.

By way of example, imagine that your organization decided to implement a new scheduling software to help manage employee work schedules in all departments more efficiently. The new software will help with scheduling errors and provides a better database for on-call employees who can fill in when someone calls in sick. This would mean that all of the employees who have been responsible for scheduling by hand in the past will experience changes in their jobs. They will have to understand how to use the new scheduling software and receive communication about how the processes in their day-to-day jobs will change. They will probably also need revisions to their job description. In this scenario, these are all activities that an aPHR candidate can expect to help out with.

Popular Theories

Many theories are available to explain how to manage change. It is helpful to be aware of these theories, as they are commonly used by senior leaders during change management. We have chosen a few of the most popular for discussion here.

Lewin's Change Management Model

Kurt Lewin is sometimes called the founder of social psychology. He was one of the first to study social dynamics and organizational development. In the early part of the 20th century, Lewin concluded that there are three stages of change management[10] that are good for use with deep dives into organizational changes:

- **Unfreeze the organization**   Once recognized that change is needed, it is necessary to break down the existing organization before it is possible to create a new one.

- **Change the organization** Resolving uncertainties and actually implementing the changes needed.
- **Refreeze the organization** A return to stability of the organizational structure, with job assignments that can be maintained for a period into the future.

McKinsey 7-S Model

The McKinsey 7-S model[11] calls for analyzing seven aspects of an organization and determining how they interact with each other. This theory is helpful in planning for change and determining how it will impact various aspects of the organization. These seven aspects are outlined in Table 4-3.

Kotter's Theory

The approach used by Kotter's theory[12] relies on senior executive(s) driving a sense of urgency about the changes. Compared to other theories, this one assumes that the current conditions already demand changes be made and is mainly focused on senior leadership's role. If you are responsible for communicating change, Kotter's theory is a good one to use. Kotter suggests there are eight steps in a successful change management process:

- *Create a sense of urgency.* Explain to your team what is happening in the world that impacts your group or employer organization. Outline why it is so important to react to those threats.
- *Build a guiding coalition.* Convince your key leaders and stakeholders of the need to change.

Aspect of Organization	Definition
Strategy	The organization's goals and plan for creating or maintaining a competitive advantage.
Structure	How departments are organized and how they actually interact with each other in reality.
Systems	The processes and rules used to accomplish work, including unofficial shortcuts.
Shared Values	Linking culture and values to the change process will permit employees to move easily through known territory to the desired change result.
Style	The style of leadership in the organization.
Staff	The employees in the organization, also considering whether all the positions are filled.
Skills	What you know your staffs' skills are and the perception your customers have of what your staffs' skills are.

Table 4-3 McKinsey 7-S Model

- *Form a strategic vision.* Define your vision and the changes that will get you there.

- *Enlist a volunteer army.* Spread your ideas for change to the remainder of your organization.

- *Remove barriers and reduce friction.* If training is needed to help bring skills up to speed, make those arrangements. Clear the path for your people to do what they need to do in contributing to the change.

- *Generate short-term wins.* Spotlight the small successes achieved by employees in their effort to implement the change. Reinforce their efforts and praise their accomplishments.

- *Sustain acceleration.* This is about creating new habits, new work patterns, new skill applications, and new methods.

- *Make the changes institutional.* The culmination of the process is to be sure it is all properly documented and that the organization's culture reflects the new changes. You have a new set of ways "to do things around here."

Chapter Review

This HRCI functional area focuses on the integrated use of training and career development efforts to improve individual, group, and organizational effectiveness. The aPHR professional will have a prominent role to play in helping employees acquire the knowledge, skills, and abilities needed by the organization. These responsibilities will range from creating instructional content and facilitating training, to assisting with change management and training program evaluation. Involvement in career development practices also helps set the stage for creating a culture that supports learning.

Questions

1. Your company has decided to review the exit interviews from the past 2 years for the finance department to determine the reasons why turnover there was higher than in other departments. From the analysis of the interviews, the HR consulting firm found that exiting employees for the most part left for a promotional opportunity in other organizations. It has been suggested that a formal career counseling program be implemented to reverse the perception of lacking promotional opportunities. Which answer *best* describes the kind of program HR will be developing?

   A. Knowledge management program

   B. Succession planning program

   C. Career pathing program

   D. Talent management program

2. At the completion of an eight-module computer-based training course, the trainees are being asked to complete a survey about the training. What evaluation method is this known as?

   A. Learning

   B. Reaction

   C. Results

   D. ROI

3. ADDIE is an instructional design tool. Which of the following is not part of ADDIE?

   A. Delivery

   B. Implementation

   C. Design

   D. Development

4. Rx Pharmaceuticals is a company that employs both technical and scientific professions. What development program could it provide to have the most effective impact on retention for its employees?

   A. An employee work/life balance program

   B. A validated succession planning program

   C. Dual-ladder careers

   D. Differing telecommuting options

5. HR is modifying the supervisory trainee program and has decided that a case study should be added to the program—one that trainees would work on in a group. Which stage of the ADDIE model is HR currently in?

   A. Analysis

   B. Implementation

   C. Decision

   D. Design

6. The customer service manager in your company maintains an online log of her employees' praises or criticism from customers. She uses this information to evaluate employees' customer service skills. This is an example of what type of training evaluation method?

   A. Behavior observation

   B. Forced distribution

   C. Critical incident

   D. Supervisory logging

7. MaryLou has decided that she will give a presentation at her professional association chapter's annual conference, based on the best practices her marketing department uses. She expects to have anywhere from 150 to 300 attendees at her breakout session. Which of the following instructional methods would be best for MaryLou to use?

   A. Group discussion in pairs

   B. Case study

   C. Presentation

   D. Demonstration

8. Pita holds an advanced degree in chemical engineering and works in research and development in the Paris facility of a large global company. Pita is solely responsible for developing a new type of removable adhesive for picture hangers, which she discovered on the job while working on improvements for an existing elastic chalking product her company produces. Who will be the owner of the patent for the new adhesive?

   A. Pita, because she is the researcher and developer of the product

   B. Pita's company, because Pita is an employee and is paid to research and develop products

   C. Pita, because her discovery of the new adhesive had nothing to do with the product she was working on

   D. The French government, due to an agreement with the company having an R&D facility in Paris

9. Your boss asks you to create SMART goals. What does the acronym SMART stand for?

   A. Smart, meaningful, action-oriented, relevant, and timed

   B. Specific, measurable, achievable, relevant, and timed

   C. Smart, measurable, accurate, relevant, and timed

   D. Specific, measurable, accurate, responsible, and timed

10. The training specialist at a chain of retail stores is conducting a training evaluation after the new customer service VIP training that took place last quarter. He is analyzing data from observations, interviews, tests, and surveys to assess whether new skills were successfully transferred to the job by the trainees. The analysis he is completing is an example of what type of evaluation?

   A. Behavior

   B. Results

   C. Learning on the job

   D. Reaction

11. Which of the following is *not* a benefit of job rotation?

    A. Engagement in work for the employee

    B. Flexibility for employer staffing needs

    C. Multi-skilled workforce

    D. Reduced benefit cost

12. Girish is a recruiter, and his company is opening several new retail facilities within the next 6 months in a metropolitan area. He is having difficulty locating interested candidates for their new opening project teams that will work for the first 4 weeks at each facility. Which program should he propose to his HR director to address the staffing need?

    A. Internships

    B. Job rotation

    C. Gig workers

    D. Cross-training

13. Which statement is *not* true about in-house corporate universities?

    A. They offer collegiate-accredited degree programs.

    B. They support a common culture and loyalty.

    C. They offer training and education to employees.

    D. They help organizations promote from within.

14. According to Bloom's knowledge-based taxonomy, which of the following is *not* one of the levels?

    A. Application

    B. Evaluation

    C. Knowledge

    D. Comparison

15. Jose is responsible for assisting with a change management initiative in his department. Senior leaders are all in agreement that the change needs to happen and are ready to take action to support it. Jose has been told to create a plan that is focused on senior leadership involvement in the change. Which theory of change is most applicable in this situation?

    A. Kotter's theory

    B. Lewin's Change Management model

    C. McMahon's 5-S theory

    D. McKinsey 7-S model

16. Donald, a new hire, is starting at your branch next week. Which of the following is the best idea to help Donald develop relationships with his coworkers during orientation?

    A. E-mail his picture to all employees before he starts.

    B. Set up a group lunch with Donald's team during his first week.

    C. Invite Donald to an industry trade show.

    D. Create a detailed orientation plan for Donald.

17. Which learning principle is focused on breaking up content into small pieces and limiting how much is provided to participants at one time?

    A. Combining

    B. Categorizing

    C. Chunking

    D. Coupling

18. Idina is creating an e-learning program to train all employees on a new federal law they must follow. The material is complex, but an instructor is not needed. The team thinks a self-paced program will work just fine. Of the following options, what is the most important factor for Idina to consider when developing the content?

    A. Carefully selecting font size, graphics, and multimedia so they support learning objectives

    B. Adding animations to the training to make it more exciting to watch

    C. Hiring someone with a soothing voice to record the training

    D. Using videos that include actual employees in the training to help with employer branding

19. You created a training program and received a complaint from an employee who is hearing impaired. It is difficult for the employee to hear what the instructor is saying. What should you do?

    A. Immediately add captions to all your training videos.

    B. Begin the interactive process under the ADA with the employee.

    C. Survey employees who have completed the training so far to see if any other accessibility considerations need to be addressed for disability or cultural reasons.

    D. Evaluate the trainer and coach him on his public speaking ability.

20. ABC Trucking wants to add driver-tracking software to its trucks to help the dispatch team assign deliveries and better resolve customer complaints. Which of the following is *least* relevant to this change management initiative?

   A. Determine how the drivers feel about this change.

   B. Determine if the drivers' union is okay with this change.

   C. Determine whether dispatch has enough work to do after the software is implemented.

   D. Determine the best way to communicate the change to drivers.

Answers

1. C. Career pathing is a practice in which an employee charts a course within their organization for their career path and career development. By creating a program in which employees can perceive other possibilities for their career, it broadens their career progression opportunities and is a helpful practice for retention of talent.

2. B. The easiest method to administer and the most frequently used, the reaction evaluation method is level one of Kirkpatrick's model. It measures how participants in the training felt about the training program immediately following the conclusion of the training.

3. A. ADDIE is an instructional design model that follows the phases of assessment, design, development, implementation, and evaluation.

4. C. Dual-ladder careers provide opportunities for a parallel occupational track that recognizes and rewards different skill sets. This allows organizations to retain their technical and professional employees at a similar rate as their managerial-track employees.

5. D. During the design phase, the course developer is involved in activities related to determining which tasks participants need training on, and in this case, they have determined a case study would be the delivery method.

6. C. This example best describes the critical incident method. The critical incident method refers to when a rater logs over a period of time both desired and effective behaviors with their results and ineffective behavior incidents.

7. C. The presentation style will allow MaryLou to present her best practices to a large group of attendees at the same time, with minimal disruption.

8. B. Pita's employer pays her for this R&D work as a part of her normal job duties, and as long as this discovery occurred while Pita was on the job, the patent and discovery belong to the employer. HR needs to ensure this information is imparted to all employees, new and existing, in functions like R&D.

9. B. Goal setting using the SMART format requires that goals be specific, measurable, achievable, relevant, and timed.

10. A. Having observations, conducting interviews, giving tests, and conducting surveys describe the behavior evaluation method.

11. D. Job rotation is the shifting of an employee between different jobs and does not usually correlate with reduced benefit costs.

12. C. Gig workers are independent workers employed by an organization for short-term engagements; they have the skills and/or knowledge for a particular function.

13. A. In-house corporate "universities" are not credentialed universities that provide academic-accredited degrees.

14. D. Comparison is not a level within Bloom's knowledge-based taxonomy. The six levels are knowledge, comprehension, application, analysis, synthesis, and evaluation.

15. A. Kotter's theory is focused on senior executive support and assumes there is agreement among senior leaders about the change. To our knowledge, McMahon's 5-S theory does not exist.

16. B. A group lunch can be a great way to help develop relationships with other coworkers in a relaxed environment. Although the other ideas are helpful, they are not the best option to focus on building relationships.

17. C. Chunking is the learning principle that breaks content up into small pieces. Research has shown that we can hold five to nine pieces of information in our short-term memory at one time.

18. A. Although all of the answer options offer value in some way, carefully selecting font size, graphics ,and multimedia to support learning objectives is the best answer. It supports several different aspects of instructional design so everything is cohesive and clear without the support of an instructor.

19. C. This is a formative evaluation of the training. It seems adding captions to videos will be necessary, but there may also be other disability-related or cultural considerations you need to adapt training to.

20. C. Although the dispatch team's workload may be impacted by the new software, the dispatch team will be busy working out the kinks of the new system, so this is a consideration to file away for later. The other answer options address immediate needs in the change management process.

Endnotes

1. Jim Harter and Amy Adkins, "Employees Want a Lot More from Their Managers," accessed on October 4, 2021, https://www.gallup.com/workplace/236570/employees-lot-managers.aspx

2. B.S. Bloom, M.D. Engelhart, E.J. Furst, W.H. Hill, and D.R. Krathwohl, "Taxonomy of educational objectives: The classification of educational goals," in *Handbook I: Cognitive Domain* (David McKay Company, 1956).

3. R.K. Sawyer, *The Cambridge Handbook of the Learning Sciences, Second Edition* (Cambridge University Press, 2014).

4. G.A. Miller, "The magical number seven, plus or minus two: Some limits on our capacity for processing information," *Psychological Review*, 63, 81–97 (1956).

5. Annick Renaud-Coulon, *Corporate Universities: A Lever of Corporate Responsibility* (Global CCU Publisher, 2008).

6. L.S. Vygotsky, *Mind in Society: The Development of Higher Psychological Processes* (Harvard University Press, 1978).

7. Chuck Leddy, "The Benefits and Challenges of Job Rotation," accessed on October 5, 2021, https://www.forbes.com/sites/adp/2017/12/05/the-benefits-and-challenges-of-job-rotation/?sh=2a60f91f6ff5

8. *Chief Learning Officer*, "Don Kirkpatrick: The Father of the Four Levels," accessed on October 5, 2021, https://www.chieflearningofficer.com/2009/10/23/don-kirkpatrick-the-father-of-the-four-levels/

9. Elisabeth Kübler-Ross, *On Death and Dying: What the Dying Have to Teach Doctors, Nurses, Clergy and Their Own Families* (Scribner, 2014).

10. *MindTools*, "Lewin's Change Management Model," accessed on October 5, 2021, https://www.mindtools.com/pages/article/newPPM_94.htm

11. *MindTools*, "McKinsey 7-S Framework," accessed on October 5, 2021, https://www.mindtools.com/pages/article/newSTR_91.htm

12. John Kotter, "The 8-Step Process for Leading Change," accessed on October 5, 2021, https://www.kotterinc.com/8-steps-process-for-leading-change/

Compensation and Benefits

The functional area Compensation and Benefits weighs in at 17 percent of the Associate Professional in Human Resources (aPHR) exam.

Compensation and benefits, collectively identified as *total rewards,* are functions that are valuable to business owners and managers and are significantly important to employees. An organization's total rewards program can make a big impact on successfully hiring, retaining, and motivating employees. As a human resource (HR) practitioner, you should expect to be involved in a wide range of compensation and benefits activities that require knowledge ranging from legal compliance to implementing creative total rewards strategies that best fit your workplace. Regardless of your role in this functional area, this chapter will provide an overview of basic compensation and benefits requirements you will need to know to be successful in your job.

The Body of Knowledge (BoK) statements outlined by HR Certification Institute (HRCI) for the Compensation and Benefits functional area by those performing early-career HR roles are as follows:

Knowledge of

- **01** The elements involved in developing and administering an organization's compensation strategy, such as pay structures, pay adjustments and incentive programs; for example, external service providers, market analysis, job evaluation/classifications, merit increases, pay scales/grades, cost of living adjustments, and service awards

- **02** Health benefit and insurance programs, including eligibility requirements, enrollment periods, and various designs; for example, high-deductible plans, health savings accounts, flexible spending accounts, preferred provider organizations, and short or long-term disability

- **03** Supplemental wellness and fringe benefit programs commonly offered by organizations; for example, employee assistance programs (EAPs), gym membership, online therapy, housing or relocation assistance, and travel/transportation stipends

- **04** Employee eligibility for and enrollment in retirement plans as well as rules regarding contributions and withdrawals; for example, 401(k), 457(b), catch-up contributions, and hardship withdrawals

- **05** Components of wage statements and payroll processing; for example, taxation, deductions, differentials, garnishments, leave reporting and final pay, and total reward statements

Laws and Regulations

Many federal laws impact the compensation and benefits function. Just by seeing the number of federal laws that have been passed in this area, you can get a sense of the importance of legal compliance. This section will highlight all 32 of those laws in Table 5-1 as well as place a focus on the ones you'll probably encounter most in your day-to-day responsibilities. Many of these laws will be on your aPHR exam, and you can find additional information on them in Chapter 2.

Federal Laws That Apply to Compensation and Benefits	
The Consumer Credit Protection Act	The Service Contract Act
The Copeland "Anti-Kickback" Act	The Small Business Job Protection Act
The Davis-Bacon Act	The Social Security Act
The Dodd-Frank Wall Street Reform and Consumer Protection Act	The Tax Reform Act
The Economic Growth and Tax Relief Reconciliation Act (EGTRRA)	The Taxpayer Relief Act
The Employee Retirement Income Security Act (ERISA)	The Unemployment Compensation Amendments (UCA)
The Equal Pay Act (amendment to FLSA)	The Uniformed Services Employment and Reemployment Rights Act (USERRA)
The Fair Labor Standards Act (FLSA)	The Walsh-Healey Act (Public Contracts Act)
The Health Information Technology for Economic and Clinical Health (HITECH) Act	The Work Opportunity Tax Credit (WOTC)
The Health Insurance Portability and Accountability Act (HIPAA)	The Genetic Information Nondiscrimination Act (GINA)
The IRS Intermediate Sanctions	The Lilly Ledbetter Fair Pay Act
The Omnibus Budget Reconciliation Act (OBRA)	The Consolidated Omnibus Budget Reconciliation Act (COBRA)
The Pension Protection Act (PPA)	The Family and Medical Leave Act (FMLA)
The Portal-to-Portal Act (amendment to FLSA)	The Mental Health Parity Act (MHPA)
The Retirement Equity Act (REA)	The Mental Health Parity and Addiction Equity Act (MHPAEA)
The Revenue Act	The Patient Protection and Affordable Care Act (PPACA)

Table 5-1 Federal Laws That Apply to Compensation and Benefits

There are eight laws in Table 5-1 that play an important role in many day-to-day compensation and benefits responsibilities. The remainder of this section provides a short recap of these laws. Further detail on them can be found in Chapter 2.

The Employee Retirement Income Security Act (ERISA)

ERISA applies to retirement plans. It does not require employers to establish retirement plans, but it outlines how they should be managed once they have been established. The IRS also oversees annual retirement plan reporting requirements under this law.

Fair Labor Standards Act (FLSA) (1938), as Amended

The FLSA establishes minimum wage, overtime pay, recordkeeping, and youth employment standards. Here are a few of the most common provisions that impact an HR professionals' responsibilities:

- **FLSA minimum wage**   The federal minimum wage is $7.25 per hour as of this writing. Many states also have minimum wage laws, and it is important to stay current on these laws. In cases where an employee is subject to both state and federal minimum wage laws, the employee is entitled to the higher minimum wage.

- **FLSA overtime**   Covered nonexempt employees must receive overtime pay for hours worked over 40 per workweek (any fixed and regularly recurring period of 168 hours, which is seven consecutive 24-hour periods) at a rate not less than one-and-a-half times the regular rate of pay. There is no limit on the number of hours employees 16 years or older may work in any workweek. The FLSA does not require overtime pay for work on weekends, holidays, or regular days of rest, unless overtime is worked on such days. Many state laws also impact overtime regulations. Although state laws will not be covered on the exam, be sure to refer to your state's laws in this area as well.

- **Hours worked**   Hours worked ordinarily include all the time during which an employee is required to be on the employer's premises, on duty, or at a prescribed workplace.

- **Recordkeeping**   Employers must display an official poster outlining the requirements of the FLSA. Employers must also keep employee time and pay records.

- **Child labor**   FLSA provisions are designed to protect the educational opportunities of minors and prohibit their employment in jobs or conditions detrimental to their health or well-being.

Health Insurance Portability and Accountability Act (HIPAA)

This law provides privacy requirements related to medical records for individuals as young as 12 years old. It ensures that individuals who leave or lose their jobs can obtain health coverage even if they or someone in their family has a preexisting health condition. It also restricts the ability of employers to impose actively-at-work requirements as preconditions for health plan eligibility, as well as a number of other benefits.

Social Security Act

This law supports many programs through payroll taxes that come from employer and employee contributions. These programs include retirement benefits, survivor benefits, disability insurance, and several different types of health insurance programs—one of these programs being Medicare for older or disabled individuals.

The Uniformed Services Employment and Reemployment Rights Act (USERRA)

USERRA covers employees serving in the U.S. military. It requires that employers continue paying for the employee's benefits to the extent they paid for those benefits before the call to duty. It also requires that employers continue giving credit for length of service as though the military service was equivalent to company service. This law requires HR professionals to administer leaves of absence for military service, ensuring that all the requirements of the law are followed.

Consolidated Omnibus Budget Reconciliation Act (COBRA)

Applying to employers with 20 or more employees, COBRA provides continuing coverage of group health benefits to employees and their families upon the occurrence of certain qualifying events where such coverage would otherwise be terminated. Many employers partner with a COBRA vendor who administers COBRA benefits for former employees and manages the required communication notices under the law.

Family and Medical Leave Act (FMLA)

Applying to employers with 50 or more employees, the FMLA sets in place leave benefits for eligible employees with personal medical, family, or military-caregiver-related emergencies. FMLA provides for leaves lasting up to 12 weeks in a 12-month period, and it is unpaid unless the employer has a policy to pay for the leave time. If the need for leave can be reasonably anticipated, employees must give their employers 30 days' notice. During the leave, it is an obligation of the employer to continue paying any benefit plan premiums that the employer would have paid if the employee had remained on the job. If there is a portion of the premium for health insurance that is normally paid by the employee, that obligation for copayments continues during the employee's leave time. The 12 weeks of leave may be taken in increments of 1 day or less.

Patient Protection and Affordable Care Act (PPACA)

Applying to employers with 50 or more employees, this law is also known as the "Affordable Care Act" or "Obamacare." It created health insurance trading centers in each state where employees and those who are unemployed can shop for health insurance coverage. In 2017, changes in the Affordable Care Act included elimination of the financial penalties for individuals who did not sign up for health insurance. Consequently, the number of people who are underinsured has increased, and this legislation continues to be a hot topic in Washington, D.C.

Total Rewards

People seek and stay at jobs that reward them financially and enrich their lives. Developing and maintaining total rewards programs that attract and retain employees is an important HR function.

A total rewards program includes compensation that is both direct and indirect. Direct compensation (for example, "cash") applies to a variety of pay programs that are, in one way or another, cash-based, whereas indirect compensation (for example, "benefits") applies to programs primarily designed to provide recognition and benefits and, therefore, are indirectly cash-based. Common examples of these two types of compensation are listed in Table 5-2.

Some of the direct compensation programs are discretionary, meaning that employers have some flexibility in how they structure them. Examples include cash awards, differential pay, and bonuses. Other direct compensation programs like base pay are mandatory and governed by federal, state, and in some cases, local laws and regulations.

Some of the indirect compensation programs are also discretionary. They include paid vacation, paid time off, 401(k) and retirement plans. Finally, some benefits are mandatory and governed by laws and regulations. Social Security, workers' compensation, and unemployment insurance are examples. Paid sick leave benefits are also mandatory in some states. Even discretionary programs are subject to regulation when they are employed.

 EXAM TIP   The single difference between direct and indirect compensation is that direct compensation results in some form of a cash reward while indirect compensation results in some form of a desired benefit for the employee.

While Table 5-2 lists many common total rewards programs, this is an area of constant innovation in the human resources field. Attracting, retaining, and motivating employees is equally as important as it is challenging. As such, it continues to be an area where new and innovative programs are top of mind for employers. From workplace gyms, childcare facilities, tuition assistance, recreation rooms, to countless different types of recognition programs, there are many ways to add value to an employee's total rewards package.

Direct Compensation (Cash)	Indirect Compensation (Benefits)
Base pay (wages and salary)	Social Security
Commissions	Unemployment insurance
Bonuses	Disability insurance
Merit pay	Profit sharing
Piece rate	401(k) and other similar programs
Differential pay	Healthcare
Cash awards	Vacation and sick leave

Table 5-2   Direct and Indirect Compensation

As a result, there are many different kinds of external service providers that focus on total rewards programs. Some assist with job evaluation or help create compensation plans. Others focus on recognition and rewards programs. You'll also find many benefits services that help with COBRA or leave of absence compliance based on federal law. This leaves HR professionals in the benefits and compensation arena with options on how to best support the organization's total rewards program.

Secrecy or Transparency?

The debate over the question of how open an organization should be about its total rewards program is an age-old one that has challenged most HR professionals at some point in their career. These are some points to consider when thinking about this topic:

- The essential elements of individual employee pay and benefits should be considered and treated as confidential. Employees should expect that the organization will maintain appropriate controls and limit access to sensitive employee data and information.

- Notwithstanding the previous bullet point, some leakage of information is difficult to avoid because of the inevitable sharing of information, whether that be from the employees themselves or a business unit leader (or occasionally even an HR staff member).

- A primary objective of any total rewards program should be to attract, motivate, and retain a workforce that can advance the organization's mission and business objectives. Keeping the key components and drivers of that program a secret from employees will seriously limit an organization's ability to achieve this objective.

- Communication is the foundation of transparency. Communicate early, often, and in multiple media formats. If a leakage of information does occur, it is important to manage the message. In the absence of any official communications, employees are apt to fill the void with rumors, pay related or otherwise.

That said, federal contractors are prohibited from banning discussions about compensation among their employees. Executive Order 13665 (signed by President Obama on April 8, 2014) amended Executive Order 11246. It says, "The contractor will not discharge or in any other manner discriminate against any employee or applicant for employment because such employee or applicant has inquired about, discussed, or disclosed the compensation of the employee or applicant or another employee or applicant...."[1] Be sure to check your state laws because some state laws also speak to this issue.

Job Evaluation

Job evaluation is a process for assessing the "worth" of jobs within an organization. Conducting a job evaluation is an essential first step in creating a fair wage structure. An analysis of each position's tasks, responsibilities, knowledge, and skill requirements is used to assess the value of the job to the employer and provide an internal ranking of the jobs.

Market compensation surveys are frequently used in this process. They are a tool that enables organizations to understand and recognize fair compensation for positions. Paying people fairly is good for business. If you underpay, employees will eventually look for a better offer. If you overpay, the payroll budget and profitability will suffer. That's why companies use market data to research the value of their jobs.

To determine the prevailing rate for a job, a company can "benchmark" jobs against compensation surveys that are detailed and specific to the company's industries and regions. A good compensation survey uses standard, proven methods of data gathering and statistical analysis to determine how much companies pay for a specific job in a specific industry. A number of organizations conduct salary surveys, including compensation consulting firms, industry associations, educational institutions, and state and federal governments.

Job Evaluation Methods

Job evaluation methods can be quantitative or nonquantitative. Quantitative methods use actual numbers. Nonquantitative methods often are referred to as *whole-job* methods because they rank jobs as a whole based on their perceived worth without placing a numerical value on each job. An example of a nonquantitative method would be to rank a clerical job below a supervisory job on the basis of the job's relative, nonquantitative worth.

 EXAM TIP   Job ranking and job classification are considered nonquantitative whole-job systems because they do not produce a specific numerical score; rather, they measure the worth of the "whole job" compared to other jobs.

Quantitative job evaluation methods include *point-factor* and *factor comparison* methods. Quantitative methods evaluate factors on a defined, measurable scale and provide a score as a result that is a measurable comparison of one job to another. See Table 5-3 for a summary of common job evaluation methods.

Job-Ranking Method

The job-ranking method is often called a *whole-job* comparison because it is a comparison of the whole job compared to another whole job rather than a comparison based on each job's measurable factors. Job ranking is quick and easy but not very precise. It is easy to explain, which is why it is popular, but it leaves unanswered why one job is worth more than another, as well as how much of a "gap" exists between jobs.

When there are a large number of jobs to evaluate, a paired-comparison method of ranking can be used. This method enables each job to be compared with every other job.

Type of Comparison	Nonquantitative Methods	Quantitative Methods
Job-to-job comparison	Job ranking	Factor comparison
Job-to-predetermined-standard comparison	Job classification	Point-factor

Table 5-3   Job Evaluation Methods

Jobs are methodically compared to the next job and, depending on the perceived worth, moved up or below the next job. Ultimately, the job with the highest number of upward movements is the highest ranked. Other jobs are ranked accordingly.

In a job-ranking method, jobs are arranged in order of their value or merit to the organization. Accordingly, the jobs at the top of the list provide more value to the organization, and the relative importance keeps decreasing as you move down the list.

The worth of a job is usually based on judgments of the following:

- Skill
- Effort (physical and mental)
- Responsibility
- Working conditions

Because of its simplistic nature, this method works well for small organizations but is not very effective for big organizations where the jobs are large in number, and thus this becomes a complex process.

Job Classification Method

Jobs can be compared to an outside scale. This also can be done on a whole-job basis called a *job classification* method. Job classification is the result of grouping jobs into a predetermined number of grades or classifications. Each classification has a class description. The federal government has a classification system known as the General Schedule (GS). The GS is the predominant pay scale for federal employees, especially employees in professional, technical, administrative, and clerical positions. The system consists of 15 grades, from GS-1, the lowest level, to GS-15, the highest level.[2] There are also ten steps within each grade. The grade level assigned to a position determines the pay level for that job.

Classes can be further identified by using benchmark jobs that fall into each class. Benchmark jobs have the following characteristics:

- The essential functions and knowledge, skills, and abilities (KSAs) are established and stable.
- They represent the entire range of jobs in each class.
- A significant percentage of workers are employed in these jobs.
- External market rates for these jobs are an acceptable basis for setting wages.

In the job classification method, a job may be compared to a similar job or to other jobs in the General Schedule to determine its relative ranking. This is considered a non-quantitative method called a *job-to-predetermined-standard comparison*. Job classification comparisons are a good method when evaluating a large number of jobs but may not be effective when jobs overlap, as they look only at whole jobs.

Job classification is most frequently performed in large companies, civil service and government employment, nonprofit agencies, and colleges and universities. The results of a job classification analysis are designed to create uniformity in job titles, consistent job levels within the organization hierarchy, and salary ranges that are determined by identified factors. These factors include market pay rates for people doing similar work in similar industries in the same region of the country; pay ranges of comparable jobs within the organization; and the level of knowledge, skill, experience, and education needed to perform each job.

Point-Factor Method

The most commonly used quantitative job evaluation method is the *point-factor method*, which uses specific compensable factors as its reference points to measure relative job worth. Compensable factors are significant job characteristics that contribute to the value of the work and the organization as a whole. The following are two well-known systems used to identify compensable factors:

- **The Hay plan**   Uses a standard criteria comprising three compensable factors: know-how, problem-solving, and accountability.

- **The factor evaluation system (FES)**   Determines levels of duties and responsibilities using a point rating system to evaluate selected positions. FES uses weighted factors to address the position's major characteristics of responsibility, education, experience, job conditions, physical requirements, supervision, training, and so on.

These are the five steps in the point-factor method of job evaluation:

1. *Identify key jobs.* These are benchmark jobs, not necessarily the most important jobs in the organization, but jobs that are equitably paid, stable, and well defined.

2. *Identify the compensable factors.* These are the factors that will be used to distinguish one job from another. Six to eight factors are generally sufficient. Experience, responsibility, knowledge, degree of difficulty, and education are most often used. Other factors that can be considered, depending on their general applicability, include physical demands, mental requirements, skill, working conditions, and supervisory responsibilities.

3. *Weigh the factors according to their overall worth.* Usually, the most heavily weighted factors are knowledge, responsibility, experience, education, degree of difficulty, and supervisory responsibilities.

4. *Divide each job factor into degrees that range from high to low.* Assign points to each degree. The number of points assigned to each degree should correspond with the weighting of the factors. As an example, if the factor for skill is weighted 40 percent, the factor of working conditions is weighted 10 percent, and both factors have 5 degrees, then degree 2 for skill should have 4 times as many points as degree 2 for working conditions.

5. The final result will be a table (see Table 5-4) that gives a complete range of points from 50 (the least number) to 200 (the most). Based on the assigned point values, the job in this example is 126 on a scale of 50 to 200 points. Points usually determine the pay grade to which the job will be assigned.

Point-Factor Job Evaluation Method						
Compensable Factor	**Weighted Percentage**	**Degrees/Points**				
		1	2	3	4	5
Skill	(40%)	20	32	48	72	100
Responsibility	(30%)	15	24	36	54	75
Effort	(20%)	10	16	24	36	50
Working Conditions	(10%)	5	8	12	18	25
Example: Machine Operator	**Compensable Factor**	**Degree**		**Points**		
	Skill	3		48		
	Responsibility	2		24		
	Effort	4		36		
	Working Conditions	4		18		
	Total points			*126*		

Table 5-4 Point-Factor Job Evaluation Method

Factor Comparison Method

The factor comparison method is more complex than ranking, classification, or the point-factor methods and is only occasionally used. It involves ranking each job by each compensable factor and then, as an additional step, identifying dollar values for each level of each factor to develop an actual pay rate for the evaluated job.

The factor comparison method is most often used in union negotiations as part of a labor contract and in limited cases where wages are steady over a period of time and the organization uses a flat rate for each job.

Factor comparison breaks down a job into a small number of key factors, such as skills, effort, knowledge, and responsibilities. The next stage is to identify benchmark jobs, which are well-known positions that are consistent across different companies and organizations. Each job is then assigned a salary, which is further broken down for each factor.

Advantages of factor comparison include its broad application; it can be applied to a wide range of job roles and industries and can also be applied to new roles in order to compare them to similar positions. Distilling the value of the job in monetary terms can also help organizations make sure their recruitment methods provide a decent return on investment (ROI). One of the main disadvantages is that someone has to make a decision on the relative worth of each factor. For example, someone may believe knowledge is worth more than skills and give this factor "too much" salary.

Hay Group Guide Chart/Profile Method

Hay job evaluation is a proprietary point-factor job evaluation methodology developed by the Hay Group[3] and used by organizations to map out their job roles in the context of the organizational structure. The general purpose for using this job evaluation method is to enable organizations to map and align their jobs. Typically, Hay evaluations are carried out in a series of steps within any organization that chooses to use the method. These steps are as follows:

1. Train representatives from major departments and HR functions in the use of the method.

2. Revise all job descriptions across the organization with HR assistance.

3. Create job evaluation boards, which include a mix of line management, HR, and experts deciding on the plotting of jobs.

4. HR works with senior management to put together a banding proposal expressed in Hay points by grading staff and describing the benefits that will be attracted by each band.

5. Once the jobs are all rated and mapping is completed, the company board of directors (or equivalent) reviews the summary, the banding proposals, and cost (if any) with the company and recommends for the activities to go live. If the changes are approved, the project manager then moves to implement them.

Pricing and Pay Rates

Compensation surveys are essential tools for establishing the pay level of positions and staying competitive in the marketplace. In the "golden gilded age" of compensation management (1990s to early 2000s), HR was delighted with the increased availability and access to market data, thanks to technology. Compensation information enabled companies to balance their internal pay structures with what the local market was providing for high-demand talent. The data was imperfect, but it was credible when HR would show data to support their conclusions for talent bleeding (the loss of key and high-potential employees). More available market data also reduced the need to work with high-cost compensation consulting firms to gather information.

In more recent decades, the focus of compensation surveys has shifted to calibrating pay levels primarily with the external market, and that in turn has created enormous pressure to obtain and ensure the data is accurate, timely, and "apple-to-apple" in terms of usefulness. Today there are thousands of published surveys that an HR professional can obtain for various job families, industries, geographical areas, and just about everything else you can sort data on. So, there is a wealth of information at your fingertips. However, you still need to be aware that just because you read something on the Internet doesn't mean it's true.

Here comes the bad news: only a fraction of companies participate in surveys. There are millions of organizations, large and small, in the United States, yet a very low percentage participate in compensation surveys. A survey that has 2,500 participants might sound great, yet 2,500 participants represent less than 1 percent of all companies that have more than 500 employees. What is most disturbing is that more companies use compensation survey data than contribute to the surveys as participants. Additionally, those companies participating are normally participating in multiple surveys, causing data to be two-dimensional.

 NOTE When comparing jobs to market compensation data, it is important to compare duties, scope, and reporting relationships and not just job titles because they are often misleading.

Pay Grades and Ranges

After an organization has determined its relative internal job values (that is, through a job evaluation) and collected appropriate market survey data through pay surveys, work begins on developing the organization's pay structure, including creating pay grades and establishing pay ranges.

Pay grades, or job groups, are the way an organization organizes jobs of similar values. The valuation is a result of the job evaluation process. Jobs of the same or similar value, even though dissimilar in function, are paid within the same pay grade.

No fixed rules apply to creating pay grades; rather, the number of pay grades and their structures are more a reflection of organizational structure and philosophy. Issues that should be considered include the following:

- The size and structure of the organization
- The "distance" between the lowest and highest jobs in the organization
- The organization's pay increase and promotion policy
- The grouping of nonexempt and exempt jobs as well as job families (that is, clerical, technical, professional, supervisory, and management jobs)
- Creating enough grades to distinguish job difficulty levels but not so many that the difference between neighboring grades is too small

Well-structured pay grades enable management to develop a well-coordinated pay system rather than having to create a separate pay range for each job. Pay ranges establish the upper and lower boundaries of each pay grade. Market data for a benchmark job (ideally, a "key" job that will link to market value) in each pay range helps to determine the range midpoint. The range spread reflects the equal dispersion of pay on either side of the midpoint to the lower and upper range boundary. Quartiles and percentiles show the spread of data throughout a range. These are commonly recognized reference points an organization uses to measure its position against the market as well as for internal compensation management purposes.

The range spread is the dispersion of pay from the lowest boundary to the highest boundary of a pay range. Range spread is calculated by subtracting the range minimum from the range maximum and dividing that figure by the range minimum:

$$\frac{\text{Maximum} - \text{Minimum}}{\text{Minimum}}$$

Range spread is expressed as a percentage For example, the range spread for a pay range with a $30,000 minimum and a $45,000 maximum would be as follows:

$$\frac{\$45,000 - \$30,000}{\$30,000} = 50\%$$

Typical range spreads in organizations are as follows:

- Nonexempt jobs: 40%
- Exempt jobs: 50%
- Executive jobs: 60%

Generally, lower-level jobs have a narrow range between minimum and maximum pay ranges. Jobs at a lower level tend to be more skill based, which provides for more movement opportunity than higher levels where jobs are more knowledge based and progression is slower.

Ranges should overlap so that progression is steady within a pay grade. As a worker's pay increases with movement to a higher-range quartile, the opportunity for career progression is possible in a measured way.

There also should be a large enough distance between range midpoints so that pay compression between a lower pay grade and a high pay grade does not occur.

Broadbanding is a recent concept that combines several pay grades or job classifications that have narrow range spreads with a single band that has a wider spread. Organizations usually adopt broadbanding as a way to simplify their pay levels and reduce management oversight requirements. As a result, broadbanding typically is more popular in large organizations than in smaller ones.

While broadbanding has some advantages, it also has some disadvantages. In some cases, broadbanding does not work well with the organization's compensation philosophy. This is particularly true in organizations that focus on promotional opportunities. The reduction of pay grades as a result of broadbanding correspondingly reduces the number of opportunities for promotion.

Broadbanding can also be used against an organization in equal pay analysis. If it is assumed that all jobs are equal within a broadband, the government has claimed that all jobs should be paid the same. If the jobs are not paid the same, differences can be computed and analyzed for statistical significance. Excesses can be claimed to represent illegal pay discrimination. For example, an HR manager, an accounting manager, and a facilities manager are all in the same broadband. They are not all paid the same, however. Differences can be hard to defend against discrimination charges. Broadbanding should be used with care, particularly in an organization that is a federal contractor.

Compa-ratios are indicators of how wages match, lead, or lag the midpoint and are normally an indicator of market value. Compa-ratios are computed by dividing the worker's pay rate by the midpoint of the pay range.

The compa-ratio formula is as follows:

$$\text{Compa-ratio} = \frac{\text{Pay rate}}{\text{Midpoint}}$$

Compa-ratios less than 100 percent (usually expressed as a "compa-ratio less than 1.00") mean the worker is paid less than the midpoint of the range. Compa-ratios greater than 100 percent (1.00) mean that wages exceed the midpoint.

EXAM TIP Compa-ratios can be used for budgetary controls as well as to investigate discrimination in that a difference between one group and another can indicate the possibility of discrimination.

Variations in Pay: Red and Green Circle Rates

Pay ranges must be periodically evaluated and adjusted to reflect organizational and market changes. Red circle rates, green circle rates, and cost-of-living adjustments are some of the techniques used to adjust to these changes.

Red Circle Rates

Organizations use red circle rates as a method to increase an employee's pay to a new rate higher than the maximum for the assigned pay range. This situation occurs more often in smaller organizations where promotional opportunities may be limited. When this happens, an employee's next pay raise indicated by the organization's merit guidelines might place the new pay level above the maximum for the applicable pay range.

An example of this is the accounting manager who is paid $95,000 per year. The top of the range for the accounting manager position is $100,000. Based on job performance, the manager would be entitled to a 7 percent increase. The next promotion step is the chief financial officer (CFO) job. In this case, the company may decide to process the 7 percent increase as a red circle rate 2 percent above the range maximum for an accounting manager. Typically when this is done, the new pay level is frozen until the maximum of the pay range moves upward to exceed the accounting manager's pay level. This would usually happen when the comparative market numbers increase, thereby allowing a change to the pay range.

Green Circle Rates

Green circle rates occur when a new employee is hired at a pay rate lower than the minimum rate for the applicable grade. It can also happen when a "fast track" employee is promoted to a new job in a high pay grade under circumstances where the percentage pay increase needed to reach the new grade is excessive and might create an unwanted precedent. In this case, the pay increase may result in a pay level below the minimum level of the new pay grade, thus creating a green circle rate.

Situations such as this should be avoided whenever possible and should be allowed only as a last resort because they can create serious morale issues and, even worse, may create an arguable case of pay discrimination. In any case, such actions should be carefully considered and justified in writing after all of the possible consequences are considered.

Base Pay Systems

After an organization has analyzed, evaluated, and priced its jobs, as well as designed its pay structure, the next step is to determine a type of base pay system. In most cases, employees receive some type of base pay, either as an hourly wage (paid to hourly employees) or as a salary (a fixed wage that doesn't change regardless of the hours worked).

Base pay system choices include single or flat-rate systems, time-based step rate systems, performance-based merit pay systems, productivity-based systems, and person-based systems. Each of these systems is designed to best achieve the objectives of attracting, motivating, and retaining employees under a different set of circumstances.

Single or Flat-Rate System

In the single or flat-rate system, each worker in the same job has the same rate of pay regardless of seniority or job performance. This pay system is most commonly found in elected public-sector jobs or in a union setting. The single pay rate (or flat pay rate) usually is directly linked to an applicable market survey. This system is also used as a training rate under circumstances when the worker is being trained for a job.

Time-Based Step Rate Systems

The time-based step rate system bases the employee's pay rate on the length of time in the job. Pay increases are published in advance on the basis of time. Increases occur on a predetermined schedule. This system has four variations, as described in the sections that follow.

Automatic Step Rate System

In the automatic step rate system, the pay range is divided into several steps, each a predetermined amount apart. At the prescribed time interval, each employee with the required seniority receives a one-step pay increase. This system is common in public-sector jobs and in a union environment.

Step Rate with Performance Considerations

The step rate with performance considerations system is similar to the automatic system except that performance can influence the size or timing of the pay increase.

Combination Step Rate and Performance

In the combination step rate and performance system, employees receive step rate increases up to the established job rate. Above this level, increases are granted only for superior job performance. To work, this system requires a supporting performance appraisal program, as well as good communication and understanding by the workers paid under this system.

Cost-of-Living Adjustments (COLAs)

A cost-of-living adjustment is a pay increase given to all employees on the basis of market pressure, usually measured against the consumer price index (CPI), which is a measure of the price of goods and services in a given area over a period of time. COLAs can be paid as a lump sum or over a period of time and usually are a negotiated practice in a unionized environment. Non-union employers typically resist the pressure to provide COLAs because, once started, they are difficult to stop, thereby diminishing the organization's ability to control its labor costs.

Performance Rating	1st Quartile	2nd Quartile	3rd Quartile	4th Quartile
Exceeds Performance Objectives	6–7%	5–6%	4–5%	3–4%
Meets Performance Objectives	4–5%	3–4%	2–3%	1–2%
Needs Improvement	2–3%	1–2%	0–1%	0%

Table 5-5   Merit Guidelines Example

Performance-Based Merit Pay System

The performance-based merit pay system is based on an employee's individual job performance. A performance-based pay system is often referred to as *merit pay* or *pay for performance*. In this system, employees are typically hired at or near the minimum for their applicable pay range. Pay increases are normally awarded on an annual basis (or annualized if awarded on other than an annual basis) and influenced by the individual's overall job performance. A document identifying the percent pay increase linked to levels of performance and the individual's position in the applicable pay range is communicated to employees as an incentive to increase their performance, thereby earning a higher percentage increase. This document is known as Merit Guidelines. Table 5-5 illustrates a Merit Guidelines example.

To be effective, the merit pay system must be understood by employees affected by the system. In addition to the merit pay system, a clearly stated performance appraisal program is required to support the merit pay system. Key points that should be addressed in designing and implementing an effective merit pay system include the following:

- Merit pay figures can be either a range or a single number. A range can be easier for experienced raters, while a single number can ensure more consistency for inexperienced raters.
- Performance ratings should clearly link to documented pre-agreed performance objectives.
- The gap between one performance level and the next should be large enough (around 2 percent) to be a significant incentive.
- "Needs Improvement" ratings should be placed into a Performance Improvement Program with a defined period (usually not more than 90 days) to improve overall performance.
- Feedback is very important in a merit pay system. Employees must be able to understand, in writing, why they were granted a certain merit increase and associated performance rating.

Productivity-Based Systems

In the productivity-based system, pay is determined by the employee's output. This system is mostly used on an assembly line in a manufacturing environment. The following sections describe two types of productivity-based systems.

Straight Piece-Rate System

With the straight piece-rate system, the employee receives a base rate of pay and is awarded additional compensation for the amount of output produced.

Differential Piece-Rate System

In the differential piece-rate system, the employee receives one rate of pay up to the production standard and a higher rate of pay when the standard is exceeded. Both the straight piece-rate system and the differential piece-rate system focus on quantity rather than quality. As a result, other quality control programs may be required to ensure the required quality standards of the job are met.

Person-Based Systems

In the person-based system, employee capabilities, rather than how the job is performed, determine the employee's pay. For example, two employees do the same work, but one employee with a higher level of skill and experience receives more pay. There are three types of person-based systems, as described next.

Knowledge-Based System

In the knowledge-based system, a person's pay is based on the level of knowledge they have in a particular field. This system is often used for professions requiring a certain level of education, such as lawyers and doctors.

Skill-Based System

Employees paid in the skill-based system are paid for the number and depth of skills they have that are applicable to their job. Heavy-equipment operators are typically paid in this system.

Competency-Based System

In the competency-based system, pay is linked to the level at which an employee can perform in a recognized competency. In HR, a professional with specialty skills in organizational development or labor relations will typically be paid for their competency.

Financial Incentives

Financial incentives are a monetary benefit to encourage behavior or actions that otherwise would not take place. It is an excellent way to motivate employees and reward them for things such as higher performance, output, or longer work hours.

Differential Pay

A pay differential is additional compensation paid to an employee as an incentive to accept what would normally be considered adverse working conditions, usually based on time, location, or situational conditions. The same pay differential is paid to all employees under the same circumstances or conditions. Pay differentials benefit the employer by incentivizing employees to accept work they might not otherwise accept. They also benefit the employee as additional compensation for accepting the work.

Overtime Pay

The Fair Labor Standards Act requires employers to pay nonexempt employees one-and-a-half times their regular rate of pay when they work more than 40 hours in a single workweek. Some employers voluntarily pay more than the legally required time-and-a-half rate for overtime. The FLSA allows employers, at their discretion, to pay more than the FLSA requires; they may not pay less. State laws and wage orders will not be on the exam, but they also often dictate overtime pay.

Regular Rate of Pay

The FLSA requires employers to pay overtime based on an employee's regular rate of pay. Where an employee in a single workweek performs two or more different types of work for which different straight-time rates have been established, the regular rate for that week is the weighted average of such rates. That is, the earnings from all such rates are added together, and this total is then divided by the total number of hours worked at all jobs.

Hazard Pay

Hazard pay occurs when employees are called to work under adverse conditions either caused by the environment or due to the circumstances. Work generally considered putting an employee at risk for safety or health purposes would typically qualify for a hazard pay differential.

Shift Pay

Shift pay is a time-based differential pay that rewards the employee who works hours normally considered undesirable, such as a night shift or hours that are in addition to the employee's regular work schedule (for example, overtime). Time-based differential pay may be a specified amount per hour or a percentage of the employee's regular rate of pay. Except for overtime, federal law does not legally require employers to pay a differential rate of pay, although state requirements may differ.

Reporting Time Pay

Reporting time pay is a guarantee of at least partial compensation for employees who report to their job expecting to work a specified number of hours but who are deprived of that amount of work because of inadequate scheduling or lack of proper notice by the employer.

On-Call Pay

An employee who is required to remain on their employer's premises or so close to the employee's work location that they cannot use the time effectively for their own purposes is working while on-call. Whether hours spent on-call are hours worked is a question to be decided on a case-by-case basis. All on-call time is not necessarily hours worked.

On-call situations vary. Some employees are required to remain on the employer's premises or at a location controlled by the employer. One example is a hospital employee who must stay at the hospital in an on-call room. While on-call, the employee is able to sleep, eat, watch television, read a book, and so on, but is not allowed to leave the hospital. Other employees are able to leave their employer's premises but are required to stay within so many minutes or so many miles of the facility and be accessible by telephone or by pager. An example of this type of employee is an apartment maintenance worker who has to carry a pager while on-call and must remain within a specified number of miles of the apartment complex.

Callback Pay

Callback pay applies when employees are "called back" to perform work beyond regularly scheduled hours. The Fair Labor Standards Act does not guarantee employees a minimum number of hours of work when they are called back. However, FLSA guidelines require that the hours they do work must be paid for at the employees' base rate or at the applicable overtime rate.

Geographic Differentials

Geographic differentials are differences in pay for similar or identical jobs that are based on variations in costs of living in labor markets in particular geographic regions. Large cities, notably New York and San Francisco, often include a portion of an employee's wages, typically a percentage of the basic salary, as a supplement to cover the increased costs of living in a "high-cost" city.

Weekend and Holiday Pay

An employer is required to pay hourly employees only for time actually worked. On the other hand, exempt employees (salaried employees who do not receive overtime) who are given the day off must be paid their full weekly salary if they work any hours during the week in which the holiday falls.

Team and Group Incentives

Team-based incentive plans are designed to encourage and reward exceptional levels of team achievement. Employers use incentives in business as motivators for employees to work collectively. It is also a way for business owners to boost overall productivity and earnings while simultaneously rewarding employees for a job well done. The objective of team incentives is to encourage group goal setting, collaboration, and teamwork.

Organization-Based Pay

Often referred to as *pay-for-performance (PFP)* plans, these plans tie compensation directly to specific business goals and management objectives. In PFP systems, employees' compensation is composed of a fixed base salary and a variable component. The most commonly used variable components are profit-sharing and gainsharing plans, described next.

Profit Sharing

A profit-sharing plan, also known as a *deferred profit-sharing plan,* is a plan that gives employees a share in the profits of a company. Under this type of plan, an employee receives a percentage of a company's profits based on its quarterly or annual earnings. The company contributes a portion of its pretax profits to a pool that will be distributed among eligible employees. The amount distributed to each employee may be weighted by the employee's base salary so that employees with higher base salaries receive a slightly higher amount of the shared pool of profits.

Gainsharing

Gainsharing is best described as a system of management in which an organization seeks higher levels of performance through the participation of its people. As organizational performance improves, employees share financially in the gain. It is a team approach; generally all the employees at a site or operation are included. The typical gainsharing organization measures performance through a predetermined formula. The organization's actual performance is compared to baseline performance (often a historical standard) to determine the amount of the gain. Employees have an opportunity to earn a gainsharing bonus (if there is a gain) generally on a monthly or quarterly basis.

 EXAM TIP The difference between gainsharing and profit sharing is that gainsharing is a reward based on improved productivity, whereas profit sharing is reward based on a percentage of profits.

Payroll

Payroll is a function that directly impacts compensation and thereby traditionally affects every employee in the organization. It has traditionally been treated as an administrative function responsible for issuing paychecks and maintaining payroll records. Today's payroll function is responsible for the following:

- Legal compliance (federal, state, and local)
- Ongoing reporting
- Record generation and maintenance
- Control and security

The cost and quality of legally compliant payroll services are issues that influence the organization's approach to its payroll function. Payroll may be an in-house function, an outsourced function, or some combination of these approaches. In some cases, payroll responsibility may be an HR responsibility, although, in most cases, payroll is part of the organization's finance and accounting function. In any case, payroll extensively interacts with HR, and vice versa.

Most organizations rely on a combination of technology and automation in an effort to reduce payroll processing costs and the amount of transactional work involved. Employees expect their paychecks to be issued in the correct amount and on time. Their expectations are reinforced by a multitude of legal requirements associated with payroll.

Payroll Administration

Administering the payroll function is complex, given the multitude of requirements that must be met. There is a need to comply with federal, state, and local legal requirements, as well as the regular administrative burden of issuing paychecks.

Employers are required to keep a master file of employment records for the federal government in addition to an accurate master file to track their labor costs and maintain an organized pay process. This master file contains information such as the following:

- Personal data on each employee (including name, gender, birth date, and Social Security number)

- Employment data (including date of hire, hours worked per day and per week, and employee's regular rate of pay)

- Tax and payroll data on each employee (including Form W-4 data, allowances claimed, marital status, time records, and Form W-2 for individual income tax purposes)

- Form 1099 for independent contractors who earn $600 or more for services they provide

- Payroll data for the organization, including Form 941, the employer's quarterly federal tax form with local wages subject to federal, state, and local income taxes; total income; Social Security and Medicare tax withheld; payroll ledgers, worksheets, reconciliation; copies of payroll tax deposit information; and Form W-3 (Transmittal of Wage and Tax Statements sent to the Social Security Administration)

Under the Fair Labor Standards Act (FLSA) and the Age Discrimination in Employment Act (ADEA), employers must retain payroll records for 3 years. States may have longer retention requirements. Employers may want to retain payroll records at least as long as the applicable state statute of limitations for contracts claims.

When an employee leaves an organization, some state laws require final paychecks to be granted to employees immediately (on their last day of work). This requires close communication between the HR and payroll functions. After an employee's termination of employment, payroll records should include a copy of the termination record as well as all wages, salaries, commissions, and any other compensation paid to the employee.

Payroll Systems

Most organizations use a computerized payroll system either outsourced or linked to an in-house server. A customized system often includes integrated human resource information systems (HRISs) and payroll capabilities. Many employee self-service (ESS) systems, which will be described later in this chapter, also include benefits data. This minimizes the chance for data-processing errors, eliminates redundancies, and ensures data is current and synchronized.

When selecting a payroll system, the following issues should be considered:

- The system's capability to service the organization's needs. Employees depend on the payroll system to receive timely and accurate paychecks. The organization needs a cost-efficient system that can reliably and dependably meet all of its payroll requirements.

- A good payroll system includes a series of checks and balances designed to accurately produce results with the capabilities to detect error, fraud, or any misuse of data.

- The HRIS and the payroll systems must be compatible. They must be able to share data and make changes to data so that records in one system are accurately and timely reflected in the other system. It is especially helpful when an organization's system has the capabilities to track vacation time, leaves of absence, and payroll. When a system contains information on employee time off, it is much easier to process paychecks based on hours worked.

- Outsourced payroll services are designed to provide the advantage of overall cost savings, better payroll expertise, accuracy, reliability, and accountability. Choosing a payroll vendor is an important decision that must be carefully made given the significance of the payroll function and, by extension, its link to the HRIS, which are both critically important to the organization.

Wage Statements

The FLSA requires that employers keep accurate records of employee wages, and many state laws require wage statements for each employee's paycheck. As such, wage statements, often known as *pay stubs,* have become a common feature in most payroll systems. Pay stubs outline employee compensation for the payroll period, and they can be very helpful in pointing out wage differentials in a pay period, such as hours worked at an employee's base pay rate and overtime pay rate.

Pay stubs also outline deductions from pay. Some deductions from pay are required by law, such as the employee contributions to Social Security and Medicare. Federal and state taxes are also deducted from pay based on an employee's selections on their W-4 form. Other deductions may be required by court order, such as garnishments. Common garnishments include child support and spousal support.

Employee Benefits

Benefit programs are referred to as *indirect compensation* (compared to compensation, which is a direct benefit). They are designed to help employees by rewarding continued employment, enabling employees to live healthy lives, help them care for their families, and provide retirement benefits. In addition to helping employees, benefits programs help employers by attracting and retaining talent as well as increasing employee loyalty to the organization. Table 5-6 lists the most significant employee benefit programs.

Government-Mandated Benefits

Some benefits are mandated by law. They must be provided and cannot be altered by the employer, even when the employer may feel they are not necessary. Currently, federal law mandates Social Security, Medicare, healthcare under the Patient Protection and Affordable Care Act (PPACA), unemployment insurance, workers' compensation, COBRA, and the Family and Medical Leave Act (FMLA). The PPACA, COBRA, and FMLA are described in detail in Chapter 2.

Social Security

Social Security originally was intended to provide retirement income for older workers. It has since expanded to include retirement, disability, death, and survivors' benefits. Social Security is the largest social welfare program in the United States. For tax purposes, the

Employee Benefits	Healthcare Benefits
Social Security	Marketplace plans (ACA)
Workers' compensation	Managed healthcare plans
Unemployment compensation	Fee-for-service plans
Disability benefits	Health maintenance organization (HMO)
Life insurance	Preferred provider organization (PPO)
Long-term care (LTC) insurance	Point of service (POS)
Employee assistance programs (EAPs)	Health insurance purchasing cooperatives (HIPCs)
Retirement plans	High-deductible health plans (HDHP)
Supplemental unemployment benefits (SUBs)	Health reimbursement accounts (HRAs)
Paid holidays	Health savings accounts (HSAs)
Paid vacation	Flexible spending accounts (FSAs)
Paid sick leave	Prescription drug plans
Paid time off (PTO)	Dental plans
Sabbaticals	Vision care plans
Bereavement leave	
Jury duty leave	
Personal (floating) days	
Severance packages	
Supplemental benefits programs	

Table 5-6   Employee Benefits

system is split into two programs: Social Security and Medicare. To qualify for Social Security, a person must earn a number of "quarters," usually 40 quarters, which takes at least 10 years. Medicare is a healthcare program that provides insurance for retired individuals and those with qualified disabilities.

There is no age limit for Social Security. Employees who continue to work while receiving Social Security payments must also pay into it. The employer matches the employee's contributions. Independent contractors and self-employed individuals pay both the employer's and the employee's share of the tax. The amount of monthly retirement income depends on the individual's average earnings on jobs covered by Social Security. Workers can begin to receive reduced benefits at age 62 but are entitled to full benefits if they wait until their retirement age, which is determined on a graduated scale.

Unemployment Insurance

Unemployment insurance provides workers whose jobs have been terminated through no fault of their own monetary payments for a given period of time or until they find a new job. Unemployment payments are intended to provide an unemployed worker with time to find a new job equivalent to the one lost without financial distress. Without employment compensation, many workers would be forced to take jobs for which they are overqualified or would end up on welfare. Unemployment compensation is also justified by sustaining consumer spending during periods of economic adjustment.

In the United States, unemployment insurance is based on a dual program of federal and state statutes. The program was established by the federal Social Security Act in 1935. Much of the federal program is implemented through the Federal Unemployment Tax Act. Each state administers a separate unemployment insurance program, which must be approved by the secretary of labor, based on federal standards. There are special federal rules for nonprofit organizations and governmental entities. A combination of federal and state law determines which employees are eligible for compensation, the amount they receive, and the period of time benefits are paid.

Workers' Compensation

Workers' compensation is a type of insurance paid for by the employer that provides wage replacement income and medical care benefits to employees who suffer work-related injuries or illnesses in return for giving up the employee's right to sue their employer for negligence. Benefits are regulated by the states, not the federal government. Individual states prescribe the rules governing coverage, eligibility, types of benefits, and the funding of benefits.

Workers' compensation will pay hospital and medical expenses that are necessary to diagnose and treat the injury. It also provides disability payments while the employee is unable to work (typically, about two-thirds of the regular salary) and may pay for rehabilitation, retraining, and other benefits as well.

EXAM TIP   The basic concept behind workers' compensation is that the basis of workers' compensation laws is "liability without fault." This means the injured employee is entitled to reasonable compensation regardless of who causes the accident.

Healthcare Benefits

Health insurance is a major benefit to the American worker. Although considered an essential part of a worker's benefits package, healthcare benefits were not legally mandated until the 2010 enactment of the Patient Protection and Affordable Care Act (PPACA), also referred to as the "Affordable Care Act" (ACA) or "Obamacare." The goal of this law is to increase the quality and affordability of health coverage by expanding public and private insurance coverage and reducing the costs of healthcare for individuals and the government. The original law included mandates and subsidies as well as created new insurance exchanges to accomplish its goals. In the first few years after ACA implementation, health insurance coverage was mandatory for individuals either through their employers or through newly created state health insurance exchanges.

As a result of President Trump's Tax Reform Plan signed into law in 2017, the insurance coverage mandate of the ACA was affected. Fines associated with not having health coverage were no longer enforceable beginning in 2019. At the time of this book's writing, the law and its implementation continue to face challenges from government, certain advocacy groups, and private business associations.

Regardless of the current legal and political landscape associated with offering medical insurance to employees, most employers offer one or more types of medical plans. It remains one of the key aspects of an employee benefits package.

Health Benefits Eligibility

Although employers have some flexibility in who they choose to offer health benefits to, there are a few federal laws that regulate eligibility. The first is the ACA, which requires that health benefits be provided to employees working at least 30 hours per week (or 130 hours per month). Additionally, the Employee Retirement Income Security Act (ERISA) requires that employees are eligible to participate in retirement plans after completing 1,000 hours of service in a 12-month period.

So, based on the requirements noted earlier, an organization should offer benefits to all full-time employees and part-time employees who meet the requirements of federal law. As part of their total rewards strategy, many employers choose to offer supplemental benefits such as tuition reimbursement, child care, therapy, or wellness benefits to all employees.

Health Benefits Enrollment

Benefits enrollment in employer-sponsored health plans is often an early-career HR responsibility. Benefits enrollment timelines for new employees will be dictated by your organization's plan rules. Typically, new employees are eligible for healthcare benefits somewhere between 30 and 90 days after their date of hire with the organization. Enrollment for retirement benefits is usually 6 to 12 months after an employee's date of hire.

Every year, all employees eligible for the organization's benefits plan have an opportunity to make changes to health benefits elections during *open enrollment*. Prior to open enrollment, employers examine the cost of various benefit plan options and sometimes make changes to plan offerings. Open enrollment is typically a busy time for HR. A close relationship with the organization's contracted benefits broker to help with new plan selection and employee communication is essential.

Some mid-year changes are also permitted to benefits plans, depending on the type of plan. For health, dental, or vision plans, tax code Section 125 allows employees to change their benefits elections within 30 days of a *qualifying event*. Some examples of qualifying events include marriage, divorce, job change, birth or adoption of a child, or a dependent child reaching the age of 26. On the other hand, for contribution changes to retirement plans or health savings accounts (HSAs), employees may make changes at any time, for any reason.

Healthcare Plan Designs

There are a variety of options for employers to choose from when deciding which healthcare option to offer employees. Decisions are often made based on the organization's total rewards strategy, size, and cost of plan options. This section will review the most common healthcare plan designs, and some of the advantages and disadvantages of each one.

Marketplace Plans Under the Affordable Care Act (ACA)

The ACA requires organizations to minimally cover the following categories, called *essential health benefits:*[4]

- Ambulatory patient services (outpatient care provided without being admitted to a hospital)
- Emergency services
- Hospitalization (surgery and overnight stays)
- Pregnancy, maternity, and newborn care (both before and after birth)
- Mental health and substance use disorder services, including behavioral health treatment (includes counseling and psychotherapy)
- Prescription drugs
- Rehabilitative services and devices (services and devices to help people with injuries, disabilities, or chronic conditions gain or recover mental and physical skills)
- Laboratory services
- Preventive and wellness services and chronic disease management
- Birth control coverage
- Breastfeeding coverage
- Pediatric services, including oral and vision care (but adult dental and vision coverage aren't essential health benefits)
- Medical management programs (for specific needs such as weight management, back pain, and diabetes)

Managed Healthcare Plans

Managed healthcare plans are a type of health insurance. They have contracts with healthcare providers and medical facilities to provide care for members at reduced costs. These providers make up the plan's network.

Fee-for-Service Plans

Fee-for-service (FFS) is a payment model where services are unbundled and paid for separately. In healthcare, it gives an incentive for physicians to provide more treatments because payment is dependent on the quantity of care, rather than the quality of care.

Health Maintenance Organization (HMO)

HMO plans offer a wide range of healthcare services through a network of providers who agree to supply services to members. They are the most common type of managed healthcare plan. With an HMO, members will likely have coverage for a broader range of preventive healthcare services than they would through any other type of plan.

Members of HMOs are required to choose a primary care physician (PCP). The PCP will take care of most of the member's healthcare needs. Before seeing a specialist, members need to obtain a referral from their PCP.

Though there are many variations, HMO plans typically enable members to have lower out-of-pocket healthcare expenses. They may not be required to pay a deductible before coverage starts, and the copayments will likely be minimal. Members also typically won't have to submit any of their own claims to the insurance company. However, keep in mind that they will likely have no coverage for services rendered by out-of-network providers or for services rendered without a proper referral from the PCP.

Preferred Provider Organization (PPO)

PPO plans are some of the most popular types of plans in the individual and family market. PPO plans allow members to visit any in-network physician or healthcare provider without first requiring a referral from a PCP.

Members of PPO plans are encouraged to use the insurance company's network of preferred doctors and usually won't need to choose a PCP. No matter which healthcare provider a member chooses, in-network healthcare services will be covered at a higher benefit level than out-of-network services. It's important to check whether the provider accepts a health plan in order to receive the highest level of benefit coverage.

Members usually have an annual deductible to pay before the insurance company starts covering their medical bills. They may also have a copayment of about $10 to $30 for certain services or be required to cover a certain percentage of the total charges for medical bills.

Point of Service (POS)

A point of service (POS) plan has some of the qualities of HMO and PPO plans with benefit levels varying depending on whether a member receives care in or out of the health insurance company's network of providers.

PART II

POS plans combine elements of both HMO and PPO plans. Like an HMO plan, members may be required to designate a PCP who will then make referrals to network specialists when needed. Depending upon the plan, services rendered by a member's PCP are typically not subject to a deductible, and preventive-care benefits are usually included. Like with PPO plans, members may receive care from non-network providers but with greater out-of-pocket costs. Members may also be responsible for copayments, coinsurance, and an annual deductible.

Health Insurance Purchasing Cooperatives (HIPCs)

HIPCs act as purchasing agents for a group of several employers. They use the size of the cooperative over the size of the individual organizations to negotiate and purchase health insurance plans for their members. Their goal is to provide small organizations the advantage of their size in negotiating health plan contracts.

High-Deductible Health Plans (HDHP)

High-deductible health plans (HDHP), defined narrowly, refer to third-tier health insurance plans that protect employees from catastrophic medical expenses. High-deductible policies cost less, but employees are responsible for medical costs until the deductible has been reached.

HDHPs are often paired with health savings accounts (HSAs), health reimbursement accounts (HRAs), or similar medical payment products to pay routine healthcare expenses directly. The combination of an HDHP and a tax-advantaged plan for covering medical costs prior to reaching the deductible is known as a *consumer-driven health plan* (CDHP).

Health Reimbursement Account (HRA)

A health reimbursement arrangement, commonly referred to as a *health reimbursement account,* is an IRS-approved, employer-funded, tax-advantaged employer health benefit plan that reimburses employees for out-of-pocket medical expenses and individual health insurance premiums. An HRA is not health insurance. A health reimbursement arrangement allows the employer to make contributions to an employee's account and provide reimbursement for eligible expenses. An HRA plan is an excellent way to provide health insurance benefits and allow employees to pay for a wide range of medical expenses not covered by insurance.

Like a health savings account, there is a limit to the amount of money an employer can contribute to certain HRAs. As of the time of this writing, annual employer contributions for small-business HRAs are capped at $5,300 for a single employee and $10,700 for an employee with a family.

However, for other HRAs, such as an integrated HRA or a one-person stand-alone HRA, there are no annual contribution limits.

An HRA may reimburse any expense considered to be a qualified medical expense under IRS Section 213 of the Internal Revenue Code, including premiums for personal health insurance policies. Within IRS guidelines, employers may restrict the list of reimbursable expenses in any way they choose for their HRA plan.

HRA balances may roll forward from month to month or from year to year, depending on which HRA plan an employer chooses. Small-business HRAs may roll forward from month to month only; no annual rollover is permitted.

Health Savings Account (HSA)

A health savings account is a tax-advantaged medical savings account you can contribute to and draw money from for certain medical expenses, tax free. HSAs can be used for out-of-pocket medical, dental, and vision. HSAs can't be used to pay health insurance premiums. HSAs can be used with only high-deductible health plans that count as minimum essential coverage (MEC).

The funds contributed to an HSA account are not subject to federal income tax at the time of deposit. Unlike a flexible spending account, HSA funds roll over and accumulate year to year if they are not spent. HSAs are owned by the individual, which differentiates them from company-owned HRAs, which are an alternate tax-deductible source of funds paired with either high-deductible health plans or standard health plans.

Flexible Spending Account (FSA)

A *flexible spending account* (also known as a *flexible spending arrangement*) is a special account you put money into that you use to pay for certain out-of-pocket healthcare costs. You don't pay taxes on this money. This means you'll save an amount equal to the taxes you would have paid on the money you set aside. However, FSA money does not roll over year to year, so the amount you elect in a given year must be used in that year.

At the time of this writing, FSAs are limited to $2,750 per year per employee. If you're married, your spouse can put up to $2,750 in an FSA with their employer too. Every year, the annual cap for FSA funds is evaluated by the IRS and often increases slightly.

You can use funds in your FSA to pay for certain medical and dental expenses for you, your spouse, and your dependents. You can spend FSA funds to pay deductibles and copayments, but not for insurance premiums. You can spend FSA funds on prescription medications, as well as over-the-counter medicines with a doctor's prescription. Reimbursements for insulin are allowed without a prescription. FSAs may also be used to cover costs of medical equipment such as crutches, supplies like bandages, and diagnostic devices like blood sugar test kits.

There are also FSAs for dependent care costs such as child care or elder care, known as a *dependent care flexible spending account*. This type of FSA has a higher annual limit than FSAs for healthcare costs.

Prescription Drug Plans

Prescription drug plans are often included as part of an organization's medical plan. Most non-Medicare prescription drug plans require a minimum copayment for prescriptions or a percentage of the cost. In some cases, plans may also require the use of generic-brand drugs or the use of formulary drugs. A drug formulary may include generic or brand-name prescription drugs that are covered by the health plan. Some plans require subscribers to fill their prescriptions at specified pharmacies at a predetermined cost.

Dental Plans

Dental plan coverage is generally subject to a high adverse selection rate; that is, subscribers with dental issues are more likely to enroll in a dental plan than those who do not have dental issues. This affects the cost of coverage. To avoid the resulting cost issues, high employee enrollment with a cap on benefits is normally necessary for dental plans. Other approaches include a managed care form of coverage with coverage restricted only to network providers.

Vision Care Plans

Vision plans generally limit the frequency of coverage along with a monetary cap on coverage. The majority of plans limit new lenses, frames, or contact lenses. In addition, most plans place a monetary cap on allowances for a standard set of lenses, frames, or contact lenses. Some plans provide discounts for laser vision correction surgery.

Healthcare Costs

All organizations are concerned with their ability to manage or control their healthcare costs. You will likely be involved in this discussion with management at some point in your HR career. The following are some actions that can help with this effort:

- *Change the delivery system.* The type of healthcare delivery system has a major effect on costs. HDHPs are often cheaper than HMO, PPO, and POS plans. HIPCs can help by negotiating better terms than might otherwise be possible with direct negotiations between the carrier and the organization.

- *Let employees choose.* Provide a benefits program with choices such as an HMO and a PPO. This is a way to avoid offering healthcare services that are not wanted or needed.

- *Redesign the programs.* Examine the balance between the employer share and the employee share of the premium. Changing the balance can also include the following:
  - Increasing deductibles and out-or-pocket requirements. Employers can mitigate shifting the burden to employees by allowing employees to pay these costs through pretax Section 125 healthcare spending accounts.
  - Requiring generic prescription drugs and/or mail-order drugs.

- *Promote prevention and wellness.* A number of programs can help:
  - Incentives for quitting smoking
  - On-site fitness facilities and/or discount memberships to off-site facilities
  - Health wellness programs
  - Encouraging healthy and safe behaviors (for example, promoting bicycling and so on)

Common Benefits Provided to Employees

In addition to medical, dental, and vision benefits, a number of benefits are commonly part of an employer's benefit package:

- Disability benefits
- Life insurance
- Long-term care (LTC) insurance
- Employee assistance programs (EAPs)
- Retirement plans
- Supplemental unemployment benefits (SUBs)
- Paid leaves

Disability Benefits

Employer disability plans typically come in two forms:

- **Short-term disability (STD)**   This coverage usually begins where any employer-provided sick leave ends. STD typically covers only a portion of lost income and may require a waiting period. In some cases, organizations may self-fund their STD. Typically, STD provides up to 50 to 70 percent of coverage of the employee's base salary up to 6 months. Five states have mandated short-term disability plans: California, Hawaii, New Jersey, New York, and Rhode Island. In addition, Puerto Rico also has mandatory insurance requirements.

- **Long-term disability (LTD)**   LTD coverage usually begins after short-term disability coverage ends. LTD is always underwritten by a commercial insurance company due to the risk associated with the coverage. When a disabled employee is also eligible for Social Security disability benefits, the LTD is often integrated with the Social Security coverage to avoid duplication of coverage. When employees go on LTD, their employment ends with their organization, even though they are collecting LTD benefits.

During their first 2 years of LTD coverage, individuals must be unable to perform their own occupation. After 2 years, a person must be unable to engage in any occupation or do any work to continue on LTD (unless their plan indicates otherwise). Benefits cease when a person returns to work or dies prior to normal retirement age. There are no income levels applicable to LTD coverage.

Life Insurance

Employees are concerned about care for their families if they were to die prematurely, leaving their families without adequate resources. Group term life insurance provides benefits that address this issue.

PART II

Group term life insurance provides a lump sum benefit to beneficiaries. The benefit may be in the form of a flat amount or a multiple of salary. Also, the amount may vary by length of service or position.

> **NOTE** Many employers keep the value of the group term life insurance to $50,000 because plans kept at that level or less are not taxable when nondiscriminatory. When plans are over $50,000, the amount over $50,000 is referred to as excess group term life insurance and treated by the IRS as imputed income subject to tax. Imputed income is added to other income and appears on the employee's W-2 Form.

Long-Term Care (LTC) Insurance

Long-term care (LTC) insurance covers the cost of long-term care in a number of settings, including care at home, in an assisted living facility, in a nursing home, or as an inpatient in a hospice. If LTC is offered, it must provide care for people who are chronically ill for at least 90 days. The premium payments are not counted as employee income, and employers can deduct their part of the insurance premiums from their annual income tax liability.

Employee Assistance Programs (EAPs)

Employee assistance programs (EAPs) are employer-sponsored benefits that provide a number of services that help promote the physical, mental, and emotional wellness of individual employees who otherwise would be negatively impacted by health-related crises. EAPs help employees find professional resources to deal with their problems. Services are provided by licensed counselors, typically through third-party organizations with a high degree of confidentiality for employees. Depending on the specific program, services can help employees meet personal goals, reduce stress and anxiety, and improve overall emotional and physical health. Online therapy is one of the most popular benefits offered by EAPs.

Retirement Plans

Retirement plans can take many forms. Whatever plan is selected, the goal of the benefit is ultimately to help employees save money for retirement and invest in their financial security. There are two different types of retirement plans covered by the Employee Retirement Income Security Act (ERISA): defined benefit plans and defined contribution plans.

Defined Benefit Plans

A defined benefit plan provides a specified monthly benefit at retirement. Its popularity has decreased significantly in recent decades, and many plans have been replaced by defined contribution plans. This type of plan is more common in the public sector in the form of pensions.

Defined Contribution Plans

The most common type of defined contribution plan is a 401(k) plan. In these plans, contributions are made to an account through payroll deduction, and the balance of the account is available, including any investment gains, once the employee reaches retirement age. As interest compounds over time, small contributions can grow into significant retirement savings.

Employee-contributed dollars may also be matched up to a certain percentage by employers to provide an added benefit to participating in the plan, essentially "free money." Any contributions made by an employee to a retirement plan are *vested* in the plan immediately. Once money has been vested in an employee's retirement plan, it is an employee's asset that cannot be taken away by a third party. Oftentimes, there is a vesting schedule for employer-contributed money. It is usually a percentage amount that increases every year to incentivize employees to stay at an organization. Any portion not vested may be forfeited under certain conditions, such as termination of employment.

As of this writing, such plans have an annual maximum contribution limit of $19,500. There are also additional contributions allowed for employees over the age of 50, called *catch-up contributions*. Since the plans are intended to provide a retirement benefit, there are taxes and penalties associated with removing funds from a plan before retirement age. However, plans typically allow for *hardship withdrawals* up to a certain amount for defined reasons without penalty.

Nonqualified Retirement Plans

Another type of defined contribution plan that is available to public and nonprofit employers is a 457(b) plan. This is called a nonqualified retirement plan because it is not governed by ERISA. This type of plan operates very similarly to a 401(k) plan, but some aspects such as catch-up contributions, early withdrawals, and hardship withdrawals are handled differently. Some public employers choose to offer both a 401(k) and 457(b) plan to their employees to allow them to contribute maximum amounts to both types of plans.

Supplemental Unemployment Benefits (SUBs)

Supplemental unemployment benefits (SUBs) are unemployment benefits in addition to government benefits offered by some employers. SUBs are common in union environments. Under the Internal Revenue Code, SUBs may be exempt from federal income taxes for employers but not for employees.

Paid Leaves

Many employers have found that paid time off as a reward for service provides the employee with relief from the ongoing demands of work as well as benefits the employer with increased morale and commitment. Various types of paid leave are described in the sections that follow.

Paid Holidays

While paid holidays are not legally required, employers find that both employers and employees benefit from them. The number of paid holidays vary from 6 to 12 per year, generally including New Year's Day, Memorial Day, Independence Day, Labor Day, Thanksgiving Day, and Christmas Day. Paid holidays are generally paid on the basis of the employer's schedule for a regular workday.

Paid Vacation

A standard employee vacation benefit is based on an accrual system measured based on an employee's length of service. Employers may choose the amount of vacation to offer employees based on their length of service, but state laws dictate how plans are managed.

State laws vary on the management of vacation accrual. Some states do not allow a "use-it-or-lose-it" policy in which vacation benefits do not carry over to the next year if they are not used. In some cases, vacation can be carried over from year to year with a provision for a reasonable cap. Many employers have a cash-out policy that allows an employee to receive cash back for their unused vacation. Generally, employees must receive advance approval to use their vacation to avoid disrupting the employer's work flow.

Paid Sick Leave

Organizations that otherwise have paid vacation policies usually also have paid sick leave policies to provide for time off due to illness or injury. These sick leave programs are primarily intended for the benefit of the employee, although in recent years, sick leave programs have often been expanded to cover an employee's time off to care for a family member. Several states have implemented laws requiring paid sick leave programs. Some states mandate that a portion of the employee's sick leave accrual must be allowed for family care.

Paid Time Off (PTO)

Many employers combine vacation and sick leave into a single program called *paid time off* (PTO). PTO is a concept that allows employees to accrue time off that the employee can then use whenever circumstances require that they be absent from work. PTO does not require justification for a certain type of absence (sick, vacation, or personal time), but simply an approval in the event of a planned absence or the accrued balance to be used in an unplanned absence.

 NOTE PTO accrual is treated in the same manner as vacation; that is, PTO is subject to the same rules applicable to vacation.

Sabbatical

Some professions or industries allow long-term employees to take a paid leave of absence as a way to complete a course of study, do research, or engage in other pursuits. This practice is particularly evident in the teaching profession, although not restricted only to that profession. Some organizations allow its long-term employees with high-balance sick leave accounts to take extended unpaid time off with the opportunity to use a portion of their sick leave for paid time off during this absence.

Bereavement Leave

Most organizations have policies that provide for paid time off to attend a funeral of a family member. In some cases, this benefit is available to extended family members as well as close friends.

Jury Duty Leave

When a person is called for jury duty in the United States, that service is mandatory, and the person summoned for jury duty must attend. Failing to report for jury duty is not technically illegal and usually results in the individual simply being placed back into the selection pool to be called for another trial. However, repeatedly ignoring a jury summons can result in strict penalties, which may include being fined or jailed for contempt of court.

Employers cannot fire an employee for being called to jury duty, but they are typically not required to pay wages during this time. Employers typically offer jury duty leave as an unpaid leave benefit, but some employers choose to pay employees the difference between their regular pay and pay received while serving on a jury for a portion of the leave period.

Personal (Floating) Days

Many organizations allow a limited number of paid days off for employees' personal needs. These are often referred to as "floating holidays" because when they are taken is determined by the employee. Typically, approval is required in advance. Because these paid days off are determined by the employee, some states apply the same rules to these days as they do to vacation or PTO.

Severance Packages

While not legally required, some organizations give employees who are terminated for a reason other than cause a severance package, which may include:

- Salary continuation for a specified period of time (for example, 1 week of pay for each year of service)
- Outplacement services such as résumé assistance, interview preparation and placement counseling, testing, and job search assistance
- Retraining in some cases
- Paid benefits premium assistance for a limited period of time

Severance packages often have legal implications. As such, legal assistance should be sought whenever circumstances arise that include a potential severance package.

Supplemental Benefits

Employers have other benefits options to consider. Over the past several years, supplemental benefits have become much more common. To remain competitive, organizations should consider adding supplemental benefits to their employee offerings. It is a good practice to describe eligibility for supplemental benefits in an employee handbook as a way to ensure consistent and fair treatment of employees as well as for legal liability protection.

Tuition Reimbursement

Many employers support employee education and development by providing financial support to employees who undertake educational courses related to their work or for general professional development purposes. In some cases, employer tuition reimbursement programs also provide financial support for books and other ancillary supplies. In most cases, employers require a passing grade in order to qualify for tuition reimbursement support. There is an annual dollar limit on the amount of reimbursement eligible for income inclusion for tax purposes.

Paid Volunteer Time

A growing trend that aligns with corporate social responsibility programs in organizations is paid volunteer time. Employees are paid their normal wages while volunteering for a nonprofit or underserved community organization. Paid volunteer time is often offered in increments of 1 day. Not only can this be a great team-building activity to get employees out of the office and establish a sense of pride for supporting a good cause, it also provides a benefit to the organization being served.

Workplace Amenities

With demands for 24/7 services in some industries like hospitality and information technology, workplace amenities offer employees an opportunity to make the workplace "a home away from home." Workplace eateries and cafeterias, recreation and game rooms, onsite gyms and fitness classes, and even nap pods are some of the amenities being offered at various organizations.

Employee Recognition Programs

Many organizations offer recognition programs such as employee of the month. On-the-spot recognition programs are also a popular way to reward employees for exhibiting an organization's core values or providing excellent customer service. Recognition programs may also be tied to an employee's length of service with an organization, such as 5, 10, or 20 years of service. Some organizations also provide recognition for personal milestones such as an employee's birthday or the birth or adoption of a child.

There are many options for recognition programs. They can be highly motivating to employees if selected properly. Conducting an employee opinion survey to determine which programs are most valued by employees is a good way to figure this out.

Childcare Services

Employers can provide a variety of childcare services to help working parents deal with the ongoing needs of preschool or school-aged children:

- Supportive time-off policies
- Resource and referral services to identify available community services and childcare providers
- Tax advantages through a dependent care flexible spending account
- A flex-time program for working hours
- Work options such as job sharing and part-time work

Elder Care

Demographic changes often place family support pressures on employees and their elders as well as their children. Organization support services include the following:

- Supportive time-off policies
- Employer-sponsored group long-term care insurance
- Counseling assistance through an EAP
- Resource and referral services to identify elder care services and providers
- Tax advantages through a dependent care flexible spending account
- A flex-time program for working hours

Commuter Assistance

Most organizations have a significant number of employees who commute to work in their own car because public transit is either too expensive or not easily accessible to satisfy the employee's work requirements. Some organizational support services that can help include the following:

- A flex-time program for working hours
- Mass transit cost assistance (tokens, transit passes, and so on)
- Van pooling or carpooling assistance
- Dedicated parking for employees at or near the employee's place of employment

Prepaid Legal Insurance

Although not as popular as it was several years ago, some employers continue to provide prepaid legal insurance that covers the cost of routine legal services such as developing a will and assistance with real estate matters, divorces, and other basic legal assistance.

This often is a relatively high-cost benefit that is utilized by a few employees, which may explain why this benefit is not widespread. Some EAP programs bundle this type of benefit with their offerings.

Gym Membership

Having healthier employees ultimately results in reduced healthcare costs for the organization. So, offering benefits that give employees the opportunity to stay healthy can also benefit the employer. One common way organizations do this is by offering a free or discounted gym membership to employees. Some organizations even set aside space in the office and create a gym employees can utilize on their break time.

Housing or Relocation Assistance

As the workplace has become more "global," employers are often recruiting employees from other states, and even other countries. As a result, offering assistance to relocate employees to their new place of work has become a valued benefit offering. Assistance often comes in the form of temporary housing or coverage of moving costs up to a certain amount of money.

Travel Stipends

When employees are required to travel as part of their job, it is helpful to employees when the employer makes traveling as seamless as possible. So, employers usually offer a stipend and/or expense reimbursements to cover the cost of travel, lodging, and meals. It is important to have procedures on travel stipends and expense reimbursements well documented in the employee policy manual to avoid any confusion. The accounting department will also have requirements to provide receipts for travel-related expenses.

Legal Compliance

As noted earlier in the chapter, 32 federal laws apply to the compensation and benefits function. That's a whole lot of laws! As an early-career HR professional, you will likely be responsible for tasks that help keep the organization in compliance with these laws.

Taxable and Nontaxable Benefits

Employee benefits fall into two categories: taxable and nontaxable benefits. Both categories include direct compensation and indirect compensation (employer-paid coverage or reimbursements). Table 5-7 identifies some of the benefits we've discussed in this chapter in each category (the list is only generally indicative; it is not all-inclusive).

	Taxable Benefits	Nontaxable Benefits
Direct Compensation	Base pay Differential pay Severance pay Paid time off	Wages paid after death in a new year
Indirect Compensation	Disability benefits when employer pays the premium Life insurance when employee pays with pretax dollars Gifts, prizes, and awards over $25 Personal use of a company vehicle Sick pay	Work-related expense reimbursements Childcare (subject to limitations) Company vehicle use (only work-related) Gifts, prizes, and awards valued at less than $25 Group life insurance plans, $50,000 or less coverage Educational expenses (subject to annual limits) Medical, dental, health plans (employer contributions) Employee-paid disability benefits when purchased with after-tax dollars

Table 5-7   Taxable and Nontaxable Benefits

Communication Required by Law

ERISA-required reporting and communication requirements that must automatically be distributed to every employee include the following:

- **Summary plan description (SPD)**   Contains information on what the benefits plan provides in layperson terms. Distribution is required within 120 days after the plan's establishment or 90 days after eligibility. The SPD must be updated no less frequently than every 5 years.

- **Summary annual report (SAR)**   Contains financial information about the plan. Distribution is required within 9 months after the end of the plan year.

- **Summary of material modifications (SMM)**   Required whenever any of the plan's features have been significantly changed or within 210 days after the end of the plan year.

Other required or highly recommended communications include the following:

- An FMLA policy statement in all employee handbooks (for employers with 50+ employees)

- General notification of federal (and state if applicable) COBRA rights (employers with 20+ employees)

- Notice of special HIPAA enrollment rights and privacy rights

The preceding list is not all-inclusive. Due diligence is required so that all organizations understand the requirements of applicable laws, regulations, and instructions for any official forms or other official guidance.

Benefits Communication

In addition to legally required communication, benefits programs can be complex, and it is important for employees to understand their value. Implementing a costly benefit program that employees fail to participate in because they do not understand it can be a big human resource and financial problem.

Contracted benefits brokers can be helpful with this process, as they often create materials that explain benefits offerings in simple terms. Group presentations are also common during open enrollment periods to present benefits offerings and answer questions.

Total Rewards Statements

Total rewards statements evolved from wage statements as a way to outline all aspects of an employee's total rewards package. They are often used as a recruitment and retention tool to communicate information on direct and indirect compensation. Oftentimes, employees are not aware of the cost of employer contributions to various benefits programs, so total rewards statements can offer more clarity in this area.

Common components of total rewards statements include the following:

- Annual compensation
- Bonus amounts
- The cost of paid holidays, paid vacation, and paid sick time (at the employee's rate of pay)
- Employer contributions to health benefits
- Employer contributions to retirement benefits
- Employer contributions to supplemental benefits related to wellness, mental health, tuition assistance, and so on

Communicating Through Employee Self-Service (ESS) Technologies

The communication requirements described in this section are influenced by the introduction of self-service technologies that are rapidly improving the communication capabilities of organizations. These systems often integrate payroll, benefits, and HR information into one place. Employee self-service (ESS) applications provide quick and easy access to information, which benefits the organization in the following ways:

- By increasing the accuracy of employee data
- By improving the timeliness of employee transactions
- By reducing HR costs associated with traditional delivery channels

With increased benefits, ESS brings responsibilities:

- The application must be protected from hackers.
- Unauthorized internal and external access must be managed.
- Access to payroll data and benefits information must be protected.

HR can help promote the success of ESS technology by ensuring that employees do the following:

- Understand the purpose of this technology, what functions are available, and how to apply the functions to meet their needs.
- Recognize the benefits of ESS technology when compared to traditional methods.
- Make the effort to use the technology to their advantage.

Chapter Review

In this chapter, we examined the important role of compensation and benefits in all aspects of the organization. This is an important topic to know and understand for the exam and because of its direct impact on all of the organization's stakeholders.

You learned that compensation is a systematic approach to providing value to employees in return for the work they perform for the organization. This "system" provides methods for maintaining a balance between the organization's needs while attracting, developing, retaining, and rewarding employees. As part of exploring the "system," we reviewed the purpose of job evaluation as a systematic way of determining the value or worth of a job in relation to other jobs in an organization. We reviewed different methods of job evaluation, including job ranking, job classification, the point-factor method, the factor comparison method, and the Hay plan.

We also examined the theory behind pay grades and ranges along with the basis of pay rates. We reviewed financial incentives, including differentials, team- and group-based incentives, and organization-based pay such as profit sharing and gainsharing.

Going hand in glove with a good compensation program is a good benefits program. Although expensive, there are many reasons to provide employees with a comprehensive benefit program. For most organizations, the ability to find and keep highly qualified staff is the key driver. The more progressive the organization, the more flexible the structure is in response to today's challenges. Employers who continue to provide a more traditional and limited program will likely find it more difficult to attract and keep different types of employees.

In the section "Employee Benefits," we reviewed various healthcare plans, as well as the administration of benefits accounts and programs. We also looked at supplemental benefits programs and various leave-of-absence formats, as well as their value to employees and the organization. Some of these leaves are mandated by law, while others are prescribed by policy. Either way, they will be an important part of your practice as a human resource management professional.

All of these topics are important to you, not only because some will likely appear as subject matter on your exam, but also because they are basic concepts you need to know as you move forward in your professional HR career.

Questions

1. A window manufacturer guarantees its installers a base wage plus an extra $25 for each job completed to specifications. The employer is using a
   _____.

   A. merit pay system

   B. productivity-based pay system

   C. competency-based system

   D. flat-rate system

2. Under the factor comparison method, jobs are evaluated through the use of
   _____.

   A. predetermined wage classes

   B. a wage/salary conversion table

   C. a scale based on compensable factors

   D. a comparison with market pricing

3. Which of the following is not a pay differential?

   A. Hazard pay

   B. Shift pay

   C. Base pay

   D. Overtime

4. If a leave under FMLA can be reasonably anticipated, how much notice must the employee give the employer?

   A. 7 days

   B. 14 days

   C. 30 days

   D. 90 days

5. Which of the following terms refers to collapsing multiple pay ranges into a single-wide pay range?

   A. Wide banding

   B. Pay compression

   C. Green circle rates

   D. Broadbanding

6. Which of the following laws does *not* directly relate to a company's compensation or benefits program?

   A. Equal Pay Act

   B. Fair Labor Standards Act

   C. Port-to-Portal Act

   D. Uniform Guidelines on Employee Selection Procedures

7. Social Security, COBRA, and Medicare are examples of _____.

   A. medical benefits

   B. social benefits

   C. government-regulated benefits

   D. employer-sponsored benefits

8. _____ is the right of employees to receive benefits from their retirement plans.

   A. Transference

   B. Portability

   C. Social Security

   D. Vesting

9. Which job evaluation method is most difficult to use?

   A. Factor comparison method

   B. Ranking method

   C. Classification method

   D. Point-factor method

10. The simplest method of job evaluation is the _____.

    A. job-ranking method

    B. point-factor method

    C. classification method

    D. factor comparison method

11. A(n) _____ system is a productivity-based system in which an employee is paid for each unit of production.

    A. incentive

    B. merit

    C. results-oriented

    D. piece-rate

12. The Equal Pay Act prohibits wage discrimination on the basis of
_____.

    A. race

    B. sex

    C. seniority

    D. merit

13. Which of the following compensates employees who arrive at work but find that no work is available?

    A. On-call pay

    B. Reporting time pay

    C. Premium pay

    D. Travel pay

14. Which of the following statements about workers' compensation is true?

    A. It covers all of workers' health problems.

    B. It is funded by employers and regulated by the federal government.

    C. It is paid even if an accident is the employee's fault.

    D. It pays all injured workers the same benefits.

15. A consumer-driven health plan combines a tax-advantaged plan for covering medical costs and which of the following types of health plans?

    A. HDHP

    B. PPO

    C. POS

    D. PPA

16. The concept of broadbanding was developed to
_____.

    A. limit the autonomy of line managers

    B. reduce employee mobility with the organization

    C. work with flatter organization structures

    D. provide narrower salary ranges

17. A worker is paid $8.50 an hour when the pay range for that assigned grade is $7 to $8 an hour. This is referred to as a _____.

    A. green circle rate

    B. pay differential

    C. red circle rate

    D. compressed salary

18. Which of the following statements about a single-rate pay system is true?

 A. It provides opportunity for progression within a single grade level.

 B. It is typically used for exempt jobs.

 C. It disregards performance or seniority.

 D. It is not applicable in a union environment.

19. Which of the following is *not* regulated by the FLSA?

 A. Exempt status

 B. Employee benefits

 C. Minimum wage

 D. Overtime pay

20. Workers' compensation is regulated by the _____ .

 A. U.S. Department of Labor

 B. States

 C. Private insurance companies

 D. Social Security Administration

Answers

1. **B.** The employer is using an incentive program based on performance results, which is considered a productivity-based pay system. A merit-based pay system does not address incentive pay. A competency-based system addresses capabilities, whereas a flat-rate system establishes a fixed rate of pay.

2. **C.** The factor comparison job evaluation method involves a set of compensable factors identified as determining the worth of jobs. Typically, the number of compensable factors is small. Next, benchmark jobs are identified. Benchmark jobs should be selected as having certain characteristics, such as equitable pay and being distributed along a range. The jobs are then priced, and the total pay for each job is divided into pay for each factor. This process establishes the rate of pay for each factor for each benchmark job. The other jobs in the organization are then compared with the benchmark jobs, and rates of pay for each factor are summed to determine the rates of pay for each of the other jobs.

3. **C.** Hazard pay, shift pay, and overtime are all differentials. Base pay is the foundation of an employer's compensation program.

4. **C.** The FMLA allows employers to require 30 days' advance notice when the leave can be reasonably anticipated. The other choices are incorrect.

5. **D.** Broadbanding is a term that refers to pay ranges with a wide spread. This is often done to facilitate the management of pay levels within the pay range. A side effect of broadbanding is reducing the opportunity for promotions because of a smaller number of ranges. That can adversely affect morale.

6. **D.** In 1978, the Civil Service Commission, the Department of Labor, the Department of Justice, and the Equal Opportunity Commission jointly adopted the Uniform Guidelines on Employee Selection Procedures to establish uniform standards for employers for the use of selection procedures and to address adverse impact, validation, and recordkeeping requirements. The other choices are laws that directly relate to employers' compensation programs.

7. **C.** Social Security, COBRA, and Medicare are all government-regulated benefits.

8. **D.** Vesting is the absolute right to an asset that cannot be taken away by any third party, even though one may not yet possess the asset. The portion vested cannot be reclaimed by the employer, nor can it be used to satisfy the employer's debts. Any portion not vested may be forfeited under certain conditions, such as termination of employment.

9. **A.** The factor comparison method is a systematic and scientific method of job evaluation. It is the most complex method of the four recognized methods. Under this method, instead of ranking complete jobs, each job is ranked according to a series of factors. These factors include mental effort, physical effort, skill needed, responsibility, supervisory responsibility, working conditions, and other such factors. Pay is assigned in this method by comparing the total value of the factors required for each job and dividing the result among the factors weighted by importance. Wages are assigned to the job in comparison to its ranking on each job factor.

10. **A.** The simplest method of job evaluation is the ranking method. According to this method, jobs are arranged from highest to lowest, in order of their value or merit to the organization. Jobs can also be arranged according to the relative difficulty in performing them. The jobs are examined as a whole rather than on the basis of important factors in the job; the job at the top of the list has the highest value, and obviously the job at the bottom of the list has the lowest value. The ranking method is simple to understand and practice; it is best suited for a small organization. The downside is that this kind of ranking is highly subjective in nature.

11. **D.** The piece-rate pay method compensates employees a set amount for each unit of work completed. For example, in a manufacturing setting, an employee receives a set amount for each item they produce, regardless of how fast or slow they work.

12. **B.** The Equal Pay Act requires that men and women be given equal pay for equal work in the same establishment. The jobs need not be identical, but they must be substantially equal. It is job content, not job titles, that determines whether jobs are substantially equal.

13. **B.** Reporting time pay is a guarantee of at least partial compensation for employees who report to their job expecting to work a specified number of hours but who are deprived of that amount of work because of inadequate scheduling or lack of proper notice by the employer. On-call pay is pay legally required for time an employee must be on duty, on the employer premises, or at any other prescribed place of work. Premium pay is additional pay provided to employees for working certain types of hours or under certain types of conditions. Travel pay that is home-to-work travel is generally not compensable.

14. **C.** Workers' compensation is a "no-fault" insurance plan that is paid even if an accident is the employee's fault. The other three choices are incorrect.

15. **A.** A high-deductible health plan (HDHP) that includes a tax-advantaged health savings account to pay for the cost of the deductible is known as consumer-driven healthcare.

16. **C.** Broadbanding is the term applied to having extremely wide salary bands, much more encompassing than with traditional salary structures. Whereas a typical salary band has a 40 percent difference in pay between its minimum and maximum, broadbanding would typically have a 100 percent difference. This is done to reduce an organization's hierarchy that facilitates movement within the organization. The other three choices are incorrect.

17. **C.** When an employee is overpaid, a salary term describes their base pay as a red circle rate, or a rate of pay that is above the maximum salary for a position. A red circle policy is a common approach to addressing this situation and allowing the market to catch up with the employee's pay. A green circle rate denotes any individual employee's salary that falls below the minimum of the organization's pay range. Pay differential is simply a difference in pay in response to external factors. A compressed salary situation occurs whenever the difference in salary levels reaches a minimum difference between one level and the other. This occurs when external factors artificially inflate applicable salary levels.

18. **C.** This is a policy of compensation whereby employees are all paid at the same rate as opposed to being paid within a pay range. This is typical in a situation where the job being performed is so similar that there really isn't room for a wide range of skill level.

19. **B.** Employee benefits are regulated by the Employee Retirement Income Security Act (ERISA). The other three choices are regulated by the Fair Labor Standards Act (FLSA).

20. **B.** Workers' compensation is regulated by the states. At the turn of the twentieth century, workers' compensation laws were voluntary for several reasons. Some argued that compulsory workers' compensation laws would violate the 14th Amendment due process clause of the U.S. Constitution. Many felt that compulsory participation would deprive the employer of property without due process. The issue of due process was resolved by the United States Supreme Court in 1917. After the ruling, many states enacted new compulsory workers' compensation laws. The other three choices are incorrect.

Endnotes

1. 79 FR 20749, accessed on October 18, 2021, https://www.govinfo.gov/app/details/FR-2014-04-11/2014-08426

2. Office of Personnel Management Policy Data and Oversight, accessed on October 18, 2021, https://www.opm.gov/policy-data-oversight/pay-leave/pay-systems/general-schedule/

3. Korn Ferry Hay Group, "Job Evaluation: Foundations and Applications," accessed on October 19, 2021, https://www.kornferry.com/content/dam/kornferry/docs/pdfs/job-evaluation.pdf

4. Healthcare.gov, "What Marketplace Health Insurance Plans Cover," accessed on October 22, 2021, https://www.healthcare.gov/coverage/what-marketplace-plans-cover/

Employee Relations

The functional area Employee Relations will be 24 percent of the Associate Professional in Human Resources (aPHR) exam weighting. For both human resource professionals and managers, employee relations is a very important responsibility because it is focused on "people." No organization can run without people to do the work necessary to accomplish organizational goals.

For early-career HR roles, employee relations is concerned with many things, from how the organization communicates with employees and creates policies, to managing conflict and performance. Many of these responsibilities are guided by federal, state, and local laws. That's why the Employee Relations function partners closely with a labor attorney. However, while a labor attorney can be a helpful guide, HR is responsible for applying the laws in practical terms so managers and employees alike are able to perform their functions appropriately.

The Body of Knowledge (BoK) statements outlined by HR Certification Institute (HRCI) for the Employee Relations functional area by those performing early-career HR roles are as follows:

Knowledge of

- **01** The purpose and difference between mission, vision, and value statements as well as how they influence an organization's culture and employees

- **02** How HR supports organizational goals and objectives through HR policies, procedures, and operations; for example, functions of human resource information systems (HRISs), organizational structures, preparing HR-related documents, basic communication flows and methods, SWOT analysis, and strategic planning

- **03** Techniques used to engage employees, collect feedback, and improve employee satisfaction; for example, employee recognition programs, stay interviews, engagement surveys, work/life balance initiatives, and alternative work arrangements

- **04** Workforce management throughout the employee lifecycle, including performance management and employee behavior issues; for example, goal setting, benchmarking, performance appraisal methods and biases, ranking/rating scales, progressive discipline, termination/separation, offboarding, absenteeism, and turnover/retention

- **05** Policies and procedures to handle employee complaints, facilitate investigations, and support conflict resolution; for example, confidentiality, escalation, retaliation, and documentation

- **06** The elements of diversity and inclusion initiatives and the impact on organizational effectiveness and productivity; for example, social responsibility initiatives, cultural sensitivity and acceptance, unconscious bias, and stereotypes

Laws and Regulations

As with all the other chapters, you will find more details about laws that apply to employee and labor relations in Chapter 2. Look to that chapter for information each time you come across a reference to a law you don't understand or have yet to hear about. Figure 6-1 lists some of the federal laws that apply to this functional area.

EXAM TIP Whenever you see the term *labor relations,* it means you are talking about employees who are represented by a union.

State Laws

Each state can pass its own employee relations laws—and many have. At the state level you will find such coverage as these, governing the following topics:

- Expansion of benefits beyond those provided for in federal law
- State disability insurance programs
- Unemployment insurance programs
- Paid sick leave
- Equal employment opportunity protections for classes beyond those in federal law
- Wage and hour requirements for overtime rates and rules of application

It is often the case that a state law covers the same topic as a federal law but offers more protections for employees. In this scenario, you should follow whichever law is more "generous" to employees.

Federal Regulations

When Congress passes a law, it is up to the appropriate department (or agency) such as the U.S. Department of Labor (and the National Labor Relations Board) to develop and publish proposed regulations that will implement the new law. Once the proposed

• Davis-Bacon Act of 1931	• Electronic Communications Privacy Act of 1986
• Employee Polygraph Protection Act of 1988	• Equal Pay Act of 1963
• Fair and Accurate Credit Transactions Act of 2003	• Fair Credit Reporting Act of 1970
• Fair Labor Standards Act of 1938	• Immigration and Nationality Act of 1952
• Immigration Reform and Control Act of 1986	• Labor-Management Relations Act of 1947 (Taft-Hartley Act)
• Labor-Management Reporting and Disclosure Act of 1959 (Landrum-Griffin Act)	• National Labor Relations Act of 1935
• Norris-LaGuardia Act of 1932	• Portal-to-Portal Act of 1947
• Railway Labor Act of 1926	• Service Contract Act of 1965
• Federal Insurance Contributions Act of 1935 (Social Security Act)	• Uniformed Services Employment and Reemployment Rights Act of 1994
• Vietnam Era Veterans Readjustment Assistance Act of 1974	• Wagner-Peyser Act of 1933 (Amended by Workforce Investment Act of 1998)
• Walsh-Healey Act of 1936 (Public Contracts Act)	• Civil Rights Act of 1964 (Title VII)
• Civil Rights Act of 1991	• Drug-Free Workplace Act of 1988
• Genetic Information Nondiscrimination Act of 2008	• Lilly Ledbetter Fair Pay Act of 2009
• Pregnancy Discrimination Act of 1978	• Uniform Guidelines on Employee Selection Procedures of 1976
• Age Discrimination in Employment Act of 1967	• Worker Adjustment and Retraining Notification Act of 1988
• Occupational Safety and Health Act of 1970	• Needlestick Safety and Prevention Act of 2000

Figure 6-1 Key federal laws impacting employee and labor relations

regulations are published, there is a requirement for a public comment period. At the close of the public comment period, the department will review the comments, make any changes it believes appropriate in the regulation proposal, and publish either the final regulations or a revised proposal with a new public comment period. Once published as final, the regulations will carry an implementation date (or dates for individual components of the law's requirements). Once that date has arrived, all employment organizations subject to the new law and regulations will be obligated to comply.

Rights and Responsibilities

One important aspect of employee relations is rights and responsibilities. As with any relationship, each party (employee and employer) must allow for certain rights and responsibilities for the relationship to continue in a healthy and productive way. Doing this is part of complying with the laws that are passed.

Employer

Employer responsibilities include such things as treating employees in accordance with the principle of "good faith and fair dealing." It is more than an ethical requirement. Good faith and fair dealing is a legal covenant. Employers are expected to honor commitments made to employees when employees are convinced to act based on those employer promises. For example, when a manager interviews the best qualified job candidate and says, "We really want you to move out to our state and be part of this organization. We will have a job for you for as long as you want it," the employer has enticed the candidate into action based on the promise of permanent employment. If the employer cuts the new employee off the payroll when downsizing the organization, it has broken its obligation under the covenant of good faith and fair dealing. The result can be a lawsuit based on contract law.

Employer rights include the expectation that employees will work for a full 8 hours each day they are scheduled for 8 hours. The employer has a right to ensure worker behavior while on the job meets with policy requirements, and the employer has the right to inspect employee work product, work space, and communication related to work.

Employee

Employees have the right to expect they will be treated with good faith and fairly by their employer. They have the right to proper wage calculation and prompt payment. They have the right to full benefit provisions as provided by organizational policy and contract provisions.

Employees also have responsibilities. Those include the responsibility to give a full 8 hours of effort for an 8-hour workday, compliance with all employer policies, and treatment of everyone in the workplace with civility.

Organizational Strategy

Employee relations programs should be aligned with an organization's vision, mission, values, goals, and objectives. All employee relations programs communicate organizational strategy in some way. For example, a performance evaluation usually rates employee performance based on certain expectations, outputs, and behaviors. These may be attendance, customer service, following policies, creativity, and so on. The options are endless. However, what is important is that the categories chosen for the performance evaluation align with the things the organization cares about and hopes to accomplish.

Employees and the organization are ultimately more successful when there is a shared understanding of the things that are important. For example, a core value of "honesty" may not be relatable to employees if there are not programs for constructive feedback, mediums for reporting employee concerns such as an open-door policy, or an option for anonymous reporting of serious breaches of organizational policy.

Mission

A mission is a written declaration of an organization's core purpose and focus that normally remains unchanged over time. Properly crafted mission statements do the following:

- Serve as filters to separate what is important from what is not
- Clearly state which markets will be served and how
- Communicate a sense of intended direction to the entire organization

Vision

A vision is different from a mission. A mission is something to be accomplished, whereas a vision is more of an inspirational statement. It describes what the organization envisions for the future if it fulfills its mission. A vision is intended to serve as a clear guide for choosing current and future courses of action.

Values

Values are important and lasting beliefs or ideals shared by the members of a culture about what is good or bad and desirable or undesirable. Values have a major influence on a person's behavior and attitude, and they serve as broad guidelines in all situations. Some common business values are fairness, innovation, and community involvement.

Goals and Objectives

Objectives define strategies or implementation steps to attain the identified goals. Unlike goals, objectives are specific and measurable and have a defined completion date. Objectives follow the SMART test (specific, measurable, achievable, relevant, and timed). They outline the "who, what, when, where, and how" of reaching the goals.

Strategic Planning

Strategic planning is a regular process that executive management in all functional areas is involved in. It flows from an organization's mission, vision, values, goals, and objectives. It describes the direction the organization wants to go in and how resources should be allocated to pursue this direction. The annual budget each year is usually an output of strategic planning.

A common technique for strategic planning is a SWOT analysis. SWOT stands for strengths, weaknesses, opportunities, and threats. Strengths and weaknesses are looked at as internal factors within the organization that can be managed. Opportunities and threats are controlled by external forces. SWOT analysis is a long-standing simple process used in strategic planning for collecting information about an organization's current state. Four foundational questions are posed:

- **S:** What are the organization's strengths?
- **W:** What are the organization's weaknesses?

Organizational Need	HR Contribution
Cost containment	• Payroll costs • Benefit plan costs (for example, health insurance, life insurance, disability insurance, and time-off policies) • Union contract provisions • Recruiting expenses
Employee and management support	• Recruiting • Training • Coaching for supervisors and managers • Safety program planning and implementation
Data management	• HRIS • Reporting service (for example, safety, recruiting and hiring, employee service reports, and retention)

Table 6-1 HR's Contribution to the Strategic Plan

- **O:** What external opportunities might help the organization to progress toward its vision?
- **T:** What external threats could foil the organization's plans and business?

HR's role in the strategic plan is to align its initiatives with the organization's objectives. Having the right number of people, with the right capabilities, at the right times, and in the right places, engaged and motivated to do the right things is HR's primary support role for the organization. For example, recruitment initiatives must align with plans for opening a new facility. Retention incentives such as compensation and benefits should fit into the organization's plans for holding on to key employee groups.

What will be the human resource department's contribution to the enterprise strategic plan? Table 6-1 outlines some things that are fairly common.

Organizational Structure

A business structure, otherwise known as an *organizational structure,* defines how activities such as task allocation, coordination, and supervision are directed toward the achievement of organizational aims. It can also be considered the viewing glass or perspective through which individuals see their organization and its environment.

The four main types of organizational structure are flat, functional, divisional, and matrix, as detailed next:

- **Flat**   A flat organization (also known as a *horizontal* organization or delayering) has an organizational structure with few or no levels of middle management between staff and executives. The advantages of this type of structure are that it elevates the employees' level of responsibility in the organization, and it removes excess layers of management, which improves the coordination and speed of communication between employees. Fewer levels of management encourage an easier decision-making process among employees. The disadvantages are that employees often lack a specific boss to report to, which creates confusion and possible power struggles among management. Also, flat organizations tend to produce a lot of generalists but no specialists, and the specific job functions of employees may not be clear. A flat structure may limit the long-term growth of an organization; management may decide against new opportunities in an effort to maintain the structure. Larger organizations struggle to adapt the flat structure, unless the company divides into smaller, more manageable units.

- **Functional** A functional structure is set up so that each portion of the organization is grouped according to its purpose. In this type of organization there may be a marketing department, a sales department, and a production department. The functional structure works well for small businesses in which each department can rely on the talent and knowledge of its workers and support itself. One of the drawbacks to a functional structure is that the coordination and communication between departments can be restricted by the organizational boundaries of having the various departments working separately.

- **Divisional** A divisional structure typically is used in larger companies that operate in a wide geographic area or that have separate smaller organizations within the umbrella group to cover different types of products or market areas. Many automotive manufacturers such as Toyota have a divisional structure, with divisions for each car brand, a parts division, and divisions for each geographic area. The benefit of this structure is that needs can be met more rapidly and more specifically; however, communication is inhibited because employees in different divisions are not working together. Divisional structure is costly because of its size and scope. Small businesses can use a divisional structure on a smaller scale, having different offices in different parts of the city, for example, or assigning different sales teams to handle different geographic areas.

- **Matrix** The matrix structure is a hybrid of the divisional and functional structures. Typically used in large multinational companies, the matrix structure allows for the benefits of functional and divisional structures to exist in one organization. This can create power struggles because most areas of the company will have dual management—a functional manager and a product or divisional manager working at the same level and covering some of the same managerial territory.

 EXAM TIP The advantage of a functional structure is that it promotes skill specialization; the disadvantage is that it reduces communication and cooperation between departments.

Organizational Communication

Following from organizational structure is the consideration of how communication flows through the organization. Depending on an organization's structure, communication may be easier or more difficult. For example, in a flat organizational structure, employees in all departments may work together closely, and communication is relatively seamless. In a divisional structure, especially where employees are separately geographically, other departments can be "out of sight, out of mind," resulting in strained communication.

Workplace communication is the process of exchanging information, both verbal and nonverbal, within an organization. An organization may consist of employees from different parts of the society. They may have different cultures and backgrounds and can be used to different norms. To unite activities of all employees and restrain from any missed deadline or activity that could affect the company negatively, communication is crucial. Workplace communication is tremendously important to organizations because it increases productivity and efficiency. Ineffective workplace communication leads to communication gaps between employees, which causes confusion, wastes time, and reduces productivity.

Communication starts from the top. Management should always be thinking about whether communication is effective and which new methods of communication could be more productive. For example, are more meetings needed between departments? A monthly newsletter to all employees? More e-mails updating employees on the status of projects? The options are endless. Whether interacting with colleagues, subordinates, managers, customers, or vendors, employees' ability to communicate effectively using a variety of tools is essential.

Also, nonverbal communication must be taken into consideration. How a person delivers a message has a lot of influence on how it is perceived. HR is often responsible for management communication training, which emphasizes skills for nonverbal and verbal communication.

E-mail Communication

As technology becomes even more prevalent, workplaces find themselves communicating via e-mail more than ever. E-mail communication is an art. It is easy for a reader to construe a whole different meaning from an e-mail message than what was originally intended.

Here are some tips concerning e-mail etiquette:

- Start on a personal note.
- Tame the emotions.
- Keep it short and sweet.
- Read it twice.
- Master the subject line by making it clear and concise.

Human Resource Information Systems (HRISs)

HR professionals coordinate a wide variety of employee activities that involve large amounts of data over time, so having a human resource information system (HRIS) can be an important part of the HR strategy. An HRIS provides data management and accurate and timely information for decision-making. It also streamlines

HR processes by reducing the amount of time spent on daily transaction activities, such as tracking employee status changes. It frees the HR team to work on tasks that are more aligned with the organization's goals and strategy.

An HRIS functions as a productivity tool for HR. Increased speed and accuracy result when HR transactions are performed with computer software rather than manually. Routine transactions such as employee headcount, payroll tracking, and time and attendance reporting become automated and more cost effective.

Data for legal compliance and reporting can also be housed in an HRIS, such as data about staffing, turnover, benefits, and regulatory compliance issues. HR staff can provide reports on the total number of employees, cost to hire, vacant positions, benefits costs, required reports such as EEO-1, and the cost of raises and bonuses.

A company's HRIS also functions as an executive information system to aggregate high-level data for long-range planning such as succession planning. The system provides information for strategic needs such as forecasting, staffing needs assessment, and employee skills assessment.

Lastly, an HRIS can also function as an office automation system to design employee documents such as job applications and requisitions, to schedule shared resources such as a conference room, and to schedule and track employee training. All employee communication, such as newsletters, employee handbooks, and benefits changes, can also be housed in an HRIS.

Human Resource Policies

HR policies are guidelines on the approach the organization intends to adopt in managing its people. HR policies are written statements of the company's standards and objectives and include all areas of employment. They contain rules on how employees must perform their jobs and interact with each other.

EXAM TIP   HR policies serve three major purposes: to reassure employees they will be treated fairly and objectively, to help managers make rapid and consistent decisions, and to give managers the confidence to resolve problems and defend their decisions.

Employee Handbook

The terms *employee handbook* and *policy manual* are often used interchangeably. Regardless of the term used, this document sets forth expectations for employees and describes what they can expect from the company. It should also describe legal obligations such as the employer's and employees' rights.

Many states have rather strict laws about employment policies and their communication with workers. Generally, it is not acceptable to make policies effective retroactively. Plan to circulate any policy changes or additions to your employees with sufficient time for them to digest and adjust to the requirements before the implementation date.

NOTE Attorneys recommend having employees sign a document acknowledging receipt of the employee handbook. It doesn't mean they agree with everything in the handbook but rather that they have received a personal copy. This is helpful in preventing legal claims.

Developing an employee handbook can take a short amount of time or a considerable amount of time. It is important to involve other departments and employees in the process to make sure the handbook is both legally compliant and accurately communicates organizational values and goals. If the organization has unions, it may be necessary to negotiate policy changes through the collective bargaining process.

When writing an employee handbook, keep in mind that it typically includes the following topics:

- **ADA policy**   The duty to provide reasonable accommodation is required under the Americans with Disabilities Act (ADA). To comply with the ADA, attain diversity goals, access a larger labor pool, and take advantage of tax incentives, most employers adopt a written policy with a formal, comprehensive approach to employing people with disabilities.

- **EEO policy**   Employees must be informed of their right to be free from workplace discrimination and retaliation. EEO policies also apply to vendors, contractors, and other third parties with whom the employer conducts business. State or local laws may expand the list of protected categories.

- **Harassment policy**   It is important for employees to understand that the organization has zero-tolerance for harassment and what avenues are available for reporting and resolving complaints.

- **Non-disclosure agreements (NDAs) and conflict-of-interest statements** Although NDAs are not legally required, having employees sign NDAs and conflict-of-interest statements helps to protect company trade secrets and proprietary information.

- **Compensation**   Clearly explain to employees that the organization will make required deductions for federal and state taxes, as well as voluntary deductions for the company's benefits programs. In addition, the handbook should outline legal obligations regarding overtime pay, pay schedules, performance reviews, salary increases, time-keeping records, breaks, and bonuses.

- **Workers' compensation**   Clearly describe applicable employee rights and benefits as provided for under the organization's workers' compensation program.

- **Work schedules**   Describe work hours and schedules as well as procedures for tracking attendance, maintaining punctuality, and reporting absences, along with guidelines for flexible schedules and telecommuting.

- **Standards of conduct**   Document expectations of how the organization wants employees to conduct themselves, including dress code and ethics. In addition, remind employees of their legal obligations, especially if the organization is engaged in an activity that is regulated by the government.

- **Progressive discipline**   Progressive discipline generally includes a series of increasingly severe penalties for repeated offenses, typically beginning with counseling or a verbal warning. Such procedures help ensure consistent treatment of employees and can minimize exposure to discrimination claims.

- **Employee lifecycle information**   An employee handbook should include an overview of the employee lifecycle, including job classifications, employee referrals, employee records, job postings, performance reviews, termination and resignation procedures, transfers and relocation, and union information, if applicable.

- **Safety and security**   Safety policies should focus on commitment to a safe and secure work environment. The Occupational Safety and Health Administration's laws require employees to report all accidents, injuries, potential safety hazards, safety suggestions, and health- and safety-related issues to management. Safety policies should also include policies regarding bad weather, hazardous community conditions, and locking file cabinets or computers when not in use.

- **Computers and technology**   Outline policies for appropriate computer and software use and the steps employees should take to secure electronic information, especially any personal identifiable information you collect from your customers.

 EXAM TIP   Employers need to be cautious when using employee handbooks to prohibit undesirable behavior outside of the workplace, especially with respect to social media because of freedom of speech under the First Amendment to the U.S. Constitution.

Employee Engagement Programs

When you consider that full-time employees spend about 2,000 hours per year at work, more of employees' waking hours may be spent in the workplace than in their homes. For employees to be productive, there needs to be a certain degree of satisfaction. More satisfied employees perform better and are more likely to stay with an organization long term. This is the ultimate goal of employee engagement programs and why they are so important.

Recognition

The larger an organization grows, the greater the likelihood that its recognition programs will be structured. In small organizations, recognition can be given in many forms, often as events unfold and accomplishments are achieved.

Employee recognition works best when it is meaningful to employees. Therefore, it follows that every organization will have a slightly different kind of recognition program. However, the most common types of programs include service anniversary awards, employee-of-the-month awards, employee suggestion awards, sales achievement awards, team achievement awards, individual achievement awards, or peer-to-peer awards. Obviously, that is not an exhaustive list. You can add others and apply them as your organization finds a fit between the recognition and the accomplishment.

Service Anniversary Awards

Employee recognition often includes anniversary awards recognizing years of service with an organization. Some organizations provide plaques, certificates, or pins. A growing number of recognition program service providers can also offer employees a catalog of award choices based on their service milestone.

Employee-of-the-Month Awards

Employee-of-the-month awards are a great way to recognize employee achievements on a regular basis. Rewards can include designated parking spaces, plaques or bulletin board posting, or a special benefit like a dinner gift card.

Employee Suggestion Awards

Cost savings suggestions offered by employees benefit the employer and should be rewarded. Common rewards range from cash to paid time off or even paid travel excursions.

Sales Achievement Awards

Sales achievement awards are dependent on reaching certain pre-announced sales goals. Often rewards in this category involve some type of financial benefit to the employee. It can be cash, paid travel, or gift cards that can be spent on something the employee really would like to have.

Team Achievement Awards

Team achievement awards come into play when the team of workers has pre-established work goals that will result in a benefit to the company if achieved. It can be a production goal, a safety record, or absence control. The reward can be anything from a pizza party to a free night at the movies or a dinner out. Sometimes, teams are awarded paid time off for their accomplishments. It is something the employer can customize to its own culture.

Individual Achievement Awards

Individual achievement awards are like team awards in many respects. The rewards can be much the same, and they are made because of a special achievement by an individual employee. It could be a production award, an accomplishment in production quality, contribution of suggestions for improving the workflow, or any other personal idea.

Peer-to-Peer Awards

When peers receive recognition from coworkers, it has special meaning. Getting colleague approval is a great motivator. Many HRISs and recognition programs now include peer-to-peer recognition in the form of a company social media website, operating like a Facebook or Instagram feed.

Work/Life Balance

One of the main reasons employees work is to earn money to secure a better quality of life for themselves and their families. Therefore, giving employees the time and flexibility to enjoy their personal lives is a valued benefit. This may come in the form of flexible work hours to attend to family or personal matters or more vacation time.

Work/life balance can also be improved with technology. There are many ways to accomplish work from anywhere nowadays. There are also technologies to make collaboration and information sharing more efficient than ever. That said, technology can have its downsides if not used properly. Managers must be mindful of e-mailing or texting employees 24/7, especially when they are on vacation.

Alternative Work Arrangements

In recent years with the growth of technology, it has become possible for employees to work from anywhere, at any time. In 2020, a survey by the Pew Research Center indicated that 71 percent of workers were capable of working from home all or most of the time.[1] As long as the organization's expectations are met for the quality and quantity of work, working remotely can be effective and a highly desired employee benefit.

Alternative work arrangements also come in the form of compressed workweeks (three 12-hour shifts or four 10-hour shifts), half workdays on Friday, or earlier or later work shifts. This list is not exhaustive. The right arrangement depends on the balance between the organization's needs, the job's responsibilities, and the employee's needs.

Special Events

There are many types of special events. They can include company parties, holiday celebrations, company days at the local amusement park, paid excursions, or a night out. Special events offer a thank-you and recognition to the entire group of employees.

Company Parties

Company parties are a common way of rewarding groups of people at one time. A common version of this event is a company day out at the local amusement park. Whether it is a water park in August or Disneyland in January, sponsoring these events is a way for a company to acknowledge the hard work put in by its employees.

Company picnics are another common offering that allows an employer to say "thank you" to its employees by inviting their families to participate. What is better than a fire-roasted hot dog and an ice cream cone after a three-legged race with coworkers? Consumption of alcohol at such events has been reduced in recent years because of liability issues faced by company hosts. Some say that alcohol will not be served just to avoid the liability of people driving while intoxicated.

Holiday Celebrations

Holiday parties happen around December celebrations such as Christmas, Hanukkah, and Kwanzaa. They are year-end events that acknowledge all that has happened during the year and all the work put in by employees to help the company achieve its objectives.

Parties can be held in the office with light refreshments, or they can be more elaborate celebrations with meals involving employees only or employees and their families. Budget is the main controller of the agenda.

Some people really enjoy decorating for the holidays. Independence Day, Halloween, Thanksgiving, Christmas, Hanukkah, and Kwanzaa decorations tend to make a workplace livelier. They help lighten the atmosphere at work. Sometimes, the HR department is placed in charge of decorating, and other times a committee of interested workers can handle the effort. Company funding of the decorative materials is usually provided.

Employee Feedback

Employee feedback is necessary to assess many conditions in the workplace, including morale, job satisfaction, and ideas for innovation and improvements. Common methods of soliciting feedback include employee surveys, stay interviews, or focus groups.

 EXAM TIP   Since employee feedback is so critical to successful business operations today, you can expect that the certification exam will contain questions about the methods of collecting employee feedback and how it can be used.

Employee Surveys

There are a host of methods for assessing employee morale, work satisfaction, and communication quality and effectiveness. One method that is held as extremely helpful in providing direct feedback is the survey format. Employee surveys can be used to gather information directly from employees and can be applied immediately following a major employment event. For example, when new benefit programs are introduced, surveys can be used to identify employee reactions to the new offerings and the ease with which they have access to those programs. Surveys are most commonly used to determine how engaged workers are within the organization.

Engagement Surveys

Employee engagement surveys are used to improve morale, productivity, engagement, and to reduce turnover by gathering actionable feedback on job experiences. These surveys are usually prepared and administered by professional consultants. When professionals prepare a survey, there is more assurance that the survey is valid and measures what you want it to. Also, when an outsider administers the survey and tabulates results, employees can be sure that their responses are confidential. Some vendors also offer standard engagement surveys that are less expensive than a customized version.

Topics covered in employee engagement surveys can include job-related training, supervisor treatment, employment policies and their impact on individual employees, satisfaction with compensation programs, and satisfaction with benefit programs such as healthcare insurance and vacation policies. Responses can be offered on a scale such as "more likely" to "less likely" or "strongly agree" to "strongly disagree."

At some time, it is generally helpful to get feedback about employee attitudes on all topics that touch their lives as workers. Many employers conduct engagement surveys annually to measure changes from year to year.

360/180 Degree Surveys

Taken literally, 360 degree surveys ask everyone around an employee to provide feedback about that person's competencies, behaviors, and contributions. In one common application, managers use these surveys to get feedback from their subordinates as well as their peers and supervisors. Usually feedback is provided anonymously.

Non-management individuals can't literally be the subject of a 360 degree feedback program because they have no subordinates, so 180 degree surveys are used where only their manager, coworkers, and internal customers are asked to provide input. Peers and supervisors can offer input to non-management people that can help with interpersonal skill development and grooming for promotional opportunities.

Stay Interviews

A stay interview is a one-on-one meeting between a manager and a highly valued employee who may be at risk of leaving the organization. The purpose is to identify the factors that will entice the employee to stay with the employer rather than change jobs. If it is possible to identify conditions or "triggers" that might cause the employee to leave, the employee's exit may be preventable. These meetings can be used by any sized organization to increase retention of people who are major contributors to achieving objectives. While it is not always possible to meet all conditions, just listening to the employee can go a long way in making them feel that they are valued by the employer.

Processes for Obtaining Feedback

There are many ways to collect feedback from employees. Here are some of the most common processes used today. All have been used for decades, yet they remain the best tools for gathering input from groups of people.

Paper Surveys

Using paper and pencil seems like the most basic approach to recording opinions. Yet, that process is still one of the most effective. Properly prepared questions will yield a wealth of information that can be digested and then used to produce actionable items. If there is a new policy to be considered, employee attitudes about such a change can be invaluable before the change is made. Avoiding decisions that employees view as undesirable is preferable to correcting the bad decision after it has been implemented.

Even though we live in a digital age, there are many employees, and even entire workplaces, that lack computers. Factory workers are a good example. In some cases, computers may be brought in and set up on kiosk displays to overcome that deficiency. In other instances, introducing computers may not be an option, so paper and pencil surveys remain the standard. Making survey responses anonymous can be achieved if employees return them by mail to an address that is not a company work location. Having a third party summarize the responses can ensure confidentiality.

Computer-Based Surveys

When computers are available, presenting surveys digitally can be a good option. Advantages include the speed of response summaries and the ability to track which employees have responded and which have yet to log on and take the survey. That isn't the same as tracking individual responses. Just knowing who has yet to participate can increase the feedback percentage substantially.

Computer-based surveys can be made available on employee personal computers so the surveys can be accessed from home. Usually, when computers are made available to workers on the job, the survey is taken at work during work time.

Computer-based surveys can often be accessed from smart phones, laptops, tablet computers, or desktop computers. That flexibility of access can increase initial participation rates substantially.

Focus Groups

For an in-depth exploration of issues and testing of alternatives, focus groups offer an excellent opportunity to probe initial survey responses and go into more detail. With a properly skilled facilitator, focus groups can provide excellent information about employee beliefs. For example, when options exist for increasing employee benefits, getting employee input about preferences can be extremely helpful in the decision-making process. Perhaps the company has budget available to increase either paid-vacation allotment or retirement pay computations. Which would employees prefer? How strongly do they feel about their preference? Would they actually like a third or fourth alternative? Focus groups provide the environment in which to probe those choices. The downside of focus groups is that they are not anonymous. Therefore, they do not apply in every situation and are sometimes best used to gather more detailed data after an all-employee survey has already been conducted.

Diversity and Inclusion Programs

Diversity and inclusion (D&I) programs help make an organization more effective by employing individuals with diverse backgrounds and experiences. For example, when employees come from different backgrounds and experiences, the way they view a problem and possible solutions may be different. Adding up all of these viewpoints and possible solutions together can be much more effective in addressing organizational problems. Also, everyone likes to have their personal heritage acknowledged, and modern workforces have representation of many diverse heritages.

Managing people from extremely different cultural backgrounds and with different generational representation is a challenge that can be addressed through a good D&I program. While it may be human nature to feel most comfortable with people like ourselves, it is becoming more and more necessary to push that comfort boundary and include other people for an organization to be successful.

Common employee activities in a D&I program are *employee resource groups* (Black engineers, Hispanic professional women, and Veteran employees, among others). These groups are endorsed by employers in many cases and are sometimes provided with facilities in which to conduct meetings or informal gatherings. When employees have an opportunity to meet with people like themselves and discuss issues associated with succeeding in the workplace, they can adjust more readily and feel better about their employer and themselves. They can also offer valuable feedback to the organization.

Some employers schedule special events or celebrations based on specific cultural groupings, such as LGBTQ+ Pride. Almost anything that recognizes and supports differences between people and cultures can expand individual employee tolerance and add value to decision-making processes. As conversations about social justice and equity have increased over the past few years, it is especially important for employers to show their commitment to these important topics.

Cultural Sensitivity and Acceptance

The topic of cultural sensitivity and acceptance usually requires an educational component. Employees are likely to know much more about their individual culture than cultures that differ from their own. Therefore, many organizations have integrated this education throughout the employee lifecycle.

This education often starts at employee orientation. Employees should be made aware of the importance of diversity to the organization and all the ways in which it is celebrated, such as through employee resource groups. Employees should also be taught to be sensitive to diversity. This might include how to respond to inquiries about office closures on religious holidays or how to assist employees or customers with disabilities.

Some employers have created entire departments focused on D&I within the HR function. These departments usually offer regular training, ensure feedback from employee resource groups is collected and communicated to management, and are in charge of cultural celebrations and social responsibility programs.

Unconscious Biases and Stereotypes

Biases and cultural stereotypes are a long-standing problem. The term *unconscious bias* is often used because thoughts or feelings about other cultures are not intentional but rather are formed in the subconscious mind as a result of society, family, and institutional influences. In order for everyone to contribute equally and effectively within an organization, biases and stereotypes must be rectified. The Implicit Association Test[2] created by Harvard University is a good way to reflect on all of the unconscious biases we hold.

Sometimes biases and stereotypes can be reduced by creating diverse project teams so employees get a chance to work closely with individuals from another cultural background and "learn while doing." Oftentimes, unconscious bias training is a formal program to help employees understand how their actions and reactions can influence others.

Cultural Celebrations

Recognizing celebrations of different cultures is a good way to show appreciation for cultural differences and educate employees on other cultural backgrounds. It can be an opportunity to give groups of employees a voice during their cultural celebrations. Table 6-2 provides a current listing for the year 2022 of cultural and religious holidays that are sometimes recognized in the United States.

Social Responsibility

Celebrating diversity and inclusion in the workplace has expanded to a broader topic called *social responsibility*, which is when organizations make strides or set goals to improve the society around them. Supporting social activism like the Black Lives Matter movement, setting targets for waste reduction, or engaging in charity work are just a few examples. Instead of simply putting an affirmative action plan on paper or creating a policy about equal employment opportunity, attending a rally to support equal pay in the workplace or sponsoring a Veterans-focused job fair helps turn words into actions.

Month	Day	Celebration
January	1	Emancipation Proclamation (Black American)
	4	Birthday of Louis Braille (People with Disabilities)
	6	Feast of the Epiphany (Christian)
	14	Makar Sankranti (Hindu)
	17	Martin Luther King Jr. Day (Black American)
	27	International Day of Commemoration in Memory of Victims of the Holocaust (United Nations)
February	All Month	Black History Month
	1	Chinese New Year
	11	Birthday of Tammy Baldwin (LGBTQ+)
	14	Birthday of Frederick Douglass (Black American)
	15	Nirvana Day (Buddhist), Birthday of Susan B. Anthony (Women)
March	2	Ash Wednesday (Christian)
	8	International Women's Day
	10	Birthday of Harriet Tubman (Black American)
	17	St. Patrick's Day (Irish)
	19	Holi (Hindu)
	21	International Day for the Elimination of Racial Discrimination (United Nations)
April	2	Ramadan (Islamic), World Autism Awareness Day (People with Disabilities)
	15	Passover (Jewish)
	17	Easter (Christian)
	22	Earth Day (International)
	21–23	Gathering of Nations (Native American)
May	All Month	Mental Health Awareness Month, Jewish American Heritage Month, Asian American and Pacific Islander Heritage Month
	5	Cinco de Mayo (Mexican American)
	8	Birthday of the Buddha (Buddhist)
	17	International Day Against Homophobia, Transphobia, and Biphobia (LGBTQ+)
	19	Birthday of Malcolm X (Black American/Muslim)
June	All Month	LGBTQ+ Pride Month, Caribbean American Heritage Month
	2	Indian Citizenship Act of 1924 (Native Americans)
	12	Loving Day (Black American)
	12	Puerto Rican Day Parade (Puerto Rican)
	19	Juneteenth (Black American)
	27	Birthday of Helen Keller (People with Disabilities)

Table 6-2   Calendar of Some Cultural and Religious Holidays[3] (*continued*)

Month	Day	Celebration
July	2	Birthday of Thurgood Marshall (Black American)
	6	Birthday of the 14th Dalai Lama (Tibetan), Birthday of Frida Kahlo (Women, Mexican)
	7	The Hajj (Islamic)
	18	Birthday of Nelson Mandela (South African)
	25	Pioneer Day (Church of Jesus Christ of Latter-day Saints)
August	9	International Day of the World's Indigenous People (United Nations)
	15	Feast of the Assumption (Roman Catholic)
	18	Birth of Lord Krishna (Hindu)
	26	Women's Equality Day (Women)
	30	Al-Hijri (Islamic)
	31	Ganesh Chaturthi (Hindu)
September	All Month	National Hispanic Heritage Month (9/15–10/15), National Recovery Month
	22	Autumnal Equinox (Various Religions)
	25–27	Rosh Hashanah (Jewish)
October	All Month	Global Diversity Awareness Month, National Disability Employment Awareness Month, Breast Cancer Awareness Month, National Polish American Heritage Month
	10	Indigenous Peoples' Day (United States), World Mental Health Day (People with Disabilities)
	21	Spirit Day (LGBTQ+)
	24	Diwali (Hindu)
November	All Month	Native American Heritage Month
	10/31–11/2	All Saints Day/All Souls Day/Día de los Muertos
	16	International Day for Tolerance (United Nations), Dutch American Heritage Day
	20	Transgender Day of Remembrance (LGBTQ+)
December	1	World AIDS Day
	3	International Day of Persons with Disabilities (United Nations)
	10	International Human Rights Day (United Nations)
	16–24	Las Posadas (Mexican)
	18–26	Hanukkah (Jewish)
	21	Winter Solstice/Yule
	25	Christmas (Christian)
	26	Kwanzaa (Black)

Table 6-2   Calendar of Some Cultural and Religious Holidays[3]

Measuring Diversity

Measurements are easy to construct. The important point to remember is that we must be careful about how we define the thing to be measured. What gets measured is what gets done. Whatever the boss emphasizes and keeps coming back to every week or month is what people will spend their days working on. If turnover of a given racial group is extremely high, we should ask why. Measurements give us information that allow further exploration into the reasons things are happening. Some of the most common measurements include workforce representation, turnover rates or longevity, the number of complaints received, and the extent to which senior management is involved in the process of improving diversity of the workforce.

Workforce Representation

Determine the percentage representation of each ethnic group in the workforce. Divide the number of individuals identifying as Hispanic by the total number of people on the payroll. Multiply that by 100, and the result is a percentage. The same can be done for any subset of the employee population. If racial or ethnic groups are underrepresented in the workplace compared to the percentage of that group in the population, ways to rectify this imbalance should be considered through hiring and employee engagement programs.

Turnover Rates (Longevity)

Another measurement of interest is the turnover rate. Again, a percentage is derived by dividing the number of individuals in a given group by the total population and then multiplying the result by 100 to get the percentage. If a given group is leaving the payroll at a faster rate than all others, there is reason to investigate further. It is also helpful to examine differences between voluntary and involuntary separations for a given group to take a closer look at the reason for separation.

Complaints Received

Is a given group generating more complaints than other groups? Determine the percentage of complaints for individual groups and compare the percentages.

Management and Executive Involvement

It is up to the executive team in any employment organization to set the pace for others to match when it comes to diversity issues. Accepting people into the workforce along with their cultural background is achieved only when executives demonstrate that acceptance is the way things are done in the organization. Having a policy that is not followed by executives is a recipe for problems.

Performance Management

Performance management is a systematic process that helps improve organizational effectiveness by providing feedback to employees on their performance results and improvement needs. It is employee accomplishments and contributions that drive the business results of an organization, so a regular feedback system discussing individual performance is at the core of a good performance management system. It ensures that employees are on course for the completion of tasks and goals that are aligned with the organization's goals, and that the resources and support are provided for the employee to perform such functions.

Employee performance management systems include the following:

- Delegating and planning work
- Setting expectations for performance results
- Continually monitoring performance
- Developing a capacity to perform to new levels for personal and professional growth
- Periodically rating performance in a summary fashion
- Providing recognition and rewarding good performance

As discussed earlier in this chapter, creating and communicating the organization's vision, mission, strategies, specific goals, and values form the foundation that is needed for the performance management system. Then, performance standards are agreed upon by both the line management and the employee on what the job requires and what will be measured. At this stage, it is essential that employees clearly understand the standards, including expected behavior standards set forth for their jobs. Feedback is the next stage and can be both informal and formal. Formal feedback would entail a written performance appraisal.

Performance Standards

Employees need to know the performance and behavior expectations of their jobs. This communication begins with the very first discussion in a job interview and certainly with the job offer and new hire onboarding orientation. The discussion continues on a consistent basis with the reinforcement of organizational standards that are outlined in employee handbooks and other written material as well as with performance appraisal review sessions. The clearer the expectations set for employees, the greater the success in having expectations met.

 NOTE In order for employees to meet job expectations, there needs to be a direct relationship between the job description's competency requirements and the performance objectives.

Performance Appraisal Methods

Most organizations conduct performance appraisals or reviews on a regular basis. The frequency of reviews depends on the organization, but common timeframes are at the 90-day mark for newly hired, transferred, or promoted employees and on an annual basis. There are varying opinions in regard to the benefits of performance reviews, but many of the benefits tie back to the employee relations function. A few of these benefits are listed here:

- Provide honest feedback to employees
- Improve organizational and departmental communication
- Make employees feel valued
- Clearly define performance expectations
- Resolve grievances
- Document poor performance
- Set goals and refocus the team

Performance appraisals can also allow an organization to *benchmark* skills that need improvement. Performance ratings on a certain job skill or behavior can be compared across the organization. By comparing this data, the organization can determine if there are departments that need more training, if more emphasis needs to be placed on this skill in HR programs, and how ratings have changed from the previous year.

Whatever the reason for doing a performance review, it is important to remember that all performance review documents should be reviewed by a human resource professional before being presented to an employee. A minor wording mistake or large fluctuation in ratings between review cycles may lead to legal issues for an employer. For example, stating that an employee needs to be more "energetic" might lead to an age discrimination claim if only the oldest worker in the department received this feedback. Also, terminating an employee for poor performance after they have received a glowing performance review a few months prior would likely receive some criticism from a judge during a wrongful termination case.

The most common performance appraisal method involves just two people: the employee and their direct supervisor. In some companies, others are asked to be involved in the appraisals, such as peers, another level of management, and sometimes colleagues in the organization whose job function interacts with the employee. These are known as 360 degree appraisals.

Category Ratings

Methods for rating performance can vary greatly, from narrative to systematic ratings. The least complex of the rating methods is the category rating, where the reviewer simply checks a level of rating on a form. Three types of rating formulas are typically used in category ratings:

- **Graphic scale**   The most common type, where the appraiser checks a place on the scale for the categories of tasks and behaviors that are listed. A typical scale is 5 points, where 1 means not meeting expectations or low, and 5 means exceeding expectations or high. These types of performance appraisals normally have a comments section that the appraiser completes that provides justification for the rating.

- **Checklist**   Another common appraisal rating in which the appraiser is provided with a set list of statements or words to describe performance. The appraiser selects the one word or statement that best describes the performance—for example, "Employee consistently meets all deadlines" or "Employee consistently misses deadlines."

- **Forced choice**   A variation of the checklist approach, but in the checklist method, the appraiser is required to check two of four statements. One check is for the statement that is most like the employee's performance and the other check is for the statement that is least like the employee's performance—a combination of positive and negative statements. This method can be difficult for employees to understand.

Comparative Methods

With comparative methods, employee performance is compared directly with others in the same job. The appraiser will rank the employees in a group from highest to lowest in performance. This causes a forced distribution known as a bell curve. Ten percent will fall in the highest and lowest parts of the rating scale, another 20 percent will fall on either side, and then 40 percent will meet job standards and expectations. An obvious fault with this type of system is suggesting that a percentage of employees will fall below expectations. Figure 6-2 displays a bell curve distribution.

Narrative Methods

Narrative evaluations are time-consuming for an appraiser to complete, yet they can be the most meaningful to the employee being evaluated. Three methods are the most common for the narrative appraisal.

- **Essay format**   The appraiser writes an essay type of narrative describing each category of performance.

- **Critical incident**   The appraiser logs dates and details of both good and not-so-good performance incidents. This method requires the appraiser to keep good, detailed notes on a routine basis during the appraisal period and not rely solely on an employee's most recent performance.

Figure 6-2
Bell curve
distribution

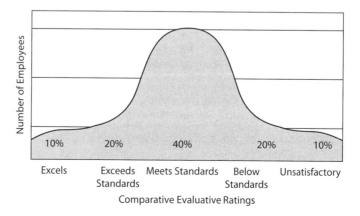

- **Behaviorally anchored rating methods**   Referred to as BARS, this appraisal method describes desirable behavior and undesirable behavior. Examples are then compared with a scale of performance level for the rating. BARS works well in circumstances in which several employees perform the same function. A BARS appraisal system requires extensive time to develop and maintain to keep the performance dimensions up to date as the job functions change. However, the BARS method offers a more accurate gauge of performance measurement, provides clearer standards to employees, and results in more consistent ratings.

Self-Assessment

Coupled with the direct supervisory management evaluation, many employees are asked to self-assess their performance. This approach creates a true two-way dialogue in the evaluation and offers an opportunity for the employee to provide their own perception of their performance. Additionally, it allows employees to create their own goals and objectives, along with triggering a discussion about career development.

Shortcomings of Performance Appraisals

As with any subjective system—and performance appraisals are subjective because they are based on people's perceptions and opinions—there can be shortcomings. Here are the most common errors made on the part of appraisers:

- **Halo**   This occurs when the employee is doing well in one area and is therefore rated high in all areas.

- **Horn**   This occurs when an employee is demonstrating a strong weakness and is thus rated low in all other areas.

- **Bias**   This happens when the evaluator's bias (consciously or unconsciously) influences and distorts their perspective.

- **Recency**   A recency error occurs when more emphasis is placed on a recent occurrence, and all earlier performances during the review period are discounted.

- **Primacy**   The opposite of recency. The evaluator gives more weight and emphasis to earlier performances, discounting more recent performance.

- **Strictness**   The evaluator is reluctant to give high ratings, and their standards are higher than other evaluators.

- **Leniency**   The evaluator does not provide low scores and instead gives all employees a high rating on their appraisals.

- **Central**   The evaluator rates all of their employees in the same range and does not consider differences of actual performance among the group rated.

- **Contrast**   The evaluator is providing an employee rating based solely on a comparison to that of another employee, and not objective standards.

NOTE These common errors can be avoided with narrative format methods, or appraisals that include rating and narrative responses to help catch potential biases in ratings.

Performance Improvement Plan (PIP)

If an employee is performing below expectations, the next step to improve poor performance is often a performance improvement plan (PIP). A PIP outlines areas where performance improvement is needed, the expected timeline for improvement, and resources and support for improvement. Employees are often placed on a PIP for a certain period of time. During this time period, generally 60 or 90 days, job performance is monitored closely. Employees are expected to make noticeable performance improvements and make use of the resources assigned to or made available to them. If an employee does not successfully complete a PIP, involuntary termination is generally the next step.

Before issuing a PIP to an employee, it is wise to obtain a legal review of the document. Because PIPs are generally the final document that supports a termination decision, there will be much scrutiny of the document if the employee sues the organization after termination.

Workplace Behavior

Behaviors are things that we do or say. Behaving is the act of saying something or doing something. There are good behaviors and bad behaviors from the viewpoint of an employer. Workplace policies usually include a description of acceptable behaviors and/or unacceptable behaviors. Workplace behavior is a factor to be considered in an employee's performance evaluation.

Attendance and Absenteeism

Actually showing up to work and being on time is viewed as a requirement by many employers. An employee who can't do one or the other may not be acceptable in the eyes of the employer.

Identifying Standards

Each employer must establish its own standards for attendance and punctuality. That means it must answer questions like "How many minutes after the beginning of a work shift should be allowed before an employee is considered tardy?" Standards for employee absence can be developed by using questions like "How many days will we allow an employee to be missing from work without proclaiming them to have an absenteeism problem?"

Establishing standards is a key step in managing these two behaviors that have a great impact on work performance. Even in organizations that have adopted an "unlimited vacation" policy, there must be some limit. If not, the standard is wide open, and employees can be absent as much as they wish. The policy then is really a "not to exceed" limit that can be substantial. For example, an "unlimited vacation policy" can permit up to 90 days in any given calendar year, and the quantity of days that will be paid can be determined based on company tenure, like in other circumstances. If an employee decides to take 6 or 7 months off work, is that permissible under the policy? If not, when does it cross the line?

Violation of Standards

When the standard is not met, what happens? Sometimes nothing. Appropriately, what should happen is disciplinary action. That means beginning with a discussion and working through the progressive discipline process until the problem is solved because the behavior has changed. When the employee begins showing up for work again and/or begins arriving on time each day, the behavior has changed, and it is no longer necessary to move further through the discipline progression.

As with all other disciplinary programs, these standards should be consistent from one situation to another when circumstances are the same. Treating employees inconsistently can result in charges of illegal discrimination.

Improvement Programs

An improvement program is a formalized approach to correcting inappropriate behavior. If an employee needs to improve attendance, it may be necessary to create an improvement program for their attendance problem. It might look something like this:

Sample Attendance Improvement Program

1. Have the initial meeting with the employee to review the attendance record.

2. Compare the attendance record with the standard expected of all employees.

3. Explain that the employee will be expected to have no absences (paid or unpaid) during the coming 30 days.

4. Any absence in the next 30 days will result in an unpaid suspension of 2 days and a final warning.

5. After the suspension, a new 30-day period will begin. Any absence during that 30-day period will result in termination of employment.

6. It is common for the supervisor to have the employee sign the improvement program, making a contract out of the expectations for improved behavior.

Violation of Code of Conduct

A *code of conduct* is a list of behavioral expectations the employer has. Violations of the code of conduct can fall along a spectrum from "minor" to "worthy of immediate dismissal." All of these expectations should be identified in the employer's handbook. That way, there are no surprises.

EXAM TIP   Even in today's work environment of greater sensitivity to employees and their needs, it is still necessary for employers to establish and maintain employee codes of conduct. You should expect that there will be questions on the exam about what a code of conduct is and how it should be administered.

Employee Behavior

We have already reviewed the nature of behavior. When someone does or says something that is unacceptable, there should be consequences of some sort. Minor violations of a code of conduct can include the following:

- Frequent tardiness
- Frequent absence (excused, unexcused, or both)
- Minor insubordination, which means not following management directives
- Taking employer supplies for personal use
- Frequent incomplete or inaccurate work product
- Abuse or misuse of office equipment
- Arguments with coworkers

Moving up along the scale of unacceptable behavior, serious code of conduct violations might include the following:

- Bringing weapons to work
- Threats of violence or actual violence against others in the workplace
- Blatant insubordination
- Embezzlement or misappropriation of company funds
- Theft of equipment
- Filing false reports

Serious infractions of the code of conduct can result in discipline and could even include immediate termination for the most serious of violations. Workplace violence is an example of behavior that can result in immediate termination. Less serious infractions can result in progressive discipline that begins with a written warning or even a final warning.

Ethics

Unethical behavior is something most employers do not tolerate. Given the U.S. laws that prohibit kickbacks to government representatives or bribes to foreign institutions, ethics is an expectation in the employment relationship. It is not only compliance with the letter of the law but the intent of the law that counts.

PART II

Here are some examples of ethical expectations that might be included in a code of conduct, each of which would be a violation of the code of conduct:

- Misusing company time (not focusing on work production for the entire workday)
- Bullying or other abusive behavior
- Theft of any kind (from supplies to misusing a company car)
- Lying to anyone in the workplace about anything
- Taking credit for work done by someone else
- Undermining or sabotaging someone else's work
- Following your boss's instructions even though you know it to be wrong
- Deliberate deception of a customer, vendor, media representative, boss, or coworker

Employee Conflicts

It is natural that people will disagree from time to time. This happens in the workplace as well as at home, in clubs, and at the ballpark. When these disagreements happen at work, it is incumbent on all parties to work civilly with one another to resolve the problem.

Work Assignment Conflicts

If a boss tells a worker to do something that is considered a bonus or premium assignment, another employee may actually prefer that work assignment. It is possible that an argument can arise between the two employees over the work assignment. No matter what the argument is about, the employer's expectation should be that it will be resolved without resorting to bad behavior on the part of any participant.

Personal Conflicts

Sparks can fly when two people have a conflict resulting from personal involvement either in or out of work. If two coworkers want to date the same person, it is easy to imagine that such a conflict can result in heated arguments or worse. It doesn't have to be that way, but often is. It is the responsibility of all employees to act in a civil manner to every other person in the workplace. Allowing escalation of emotions during such conflicts is unacceptable to most employers. That is because escalating emotions lead quickly to escalating behavioral issues. First, words are said that carry strong impact, and then an actual physical knock-down, drag-out fight takes place with physical impact. None of that is desirable or permitted by most employers.

Workplace Harassment

Harassment can take many forms. What started as sexual harassment has expanded to include harassment based on race, color, religion, sex (including sexual orientation, gender identity, or pregnancy), national origin, older age (beginning at age 40), disability, or genetic information (including family medical history). Many states have more classifications that must be protected from harassment. All are illegal, not just undesirable.

Under federal laws, it is the employer's responsibility to address the harassment problem with the offending employee. Under some state laws (such as California), it is the employer's responsibility to be sure the harassing behavior does not occur again. That goes beyond simply addressing the problem. Both employees and job applicants are included in the legal protections against harassment on the job.

Sexual Harassment

Sex discrimination is prohibited by the Civil Rights Act of 1964, and nowhere in that law will you find "sexual harassment" as prohibited behavior. Sexual harassment has been defined by the U.S. Supreme Court over the years since the law was enacted. (The U.S. Equal Employment Opportunity Commission [EEOC] guidance also offers a great deal of employer information regarding sexual harassment.) Now we know that sexual harassment is behavior of a verbal or physical nature that is unwelcome. Supervisors (on or off the job), coworkers, and even vendors or consultants are capable of sexual harassment if it impacts the workplace in some way. Two types of sexual harassment are defined in case law, as shown in Table 6-3.

The emergence of sexual harassment as a workplace problem has resulted in the elimination of offensive photographs from office walls, prohibition of sexually explicit cartoons from bulletin boards, and banning of sexually explicit jokes and stories in the workplace.

Sexual Orientation Harassment   Also defined in case law is the issue of sexual orientation harassment. When lesbian, gay, bisexual, transgender, queer, questioning, or individuals with other sexual identities (LGBTQ+) are harassed because of their sexual orientation, the behavior is illegal. (See Appendix B, "Federal Case Laws." Look for *Oncale v. Sundowner Offshore Services* and *Price Waterhouse v. Hopkins*.) All forms of sexual orientation are protected from harassment. That includes heterosexual, homosexual, and bisexual.

Transgender Harassment   When someone strongly identifies with a gender different from the one they were assigned at birth, they may dress as their rightful gender or even have surgery to physically switch genders. Harassment of transgender employees is illegal. Employers should recognize their responsibility to protect these workers from such attacks.

Quid Pro Quo	Hostile Environment
• Submission to sexual advances is made a condition of employment.	• Sexual advances are unwelcome by the victim.
• Demands of sexual favors are made in exchange for a job benefit (pay raise, good work assignment, promotion, or not being fired).	• Sexual advances interfere with the employee's work.
• Most often the offender is a supervisor of the victim.	• Sexual advances create a hostile or intimidating work environment.
• It represents an abuse of power (the victim must acquiesce or pay the penalty).	• Behavior can be verbal, physical, or visual.

Table 6-3   Types of Sexual Harassment Defined in Case Law

EXAM TIP While sexual harassment is important and must be prevented in the workplace, it is by no means the only type of harassment. Expect that the certification exam will also have questions dealing with the other types of workplace harassment hazards.

Male vs. Female Harassment While it might seem pretty basic, harassment because of sex still happens in our American workplaces. In fiscal year 2020, the EEOC received 11,497 charges of sex-based harassment in the workplace. Of those, 4.7 percent following the agency's investigation had reasonable cause, and 51.1 percent were closed with the agency having found no reasonable cause. Some peripheral issues are reproductive protections on the job, compensation differences, and caregiver responsibilities.

Racial Harassment

Disparate treatment based on race resulted in 22,064 EEOC charges in fiscal year 2020. Employment actions that were covered in alleged discrimination cases included the gamut from hiring and firing to work assignments, training, and promotions.

Religious Harassment

In fiscal year 2020, the EEOC received 2,404 charges of illegal religious discrimination. When an employee is harassed and can't complete their work assignments because they are a target of jokes and other harassing behavior due to their religion, there may be illegal discrimination going on. Religious harassment increased after September 11, 2001. The same types of problems result in verbal, visual, and physical representations that are unacceptable in the workplace.

National Origin Harassment

National origin harassment amounted to 6,377 EEOC cases in FY 2020. This includes behaviors that poke fun at people because of their heritage. It results from the visual appearance of individuals in most instances.

Other Types of Harassment

Over time, the EEOC has been sculpting definitions of harassment that are broader and broader. It began with sexual harassment and has since grown to include race, religion, and the following categories as well.

Bullying behavior on the job can constitute harassment if it is persistent and interferes with an employee's ability to perform their job duties. Bullying can be described as browbeating, intimidating, antagonizing, heckling, persecuting, pestering, or tormenting. It's all bad any way you look at it. Management has a responsibility to intervene and end the bullying behavior. Progressive discipline is usually recommended in such cases.

Disability Harassment Disability harassment can be aimed at either mental or physical disability. Remember that disability status can include any of us at any time. It is usually the most transmutable category on the list. People don't change their race, color, or national origin. They can change their religion, but it isn't common. They can change their sex, but it is infrequent in our population. However, anyone can be disabled by accident or illness at any time. Jokes, snide remarks, cartoons, graffiti, practical jokes, or other teasing or criticizing based on disability status is illegal under federal law for covered employers according to the EEOC.

Age Harassment   Age jokes are thought to be the most benign among other possible targets. That is unless you happen to be the older person to whom the joke would apply. Then, it's not so funny. A persistent pattern of such jokes can constitute harassment, and employers have an obligation to stop such behavior without delay. Any of the other forms of age harassment are also inappropriate and illegal under EEOC rules.

Veteran Status Harassment   When someone has served the country by placing themselves in harm's way as a member of the military, it is hard to imagine that they would become the target of harassing behavior on the job. Due to a lack of public support for the Vietnam War, it happened a lot at that time, and it still happens today. HR professionals are responsible for training managers and employees on the prevention of such behavior in the workplace. There is nothing funny about harassment, regardless of the intent of those participating.

Harassment Based on Other Factors   The EEOC says any individual characteristic protected by one of the federal equal opportunity laws can be the basis for a complaint of workplace harassment. Just because it isn't sexual harassment doesn't mean there is a green light for the behavior. It is still not welcome behavior in the workplace, and HR professionals play an important role in helping control it. Medical conditions fall into this category, even if they do not rise to the level of a disability.

Complaints and Grievances

Several conditions impact how employee complaints and grievances are handled within an organization. One large determining factor is whether the employer has labor unions involved in the workplace. Labor contracts or memorandums of understanding will usually contain a structured method for dealing with employee grievances. They designate steps for handling complaints about working conditions or other provisions of the labor union contract. Complaints about issues outside of working conditions are not usually addressed within the confines of a labor union contract. Those are handled by other employer policies.

Methods of Investigation

Investigations are appropriate in several circumstances within an employer's organization. They can be helpful in a grievance-handling effort and are essential in determining the validity of harassment or discrimination complaints. Whenever there is a need to determine facts surrounding a complaint, an investigation should be conducted.

Internal HR professionals are almost always given authority in state and federal law to conduct an investigation on behalf of the employer. If the organization wants to have an external investigator handle the fact finding, there are some requirements for investigator credentials imposed by state laws. Legal advisors suggest that internal attorneys are not the best people to conduct investigations because they could be placed in the position of having to testify to their investigative activities while still providing legal advice to their employer.

Whoever is designated as the investigator should normally follow these steps:

1. **Written complaint**   The employee should write out a complaint that states they were treated differently from others in similar situations based on a legally protected category, and that category should be identified. If they can do this, they will have provided a *prima facie* case, which means it seems good at first glance.

2. **Interviews**   Next, it is necessary to interview the complaining employee, and any witnesses the employee says were there at the time. Sometimes, it is a peer who has witnessed the alleged offender. When that is the case, at least one interview of the offending party should be scheduled. The investigation should follow whatever leads are uncovered until the investigator is satisfied that all the facts have been uncovered that can be uncovered. Each step of the process should be documented in writing and maintained in a confidential complaint investigation file.

3. **Determination**   Once the facts have been determined as best as possible, a determination should be made about the validity of the complaint. If the complaint is valid, a remedy should be sought based on both legal and reasonable requirements. If the complaint is determined not to have valid grounds, that will be the determination. The decision should be documented in writing and included in the investigation file.

4. **Feedback**   The employee who filed the complaint should be given feedback about the investigation results and any decisions made as a result. It may or may not be advisable to provide specific information about disciplinary action taken against an employee. Your legal advisor can give you guidance about that in your specific circumstances.

Use an Internal Investigator (HR or Legal Professional)

It is usually less expensive to use internal personnel than hire someone from outside to conduct an investigation. Whether or not to spend the extra money will depend on the sensitivity of the situation and the availability of internal people who would otherwise do the work.

HR professionals should be trained by a legal expert in the process of investigation. HR professionals should not be asked to conduct investigations without proper training. Employee complaints can sometimes jump from simple and basic to complex and legally challenging in a brief period of time. Without proper training, an investigator can bring liability to the employer rather than offer resolution with the lowest possible cost.

Hire an Outside Investigator (Consultant, Private Investigator, Attorney)

In some circumstances, hiring an outside investigator is appropriate. That investigator can be an attorney or a licensed private investigator. HR consultants are sometimes used when a licensed private investigator is not required. Using lawyers is a good idea if the investigation is legally sensitive and the lawyer used will not also be handling the case as the company attorney. Be guided in choosing which outside resource is best for you in your circumstance by your internal HR management and company legal department.

Expert witnesses are sometimes hired by employers and their legal representatives to support their position in lawsuits. When that happens, the people hired as experts offer knowledge and experience that fit the issues being disputed.

Using an attorney can be beneficial in many ways. One key benefit is the potential for attorney-client privilege. Communication between an attorney and a client can be protected from disclosure if the attorney is dispensing legal advice in that conversation. The communication could be verbal or written. When consultants prepare fact-gathering documents or reports under the instructions of an attorney, those documents may be protected because they were prepared for use by legal counsel. Critical self-analysis, such as preparing statistical testing for disparate impact in employee hiring or promotion, can be helpful to a plaintiff in a legal challenge. If the analysis is prepared for use by legal counsel, it may be protected from disclosure even when specifically requested by the plaintiff. Your attorney can provide more help in understanding how to guard against disclosing documents containing sensitive or proprietary information.

Complaint Procedures

Remember when we discussed the doctrine of good faith and fair dealing? The same principles should apply to any system an employer develops to handle nonunion complaints. In every instance, the company should be seen as treating employees fairly and in good faith. The steps can easily follow those used in union grievance handling, which will be covered in the next chapter:

1. Submit a written complaint.

2. Conduct a supervisor-level discussion of the complaint.

3. Have a discussion with HR or the supervisor's management level.

4. Have a resolution reached by senior management.

If there is a provision either in the union contract or in company policy for arbitration, that would be the final step in both discussion ladders. The complaint should be escalated until a solution is reached. Also, the more serious the complaint, the more likely it should be escalated.

Employee complaints should also be kept as confidential as possible to protect the employee and avoid *retaliation,* which is when an employee is subject to negative consequences for bringing a complaint to management. This may come in the form of a less desirable shift, not being considered for promotion, or another form of harassment. In fact, the EEOC received 37,632 claims of retaliation in fiscal year 2020. Therefore, by keeping a complaint confidential and only involving those who "need to know" about it, it is more likely that retaliation can be avoided.

Progressive Discipline

Progressive discipline is an organized process that permits employers to meet the obligation for good faith and fair dealing with employees.

Identifying Steps of Discipline

Although each situation will be assessed based on its own requirements, there are generally four major steps in progressive discipline. Sometimes, a situation will require more than one verbal warning or more than one written warning. Be sure that each employee is treated as others in similar circumstances have been treated in the past. Length of service (time with the employer) will influence the steps to be taken in progressive discipline. Generally speaking, the longer someone's service, the more time should be permitted for demonstrating acceptable behavior and meeting of standards.

Verbal Warning

When some behavior has been unacceptable, a supervisor has an obligation to address the employee and issue a verbal warning. This is a statement such as "This is a formal warning that your attendance is unacceptable and any other absences on your part will result in further disciplinary treatment." Rather than say "will result," it is acceptable to say "may result" to permit greater flexibility in handling things as they develop further. Sometimes, more than one verbal warning will be appropriate. This is particularly true when the infraction is minor in nature.

Written Warning

When the time has come and behavior has not improved since the verbal warning, the next step is a written warning. It can be a simple memo, handwritten or electronically generated, as company systems dictate. It should include a statement such as "This is a formal written warning that further disciplinary action will/may result if you have additional absences during the coming 60 days." Saying "may" will permit management to make allowances if there is a death in the employee's family or if a leave of absence is required for medical reasons. It is sometimes necessary to use this step more than once. For example, the employee maintains perfect attendance during the 60-day improvement period but then slips back into the old pattern of absence after that. Rather than begin again with verbal warnings, it is possible to issue another written warning with expectations for a new improvement period. Generally, additional infractions that happen within a 1-year period from the first infraction should be handled progressively.

Suspension

Following a written warning, a suspension is sometimes the next step. Suspensions are usually issued in a "without pay" condition. That is to deprive the employee of some income to bring home the seriousness of the problem. Suspensions can be influenced by state laws that govern treatment of exempt versus nonexempt workers. Pay treatment may not be impacted in some states for exempt employees.

The length of a suspension will depend on how others have been treated in similar circumstances in the past and whether a union contract has influence in the situation. The length of a suspension should match the level of infraction and be mitigated by the employee's length of service.

It is common for a final warning to be issued along with the notice of suspension. It can say something like "This is a final warning that your job is in jeopardy and you may be dismissed from the payroll if you do not meet the company's attendance standards during the coming 60-day period." Almost always, a final warning needs to be issued even if there is no suspension. A final warning puts the employee on notice that they will be removed from the payroll if they don't meet expectations for behavior in the future.

Termination

The final step in any disciplinary sequence is termination from the payroll. There are fancy terms used for it, but the end result is always the same. The employee is fired, terminated, or let go. It all means the same thing. The employee is being released for cause. The cause is failure to meet behavioral standards of the job and the employer. Termination for cause can influence the eligibility of an employee for unemployment insurance, depending on the state and its rules for benefit payment.

Documenting Progressive Discipline

The holy grail for HR professionals is documentation. That is the single most important component of any supervisor and management training program. Regardless of the training topic, documentation expectations should always be on the agenda. As the saying goes, "If it isn't documented, it didn't happen." Think about the likelihood that a jury will side with an employer over the employee when the employer didn't take the time to properly document the discipline that was applied to the situation. It's the big guy against the little guy, and juries usually like the little guy. Therefore, the employer must be prepared to support its actions with appropriate documentation of its good faith and fair dealing.

EXAM TIP Progressive discipline is a key example of how employers meet their requirement for "good faith and fair dealing" under U.S. law. Knowing the application of progressive discipline is only part of your exam preparation. Knowing why it is important is even more critical.

These days, no one thinks twice about video-recording events and posting them on social media. Audio and video recordings are covered by federal and state law. In employment terms, it takes only one party to permit recording of a conversation. This is known as the one-party consent rule. Federal law requires only one-party consent. When you hear a telephone message that says, "This call may be monitored or recorded for training and quality purposes," it is designed to achieve two-party consent. If you don't object to the recording, you are consenting to it being done. Many states have their own laws about recording voice or video. Many of them require two-party consent.[4]

Timing of Documentation

Documentation should ideally be prepared immediately after the event. If a supervisor has a conversation with a worker to point out a safety violation, that conversation should be documented in writing as soon after the conversation as possible.

Some people think it is all right to prepare documentation only when a formal complaint or lawsuit has been filed. Worse, some people believe it is all right to postdate the documentation. That is never okay. If documentation was not prepared when the event took place, prepare it as a reflective document with the current date to provide an honest picture of when it was created.

Content of Documentation

Complete documentation can be brief. It doesn't have to go on for pages if that is not necessary to log what happened. All documents that meet the following content requirements will be considered satisfactory:

- **Who?** What are the names of individuals involved in the incident?
- **What?** What happened during the incident?
- **When?** When did the incident happen?
- **Where?** Where and under what conditions did this incident take place?
- **How?** How did the incident happen? Were there any events that led up to the incident being documented?

Answer those primary questions in your documentation, and you will have touched all the bases. The only remaining requirements are the date the documentation is being prepared and the name/signature of the person creating it.

When to Escalate Corrective Action

There comes a time when it may be necessary to move corrective action approval to a higher level. For example, when an employee has a given number of years of service, the employer may place a policy requirement on progressive discipline that more senior management approval is needed before implementation of the discipline. When a case arrives at a deadlock in attempting to gain consensus agreement, it may be necessary that someone more senior in management will be needed to break that deadlock. If there might be a conflict of interest or a desire to avoid a conflict of interest, senior management approval or intervention might be the right action to request.

Escalation can be within the employee's own chain of command, or it could be within the HR department's chain of command. The larger the organization, the more need there is for such policies to be prepared and published. Escalation is a policy issue, not a legal issue. However, the more that senior management is involved, the greater the employer's weighted consideration of events and consequences.

Standard Practices and Procedures

When events move in a normal, expected fashion, a normal response can be sufficient. In other words, standard circumstances require standard responses. It is normal to have written policies and procedures that deal with how things normally happen. That is because most instances will require similar treatment. It is when things jump out of the "normal" box and into the "unusual" box that you must make adjustments.

Unusual Circumstances

It is when circumstances fall outside the routine that escalation to higher management may be required. Cases such as the following might fall into that category:

- A 25-year veteran of the company suddenly develops an absence problem. Requiring senior management approval on any disciplinary program would acknowledge the duty the company has to this long-tenured employee.

- A relatively new employee has passed the training period but now has a child who was seriously injured in a bicycle accident. Senior management approval may be required to lift the normal leave of absence qualification threshold.

- An employee with 5 years of service has had a confrontation with their supervisor over work quality requirements. Later it is discovered that they have cancer and the stress of their treatment and its medication is causing behavioral changes. A more senior management person may be needed to approve less severe treatment of the insubordination incident.

Termination

When the company is going to initiate the involuntary termination of a person's employment, it is a good idea to require management review and approval. The level of approval required for the review will in large part depend on the size of the organization.

Termination should be taken reluctantly by any employer. It should be the final result of rehabilitation efforts. Also, it can be the immediate reaction to such serious behavior that there is no possible way the employee can be allowed to remain on the payroll. An example of such behavior is violation of the no weapons policy. If an employee walks into the workplace with a hunting knife in hand, waves it around, and threatens people, that is behavior that should usually result in immediate dismissal.

Voluntary Terminations

Voluntary terminations are payroll separations that are initiated by the employee without employer intervention. These include employee death, resignation, and retirement.

Death Death may not seem like a voluntary separation from the payroll, but it is most often not initiated by the employer, either. Death is treated as voluntary when it comes to payroll separation.

Resignation Resignation is voluntary unless it constitutes a constructive discharge, which occurs when the employer makes working conditions so intolerable the employee has no alternative but to resign. In fact, constructive discharge is not a resignation but a forced, involuntary termination.

A true resignation is voluntary. It results from a personal need such as a relocation brought on by a spouse's change in employment, return to school as a full-time student, or a simple desire to travel and see more of the world. It could also result from the employee receiving a job offer from a different employer. If the resignation is truly voluntary, it can be recorded that way.

Retirement   Another departure that is considered voluntary is employee retirement. It is possible for employees to separate themselves from the payroll by accepting benefits under the employer's retirement program. Benefits for voluntary retirement are frequently offered as part of a reduction in force (RIF). It is usually better to have voluntary acceptance of an enhanced retirement package than having involuntary layoffs.

Involuntary Terminations   Involuntary terminations are those over which the employee has no control. These include layoffs, performance terminations, and injury, illness, or disability.

Layoffs   A layoff is a reduction in force by an employer when revenues have dropped and payroll expenses must be cut or when work levels have shifted without an employer's ability to reclaim them. It is inappropriate for an employer to claim someone is being laid off to avoid dealing with performance or other behavioral problems that should result in a dismissal for cause.

Terminations for Cause   When employees are unable to successfully complete a performance improvement program, the result is a termination for cause due to poor performance. Terminations for cause also frequently include violations of the employee handbook or the code of conduct, such as proven cases of harassment or discrimination. It is an involuntary separation from payroll.

Injury, Illness, or Disability   None of us expects to become disabled, but it happens. Automobile accidents, accidents in the home, and industrial accidents are just a few examples of how that can come to pass. When an injury is long term, or even permanent, it may not be possible for the individual to continue performing their job, even if an accommodation of some kind could be made. Illness can strike that requires long-term treatment and prevents the person from working a normal schedule. Any or all of these circumstances can result in the employer concluding that keeping the employee on the payroll is inappropriate when filling the job vacancy would be a better business decision. In these circumstances, it is important to consider all state and federal laws that must be taken into account to protect the employee before making this decision.

Off-Boarding

We used to say "removal from payroll." Now we say "off-boarding." The result is the same. It is a process of ending someone's working relationship with an employer. It is termination of that relationship, either voluntarily or involuntarily.

EXAM TIP   You might not use contemporary terms like "off-boarding," but you should know what they mean for the exam.

Payroll Processing: Final Paycheck

Part of removing an employee from the payroll involves changing status in the payroll system. Ending issuance of future paychecks is the objective.

Time may have elapsed since the most recent paycheck was issued to the terminating employee. In that case, it will be necessary to create a final paycheck that covers the as-yet-uncompensated work time. State laws differ in requirements for when final paychecks must be issued. In California, for example, when an employee gives notice of resignation, the employer must provide the final paycheck on the final day of work. If there is no notice given, the paycheck is due within 72 hours of the resignation. Other states have different rules. Be sure you understand the rules where you work.

Benefit Processing

Benefits will sometimes end when an employee separates from the payroll. Health insurance, for example, will usually cease coverage at the end of the month in which the termination occurs. Death benefits sometimes require company involvement for an extended period of time, providing certified death certificates and processing claim requests.

For employers with 20 or more workers, compliance with the Consolidated Omnibus Budget Reconciliation Act (COBRA) is required (for more about COBRA, see Chapter 2). Separating employees must receive notice of their eligibility to continue insurance coverage through COBRA.

Documenting Reason for Separation

As mentioned earlier, documentation is a critical part of the process, and separation is actually a series of events that includes compliance with federal and state requirements. In addition to COBRA, layoffs may trigger Worker Adjustment and Retraining Notification (WARN Act) compliance (for more about the WARN Act, see Chapter 2). Also, the Internal Revenue Service requires that notices be provided in some circumstances regarding rights to retirement benefits. All of these types of actions should be properly documented, perhaps even in a checklist that permits entering completion date information.

Supervisor Documentation

Supervisors may or may not have direct involvement in terminations. If they do, it will likely be related to documenting a final performance review or delivering the supervisor's portion of the personnel file to the HR department. Any final supervisory documentation should be completed in a timely way so it can be included with the archived documents.

Exit Interviews

In some organizations exit interviews are standard procedure; in others they are optional. Since the objective of an exit interview is to obtain employee opinions about how they have been treated while with the company, supervisors are not a good choice for conducting the interview. Sometimes, employees are not as honest as they might otherwise be with someone in the HR department, for example. It is standard procedure to have the HR department conduct exit interviews in some organizations. Documenting the answers to specific questions can offer insights into unspoken issues that can be consolidated into summary reports periodically issued to senior management.

Chapter Review

In this chapter we have identified human resource functions related to employee relations and engagement. These functions start with creating structure, policies, and programs that communicate company goals and expectations. These policies and programs must also balance compliance with legal requirements and employee satisfaction. There is a middle ground that HR must find between enforcing rules and creating a workplace culture that employees want to be a part of. Also, diversity and inclusion as well as various methods of employee recognition and feedback were reviewed. Lastly, performance management and workplace behavioral issues such as harassment, complaints, conflicts, and absenteeism were addressed through the progressive discipline, termination, and off-boarding processes.

Questions

Select the single *best* answer for each of the following questions.

1. Mary has never before had an employee who caused a physical fight with another employee. The policy in her organization calls for progressive discipline. Mary isn't sure if she should just give the employee a warning or terminate him immediately. What would you recommend?

   A. This is the reason people should learn self-defense. When someone is defending themselves, there should be no reason for employer-imposed discipline. The aggressive employee should be given a written warning, though.

   B. It is hard for someone to start a fight by themselves. Both employees should be written up, skipping the verbal warning step of progressive discipline.

   C. It depends on how other aggressive behavior has been treated in the past. Even though there have not been fights per se, the employee treatment should be guided by history.

   D. Violent behavior of any kind is justification for immediate dismissal. Even if there is no policy that says violence can result in immediate termination, it is a serious violation of the code of conduct. That is how this situation should be handled.

2. Biaz has been awarded a paid day off because she delivered her product development project ahead of schedule. Does this mean every time someone delivers a job in advance of the deadline they should be given a paid day off?

   A. Maybe. If the situations are the same or similar, the reward should be the same.

   B. Maybe. Assuming that the employees had the same amount of service and their projects were similar in difficulty, they should all be given a paid day off.

   C. Maybe. With an eye on illegal discrimination, the employer should err on the side of providing a day off with pay to anyone who completes work ahead of schedule.

   D. Maybe. If the employer can describe the reward as "special" based on the circumstances, it needn't create a precedent that must be followed in each future instance.

3. Hector has heard that it is necessary to have a diversity management program under some new federal law. What would you tell Hector about that requirement?

   A. The new law won't be effective until a year after it was passed, so there is no immediate requirement for him to worry about.

   B. There is no federal law requiring diversity management programs. Sophisticated employers are moving in that direction because it is the right thing to do and production results often improve.

   C. There is no law requiring diversity management programs, and employers should not consider moving toward such programs unless they are federal contractors.

   D. The new law will require diversity management programs only for employers who have federal contracts to provide goods or services to government agencies.

4. Naji is wondering how he is going to describe the difference between his organization's employee grievance resolution process and the discrimination complaint-handling process. What would you suggest?

   A. There isn't any difference between them. The processes for handling them are the same.

   B. Employee grievances are often regarding workplace rules and work assignment processes. Discrimination complaints have more to do with equal employment opportunity issues.

   C. Grievances happen only in union-represented organizations, so Naji doesn't have to worry about that. He still has to explain how discrimination complaints can be handled in his organization.

   D. Handling grievances is not required by law, but handling discrimination complaints is a legal requirement under federal law.

5. Sophia makes it a practice to call each applicant's former employers to verify employment claims and determine whether there were any behavioral problems in prior jobs. Her company is now being sued because a new hire had an automobile accident while on a delivery run. It turned out he had a history of reckless driving charges in his past two jobs, but she wasn't told about those when she talked with the former employers. Should Sophia be worried?

   A. Yes. Almost certainly, Sophia will be blamed for negligent hiring. She has little defense. She should have found out about the new employee's previous employment issues.

   B. No. She tried to get information from the previous employers and they wouldn't talk to her. She made a good faith effort. She is off the hook.

   C. Yes. Sophia is going to have to explain to her attorney why she hired this person when there was such a bad history of workplace behavior.

   D. Yes. In this instance, she should also have conducted a search of the new employee's driving record before hiring him into a job that required driving for deliveries. She shouldn't have relied on only former employer input.

6. Malea believes that it is a good idea to conduct an employee survey each year to get input about employee attitudes. Her vice president thinks that employee surveys cost too much money and don't provide much value in the end. What should Malea tell the vice president?

   A. A well-constructed employee survey can provide information about the types of employment benefits employees would find attractive, how they feel about their managers, and if they believe they are being treated fairly. All of these feedback categories can be assigned dollar values and can be compared over time as budget impacts.

   B. Since the professional HR community is suggesting that employee surveys be conducted each year, it would be wise for Malea's organization to do that also.

   C. The organization Malea worked at before did an employee survey, and she thinks it would communicate to employees that the employer is willing to listen to them.

   D. In the modern workplace, employee attitudes are controlling factors. Surveys will help managers regain control of the workplace.

7. Why are federal regulations important?

   A. They give politicians a way to influence how government oversees the private sector.

   B. They implement laws that Congress has passed.

   C. They precede congressional action and guide Congress in the law-making process.

   D. They offer suggestions to the private sector but really have no strong influence over federal contractors.

8. Employers have which of the following rights?

   A. To treat employees any way they want in a democratic marketplace.

   B. To hire and fire people without influence from any federal law. State laws apply, though.

   C. To expect employees to work hard during the time they are on the job.

   D. To divide the workforce into teams that will all write letters to politicians opposing current legislative action.

9. Employee surveys are a good source of input about morale. Which of the following is the best way to conduct an employee survey?

   A. Calling each employee into the president's office to discuss their opinions of company policies

   B. Telling each employee to appear at a third-party contractor's office to take part in a one-on-one 360 degree feedback session

   C. Using paper-and-pencil questionnaires, online surveys, or focus groups

   D. Employing computer psychological testing that will divulge the attitude of individual employees

10. Attendance and punctuality are examples of what?

    A. Things that drive supervisors nuts

    B. Job behavior that can contribute to or detract from company goal achievement

    C. Job behavior that should never be reported to another employer in a background check

    D. Subjective performance characteristics that supervisors can document

11. Violations of the employer's code of conduct most often includes which of the following?

    A. Fighting and insubordination

    B. Sickness and excess leaves of absence

    C. Failure to meet production requirements

    D. Talking with other employees about compensation amounts

12. Which of the following is *not* an example of unethical behavior?

    A. Stealing from the employer supply cabinet

    B. Playing *Counter Strike: Global Offensive* (a computer game) during coffee break

    C. Completing a friend's time card for him when he will be late

    D. Calling in sick and then playing a round of golf

13. Sexual harassment cannot originate from which of the following individuals?

    A. A supervisor on the job

    B. A supervisor off the job

    C. A coworker who suggests a nice hot-tub relaxation party, swimsuits optional

    D. A neighbor who invites the target employee to participate in a birthday celebration for his wife

14. Illegal harassment cannot be based on which of the following?

    A. Sexual advances

    B. Racial slurs

    C. Persistent requests for a loan

    D. Persistent jokes about an employee's home country

15. In handling an employee with a disability, the employer is responsible for doing which of the following?

    A. The employer must grant discussion about a job accommodation if asked for one.

    B. The employer must not log an employee as disabled if the employee doesn't want to be identified as disabled.

    C. The employer should not distinguish between a temporary injury and long-term disability.

    D. The employer should file annual disability reports with the U.S. Department of Labor.

16. When an employee complains about unfair treatment by their supervisor, which of the following options is the best course of action?

A. The HR department should soothe the emotional complaint and encourage the employee to go back to work and pay no attention to the treatment.

B. Any employee complaint should always be investigated as possible illegal discrimination.

C. HR should suspend the supervisor for at least 2 days.

D. The CEO should be notified that a lawsuit is not far behind.

17. To foster diversity in the workplace, employers should engage in which of the following activities?

A. The employer must hire representatives of all backgrounds even if they aren't qualified.

B. Poor job performers must be retained if they are the last representatives of their cultural background.

C. Search for qualified people from many backgrounds so they can be considered for a job opening.

D. Identifying at least one person from each racial group who can be appointed to a given job title.

18. Progressive discipline policies generally involve multiple levels of which of the following?

A. Management approval before a warning is possible

B. Increasingly severe disciplinary action

C. Employee appeal before disciplinary action

D. Supervisory explanation before approval of a warning

19. Siena is the quality assurance director at her organization and reports to both the Division VP at her facility and the VP of Quality Assurance located at the headquarters office. This is an example of what type of organizational structure?

A. Flat

B. Formalized

C. Matrix

D. Chain of command

20. The statement "We aspire to be a great place to work for all employees" is an example of which of the following:

A. A values statement

B. A vision statement

C. A mission statement

D. A core competency

21. Which of the following items is an element of a performance improvement plan?

   A. Witness statements outlining the employee's performance issues

   B. A sample termination letter so the employee is aware of the consequences for not completing the plan successfully

   C. An explanation of specific behaviors or performance requiring improvement

   D. A section for the employee to waive their rights to pursuing legal action

22. Which of the following is a benefit of a narrative performance appraisal?

   A. Using this format can reduce rater bias.

   B. Supervisors are always more professional when they take the time to thoughtfully write about performance.

   C. Documentation is the holy grail for HR.

   D. It eliminates the halo effect but not the primacy effect.

Answers

   1. D. It is hard to be absolute in any recommendation; however, this situation sounds like it should result in the immediate termination of at least the aggressive employee. It may be appropriate to also discipline the other employee, depending on the outcome of an investigation.

   2. D. It is not a requirement that each person who completes their project ahead of schedule be given a paid day off. However, if a company creates a situation where people in similar circumstances are treated differently based on membership in a protected class, it could face a claim of illegal discrimination.

   3. B. Diversity management programs are not a new idea, and they are not a legal requirement. More and more employers, however, are implementing them because they help with employee satisfaction and marketplace perceptions.

   4. B. Labor relations issues are usually handled by grievance procedures, and discrimination complaints handle EEO issues.

   5. D. A background check should be tailored to the situation. For a job that requires driving, a check of DMV records and history of insurance claims should be routine. Had Sophia conducted such a check, she surely would have uncovered this history and been able to change her hiring decision.

   6. A. In fact, each category of employee feedback can be assigned a dollar value, and those can be tracked over time as budget impacts. Benefits are only one segment of the employee experience at work. Interpersonal relations with supervisors and managers are another big issue. Generally speaking, employees who feel well treated will be better performers, which also impacts the financial results.

7. B. Regulations represent the detailed implementation requirements for laws that Congress passes. They must be published and invite public comment before they may be finalized and made into legal requirements.

8. C. If an employee is to be paid for a full day, the employer has the right to expect that employee to work hard for the full day in exchange for the pay.

9. C. Paper-and-pencil questionnaires, online surveys, focus groups, and 360 degree feedback appraisals are all valid methods of conducting employee surveys.

10. B. Achieving company objectives depends on employees being at work on time on each day they are scheduled to work. Absent or tardy employees can cost the company money and detract from the company's chance to meet its objectives for financial performance and product deliveries.

11. A. Fighting and insubordination are prime examples of code of conduct violations. They are almost always cited in employee handbooks as examples of violations.

12. B. Playing a computer game during a work rest break or lunch break is perfectly acceptable as long as it is done in a safe environment. The company lunch room would qualify as a safe environment.

13. D. Sexual harassment can be based only on unwanted sexual advances in some way connected to the workplace.

14. C. Illegal harassment can be based only on a protected category under the law. These include race, color, religion, sex (including sexual orientation, gender identity, and pregnancy), national origin, older age (beginning at age 40), disability, and genetic information (including family medical history). Many states denote more classifications that must be protected from harassment.

15. A. When an employee requests a job accommodation, the employer is obligated to enter into a discussion that may or may not result in the accommodation being approved under the Americans with Disabilities Act (ADA). It may result in no accommodation or in a different accommodation that will work for the employee and be more favorable to the company.

16. B. Any employee complaint that is based on a protected category should be investigated as possible illegal discrimination.

17. C. Outreach and recruiting are tools that can help achieve a diverse workforce. Only qualified people should be included in the candidate pool, and selection decisions should be made based on the best qualified.

18. B. Beginning with verbal warnings and moving through written warnings, final warning, and dismissal, progressive discipline has increasing levels of severity.

19. C. When the organization calls for reporting to two or more supervisors, the organization is known as a matrix organization.

20. B. A vision statement is an aspirational statement that answers the questions of what the company does, who for, and what the company aspires to be in the future.

21. C. Performance improvement plans outline expected areas of performance improvement, timeline for improvement, resources available to assist the employee, and consequences for not meeting plan expectations. However, these consequences should not include a sample termination letter.

22. A. Narrative appraisals can reduce biases caused by performance ratings. They also provide a more detailed explanation of employee performance, which can be helpful to employees.

Endnotes

1. Pew Research Center, "How the Coronavirus Outbreak Has – and Hasn't – Changed the Way Americans Work," accessed on November 5, 2021, https://www.pewresearch.org/social-trends/2020/12/09/how-the-coronavirus-outbreak-has-and-hasnt-changed-the-way-americans-work/

2. Harvard University, *Project Implicit*, accessed on November 5, 2021, https://implicit.harvard.edu/implicit/takeatest.html

3. Diversity Resources, *Diversity Calendar 2022*, accessed on November 5, 2021, https://www.diversityresources.com/2022-diversity-calendar/

4. Justia, "Recording Phone Calls and Conversations," accessed on November 5, 2021, https://www.justia.com/50-state-surveys/recording-phone-calls-and-conversations/

Compliance and Risk Management

The functional area of Compliance and Risk Management covers a whopping 25 percent of the Associate Professional in Human Resources (aPHR) exam. Although that number might seem overwhelming as you near the end of this book, you have already covered much of the content in this functional area in Chapter 2. This chapter will reinforce the federal laws that apply to each of the major functional areas in the aPHR exam. It will also cover workplace safety and other business risks. When you are on the job and there is a safety problem, accidental injury, or death, you need to know what to do without spending a lot of time looking up the protocols. In addition, you must know how to complete all the required reports.

The Body of Knowledge (BoK) statements outlined by HR Certification Institute (HRCI) for the Compliance and Risk Management functional area by those performing early-career HR roles are as follows:

Knowledge of

- **01** Applicable laws and regulations related to talent acquisition, training, and employee/employer rights and responsibilities, such as nondiscrimination, accommodation, and work authorization; for example, EEOC, DOL, I-9 form completion, employment-at-will, Title VII, ADA, Immigration Reform and Control Act, Title 17 (copyright law)

- **02** Applicable laws, regulations, and legal processes affecting employment in union environments; for example, WARN Act, NLRA, collective bargaining, and alternative dispute resolution methods

- **03** Applicable laws and regulations related to compensation and benefits, such as monetary and non-monetary entitlement and wage and hour standards; for example, ERISA, COBRA, FLSA, USERRA, PPACA, and tax treatment

- **04** Applicable laws and regulations related to workplace health, safety, security, and privacy; for example, OSHA, Drug-Free Workplace Act, ADA, HIPAA, Sarbanes-Oxley Act, WARN Act, and sexual harassment

- **05** Risk assessment and mitigation techniques to promote a safe, secure, and compliant workplace; for example, emergency evacuation procedures, violence, business continuity plan, intellectual and employee data protection, and theft

- **06** Organizational restructuring initiatives and their risks to business continuity; for example, mergers, acquisitions, divestitures, integration, offshoring, downsizing, and furloughs

Laws and Regulations

Knowledge of federal laws is a significant part of the aPHR certification exam. We described federal employment laws in Chapter 2 and also noted them at the beginning of each functional area to help reinforce them throughout this book. The number of laws can certainly be overwhelming, but it becomes easier when you get a chance to apply them on the job.

Use this section as another opportunity to reacquaint yourself with federal employment laws, and continue to refer back to Chapter 2 and the beginning of each chapter for more detail on each law. Remember, practice makes perfect. The more you can familiarize yourself with these laws and think about how they will apply to your organization, or even companies you read about in the news, the easier they will be to remember on the exam.

Table 7-1 outlines the most common federal laws that apply to employment for private employers, including a brief explanation of how each law is related. The explanations in this table are intended to be brief, so don't forget to review Chapter 2 for more detail.

Federal Law	How It Applies
The Copyright Act	This law protects "original works" for authors so others may not print, duplicate, distribute, or sell their work. Using certain content in training programs may require permission from the author.
The Employee Polygraph Protection Act (EPPA)	This law prohibits the use of lie detector tests for job applicants, but there are exceptions made for certain situations, including law enforcement and national security.
The Employee Retirement Income Security Act (ERISA)	This law establishes standards and employee protections for voluntary employer health and retirement plans in the private sector.
The Fair Credit Reporting Act (FCRA)	This law requires employers to provide written disclosures to employees when credit reports or background checks are used to make an employment decision.
The Fair Labor Standards Act (FLSA)	This law covers employee treatment, such as how employees are paid, employment of young people, and how records are to be kept on employment issues such as hours of work.

Table 7-1 Common Federal Laws Related to Employment (*continued*)

Federal Law	How It Applies
The Health Insurance Portability and Accountability Act (HIPAA)	This law provides privacy requirements related to medical records for individuals as young as 12 and ensures that individuals who leave or lose their jobs can obtain health coverage even if they or someone in their family has a preexisting health condition.
The Immigration and Nationality Act (INA), The Immigration Reform and Control Act (IRCA)	These laws focus on employment eligibility and verification to work in the United States. The IRCA created Form I-9.
The National Labor Relations Act (NLRA)	This law grants employees the right to organize, join unions, and engage in collective bargaining. It also protects against unfair labor practices by employers.
The Occupational Safety and Health Act (OSHA)	This law holds employers accountable for providing a safe and healthy working environment through various standards, recordkeeping, and reporting requirements.
The Personal Responsibility and Work Opportunity Reconciliation Act	This law requires all states to establish and maintain a new hire reporting system designed to enhance enforcement of child support payments.
The Sarbanes-Oxley Act (SOX)	This law requires publicly held companies to ensure proper recordkeeping and reporting of financial information, including internal control systems to ensure those systems are working properly.
The Service Contract Act (SCA)	This law applies to federal contractors and subcontractors, other than construction services, with contract values in excess of $2,500 and calls for payment of prevailing wages and benefit requirements to all employees providing service under the agreement.
The Social Security Act	This law was passed in the heart of the Great Depression and supports social welfare and social insurance programs through payroll taxes with contributions from both the employee and the employer.
The Uniformed Services Employment and Reemployment Rights Act (USERRA)	This law protects the employment, reemployment, and retention rights of anyone who voluntarily or involuntarily serves or has served in the uniformed services.
The Vietnam Era Veterans Readjustment Assistance Act (VEVRAA), as amended by the Jobs for Veterans Act (JVA)	This veteran support legislation requires all employers subject to the law to post their job openings with their local state employment service.
The Wagner-Peyser Act, as amended by Workforce Innovation and Opportunity Act	These laws created a nationwide system of employment offices to provide job seekers and unemployment insurance recipients with job search assistance. They also offer recruitment services for employers.
The Work Opportunity Tax Credit (WOTC)	This law provides federal income tax credits to employers who hire from certain targeted groups of job seekers who face employment barriers.

Table 7-1   Common Federal Laws Related to Employment (*continued*)

Federal Law	How It Applies
The Americans with Disabilities Act (ADA), as amended by the Americans with Disabilities Act Amendments Act	Applying to employers with 15 or more employees, this law protects physically or mentally disabled individuals in recruitment, hiring, promotions, training, pay, social activities, and other privileges of employment.
The Civil Rights Act (Title VII)	Applying to organizations with 15 or more employees, Title VII of the act protects employment discrimination based on race, color, sex, religion, and national origin. Many state laws have expanded these protected categories.
The Drug-Free Workplace Act	Applying to organizations with 15 or more employees who have federal contracts of $100,000 or more, this law mandates several requirements to maintain a drug-free workplace.
The Equal Employment Opportunity Act (EEOA)	Applying to organizations with 15 or more employees, this law amended the Civil Rights Act of 1964 by giving the EEOC litigation authority. It also required a new employment poster for all covered work locations explaining that "EEO is the Law."
The Genetic Information Nondiscrimination Act (GINA)	Applying to organizations with 15 or more employees, GINA prohibits employers from using genetic information to make employment decisions.
The Uniform Guidelines on Employee Selection Procedures	Applying to organizations with 15 or more employees, this law helps prevent specific groups of people from being discriminated against in hiring decisions. This law is why pre-employment tests must be validated for the job being filled.
The Age Discrimination in Employment Act (ADEA)	Applying to organizations with 20 or more employees, this law bans employment discrimination based on age if employees are 40 years old or older.
The Consolidated Omnibus Budget Reconciliation Act (COBRA)	Applying to organizations with 20 or more employees, this law requires employers to give terminating employees the opportunity to continue their health plan coverage after they are no longer on the payroll or no longer qualify for benefits coverage because of a change in employment status, such as a reduction in hours.
Executive Order 11246 – Affirmative Action	This order applies to federal contractors with 50 or more employees and $50,000 or more in government contracts, requiring equal employment opportunity and establishing outreach programs for minorities, women, disabled, and veterans.
The Family and Medical Leave Act (FMLA)	Applying to organizations with 50 or more employees, this law requires unpaid leave lasting up to 12 weeks in a 12-month period for childbirth, adoption, or placement in foster care; to care for a seriously ill child, spouse, or parent; in case of the employee's own serious illness; or needs related to a child, spouse, or parent on active military duty.

Table 7-1   Common Federal Laws Related to Employment (*continued*)

Federal Law	How It Applies
The Patient Protection and Affordable Care Act (PPACA)	This law applies to organizations with 50 or more employees and is often known as the "ACA" or "Obamacare." It focused on increasing health increase coverage for the uninsured, but financial penalties for not signing up for insurance were revoked in 2018, so the number of uninsured Americans has increased since that time.
The Worker Adjustment and Retraining Notification (WARN) Act	This law applies to organizations with 100 or more employees and requires notification and pay protections for employees impacted by a mass layoff.

Table 7-1 Common Federal Laws Related to Employment

In addition to federal laws covering employment, there are state laws and federal agencies that will frequently impact HR responsibilities in these areas. A few key examples are noted in the sections that follow.

Employment-at-Will

Currently, *employment-at-will* exists in most states, and it is state law that usually governs these employee relationships. Employment-at-will means that unless there is an agreement to the contrary, employment can be terminated by either the employee or the employer at any time, for any reason.

Employment-at-will only exists in the absence of a contract that details the employment agreement between employer and employee. Those contracts can be related to a group, such as union memorandums of understanding, or to individuals, such as chief executive officers.

Equal Employment Opportunity Commission (EEOC)

The EEOC is a federal agency that was established by the Civil Rights Act of 1964. It is responsible for enforcing laws against employment discrimination and has offices in each state. Also, because sexual harassment is not defined under a specific federal law, it has provided much of the guidance (in addition to case law) that impacts rules against sexual harassment in the workplace.

The EEOC is responsible for three main things: investigating and resolving discrimination complaints, gathering and compiling statistical information, and running educating and outreach programs to help employers avoid illegal discrimination. In the fiscal year 2020, the EEOC received 67,448 charges of workplace discrimination and secured $439.2 million for victims of discrimination.[1] The agency also oversees EEO-1 reporting for employers with 100 or more employees or federal contracts totaling $50,000 or more.

Department of Labor (DOL)

The DOL enforces over 180 federal laws.[2] These laws range from safety and wage and hour standards to unemployment and reemployment. For any laws enforced by the agency that have poster requirements, the DOL provides free copies of required posters in multiple languages. They can be accessed through their eLaws resource at https://webapps.dol.gov/elaws/.

The DOL has the authority to investigate and penalize employers for violations of federal law. Penalties for legal violations are adjusted regularly for inflation and can surpass $100,000 for willful or repeated violations of certain laws.[3] Some states also have state labor agencies that administer state laws.

Labor Unions

In some organizations, groups of employers are represented by a labor union. All people were granted the right to form a union with the passing of the National Labor Relations Act (NLRA) in 1935 (see Chapter 2). The union is responsible for protecting the rights of the employees in the group it serves. For example, there are unions protecting occupations ranging from teachers to mine workers.

NLRB Procedures for Recognizing a Union

A specific process is required to form a union that is governed by the National Labor Relations Board (NLRB):

1. The NLRB receives a petition from a labor organization for specific bargaining unit certification. The union petition must demonstrate a "show of interest" from at least 30 percent of employees it wishes to organize into a collective bargaining unit. This show of interest is usually in the form of authorization cards the union asks employees to sign saying they would like that union to represent them.

2. If accepted by the NLRB, the employer may consent by voluntary agreement or request a hearing and election.

3. The NLRB conducts a hearing to determine the legitimacy of the election request. It determines the scope of the voting unit and whether it's a reasonable and appropriate group for collective bargaining. A *bargaining unit* is an employee group that shares a community of interest. Factors impacting that community of interest include the following:

   - Common supervision
   - Similar wages, benefits, and working conditions
   - Similarity of skills
   - Business operations in common

   Each side (employer and union) may call or subpoena witnesses to testify during the hearing.

4. Next comes a pre-election campaign by union and employer. A period of 25 to 30 days is normally allowed after the hearing decision for each side to try to convince employees of its viewpoint. The employer must provide to the NLRB an alphabetized list of employee names and home addresses who will be eligible to vote in the election. The agency will forward that list to the union so it can contact employees if it chooses to do so. That list is called an "Excelsior List"

based on the NLRB case that first required employers to offer it. Employers may actively campaign against union representation, even using company time and facilities to do so. Employers are not required to provide union representatives an opportunity to attend those sessions, or even access to company property to refute those employer meeting presentations. All campaigning must end at least 24 hours prior to the election date as required by the NLRB 24-hour rule.

5. "Blocking Charges" and charges of unfair labor practices can be filed with the NLRB by either the union or the employer. The pre-election process will be suspended while the NLRB investigates and rules on the charges. Once charges are resolved, the pre-election campaign clock can begin ticking again.

6. The NLRB conducts the election. All managers and supervisors must stay away from the location where voting takes place on election day. They are not permitted to intimidate employees during the election process. People permitted at the voting location include the NLRB agent conducting the election, employee voters, one or more non-supervisory observers chosen by the employer, and the same number of observers chosen by the union. Only employees who are determined to be in jobs within the bargaining unit are eligible to vote.

7. Either the union is elected to represent the bargaining unit or it is not (union election requires 50 percent plus one vote). The NLRB counts the votes and makes its announcement about the outcome.

Collective Bargaining

Collective bargaining is a process of negotiation that is required by the National Labor Relations Act (NLRA). Once an election has resulted in a union being certified as the representative of a work group, the next step is to develop a written contract that will lay out all the working conditions appropriate to the relationship and the work group requirements.

Contract Negotiation

Negotiating a contract requires identifying the subjects to be addressed by the agreement. Then, each party prepares its preferred position on each subject. The process of comparing those positions then begins. Often, dollars are attached to contract subjects. For example, the length of work shift, the amount of overtime to be paid, and the cost of healthcare benefits all can be represented by dollar values. If the union wants greater benefits for its members, a dollar value can be assigned to that increase. Employers argue budget restraint and use dollar values to justify their reasoning.

Establishing Contract Costs

Each component of a contract agreement can be assigned a cost in dollars. Adding all of those component costs can produce the total contract value. For example, health benefits will cost several hundreds of dollars each month to cover an employee and family members. The employer can agree to cover a percentage of that cost, with the balance being paid by the employee. A union will ask for more employer contribution to that formula. And, should the employer agree, the increased contribution can be assigned an incremental cost increase value. Adding that to other cost increases, such as increased pay schedules and overtime rates, will produce a total increase of contract costs. Each time a new proposal is made or received, a cost analysis should be made to determine the budgetary impact. Some costs will be perpetual, such as an increase in pay rates. Other costs can be limited to one time only, such as special bonus payments. There are advantages and disadvantages to costs that will be contained to one period of time (year) versus continuing into future periods of time.

Administering Union Contracts (MoU or CBA)

The thought that only large employers have union contracts is a myth. Many small employers work with union agreements. That is often the case in the construction industry, for example. Operating Engineers, Teamsters, and Laborers, among other unions, will sometimes have agreements with governmental entities that only union-represented workers will be employed on projects funded by that entity. This is common practice for cities and counties, particularly in geographical areas where labor organizations are a strong political influence.

Memoranda of understandings (MOUs) and collective bargaining agreements (CBAs) are the written contracts between employer and unions. MOU is a term usually found in the public sector, and CBA is a term normally used in the private sector.

Whether the employer is large or small, someone in the organization must be assigned the responsibility for coordinating work through unions and ensuring the employer abides by all requirements of the union contract. Sometimes, unions require that they process all job requisitions from their employer counterparts. Hiring through union "hiring halls" is the practice of notifying the union of a job opening and receiving a qualified union member as the new hire designee. It is a simple process that can provide staffing quickly, often with only one telephone call or e-mail with the employment requisition.

Large employers will have labor relations staff groups that are assigned responsibility for day-to-day interactions with labor unions, as well as carrying responsibility for contract negotiations. Small employers will rely on a part-time job duty assignment for the labor relations function because it doesn't require full-time attention. Small employers sometimes rely on their labor attorneys to fill the role of contract negotiator and grievance handler, while job requisitions are processed part time by another company employee.

Unfair Labor Practices

The National Labor Relations Act (NLRA) explains that unfair labor practices can be blamed on either employers or labor unions. Common among issues evoking such claims are those revolving around the process of union elections. Unions commonly claim the employer is blocking their organizing efforts, and employers claim that the union is harassing employees and electioneering using paid time. Another issue that generates great numbers of complaints is how management and union members behave during a work stoppage (strike).

Complaints of unfair labor practices are formally filed with the National Labor Relations Board (NLRB). The NLRB will investigate the complaints and issue a determination along with any order for corrective action or limitation on activities of the offending party.

In some instances, when an employer believes there has been a violation of civil law requirements, it will go directly to court, requesting an injunction against the union to prevent the behavior that is causing the problem. That is common when striking union pickets block access to parking lots, loading docks, or employee building entrances. Municipal laws in many locations govern how public access to property must be maintained and how public sidewalks and roadways can be used appropriately.

In other instances, unions can seek court assistance when employers are being accused of inappropriate controls on picketers. Use of physical force by private security guards could be an example.

In either situation, the remedy sought through the court is an injunction preventing the offending behaviors. With an injunction in hand, it is possible to request help from law enforcement bodies such as the police department or sheriff's department to enforce the injunction.

Complaint/Grievance Handling

Employee grievances can relate to any subject but always indicate a feeling of upset or discontent about something going on in the workplace, such as the way they are being treated, organizational policies, and the big category of "fairness."

In union-represented organizations, the union contract (MOU or CBA) will usually explain what steps exist in the grievance procedure. They are designed to permit union members the opportunity to formally protest application of any contract provision. Most will deal with working conditions such as hours of work, how shifts are assigned, or seniority practices.

NOTE   Rarely will such complaints be called "grievances" in non-union groups. That is usually a term reserved for union contracts.

Here are the typical grievance handling steps you will find in most union policies:

1. **Written grievance submission**   The employee describes in writing what is causing the upset or discontent.

2. **Grievance review**   The grievance is reviewed by the employee's supervisor and union representative to determine if it is valid.

3. **Grievance escalation**   If the grievance cannot be resolved at the first stage, the union contract will usually designate higher levels of employer management and union representatives that must attempt to resolve the issue.

4. **Arbitration**   If the grievance continues to be unresolved, many union contracts dictate that an outside arbitrator be called in to resolve the issue.

Mediation and Arbitration
(Alternative Dispute Resolution, or ADR)

Mediation and arbitration are alternative methods for dispute resolution. Some employers require one or the other in lieu of lawsuits to resolve employment problems with workers. Each requires certification by a national or state board and also requires compliance with strict ethical standards.

Mediation is the less formal of the two problem-solving methods. Since 1995, the American Arbitration Association (www.adr.org) has used a Due Process Protocol that requires fair hearing of an issue. Mediation is usually not binding on the parties involved. That means employers and employees can go through the process, arrive at a conclusion, and still not accept it, though why that would happen seems odd.

Arbitration is a stricter alternative. It is usually binding on the parties because they accept that condition before the process begins. Arbitration is nearly always conducted by an arbitrator who is a neutral party and a member of the American Arbitration Association. Binding arbitration is sometimes used as an alternative to lawsuits because the expense is considerably less than court and attorney costs, and it can be quicker.

Cost of mediation or arbitration is often split equally by the parties, although it is possible for the employer to agree to accept responsibility for paying all costs involved. In union contracts, there is frequently a provision that costs will be split between the union and the employer. The method for selecting an arbitrator is usually specified in a union contract when that step is included in the grievance-handling process.

Risk Mitigation

The HR department is responsible for controlling the risk of financial loss due to safety and health issues in the workplace. Mitigation means to lessen in severity. The following sections cover the key areas in which HR professionals focus their efforts in this regard.

Injury and Illness Prevention Plan (IIPP)

Injury and illness prevention plans (IIPPs) are not mandated by OSHA. However, some states do require employers to use them. OSHA endorses the application of IIPPs in every workplace. An IIPP is a means of communicating hazards in the workplace and how to handle them. Key elements of an IIPP include management roles and responsibilities for workplace safety, worker participation, hazard identification, hazard prevention and control, education and training, and program evaluation and improvement.

 EXAM TIP Even if you are not required to have an injury and illness prevention plan, you can expect the exam will ask you something about that topic.

Twenty-four states require IIPPs for some or all employers.[4] When states have adopted such programs, they have experienced a decrease in injuries and illnesses, as well as financial benefits. Here are a few examples:

- Alaska had an IIPP requirement for more than 20 years (1973 to 1995). Five years after the program was implemented, the net decrease in injuries and illnesses (the statewide reduction in injuries and illnesses over and above the national decrease during the same time period) for Alaska was 17.4 percent.

- California began to require IIPPs in 1991. Five years after this requirement began, California had a net decrease in injuries and illnesses of 19 percent.

- Colorado has a program that allows firms to adopt basic IIPP components in return for a workers' compensation premium reduction. The cumulative annual reduction in accidents was 23 percent, and the cumulative reduction in accident costs was between 58 and 62 percent.

- Hawaii began to require employers to have IIPPs in 1985. The net reduction in injuries and illnesses was 20.7 percent.

- Massachusetts workers' compensation program firms receive a premium credit for enrolling in a loss management program. In the first year of this program, firms participating in the program had a 20.8 percent improvement in their loss ratios.

- North Dakota has a component under its workers' compensation program for employers who have a risk management plan. The incentive is a 5 percent discount on annual workers' compensation premiums. These risk management programs contain many of the elements of an injury and illness prevention program. They resulted in a cumulative decline for serious injuries of 38 percent over a 4-year period.

- Texas had a program under its workers' compensation commission from 1991 to 2005 that identified the most hazardous workplaces. Those employers were required to develop and implement IIPPs. The reduction in injuries over a 4-year period (1992 to 1995) averaged 63 percent each year.

- Washington began requiring establishments to have IIPPs in 1973. Five years later, the net decrease in injuries and illnesses was 9.4 percent.

Identification of Risks/Dangers

A basic tenant of any safety program is workplace inspection. Identifying hazards, safety issues, and behavior problems that can cause injury are the result of such inspections. Once problems are identified, employees can be coached in how to change the way they behave in their workplace so the hazard can be reduced or eliminated. An example is leaving file cabinet drawers open after adding or removing documents. The potential for someone to walk into the open drawer is high when the cabinet is in the center of the workgroup. Opening more than one drawer at a time is another behavior problem that can result in the file cabinet tipping over onto the user.

Figure 7-1 is an example of a simple safety inspection form.

Office Safety Inspection Form

Date:	Evaluations:	S = Satisfactory
Inspector Name:		**U = Unsatisfactory**
		NA = Not Applicable to Area
Inspector Signature:		
Area Inspected: *Desks, Work Stations, Chairs*		If an unsatisfactory rating is provided for a particular item, company Form 4 must be completed for that item.

	Rating	Additional Comments
Pencils stored, points away		
No overhanging objects on desks		
Cords not a trip hazard		
Storage: Knives, letter openers		
Storage: Scissors		
Plants/water not near outlets		
Chair castors function properly		
Chair arm rests function properly		
Chair adjustments function properly		
Broken furniture is not being used		

Form 1 (1/2022)   This sheet is Page _____ of _____ pages

Figure 7-1   Sample Office Safety Inspection Form

Emergency Evacuation

One important provision of any safety plan is the preparation of emergency evacuation procedures. Employees must understand where the nearest exits are and what alternate exits are available in case the primary route out of the building is blocked. In addition, they need to know where to reassemble outside the building so the emergency operations officer can be sure everyone is safely away from the hazard.

Emergency Medical Care

When you're creating an emergency plan, considering emergency medical care is a key element. It is nice when a call to 911 will garner ambulance dispatch, but what if you can't reach 911 or there are no ambulances available when you call? Alternative plans must be made for treating and transporting injured workers to a medical facility where they can receive proper treatment.

Workplace Violence

A growing problem in this country is workplace violence. Everything in this category can cause trauma, physical or emotional. Consider how you will handle issues involving an employee who is upset and yelling at others in the workplace. What about a former employee who feels disrespected and returns to the workplace intent on killing someone? What about people who enter the workplace with weapons to take away valuable property? Any or all of these situations should be on your list of potential workplace violence incidents for which plans should be made.[5]

Health and Safety Monitoring

Human resource professionals are in a unique position to monitor employee health and safety. They usually have access to attendance reports and can identify patterns in employee wellness or illness. They can also detect issues with employee safety that occur in more than one supervisory unit. Perhaps the safety concerns span multiple work shifts within the same unit. Whatever the issue, human resource professionals should identify it and begin interventions that can mitigate the problems.

Workplace Safety Inspections

A key activity in preventing safety (and health) hazards is an active inspection program that covers all areas of the workplace. That means production facilities, office facilities, loading facilities, and shipping facilities. No location within the workplace should be exempt, and the inspections should be conducted on a regular basis. Often organizations find it helpful to apply a quarterly schedule; sometimes monthly inspections are more appropriate. It depends on how high a risk the work location faces. The higher the risk, the more frequent the inspections should be.

Handling Workplace Violence

All employees should be trained in recognizing and handling workplace violence problems. Supervisors must be trained in how to respond to workplace violence behavior and when to sound an alarm to other employees. There needs to be a management person appointed as the emergency response officer who will be responsible for talking with the media when that becomes necessary and for collecting information that can be passed on to senior management on a regular basis until the emergency has ended.

Handling Emergencies

When emergencies occur, employees need to understand how to respond. There should be some employees trained in first aid so they can provide preliminary treatment to people who have been injured. There should be some people designated to secure the facility by locking doors and closing other access points. Someone should be designated to contact law enforcement or emergency services (fire and paramedics) so employees and others can receive proper treatment. Someone should be designated as the spokesperson for media contacts and senior management briefings. Proper safety training for employees and supervisors can go a long way toward reducing injuries and achieving the appropriate emergency response when it is needed.

Business Continuity

Another important consideration is how business will continue after an emergency occurs. First, an organization must consider how to continue business in the short term by asking questions such as the following: Is it possible to keep the business open? If so, can all departments operate, or just a few? How can we keep revenues up and expenses down? Where will employees work and what changes should customers expect?

Determining the answer to all these questions is essential in preparing for an emergency. Most organizations were faced with these challenges during the COVID-19 pandemic in one form or another. However, according to a survey by Gartner, only 12 percent of employers were highly prepared for the impact of COVID-19.[6]

Workforce Restructuring

Sometimes, a long-term change in the organization is required, not just a short-term one. A workplace restructure is when an organization changes its business structure in some fashion. This can happen for many reasons. It can be a result of two or more organizations joining together, known as a *merger,* or one organization buying another organization, known as an *acquisition.* If an organization is in financial distress, it may need to reorganize or reduce internal staff to meet financial obligations. This can happen in the form of a *divestiture,* which is when an organization sells all or part of its business. Alternatively, an organization may decide to move operations to a different country, which is known as *offshoring.*

The list of reasons for why a restructure might occur are endless, but one thing that is consistent across the board is the importance of HR's involvement in the restructure process. Whether an organization is growing, downsizing, or moving, there are risks associated with these changes that must be managed.

Mergers and Acquisitions

Mergers and acquisitions (M&As) require blending the workforces of two or more organizations. Sometimes that happens quickly, and sometimes it takes years. The United Airlines and Continental Airlines merger is an example of long-term adjustment to a merger.

The unfortunate reality is that an estimated 70 to 90 percent of all M&As fail to achieve their anticipated strategic and financial objectives.[7] Oftentimes, this is a result of HR-related factors. Combining workplaces, overhauling policies and benefits programs, retraining, and adding or reducing staff members are difficult and sensitive processes. But most notably, change is difficult for people. During M&As, employees experience mixed emotions. Excitement, fear, anger, and uncertainty are only a few. That is why there is an entire HR function called *change management* dedicated to it. We reviewed change management in Chapter 4.

Government Approval Sometimes it is necessary to obtain government approval for mergers and acquisitions. The United Airlines and Continental Airlines merger is one example. Another is AT&T's purchase of Dish Network. In each case, government agencies needed to review the plans to be sure there would not be a violation of the Sherman Antitrust Act or other federal law.

Blending Policies and Culture Far more difficult than signing an agreement to merge, the actual implementation requires cultures and policies to be merged. How will union representation be determined? Which policy will prevail when there are two different policies for a given topic? How will a culture of generous work scheduling support be blended with a culture of strict scheduling rules? Those are all difficult questions to resolve.

Duplicate Workforce When NationsBank purchased Bank of America in 1998, there were a great many duplicate jobs in the headquarters organization. How can duplicate accounting personnel be reconciled with the ongoing needs for accounting workers? What happens when there are two bank branches just down the street from one another and the market can't support more than one? Duplicate workforce can be absorbed over time by placing surplus employees in other job openings that need filling. It may also involve downsizing.

Offshoring

Over the years, it has become increasingly popular to move business to another location, often to obtain a cost savings. When business is moved to another country, it is called *offshoring*. This decision is commonly made when the cost of operations or the cost to employ staff members in another location is cheaper. There are often tax benefits for organizations that decide to offshore as well. Car manufacturing in a common example. Due to the cost of production, many of the cars that we drive in the United States are manufactured in another country.

Labor laws will be entirely different in another country, so there will be many new compliance requirements when offshoring. There will also be cultural and societal differences to consider that will greatly impact what changes are made and how they are made.

Divestitures

Rather than growing, some organizations make the decision to downsize in order to meet strategic or financial goals. A divestiture can happen through a sale of part or all of a company's business. Sometimes, the decision to undertake a divestiture may come after a merger or acquisition. When two businesses merge and become fully operational, a certain business unit or location may be redundant or not perform as well financially as others.

Downsizing

During a divestiture, HR will generally be tasked with reducing staff, also known as a *downsizing*. Downsizing can happen even in the normal course of a budget cycle. If revenues are falling, expenses will have to fall as well. A very large expense is payroll. Thus, an immediate impact on budget reduction can be achieved by reducing payroll through downsizing.

Once the decision is made to reduce employees, a lot of planning and communication need to occur, such as the following:

- Forecasting the right number of staff needed to operate the business and the number of staff to reduce.

- Determining a method for staff reduction that does not violate any law or regulation, especially discrimination. How will the organization determine who stays and who does not? How will this change be executed in a fair and unbiased way?

- Checking for other laws the organization may be subject to as a result of this change. A common one is the Worker Adjustment and Retraining Notification Act (WARN Act).

- Creating a separation package for employees to assist with their transition out of the workplace.

- Determining how to communicate this change to staff members being separated from the organization and staff members who are staying. Organizational changes can be extremely difficult for the employees who stay with the organization.

Many of these steps are handled at the senior HR level. However, a divestiture or any restructure involves tremendous HR support. You may find yourself assisting with this process by gathering data about employee performance, hire dates, or demographics to help select a method of staff reduction, or you might help develop new organization charts or assist in the preparation of separation packages for employees.

NOTE Organizations often opt to reduce their workforce based on seniority, or date of hire. This means that the employees with the most recent hire date (least seniority with the organization) are selected for layoff first. This is a popular option because date of hire is the only criterion used for determining who stays with the organization and who does not. There is a low risk for discrimination or bias when using this selection method.

Furloughs

Instead of removing employees from the payroll, some organizations opt to use furloughs. A *furlough* is a temporary, unpaid leave of absence that is mandated by the employer.

So, the worker is not actually removed from the payroll but is asked to take unpaid time off for a certain period of time instead. Time off may be required in a block leave, or a certain number of hours or days within a certain period of time. The main objective is to reduce payroll costs without actually terminating the affected employees.

NOTE   If furloughing exempt employees, employers must be mindful of complying with FLSA requirements.

Security Risks

In the modern American workplace, there are a lot of potential security risks. Just in the information services context, cyber-crimes have begun climbing the activity chart. Identifying the risks is a task that should be undertaken as part of the policy development process and procedural planning. The way to do that is to inspect each element of organizational operations and ask yourself what could go wrong, or what is exposed, and then develop your plans accordingly.

If your organization is large enough to enjoy the presence of a security department, you should expect those individuals will play a key role in all of the following planning, problem identification, and response implementation.

Data Security/Cyber-Crimes

Data security is critical for human resource professionals. Maintaining a viable HR data system (human resource information system, or HRIS) is important for employee, supervisor, and HR use. Having that access blocked is a serious issue. If it is blocked because of equipment problems, that is one set of problems. If it is blocked because of a cyber-attack from someone intending to do harm, that is a different set of problems. Planning for both is something HR professionals must contribute to and sometimes take the lead in managing. Often, when there is a staff of information service professionals, they will be key allies in the planning and response process. Working with law enforcement officials is another duty that must be assigned to someone in the organization. Supporting organizations that work to prevent cyber-crimes is a consideration for medium- to larger-sized employers.

Hacker Theft

What happens when someone hacks into the HRIS and gains access to personal information about employees? HRIS data includes Social Security numbers, home addresses, names and ages of dependents, employee banking information used for direct deposit, and more. When an unauthorized person gains access to that level of sensitive data, there needs to be a rapid response to help employees protect themselves and their families. One type of support is to sponsor coverage by an organization such as the Equifax credit protection service or the LifeLock identity theft protection service. There are many such services in the marketplace. You can get advice about selecting such support from your chief financial officer and legal adviser.

PART II

A relatively new problem in the area of cyber-crime is the problem of hackers holding your data hostage. They corrupt your computer so that you cannot access or retrieve your data if you don't agree to pay them a fee to unlock your computer. This is emerging as a serious threat to employers. What if you pay and the hackers don't unlock your computer? What if you don't pay and your computer is suddenly worthless? What backup practices do you have for ensuring you can re-create your computer on a different machine with all the current data should that be necessary? Cyber-criminals are becoming very creative in their methods of attack. Almost always, their nastiness is aimed at ways they can extract money from employers for the release of the employers' information.

Employee Cyber-Theft

Disgruntled employees sometimes head for the company's databases with an eye to stealing proprietary information on products or services. They also can seek out access to employee data from payroll systems or the HRIS. You can imagine all the bad things they could do with such data if they got it. An HR professional's first duty is to plan for such problems and create plans to prevent them from happening. The second duty is to determine how to respond once a theft has occurred. Human resources normally plays a lead role in planning and implementing these plans and policies.

Inventory and Supply Security

Large organizations usually have large quantities of raw materials and completed product on hand. They also have large quantities of supplies used for office functions, medical support, employee comfort, and safety. Small organizations don't have nearly the same levels of inventory, but what they have is precious to them and a financial hardship if these supplies should go missing.

HR professionals need to work with operations managers and supervisors who have primary oversight of raw materials and product inventories and identify the risks they face and how those risks can be mitigated. Then, attention should be paid to how the organization will respond if such a theft should occur. What law enforcement will be needed? What, if any, public announcements should be made and by whom within the company?

Equipment Security

Equipment is expensive. Human resource department computer equipment expands with the size of the organization. The more there is, the greater the investment that must be made to replace the equipment should it be stolen. Many years ago, a human resource consulting firm was the victim of vandals who broke into their offices and removed every computer they had. The criminals were in and out of the facility so fast that no one saw them, and they didn't appear on any video surveillance recording because the firm didn't have any cameras installed. The data was lost. There were no backups. The firm nearly went out of business because of that theft. You can protect your organization from such a disaster if you think ahead to what you would face if someone stole your computers or other essential equipment. How can you protect that equipment? How can you prevent such a theft? What will be your recovery plan if you do experience such an attack?

Theft Prevention/Loss Prevention

In large organizations, entire departments are given the responsibility of preventing loss. There is "shrinkage" of inventory caused by shoplifting and employee theft. There is loss of money from bank accounts due to embezzlement. If it is an asset to the business, it can be stolen. HR professionals have roles to play in loss prevention, whether or not there is an independent department assigned to address those issues.

Employee Theft

Pilfering from the petty cash box in the office manager's desk drawer or diverting customer payments to personal accounts rather than company accounts are both examples of employee theft. In retail establishments, employee theft of products can be an issue.

When individuals have a predilection for stealing, they likely have a record showing they have been in trouble for such behavior in the past. Background checks should be able to unveil the record so it can be assessed and the job candidate rejected from further consideration if that is appropriate. To do that, the historical problem should be relevant to the job in question. If the job involves handling inventory, cash, or financial records, and the background shows convictions for grand theft, that might qualify as a rejection reason.

Customer Theft

Customer theft can involve a "five-finger discount" taken as the customer cruises the aisles of the employer's store. Shoplifting is America's number-one property crime according to pricegun.com.[8] On average, there are 550,000 shoplifting incidents every day. They total $13 billion of loss each year, representing a daily loss of $35 million. That is significant reason for employers to address customer theft issues.

HR professionals are involved with policy development and implementation to prevent theft in coordination with operations departments and other staff organizations. The tasks HR people may be involved with can include investigation of complaints about management treatment, investigation of policy violations, and training for employees on policy requirements.

Preventing Equipment Damage

One would normally think that preventing equipment damage falls to the operations groups that use the equipment. Yet, when arguments turn nasty, employees can resort to sabotage. *Sabotage* means deliberately destroying something so it will not work; the word comes from a century-old employee grievance over employer treatment (literally, throwing a shoe, or *sabot* in French, into the machinery to cause damage or failure of the equipment).

HR professionals can play a preventative role by properly training employees in requirements of organizational policies and investigating employee complaints of unfair or illegal treatment. Feedback to the complaining employee is critical so the communication cycle is fulfilled. The complaining employee must learn what has resulted from the complaint. Without that feedback, employee trust in the employer's handling of the issue without bias will diminish substantially.

Securing Passwords

HR professionals can help the organization with securing passwords by reviewing and training employees on the policy requirements. HR can also maintain a master log of passwords issued to each employee for the software access each person needs. If there is an information technology department, that log can be kept by the computer professionals. Preventing people from using sticky notes to write passwords and sticking them onto computer screens is important. Putting passwords on a list taped to the "breadboard" pull-out tray on a desk is also unacceptable. HR can help organizational groups determine the proper method for securing passwords for the employer.

Terrorism

Hardly a day goes by without a news story about terrorism somewhere in the world. Workplace violence is sometimes a result of terrorism and sometimes a result of disgruntled workers. It is obvious that terrorism can sometimes result in harm to employees and sometimes in loss of property. A key method for identifying situations that can involve terrorism is through employee involvement. Employee alerts to a central processing group (text message, voice call, or e-mail message) can start the wheels turning to respond and save injury and damage. Training employees in the policies for handling such incidents and how to report them is often an HR responsibility.

Workers' Compensation Compliance

The world of workers' compensation insurance is tightly regulated by state governments. States govern reporting of workplace accidents and follow the treatment for each injured worker from beginning to end. Workers' compensation insurance dictates how much will be paid for treatment and for how long. Yet there are some decisions employers get to make about their involvement with workers' compensation cases.

 EXAM TIP   Every employer is required to have workers' compensation insurance. Even though the rules governing workers' compensation are generated by each state, you can expect there will be some questions on the exam about this topic.

Reporting Requirements

Workers' compensation insurance procedures specify what information must be transmitted to the insurance company for an employer with a workplace accident. Also, these procedures specify what administrative information must be sent periodically, along with medical treatment reports. HR professionals are usually tasked with the responsibility to monitor case reports and be sure everything the insurance carrier needs actually gets to them.

Return-to-Work Policies

You might not immediately think there are policy latitudes available to employers in the handling of workers' compensation issues. Yet return-to-work policies are a good example of how employers get to determine certain employee-handling questions.

It is almost never up to the employer how early someone can return to work. That is governed by the medical evaluators. However, employers can overlay policies about the conditions under which a person can return to work.

Modified-Duty Assignments

Some people believe that modified-duty assignments are required by workers' compensation rules if there are medical restrictions when an employee is ready to return to work. In fact, employers can determine their own policy about their ability to have someone working with restrictions. That policy may vary by job type and the restrictions specified by the workers' compensation medical determinations.

If someone is going to return to work from a skiing accident with the restriction that they may not carry more than 10 pounds because of a broken leg that is still in a cast, for example, the employer gets to say whether it can have someone on the job with those restrictions. If it is not possible to have the employee lift only 10 pounds in a shipping and receiving job, it is permissible for the employer to delay the worker's return until no restrictions are required.

Likewise, if the medical restriction involves working only a few hours each day, the employer gets to determine whether it can use someone on the specific job assignment for less than full time each day.

Any decisions about these return-to-work issues should be properly documented to show both the decision and *why* that decision was the best for the circumstances. Employers may not arbitrarily block someone from returning to work without a legitimate business explanation.

Reasonable Accommodation

Reasonable accommodation in workers' compensation cases involves the same obligations that any other job accommodation request would impose on the employer. The employer must be willing to engage in an interactive dialogue process with the employee about the medical restrictions and how the job can be performed with those restrictions.

Safety is one reason for rejecting a job accommodation request. Return-to-work decisions must provide for the safe performance of job duties. If it is not possible for an injured worker to perform the job without significant safety risks, the employer may be justified in delaying the return to work by rejecting the job accommodation request.

Independent Medical Exam

Often the medical advisers on which a workers' compensation case will rely are those hired by the insurance carrier. At any time, the employer and/or the employee can choose to involve different medical people for additional opinions. Those involvements will come at the expense of the party requesting the additional opinion. When medical opinions clash, a decision must be made with concurrence of the workers' compensation insurance carrier, the employer, and the employee.

When an employee doesn't want to return to work under conditions specified by the medical experts, it may be that progressive discipline is the appropriate avenue for resolving the disagreement.

Documentation by the HR organization will be essential in case the employee decides to contest their treatment in court. Entry-level HR professionals play a key role in that documentation process, if not by writing it then by ensuring that appropriate parties submit it for the case file.

OSHA Compliance

Federal safety and health laws and regulations begin to impact an employer once the first employee is hired. The Occupational Safety and Health Act contains a General Duty Clause that requires employers to provide safe and healthy working conditions. That duty involves proper observation of workplace safety conditions and correction of any problems identified.

Workplace Safety Inspections

Larger employers have organizations that care for safety issues in all organizational units. Even though a safety department may exist, it is still incumbent upon supervisors, managers, and HR professionals to support safety rules and policies.

In smaller organizations, it may be the HR professional in concert with line supervisors who will handle safety monitoring and reporting tasks. Conducting inspections using a documentation tool such as the one shown earlier in Figure 7-1 can be helpful to document the safety status of your workplace.

Accident Reporting

Depending on your organizational size, you may have specific requirements for reporting accidents to OSHA. Even if you have only one person on the payroll, you will have reporting requirements under your workers' compensation insurance policy.

For detailed instructions about OSHA injury-reporting requirements, you should visit the agency's web site at https://www.osha.gov/recordkeeping/RKforms.html. Any changes the agency might make in the future will be posted on the web site as soon as they are approved for use. Make a habit of checking the site often.

Accidents that require only first aid are not reportable under OSHA regulations. You must identify your company's policy to determine how you should report such incidents internally. According to OSHA,[9] first aid "often consists of a one-time, short-term treatment and requires little technology or training to administer. First aid can include cleaning minor cuts, scrapes, or scratches; treating a minor burn; applying bandages and dressings; the use of non-prescription medicine; draining blisters; removing debris from the eyes; massage; and drinking fluids to relieve heat stress."

OSHA defines a recordable injury or illness as follows:[10]

- Any work-related fatality.

- Any work-related injury or illness that results in loss of consciousness, days away from work, restricted work, or transfer to another job.

- Any work-related injury or illness requiring medical treatment beyond first aid.

- Any work-related diagnosed case of cancer, chronic irreversible diseases, fractured or cracked bones or teeth, or punctured eardrums.

- There are also special recording criteria for work-related cases involving needlesticks and sharps injuries, medical removal, hearing loss, and tuberculosis.

It can be helpful to prepare a reference list showing your reporting requirements to refer to should there be an accident with one of your workers. It could look like Figure 7-2.

You should customize Figure 7-2 for your organizational policies and expectations. The priority of contact points should be resequenced for your employer. It may be that management wants notification before the workers' compensation insurance company is called. Make this tool fit your requirements. It is better to get these questions answered in advance of any actual injury and a need to use the list.

Contact	E-mail/Phone Number	Date of First Contact
First Aid Injury		
Workers' Comp Carrier	Report Line: Phone #	
Senior Management	Safety Officer Phone # Department Manager Phone #	
Minor or Nonserious Injury		
Workers' Comp Carrier	Report Line: Phone #	
Senior Management	Safety Officer Phone # Department Manager Phone #	
OSHA Incident Report	Local OSHA Office Phone #	
Serious Injury or Death		
Employee's Emergency Contact List	Employee Contact #1: Employee Contact #2:	
Workers' Comp Carrier	Report Line: Phone #	
Senior Management	Safety Officer Phone # Senior HR Officer Phone # Department Manager Phone #	
OSHA Incident Report	Local OSHA Office Phone #	

Figure 7-2 Employee Injury Reporting Contacts

Incident Reports

OSHA has a series of forms that are important for tracking injuries and illnesses and then summarizing the totals at the end of each year. OSHA Form 301, Injury and Illness Incident Report, is used to document a reportable injury. It asks for basic information such as name, address, birth date, hire date, who the tending medical provider was, what happened, and what the employee was doing just before getting injured. Current requirements call for retaining each of these incident reports for a minimum of 5 years.

Annual Accident Summary

At the end of each calendar year, employers with ten or more people on the payroll must prepare summary reports called OSHA Form 300 and OSHA Form 300A. These forms contain information about the number of days of work lost because of the accident and the number of days that the employee was on restricted duty or in a different job assignment while recovering. OSHA Form 300 is, in essence, a log of accidents that have happened during the year. This log must be summarized and documented on OSHA Form 300A. It is the summary form (OSHA Form 300A) that must be posted in a conspicuous location within the workplace from February 1 to April 30 each year. This summary does not have any personally identifiable information on it. That is all on the log (OSHA Form 300), which does not need to be posted. Form 300A must be retained for a minimum of 5 years.

Chapter Review

This chapter covered the importance of compliance, safety, and security issues. Employers are governed by many federal laws in these areas. Those laws require certain documentation and reporting of events. Some organizations also employ workers represented by unions, resulting in additional compliance requirements. You also saw how advanced planning can help prevent workplace accidents and improve workforce restructuring processes. New developments in the area of cyber-theft and network hacking are becoming more important to HR professionals. There are many tasks involved with these facets of HR management. Understanding the impact they have on your organization and its workers is critical to all HR professionals.

Questions

Select the single *best* answer for each of the following questions.

1. The ABC Company has 200 employees and needs to close one of its plants, which will cause a large number of employees to lose their jobs. Which federal law is most important for ABC Company to review in this situation?

   A. MSHA
   B. OSHA
   C. FLSA
   D. WARN

2. In an insurance company, there are few employee hazards according to its HR manager. In fact, the HR manager believes there are no federal laws that will impact safety in its operations. As the associate HR manager, what recommendation would you make to your boss?

   A. Stay the course. The HR manager is right about the freedom from federal oversight.

   B. Reconsider the conclusion. Federal oversight and office safety laws say that the employer must conduct safety training for all employees.

   C. Stay the course. The employer is specifically exempt. All insurance companies are excluded from coverage under federal safety laws.

   D. Reconsider the conclusion. OSHA requires all employers to provide a safe workplace in compliance with the General Duty Clause.

3. HIPAA does *not* apply to which of the following?

   A. Health plans

   B. A chiropractor who has retired and sold the practice

   C. A healthcare provider that sends medical records electronically

   D. A healthcare provider that keeps paper copies of medical records

4. Morton is your colleague and another Associate Professional in Human Resources. He is wondering if someone who has diabetes under control by using insulin should be considered disabled. What is your advice?

   A. Absolutely not. When a disabling condition is controlled by medication, it is no longer considered a disability.

   B. When the disability is controlled with only limited insulin injections, it is no longer considered a disability.

   C. Even if it is controlled by insulin, diabetes is still considered a disability under the ADA.

   D. Unless the diabetes has been treated for more than 5 years, it is not considered a disability.

5. The Family and Medical Leave Act will apply to which of the following employees?

   A. A new father wanting to take time off for bonding with his new son

   B. An uncle who wants to travel to the "old country" to see his new niece

   C. A mother who wants to take more time off following her vacation

   D. A sister wanting to surprise her brother for his 50th birthday

6. In which of the following instances is an injury and illness prevention plan a tool for improving safety?

   A. When a company receives a letter from OSHA saying it will soon be inspected

   B. When an employer wants to cover up hazards that have been bothering people for years

   C. When a company wants to communicate with its employees the procedures for handling certain hazards

   D. When personal protective devices are sent out for repair

7. IIPPs have been shown to:

   A. Reduce illness and injury in the workplace

   B. Improve the décor of any modern-day office

   C. Reduce the paperwork associated with injury reports to the government

   D. Increase the amount of supervisor interventions when janitorial staff performance problems arise

8. Workplace hazards are best identified through which of the following methods?

   A. Having a working committee to discuss the problems they see

   B. Conducting periodic inspections of each work location and documenting the issues identified as potential hazards

   C. Logging the accidents that employees have

   D. Employee suggestions for fixing problems they see at their workstation

9. One hazard common to all work locations is fire. Consequently, an evacuation plan should be developed and included within which of the following documents?

   A. Material Safety Data Sheets

   B. Worker's Compensation manual

   C. Injury and illness prevention plan

   D. Spreadsheet of employee problems that should be addressed

10. Workplace violence is something that most employers:

   A. Won't have to worry about

   B. Will address through the IIPP

   C. Should downplay to prevent any self-fulfilling prophecies

   D. Can prevent if they keep their doors locked

11. Which of the following is *not* considered a security risk?

   A. Employees who have a worsening attendance problem

   B. Customers who insist on seeing the way their products are assembled

   C. Retail stock that is close to an entry or exit

   D. Managers who travel with laptops containing company databases

12. What should you do if you receive an anonymous tip that one of the company employees is stealing employee data for identify theft purposes?

    A. Call the police and let them handle it.

    B. Confront the employee to get their reaction.

    C. Notify senior management and begin an investigation.

    D. Dismiss it as an unfounded story.

13. What should HR do when an employee is injured at work?

    A. Notify the proper federal and state demographic agencies.

    B. Notify the bank that there will be more workers' compensation checks needed.

    C. Notify the workers' compensation insurance carrier.

    D. Notify the parent company.

14. When an employee's doctor releases the employee to return to work with restrictions, what should happen?

    A. The employer must take the employee back and find a way to accommodate the restrictions.

    B. The employer can determine whether there is a way to accommodate the restrictions.

    C. The employer is obligated to return the employee to the same job without doing all the heavy lifting.

    D. The employer is required to pay the employee the normal rate even if there is no job available with the required restrictions.

15. An employee is ready to return to work with restrictions lasting 8 months specified by their doctor. What must the employer do?

    A. Make a job available that matches the restrictions for the entire 8 months.

    B. Pay the employee at the old earnings rate, even though the restrictions mean working at a lower-paid level.

    C. Give up to a full year of restricted-duty assignment to any worker injured on the job.

    D. Determine whether it is possible to keep the employee working with restrictions for that long a period. If it isn't, the employer may choose not to return the employee to work.

16. All employers are subject to OSHA regulations:

    A. As long as they have ten people on the payroll

    B. If they engage in interstate commerce

    C. Regardless of the number of employees

    D. Whenever state regulations don't predominate

PART II

17. How does OSHA classify an injury at work when the injury is treated with a bandage?

   A. A reportable serious injury

   B. A non-reportable serious injury

   C. A non-reportable first-aid injury

   D. A reportable first-aid injury

18. What does OSHA says you should do when someone is stuck by a syringe needle accidentally?

   A. Report the case under OSHA rules.

   B. Save the reporting until the end of the calendar year for the summary report.

   C. Report the case as a minor incident that didn't require medical treatment.

   D. Ignore the needlestick. It isn't covered.

19. When must the year-end OSHA summary report be posted?

   A. From January 1 through March 31

   B. From February 1 through April 30

   C. From March 1 through May 30

   D. From April 1 through June 30

20. You and your coworker are having a debate about your union's collective bargaining agreement (CBA). You think CBAs are contracts between a union and an employer, but your coworker disagrees. Which of the following is the best answer?

   A. You're right. They are written expressions of a set of workplace rules and benefits the employer will provide in exchange for employee work performance.

   B. You're wrong. They are guidelines only. The union will work out any deviations in the grievance process.

   C. You're both right. If the agreement says it is a contract, then it is a contract. If it doesn't claim to be a contract, then it isn't.

   D. It depends. If the employer tells the union it isn't going to enter into a contract, then the agreement is only an informal set of working rules.

Answers

1. **D.** The Worker Adjustment and Retraining Notification Act (WARN Act) applies to organizations with 100 or more employees and requires notification and pay protections for employees impacted by a mass layoff.

2. **D.** OSHA's General Duty Clause requires all employers to offer employees a safe and healthy work environment.

3. B. Since the chiropractor has sold their practice to a new owner, responsibilities for record privacy transfer to the new owner and HIPAA would not apply.

4. C. Mitigating treatment used to eliminate disability status, but not anymore. When it was amended in 2008, the ADA rules stated that mitigations may not be considered in determining disability status.

5. A. Time for bonding with a new child is a qualifying event under FMLA.

6. C. IIPP is a tool for communicating hazards and the means for handling them in the workplace. It should address the specific workplace in question.

7. A. After requiring IIPPs, states such as Alaska, California, Hawaii, North Dakota, Texas, and Washington reported double-digit decreases in workplaces injuries and illnesses.

8. B. When supervisors make inspections and record hazardous conditions, they have a record of actions necessary to make the workplace safer. Repair and improvement can be noted in future inspections.

9. C. Every IIPP should contain an evacuation plan and directions for reassembly outside the facility so it can be determined whether everyone evacuated successfully.

10. B. Both internal and external workplace violence possibilities should be addressed in the IIPP, along with the employee training plans for dealing with them.

11. A. Employee attendance records have no correlation to security risks.

12. C. Even though the allegation is from an anonymous source, you should discuss it with senior management and, with their approval, begin an investigation to determine whether there is any truth to the story.

13. C. The workers' compensation insurance carrier will open a case file and begin the process of managing examination, medical treatment, and recovery details.

14. B. The employer must evaluate the restrictions and determine whether it is possible to accommodate the employee given their performance limitations.

15. D. The employer must evaluate and document its efforts to identify a placement opportunity for that duration, but it is not obligated to create a job for the restricted employee.

16. C. OSHA rules apply to all employers. Sometimes states contract with OSHA to perform the same functions in OSHA's place.

17. C. First-aid treatment is a non-reportable event under OSHA rules.

18. A. OSHA calls needlesticks reportable injuries under special recording criteria.

19. B. The summary report must be posted for 90 days from February 1 through April 30 each year.

20. A. Collective bargaining agreements are contracts between the union and the employer.

Endnotes

1. U.S. Equal Employment Opportunity Commission, "EEOC Releases Fiscal Year 2020 Enforcement and Litigation Data," accessed on November 10, 2021, https://www.eeoc.gov/newsroom/eeoc-releases-fiscal-year-2020-enforcement-and-litigation-data

2. U.S. Department of Labor, "Summary of the Major Laws of the Department of Labor," accessed on November 10, 2021, https://www.dol.gov/general/aboutdol/majorlaws

3. U.S. Department of Labor, "Civil Money Penalty Inflation Adjustments," accessed on November 10, 2021, https://www.dol.gov/agencies/whd/resources/penalties

4. Occupational Safety and Health Administration, "Safety and Health Programs in the States White Paper," accessed on November 15, 2021, https://www.osha.gov/sites/default/files/Safety_and_Health_Programs_in_the_States_White_Paper.pdf

5. Jay C. Beighley, CPP, *War in the Workplace: A Practical Guide to a Safer Workplace* (The Management Advantage, Inc., 2016)

6. Accenture, "Continuity in Crisis: How to Run Effective Business Services during COVID-19," accessed on November 15, 2021, https://www.accenture.com/us-en/insights/operations/coronavirus-effective-business-operations

7. C.M. Christensen et al., "The Big Idea: The New M&A Playbook," *Harvard Business Review*, March 2011

8. Price Gun Store, "Shoplifting Is America's #1 Property Crime," accessed on November 15, 2021, https://www.pricegun.com/shoplifting-is-americas-1-property-crime/

9. Occupational Safety and Health Administration, "Medical and First Aid," accessed on November 15, 2021, https://www.osha.gov/medical-first-aid/recognition

10. Occupational Safety and Health Administration, "OSHA Injury and Illness Recordkeeping and Reporting Requirements," accessed on November 15, 2021, https://www.osha.gov/recordkeeping/

Early HR Career–Level Tasks

All the previous chapters focused on specific knowledge within the human resource (HR) profession. As a new HR professional, you will need to understand all of that information. In addition, you will need to understand how to apply it on the job. To that end, the Human Resources Certification Institute (HRCI) has developed a list of tasks in the Associate Professional in Human Resources (aPHR) Body of Knowledge (BoK) that is representative of what is to be found on a typical entry-level HR professional job assignment. There are no priorities assigned to the items on this list. Although there will not be any questions on the certification exam about these tasks, you should be prepared to fulfill each of these task assignments if you are asked to do so.

In large organizations, an entry-level HR professional will be expected to focus on only a few of these tasks. In smaller organizations, it may be necessary to perform most of them.

To better explain what performing these tasks will be like, one of our authors, Christina Nishiyama, will be reflecting upon her experiences when she was new to the HR profession and offer some helpful advice in the "In the Trenches" features. We hope this valuable information will help you as you embark on or continue your growth in your HR career.

What follows are the 31 tasks HRCI has outlined that an individual would likely be expected to perform at the early HR career level.

In the Trenches

Actual HR Experience

If I'm being honest, I had no idea what I wanted to be when I "grew up" after finishing college. I was not prepared to trade leisurely lunches on a grassy knoll in San Diego for a cubicle. So, I decided that a few acronyms behind my name would be a good idea. I added an MBA and then a PHR to my name, and

(Continued)

I slowly started to figure things out. Sure, there was still uncertainty, but I had a sense of direction. In the field of human resources, certifications are extremely helpful for both educational and credibility reasons. Why? Because human resources is a field where we have to stay continually educated and adapt to change. Laws change, people change, and what matters to them changes, so we must evolve to support the people who make an organization successful. So, you are absolutely making the right decision to take the aPHR exam! HR is an important seat at an organization, and continuing your education will demonstrate how important *you* truly are.

As you read the following 31 early HR career tasks that are part of HRCI's aPHR Body of Knowledge, I have inserted several experiences and tips from my early HR career days. I hope these "In the Trenches" experiences will help you keep an open mind. There are many times you may pause while reading and say, "Wait, I've never done this." That is okay, and that is why we think these experiences will be helpful to you.

I remember my first human resources job like it was yesterday. Prior to walking in the door, I spent plenty of time overeducating myself. After so many years of school, education had come naturally to me and was comfortable. Taking on a "real job" was truly the scary part. After all, what in the world would it be like to sit in one place for 8 hours every day?

My first job was in recruiting. Thankfully for me, it was a mix of the two disciplines I knew I liked: human resources and marketing. Beyond that, I had no idea what to expect. For anyone who may feel that way right now, please know that this is a perfectly acceptable feeling. It can take years to determine exactly what you want to do, and your desires and interests may continue to change throughout your career. What is most important is that you make the best of every opportunity you have. Each opportunity you take on will reveal more about you: your interests, your strengths, and your weaknesses.

Moreover, each individual work task can have a profound effect on your career. Let me explain. If anything, I have always been an expert at overcommitting myself; I'm a "yes" person to the core. I would always be the first to jump at the opportunity whenever my boss asked, "Who wants to help with a project?" Most of the time, I had no idea what the project was. Thus, I managed to commit myself to a wide range of tasks, from taking trips to the bagel shop with an exhausting list of cream cheese preferences to developing a new performance management system in 24 hours. While these tasks vary greatly in their overall impact to the business, each had a significant impact on my career. From the trips to the bagel shop, I learned that I did not enjoy the event planning function of human resources. While I can get behind any employee engagement initiative 110 percent, it is not my preference to execute them. On the other hand, had I not jumped out of my seat to pull an all-nighter to create a performance management system, I would have never considered a career in talent management. Moreover, my work would not have been noticed by our CEO, and I imagine I would not have gotten that promotion as soon as I did.

It is important to be up for any challenge as you grow your career. Sure, some of the tasks that end up in your lap may be mundane, but others can be of great benefit. As another example, I asked a former boss why he made the decision to promote me when I had very little experience. The main reason was my ambition. Being ambitious does not require years of studying or years of work experience. Open yourself up to every opportunity; you never know where it will take you.

And remember, HR is everywhere! Right now, you may be working part-time at a fast-food restaurant, teaching dance lessons, or serving as a file clerk. In any of these situations, human resources can be applied. At a fast-food restaurant, you can hone your employee relations skills by mediating an argument between coworkers and coming up with a meaningful resolution. As a dance instructor, you can heighten your training acumen and develop the best way to reach your students and guide them to success. Lastly, as a file clerk, take the extra time to read up on labor and employment laws. In this ever-changing landscape, you can quickly become a trusted authority at the organization, maintaining important documentation in the appropriate manner.

I realize that it may be hard to see these benefits now, especially on a daily basis, but be patient. Landing your first dream HR job takes time and can be frustrating. Taking the first step and attaining your certification is an important way to show that you have the knowledge, commitment, and ambition to be successful in human resources. And, do not be afraid to show off your skills. Use what you have learned in this certification journey to "wow" your supervisor and your coworkers by going the extra mile on the next project you are assigned. It may not be the first, second, or third time that you receive the recognition and growth you are seeking, but it will come eventually.

As you review the 31 tasks outlined for the early HR career level by HRCI, I'll pop in with a few examples and advice. Remember, you are sealing a brighter future for yourself in human resources by taking this exam. The aPHR foundation you are building can be applied for the rest of your career.

–Christina Nishiyama

Task #1: Access, Collect, and Provide Information and Data to Support HR-Related Decisions

As an entry-level HR generalist, you can expect to be exposed to a wide range of HR activities and processes. As a general rule, your responsibilities will be in providing support to a number of HR programs and activities (for example, recruiting, employee relations, training, safety, budgeting, needs analysis, off-boarding, and termination). You will typically work with others to access, collect, and provide information and data to support HR-related decisions.

You may be tasked with providing administrative support, such as by completing forms and documents or assembling new-hire packets (in some cases, assisting new hires as they complete a variety of forms and documents). You may be tasked with researching common

HR practices and procedures as part of the developing or updating of new HR policies and procedures. There will likely be many opportunities to provide support to your organization's training programs. Here again, you may be tasked with researching various subjects as part of assisting instructors in their preparation in presenting important training topics.

Other activities that may call for your support include sitting in on safety meetings and documenting the safety committee's decisions for the formal record and later posting for employees. Almost certainly, you will be tasked with carrying out important administrative responsibilities, such as organizing and maintaining personnel records in compliance with prevailing legal norms and practices. All the various activities in which you engage are for the most part intended to develop your HR skills and knowledge for the present, even as they help prepare you for the future and for successfully taking and passing your certification exam.

Task #2: Comply with All Applicable Laws and Regulations

In Chapter 2, we provided a list of the most common federal laws impacting human resources. Once an employer hires its first employee, it immediately becomes subject to 52 federal laws. We haven't listed all the state laws that kick into effect. Those will be important for you to identify and fold into your HR management plans. There are far too many to include here, and the aPHR exam will focus only on federal laws. Therefore, in your study plan, you should give consideration only to the federal laws. On the job, you need to concern yourself with both.

We suggest you plan to comply with all these requirements. The exam will be constructed with that expectation. Each of the laws carries equal weight in your study preparation. Don't forget that these requirements change from time to time as Congress sees fit to modify them. It is your responsibility to keep track of the changes and new requirements as they evolve.

In the Trenches

aPHR Task #2

One of my favorite things about a career in human resources is that you never stop educating yourself. Lifelong learning comes with the territory. It is so much easier to truly enjoy your career when it is ever-changing. While the responsibility of understanding so many federal and state laws may seem daunting, it becomes easier with practice. It is also important to find great resources such as HRCI and the Society for Human Resource Management (SHRM) to remain fully engaged in changes to the requirements. To boot, you will be the most popular family member at the dinner table when you can provide guidance for any employee relations issue that comes up in conversation.

—CN

Task #3: Coordinate and Communicate with External Providers of HR Services

Times are changing. Years ago, the HR function came from internal HR resources. Often, small organizations combined their resources in such a way as to utilize the capabilities of their accounting function and the HR function to provide a minimal level of capability and support in both functional areas. Unfortunately, more was lost than gained by this approach.

Today, even small organizations see the importance of having qualified knowledge staff in both areas, but it doesn't stop there. The increasingly legal complexity of the organization's many HR functions creates a need for outside third parties to augment the internal HR staff. This provides an excellent opportunity for you as an entry-level HR professional to build on your HR skills and knowledge. In addition, it provides a significant opportunity to learn even more about HR as a profession. Examples of external providers would be recruiters, COBRA administrators, and employee recognition services.

Task #4: Maintain Employee Data in HRIS or System of Record

A key task for entry-level HR professionals is maintaining employee data in the company tracking system. These are referred to as human resource information systems (HRISs). You will be required to learn the HRIS data fields, how to enter data into the database, and how to prepare reports that may be standard or customized, depending on what your boss needs for special projects.

Writing and formatting reports is a critical task requirement. You have heard the adage that databases are only as good as their input, so "garbage in, garbage out" is an accurate descriptor. Input errors or data gaps will directly influence the accuracy of report output. That does not reflect well on you or the HR organization. Commit yourself to accuracy.

In the Trenches

aPHR Task #4

This is one example where technology acumen can really pay off, even if you've learned it through playing video games and applying Instagram filters. Data entry and system maintenance may not seem like the sexiest tasks but can be approached in an innovative manner. Don't be shy about going the extra mile to become an expert on your HRIS system. You can add a great deal of value to the HR department and overall operation. Analytics is often not seen as an HR strength area by many executives, and this task abounds with opportunities to change that mindset.

–CN

Task #5: Maintain, File, and Process HR Forms

HR forms include such things as notices, announcements, new hire forms, salary forms, performance-related documents, termination paperwork, and sometimes payroll documents. Microsoft Excel has become a popular tool for data-tracking purposes. When key data elements have been assigned their own column in Excel, they can be sorted and used for database reporting. Pivot tables can be created to summarize the number of entries for each data element. They can also be used to summarize the numeric values that appear in each data element.

Large organizations will have their own programmers who can create and maintain customized HRIS databases. Small and sometimes medium-sized organizations will have to use the Excel approach or an off-the-shelf HRIS.

For example, you might need to track the hire date for each employee, so using an Excel spreadsheet, you would place each employee on an individual line in the spreadsheet. Employee names would be entered in the first column, their date of hire into another column, their job title into another column, and so on. Later, you might want to track the date a specific announcement or notice was provided to each employee, and thus another set of new columns can be added for those elements.

Keeping accurate records of employee information is part of the HR professional's responsibility. While entering data can be done by a clerical person, constructing reports is usually the task of an entry-level HR professional. Be ready to respond to your boss's requests for information. You may even find yourself receiving requests for information from your internal client organizations.

In the Trenches

aPHR Task #5

The foundation that you build with this task sets the stage for the success of many organizational functions. This is the data that is used for *everything*. You can answer all of your supervisor's questions: What should we pay our new hire? What are the salary grades and ranges for our compensation plan? Employee X is not performing; when were they hired? What is the history on other separations in this department? What is the overall cost and enrollment in our benefits plan? That's right. All these questions can be answered by the data you maintain, so do not take this responsibility lightly.

–CN

Task #6: Prepare HR-Related Documents

In most organizations, there is a schedule for generating standard reports and charts (for example, reports, presentations, and organizational charts). Some are done monthly, some are done quarterly, and others are due on an annual basis. Monthly reports can include the number of job requisitions filled and the length of time they were open. The number of people placed in training slots for essential training programs can also be a monthly report requirement. Quarterly, you may find a need to generate reports on expenses versus budget allocations. There can also be reports required for employee participation rates in benefit programs such as health coverage and life insurance programs. Annually, most organizations have an overall review of their financial performance, which is back to expenses versus budget.

In some organizations, the HR department bills internal clients for services performed related to HR activities, including recruiting, candidate screening, onboarding, initial training, exit interviews, benefit program reviews, and employee engagement in other programs offered by the employer. There will always be opportunities to practice your skills at report writing.

In the Trenches

aPHR Task #6

HR professionals often face the challenge of being pigeonholed into a certain stereotype. Being good at working with people does not always translate into being technically and financially savvy. Thankfully, this means we have an opportunity to change that mindset. Early in my career, I took it upon myself to create a thorough analysis of our benefits plan that included every cool Excel formula I could Google about. My boss was so impressed that I was promoted to oversee the finance function. This was an unexpected result from a bit of hard work, so don't be afraid to go the extra mile on this task.

–CN

Task #7: Provide Internal Customer Service by Answering or Referring HR-Related Questions from Employees as the First Level of Support

What better way to learn what to do and how to do it than to do it in a real-world setting? This is the time in your professional career when you will have the opportunity to learn not only the technical skills of HR but also the best personal skills of HR. It is often said that HR, in its best form, can be a "bridge" between an organization's management and its workers, but this doesn't happen by magic. It happens by being where "the rubber meets the road" and using your role of providing first-level support to others in the organization in a way that can only be described as a win-win for everyone.

In the Trenches

aPHR Task #7

Many of us begin a career in human resources because we love helping others. And in this day and age, it is a rarity to resolve a service concern by speaking to an actual person. In HR, we provide service to the most important customer at an organization: its employees and its management. Even if you are not able to answer an employee's question, taking the time to refer the employee to the appropriate party and following up is so appreciated by the workforce. Remember, *human* is the first word in our chosen function, and we should fully embrace the responsibility to be a helpful advocate and voice of balanced reason for the organization we work for.

–CN

Task #8: Communicate Information about HR Policies and Procedures

Effective HR organizations will review their HR policies and procedures each year. In coordination with legal counsel and with input from operations managers, the HR organization is responsible for updating and then publishing the new policies emerging from this process. Once the policies are published, as individual documents or as part of an employee handbook or policy manual, it is incumbent on HR professionals to distribute the new policies to employees. As an entry-level professional, you will likely find this responsibility falls to you. Questions must be answered prior to distribution. Will employees be asked to sign a receipt for the updated policies? When will the policies become effective? Will the policies be distributed or simply included by reference in a letter, memo, or e-mail to all employees?

You will probably be asked to draft the letter to employees once more senior management people have provided answers to these questions. Identify the preferred writing style your company uses and craft your letter in that style.

As you gain experience, you may be asked to create procedural statements. Procedures include tasks such as updating employee name changes, registering benefit selections, altering payroll documents (for example, W-4s), and updating employee data in the HRIS. You can find yourself involved in all these tasks at some time in your early career.

In the Trenches

aPHR Task #8

One of my first responsibilities in a "real" HR job was developing a policy and procedure manual. I walked out of my first meeting with a list of acronyms to be included, and I did not know what most of them meant. Fast-forward to several days on the Internet educating myself, and I quickly learned that this was more than a work task. I was getting the opportunity to shape the organizational culture and be involved in important decisions about how we would operate as a company. Even the slightest difference in how you write an appearance policy can shape your organization. Will there be uniforms? Do we allow face piercings? How should hair be styled? How are we communicating this procedure?

–CN

Task #9: Communicate the Organization's Core Values, Vision, Mission, Culture, and Ethical Behaviors

When you join an organization, specifically in the functions of HR and management, you assume a role model position wherein you support and preach the organization's core values, vision, mission, culture, and ethics. You "walk the talk" as your activities and communications align with the defined ethical behaviors and desired culture. Your actions will demonstrate the core values that drive the organization's mission and point it in the direction of its desired future, its vision.

Most organizations have *a deeper meaning* as to why they exist—that is their mission. Their mission will influence decision-making and behaviors desired at all employee levels, but it isn't well articulated throughout the rank and file. That's where HR comes in as a key contributor with employee communications, establishing a relevance with employees in a way that makes them care about the organization's reason for existing (mission) and what the organization's aspiration is to become (vision). It will be at the core of *all* your HR communications: simple, redundant, and inspiring messages that always link to the mission, ethics, values, and vision. Specific messages linked to the mission and vision become tools to help employees connect their day-to-day efforts with the strategies of the company.

Walking the talk in the role of the HR professional will include demonstrating and behaving in alignment with the expressed core values and ethics of the organization. It often requires an HR professional to make the extra effort to ensure their behavior reflects what is expected of others in the workforce. So if an organization has defined one of its core values as showing a special respect for the customer and its employees, gossiping about peers in or outside of a work setting would be the opposite of walking the talk.

The communication of the organization's mission, vision, core values, and ethical standards of behavior, along with describing the culture of the organization, will be one of the main objectives in the role of recruiting and onboarding new hires.

In the Trenches

aPHR Task #9

As the first-born child in a Sicilian family, I have always taken great pride in leading by example. This might explain the glee with which I create these "In the Trenches" for you. The task of communicating core values, vision, mission, culture, and ethical behaviors allows you to breathe life into your organization. Helping others understand the organization is the foundation for developing the employee culture and communicating that culture to the outside world. You also have the opportunity to be a leader on the HR team and within the organization by setting the example for fundamental values and behaviors.

–CN

Task #10: Identify Risk in the Workplace

Risk comes in many forms. There are safety risks, financial risks, image risks, and health risks. You may be asked to perform surveys to identify the specific types of risks in your workplace. Occupational Safety and Health Administration (OSHA) reviews will be necessary as part of the compliance requirements of federal safety law. Depending on your industry, you may have to deal with specific requirements such as bloodborne pathogens and needlesticks. General safety provisions can be identified in a survey form. You may be asked to create or update this form for your organization and then to actually perform the survey. Depending on the size of your organization and the type of workplace you have (for example, industrial, warehouse, office, or a moving work location such as a fishing boat), the survey can take from a few minutes to several days.

Risk identification is important because you must know what risks you face before you can begin to identify ways to eliminate them. You may be required to review your survey results with a safety committee, task force, or upper management. Then you may be asked to document discussions about risk resolution and participate in the implementation of action plans chosen.

In the Trenches

aPHR Task #10

Safety and risk management are deeply connected to other HR functions. For example, serving on the safety committee can generate additional knowledge on employee relations issues, training needs, or ergonomics concerns in the workplace you may have not otherwise been aware of. Even if this task is not assigned to you, be mindful of its importance. Volunteering to serve on a safety committee can help you gain a great deal of insight into the workplace and allow you to spearhead new and exciting initiatives to help the organization.

–CN

Task #11: Minimize Risk by Conducting Audits

Things that get audited in human resource systems can include Form I-9s, workers' compensation records, employee compensation history, and employee records such as the human resource information system (HRIS) or human resource management system (HRMS). Beyond surveys of the workplace, audits of records can uncover risks to the organization. For example, Form I-9 is required of all new employees. Part of the form is completed by the new employee, and part of the form is completed by the employer. If there are errors or omissions on any one of those forms, the organization may be subject to financial penalties of over $2,000 each. While there are fewer I-9 reviews by government agencies these days, it is still possible. Being sure each form is accurately completed is really important.

Workers' compensation records are also important. They must be kept current (updated each time something changes in the case) and protected from disclosure to unauthorized individuals by storage in a secure facility (locked room, locked file drawer, password-protected computer file, and so on). Correspondence in workers' compensation cases is constantly developing; correspondence to employees, insurance carriers, and medical workers must be created and filed immediately upon receipt. Determine the chain of custody and approval your organization uses to process correspondence in these cases. Be sure you follow that chain consistently.

Employee records include a vast array of documentation. The HRIS usually includes information such as name, home address, job title, hire date, job date, performance evaluation rating, training program participation, EEO-1 race or ethnicity, gender identification, department, educational background, and professional certification or licenses. That just touches on the obvious data fields. Some HRIS databases contain only current information. Others contain data history going back to the original employee hire date. Sometimes employees can update their own data records using personal passwords for access. Other times, HR is expected to maintain the database. Even when employees update their own information, HR is usually responsible for maintaining the access audit trail and individual password issuance. You will find these duties included in your job list.

In the Trenches

aPHR Task #11

For most people, the word *audit* does not trigger a sense of excitement. However, audits can be extremely valuable. A few years ago, it was time to conduct an audit of our new payroll system to ensure that direct deposit information was entered correctly. After reviewing several records, I learned that zeros in all bank account numbers were not being captured in the system. It was Thursday evening, and this meant that most employees were not going to receive their paycheck on time, resulting in a host of problems. Audits are often recommended at a certain frequency. But when in doubt, audit! Accuracy is an incredibly important part of the HR function.

–CN

Task #12: Document and Update Essential Job Functions with Support of Managers

There are two tasks here. One involves job descriptions for your job, and the other involves job descriptions for other employees. Many employers are required to perform annual reviews of their job descriptions (for example, federal contractors, both goods and services contractors, and construction contractors). The Americans with Disabilities Act and the Rehabilitation Act have brought employing people with disabilities into the mainstream. When essential job functions change, there may be need for a disability accommodation. You can be expected to keep the job descriptions current. That entails working with management or the supervisor of the job description being updated. It may mean working with incumbents in the job as well.

While no federal law currently requires job descriptions, they are advisable as a communication device and as a defense tool when the company is challenged about job accommodations. You can plan on being involved with this monitoring task.

In the Trenches

aPHR Task #12

The importance of job descriptions resides in many facets of human resources. This task is more than simply drafting a job description; it's about interacting with department heads and developing an accurate baseline for job performance. Often, job descriptions lie dormant for years and don't accurately account for responsibilities, leading to recruiting, employee relations, compliance, and even safety challenges. Consider this task an important one and take the time to establish an accurate foundation for your peers in other HR disciplines.

–CN

Task #13: Post Job Listings

Job posting is one of the most frequently required tasks of an entry-level HR professional. Job posting announcements can be placed on a company's website, on social media sites, or on Internet job boards. In larger organizations, employers will offer internal bidding, wherein a job vacancy is posted first within the organization, allowing existing employees to apply for it. This way, an organization can capitalize on the investment it has made in recruiting from current employees and employee referrals. You might use an internal intranet job bidding board that is password protected and seen or accessed by the organization's current workforce. This gives current employees the chance to indicate interest in a position that they feel qualified for before it becomes available, say in the example of an upcoming retirement.

A posting should provide a brief description of the job, including significant job duties and minimum qualifications, education, experience, and physical requirements.

Posting jobs externally is an important and creative process with the use of social media, Internet job boards, and governmental job sites. The opportunity to reach a qualified audience and to screen out applicants who do not meet the minimum qualifications has its advantages (such as assisting in employment branding of the organization to attract the talent it is seeking) and disadvantages (such as having an overabundance of applicants or missing out on potentially a cross-pollination of skills, experience, and talents of candidates due to the algorithms in the software system).

Task #14: Manage Applicant Databases

An applicant tracking system (ATS) is a database that keeps track of job applicants from the time they first apply to an organization for employment to the point when the position is filled and sometimes beyond. The database is used to enter data, access and update records, and search for and compile potential candidates for job openings as they occur. Most organizations will utilize an applicant database system software; smaller companies may use Microsoft Access or even just an Excel spreadsheet. The old adage "garbage in, garbage out" couldn't be more applicable than it is with applicant databases. Setting and monitoring the algorithms are important components when managing these systems. Not only do frequently changing laws impact the data that is kept and accessible, the sheer nature of changing employment environments requires that these databases are legally current.

Additionally, the organization's reputation can be at stake if the management of a database is incongruent or misaligned with the intentions of tracking and "courting" potential employees (for example, sending the wrong e-mail to a promising applicant awaiting their college graduation that states "no jobs are available at this time" because of a system coding glitch).

Task #15: Screen Applicants for Managers to Interview

Frontline HR professionals are given the task of reviewing application forms and résumés to choose those applicants who meet the job specifications and desired candidate profile. This basic function of the recruiting process helps save the hiring manager a lot of time by using the HR professional to screen the pool of applicants. You may find yourself screening applicants via a phone conversation, an e-mail exchange, or a face-to-face interview to gain more clarification about their experience, qualifications, and fit for the job, along with providing some rudimentary information about the job/company.

These screening interviews are generally short: 15 to 30 minutes in length. Your assessment allows you to narrow the pool of candidates to be passed on to the hiring manager to those candidates who best fit the job opening's requirements, providing them with a top tier of applicants to interview. You are known to the applicant as the "gatekeeper" (in other words, the person to get by in order to reach the hiring manager).

A difficulty to be aware of in the screening processes is to know the pitfalls of interviewing, such as the halo effect. You can find out more information about effective interviewing techniques in Chapter 3, which will help you with the task of screening applicants.

Task #16: Answer Questions from Job Applicants

Typically as the first point of contact for an applicant, and the person who organizes the interviewing process, you will be known as the gatekeeper, the person who buffers the hiring manager. The impressions you leave with potential applicants, and those who are screened out, are vital to the organization's reputation. Know this important function of your job and remember that all impressions count, especially the first impression. Your organization could be vying for a pool of candidates in a highly competitive profession, or even a large number of seasonal workers who are needed by other organizations at the same time. Your ability to answer applicant questions and to be a good, skilled communicator is an artful talent in HR.

At the same time, you must balance the best interests of the organization and the hiring manager by maintaining an ability to know what can and should not be discussed with an applicant. As an example, a job applicant for a mid- or high-level position may want to discuss salary. You should be clear on how to respond so as to not understate a range and avoid losing a sought-after candidate. Anticipating what questions might be asked and rehearsing responses are a necessity as the gatekeeper. Coordinating the responses with the hiring manager to be in sync will also be helpful in your gatekeeper role.

In the Trenches

aPHR Task #16

You may not realize this now, but when an applicant speaks to an actual person, it is a big deal. If you have ever applied for a job, you probably know that you'll send many applications over the Internet, and the likelihood of a response is slim. Thus, simply being responsive to applicants can make your company a desirable place to work. People appreciate this humanistic approach to recruiting. Even if you can't answer all the questions an applicant may ask, word will spread quickly that your company cares about its people.

–CN

Task #17: Coordinate Interview Logistics

Although coordinating the interview logistics for the hiring manager and the potential candidates may at first seem to be a function of an administrative assistant, it is much more than just coordinating calendars. For the HR professional, it will involve the review and possibly the preparation of interview questions that the hiring manager will use, ensuring that laws are complied with and the pitfalls of interviewing techniques are avoided. Many times it will most likely involve group interviewing and perhaps even mentoring a supervisor who has had no experience with hiring or interviewing.

Task #18: Interview Job Candidates

In several instances, the interviewing of job applicants and the selection of new employees may be a responsibility of the early-career HR professional. Such will be the case with many organizations that use field HR representatives, such as the retail industry, or when there is a cyclical seasonal workforce, such as a distribution center or manufacturing facility that hires temporary workers.

Learning and understanding effective interviewing and selection techniques, as Chapter 3 explains, are essential for success with this task.

In the Trenches

aPHR Task #18

From "Tell me a bit about your work history" to "What song would you choose to make your grand entrance to in front of your coworkers," interview styles can be extremely different. There are always innovations in interview techniques, and undertaking this task provides an opportunity to do some research and find the best technique for your organization. Behavioral interviews can shed a great deal of insight on an applicant's fit for a position. While interviews should always comply with legal requirements, there is an opportunity to develop some helpful tools for an organization through a bit of research and creativity.

–CN

Task #19: Arrange for Tests and Assessments of Applicants

Assessments and tests are used to determine the knowledge and skills that have been identified as essential for a job. A typical job applicant assessment may involve the completion of a created standard test that is given to all applicants to ensure they can demonstrate the skills/knowledge needed. This is common when hiring IT programmers and in the skills trade occupations. Even professional occupations have gravitated to assessments, including HR.

The HR professional may arrange for these prescreening assessments in a controlled environment (not allowing smartphones, for example), with time frames imposed, or may set them up with a third-party testing center. To ensure a successful assessment and test of applicants, it's important they are prepared for the experience and that expectations are clearly communicated as to what they will be assessed on.

In the Trenches

aPHR Task #19

The budding psychologist in all of us can rise to the occasion on this task. In this day and age, there is so much more to the hiring process than an interview. There are an array of assessments available that can uncover certain behaviors that are difficult to see in an interview. While you may only start by arranging appointments, you will ultimately have the opportunity to see the results of these tests and the insight they can provide, arming you with additional knowledge that can be applied in the future.

–CN

Task #20: Coordinate the Employment Offer

The interviews have been concluded, the references have been checked, and the assessment or employment tests are in. The hiring decision has been made, and it's time to extend a job offer. Communicating the job offer, which would include start date, salary, benefits, and so on, is typically the next step handled, and in larger organizations, that responsibility belongs to the HR department. The reason that HR would handle the job offer is to ensure again that legality issues are not breached (as can happen when a hiring manager states, "You will have a job for life in our company") and to be the first line of negotiation representing the organization (for example, salary negotiation). Having a checklist of vital information to offer is always recommended and helpful, including the desired start date, the offered salary, the benefits package, and any perks, official job title, and so on. Normally the more senior-level position offerings will be handled by the senior HR leader or even the senior management of the organization and may include employment contracts. You can fully expect to be making job offers to nonexempt position candidates. Offer letters should be approved and immediately prepared upon acceptance of the verbal offer for the candidate.

Task #21: Administer Post-Offer Employment Activities

When the offer has been accepted by the selected candidate, the transition from candidate to employee now begins. Employment relationships in many U.S. states are subject to the law of *employment-at-will,* meaning that the relationship can be ended at any time by either party, with or without a reason (more information is noted in Chapter 7). As a result, few employees will be working under an employment contract agreement. Executives, who are often key contributors, are typically the type of employee who would fall into that category.

Post-offer employment activities will include the execution of employment agreements, completing the required tax and government forms, relocation to the job site, and perhaps immigration visas. At this stage, the newly hired employee forms their first impression of what it will be like in the company. Your activities will have a spotlight shining on them, so remember that first impressions count. Get it right, make it professional, and be the example of the culture of your company.

Task #22: Communicate Compensation and Benefits Programs and Systems

In Chapter 5, you learned the many aspects of compensation and benefits that legally require effective communication and understanding. As a "total rewards program," compensation and benefits uniquely require complete understanding on the part of the organization's workers and management. The importance of excellent two-way communications comes not only from the law, which it does in many cases, but also from the moral responsibility to fully inform management and workers of their benefit entitlement obligations as well as their benefits.

Task #23: Coordinate Activities to Support Employee Benefits Programs

As an entry-level HR professional, you will have the opportunity to learn and support many benefit programs in your organization (for example, wellness and retirement planning programs). You may be tasked with helping workers understand their Social Security benefits as well as their Medicare benefits, Parts A, B, and D, as part of your real-world learning process. You may also be asked to answer basic questions about unemployment insurance, workers' compensation, the Consolidated Omnibus Budget Reconciliation Act (COBRA), the Health Insurance Portability and Accountability Act (HIPAA), and the Family and Medical Leave Act (FMLA). While you won't be expected to be an expert, you will be expected to be able to help or direct a worker with a benefits question to a knowledgeable resource as part of your organization's HR team. This means you need to have some basic knowledge and understanding to be able to provide at least some basic information regarding these programs.

Other benefits you need to know with at least a basic threshold of knowledge include state versions of family and medical leave laws in states where these laws apply. Other benefit programs that are a "need to know," at least at a basic level for the entry-level HR professional, include healthcare benefits, consumer-driven healthcare, retirement benefits, wellness programs, and the basic purpose of the Employee Retirement Income Security Act (ERISA).

In the Trenches

aPHR Task #23

Ultimately, the value you place in your organization's benefits program tells your employees how much you value them. Benefits are a key driver for recruiting and retaining top performers. While not every organization has the ability to provide the richest benefits plan, being creative with this task will go further than you think. Take the time to understand your workforce and what is important to them. Oftentimes, there are free or low-cost ways to add great value to your benefits plan. Talk to your benefits broker about programs that you may be underutilizing, such as your employee assistance program or wellness program. I've learned that it is also important to talk to your employees to find out what is important to them. Soliciting feedback can be a great way to launch a popular program at the office and engage willing participants in the process.

–CN

Task #24: Coordinate Payroll-Related Information

Many payroll activities are related to HR issues (for example, new hire forms, pay adjustments, paid time off, and terminations). This requires the payroll and HR departments to coordinate shared functions. As a junior member of this team, you will be expected to work closely with payroll in support of your organization's recruitment, processing pay increases and benefit deductions, handling paid time off and vacation leaves, and doing the paperwork needed to process employment terminations, both voluntary and involuntary. As the champion of employee relations, the HR department must be sensitive to the time devoted to payroll processing because employees will face issues directly if paychecks aren't processed correctly and on time. The payroll and HR departments are privy to confidential employee data, including financial information, Social Security numbers, and home addresses. The two departments must work together to ensure that this information doesn't fall prey to unauthorized individuals or companies.

Payroll functions are covered by either the finance department or the HR department in most organizations.[1] Essentially, payroll is number driven and calls for knowledge of tax laws and accounting. Because of this, many respondents believe that payroll should be positioned with the finance department. At the same time, payroll is considered a function of HR because it pays and deals with people. The HR side is concerned with the company preserving the employees' rights and abiding by federal and state anti-discrimination laws. At the same time, the employee must receive compensation, a finance function, in accordance with the company's policies.

Task #25: Process Claims from Employees

A primary function of HR is to ensure the company complies with federal and state labor and employment laws, such as Title VII of the Civil Rights Act of 1964 and the Occupational Safety and Health Act of 1970. Employees are the HR department's internal customers; therefore, HR's obligation to serve its internal customers is another function of the department. Within those two areas—compliance and customer service—the core responsibilities of HR include transactional and functional activities, such as establishing compensation structure, addressing employee relations matters, recruiting qualified applicants, maintaining workplace safety, and processing workers' compensation and short-term and long-term disability benefits where they apply.

Task #26: Resolve Routine Employee Compensation and Benefits Issues

HR generalists often work on compensation and benefits issues with guidance and direction from compensation and benefits specialists. In larger organizations, HR generalists often receive guidance from internal, and sometimes external, compensation and benefits specialists to develop strategic compensation plans, align performance management systems with the organization's compensation structure, and monitor negotiations for group healthcare benefits. Examples of HR generalist responsibilities include addressing and resolving routine compensation and benefits issues, monitoring Family and Medical Leave Act compliance, and adhering to confidentiality provisions for employee medical files.

HR generalists for small companies might also conduct open enrollment for employees' annual elections pertaining to healthcare coverage. This team approach provides the organization with the technical expertise it needs while benefitting junior-level HR generalists through their exposure to HR strategic responsibilities.

Task #27: Conduct Orientation and Onboarding for New Hires, Rehires, and Transfers

An HR generalist is a key person within the human resources function of an organization. Principally, the HR generalist is responsible for the day-to-day management of HR operations, which means they manage the administration of the organization's employment-related policies, procedures, and programs. HR generalists are almost universally responsible for recruiting, screening, interviewing, and recommending the selection of job candidates. They may also handle employee relations, payroll, benefits, and training. In many organizations, the work of an HR generalist is often administratively focused in nature and involves documenting grievances, terminations, absences, performance reports, and compensation and benefits information.

Task #28: Coordinate Training Sessions

Training embodies a wide range of topics. In human resource management terms, it can include logistics, materials, training record tracking, training registration, and training evaluation. Employee training can be conducted in-house or by an outside provider. Keeping records of what training experiences each employee has had will likely be your responsibility, but this task goes beyond recordkeeping.

You will probably be asked to provide administrative support to in-house training programs, particularly those related to HR topics. You may even be asked to conduct some of that training. Think about all that is required for a training program to be successful. There is more to training success than having an instructor competent in the subject matter: all of the registration functions (seat reservations and check-in), facility reservations (training room), audio/visual (AV) equipment reservations and testing for operability, reproduction of training materials, recording the names of people who actually attend the program, ordering refreshments and food if appropriate, and collecting and summarizing program evaluation forms. To successfully complete this task, you will need to develop a checklist of duties required for each training program. Using it to prepare for each program and documenting all that happened are important.

It is not uncommon for employees to attend outside training programs. You will need to keep records about who went to which training program. In addition, you may even be asked to research the training programs available for a specific application. That will mean surveying outside vendors for a program that meet the needs of your staff.

Training is a necessary component of many certification, recertification, and licensing requirements. Recertification for the aPHR designation requires continuing education in the HR profession. You will probably be required to keep records for all those requirements if the employees are not responsible for maintaining their own documentation.

In the Trenches

aPHR Task #28

As a human resource professional, training is your friend. Everyone can benefit from growth and development, and helping with this task can be rewarding. Additionally, having a pulse of the overall training function at your organization can be helpful in your position. Whenever the day-to-day HR concerns walk through your door, ask yourself, how can training make this situation better? Do we need better supervisory training? Are all employees struggling with understanding the same policy? Training sessions can be the foundation for resolving many of the challenges in the workplace.

–CN

Task #29: Conduct Employee Training Programs

As a new HR professional, you may be asked to conduct training for employees on topics such as safety regulations, emergency preparedness, presentation skills, and time management. Safety programs involve identifying safety and health hazards in the workplace, protecting workers from those hazards, and eliminating the hazards as quickly as possible. Your company will have its own documentation requirements, alert notification chain, and resolution monitors. In the absence of a dedicated safety manager, you can be asked to fill these roles. A key training requirement is the annual delivery of the emergency evacuation plan. Including workplace violence (everything from verbal assault to assault with an automatic rifle), employees must understand how to evacuate the building and where to assemble so they can be counted. It is necessary to impress upon employees the importance of identifying anyone left in the facility so rescue can be planned. Typical tragedies include workplace violence, earthquake, fire, flood, and wind storms (tornado or hurricane). You can expect to be responsible for conducting practice evacuations periodically.

Communication skills often fall within the purview of the HR department. That includes written communication training. (What is the company style? What memo and letter formats must be used? How should forms be completed?) It also includes oral communication training, which can range from one-on-one conversations to group presentations from the podium. You should expect to be in the spotlight if you are going to be an HR professional.

Time management is a common training topic. Some folks grow up not knowing how to manage their own time. Setting priorities, asking for input about priorities, and building action plans based on priorities are all components of time management. You can become the expert on the topic and share that expertise with your employee population.

In the Trenches

aPHR Task #29

For many, it is an unfortunate reality that public speaking is frightening. Even after working in HR for many years, the hairs on my neck stand up when I have to conduct a presentation in a meeting. One of my favorite quotes from Eleanor Roosevelt is, "Do one thing every day that scares you." So use this opportunity to grow! Communication is a critical component of being a good HR professional, and honing these skills can lead to growth and success in many areas. The organization will look to HR to drive the communication program for the company and its people. Smile and take on this task with pride. It will take you further than you realize.

—CN

Task #30: Coordinate the Logistics for Employee Relations Programs

The employee relations function is, by pure definition, focused on relationships in the workplace—how employees interact with each other and management, how they feel about the work they perform and the conditions in which they perform their jobs, and whether they feel treated fairly and with respect. Creating and administering programs associated with employee relations is a big chunk of the early-career HR professional's responsibilities. Examples of ER programs include service and performance recognition programs, special events like Bring Your Child to Work Day, and various diversity programs.

You may find yourself in the role of an event coordinator, organizing special functions that align with the company's culture, values, and celebrations. You could find yourself in the role of the birthday and anniversary fairy, bestowing upon employees the recognition of their special day. Ensuring that milestones such as years-of-service anniversaries and recognition awards are timely typically begins within the HR function—"the keeper of the information." Logistics will typically involve negotiating purchases of service awards, securing special recognition treats such as gift cards, and choosing the location of events such as the annual holiday bash. These are important tasks where you get to use creativity, imagination, ingenuity, and resourcefulness.

In the Trenches

aPHR Task #30

When you spend most of your waking hours with the same group of people, everyone desires to feel included and appreciated. In employee relations, we get to create programs that show the workforce how much we appreciate them, but we often become involved in challenging interpersonal situations as well. When an employee comes to you with a concern, oftentimes it matters most that you listen and help to provide a solution. There have been countless times when I have resolved an issue between two employees simply by listening to concerns and remaining diligent on follow-up. It's easy to do and shows how much you respect and value the employees at your organization.

—CN

Task #31: Monitor Completion of Performance Reviews and Development Plans

The importance of performance management as an ongoing process of providing developmental feedback to employees about their performance and expectations for new performance will continue to be an ongoing process for organizations. It's the core to creating continuing growth and expansion for both the employee and the company.

A key element of these programs is the monitoring and consistency of ensuring they occur timely and fairly. In early-level HR professional roles, the role of ensuring that supervisors follow through with their responsibilities to conduct performance reviews and set out training and development plans for their employees can be daunting, almost nagging in some instances. Yet meaningful feedback and recognition, along with clear goals and expectations, are what employees request more often than not. There are software systems, much like applicant tracking systems, that can assist you with this tracking function; use them to the full extent possible in keeping supervisors on track and compliant.

In the Trenches

aPHR Task #31

This task might not win you the popularity contest, but it is an important part of our role in HR. Historically, managers and employees are engaged at different levels in the performance review process. This typically means a lot of hand-holding for HR professionals. Communicate deadlines early and often! It is also important to make sure that reviews are inclusive of the whole monitoring period and not biased. Don't be afraid to provide feedback to managers if they are having challenges with the process.

–CN

Chapter Review

The aPHR exam is a knowledge-based exam. Candidates are responsible for knowing and understanding the five knowledge areas that were set forth in Chapters 3 through 7. The 31 tasks in this chapter are typical assignments and functions that HRCI has identified an individual would likely be expected to perform, and know, at the early HR career level. Again, they will not be part of the exam; however, they are an important basis for knowing what to expect in an entry-level HR professional job.

Endnote

1. Deloitte's 2018 Payroll Operations Survey: 51 percent of companies surveyed reported that payroll was a function of their finance departments, and 31 percent said that payroll was a function of their HR departments.

PART III

Appendixes and Glossary

- **Appendix A** List of Common HR Acronyms
- **Appendix B** Case Laws by Chapter
- **Appendix C** For Additional Study
- **Appendix D** About the Online Content
- **Glossary**

List of Common HR Acronyms

AA	1) affirmative action; 2) adverse action
AACSB	Association to Advance Collegiate Schools of Business
AACU	American Association of Colleges and Universities
AAO	Affirmative Action Officer
AAP	Affirmative Action Plan
AAR	average annual return
ABF	asset-based financing
ABM	activity-based management
ABMS	activity-based management system
ACA	Affordable Care Act
ACH	Automated Clearing House
AD&D	accidental death and dismemberment
ADA	Americans with Disabilities Act
ADAAA	Americans with Disabilities Act Amendments Act
ADEA	Age Discrimination in Employment Act
ADL	activities of daily living
ADP	Automatic Data Processing
ADR	alternative dispute resolution
AFL-CIO	American Federation of Labor and Congress of Industrial Organizations
AFSCME	American Federation of State, County, and Municipal Employers
AI	appreciative inquiry
AIDS	Acquired Immune Deficiency Syndrome
AJB	America's Job Bank
ALC	Alien Labor Certification
ALEX	Automated Labor Exchange
ALJ	administrative law judge
ALM	asset liability management
AMPS	auction market preferred stock

ANSI	American National Standards Institute
AP	accounts payable
APA	American Psychological Association
APB	Accounting Principles Board
aPHR	Associate Professional in Human Resources
APR	annual percentage rate
APV	adjusted present value
APY	annual percentage yield
AR	accounts receivable
ARRA	American Recovery and Reinvestment Act
ASB	Accounting Standards Board
ASHHRA	American Society for Healthcare Human Resources Administration
ASO	Administrative Services Only plan
ASTD	American Society for Training and Development
ATB	across the board
ATO	1) administrative time off; 2) asset turnover
ATOI	after-tax operating income
ATU	annual tax unit
AWL	actual wage loss
AWOL	absent without leave
AWW	average weekly wage
BARS	behaviorally anchored rating scale
BAT	Bureau of Apprenticeship and Training
BB	base benefits
BCP	business continuity plan
BCR	benefit/cost ratio
BFOQ or BOQ	bona fide occupational qualification
BIA	business impact analysis
BLBA	Black Lung Benefits Act
BLS	Bureau of Labor Statistics
BNA	Bureau of National Affairs
BOD	board of directors
BOT	board of trustees
BPA	blanket purchase agreement
BRB	Benefits Review Board
BU	bargaining unit
C&B	compensation and benefits
C&P	compensation and pension
CAA	Congressional Accountability Act
CAFTA	Central American Free Trade Agreement
CAI	computer-assisted instruction

CAO	chief administrative officer
CAPEX	capital expenditures
CASB	Cost Accounting Standards Board
CBA	1) collective bargaining agreement; 2) cost benefit analysis
CBO	Congressional Budget Office
CBP	cafeteria benefits plan
CBT	computer-based testing
CC	civil code
CCH	Commerce Clearing House
CCHR	Canadian Council on Human Resources
CCI	Consumer Confidence Index
CCL	Center for Creative Leadership
CCP	Certified Compensation Professional
CCPA	Consumer Credit Protection Act
CDC	Centers for Disease Control and Prevention
CDL	commercial driver's license
CEA	1) Commodity Exchange Authority; 2) Certificate of Educational Achievement
CEBS	Certified Employee Benefits Specialist
CEO	chief executive officer
CEPS	cash earnings per share
CEU	continuing education unit
CFAT	cash flow after taxes
CFO	chief financial officer
CFR	Code of Federal Regulations
CGQ	corporate governance quotient
CGT	capital gains tax
CHRC	1) Canadian Human Rights Commission; 2) criminal history records check
CHRO	chief human resources officer
CIO	1) chief investment officer; 2) chief information officer
CISO	chief information security officer
CMA	Certified Management Accountant
CMO	chief marketing officer
CO	compliance officer
COB	close of business
COBRA	Consolidated Omnibus Budget Reconciliation Act
COL	cost of living
COLA	cost of living adjustment
COO	chief operating/operations officer
CPA	Certified Public Accountant

PART III

CPE	Continuing Professional Education
CPG	consumer packaged goods
CPI	Consumer Price Index
CPI-U	Consumer Price Index for All Urban Consumers
CPI-W	Consumer Price Index for Urban Wage Earners and Clerical Workers
CPM	critical path method
CR	corporate responsibility
CRM	1) client relationship management; 2) customer relationship management; 3) credit risk management
CROGI	cash return on gross investment
CSHO	compliance safety and health officer
CSO	1) chief security officer; 2) chief strategy officer
CTO	1) compensatory time off; 2) chief technology officer
CTS	carpal tunnel syndrome
CUPA	College and University Personnel Association
CUSFTA	Canada-U.S. Free Trade Agreement
CV	curriculum vitae
CWHSSA	Contract Work Hours and Safety Standards Act
CWSP	College Work-Study Program
D&I	diversity and inclusion
D&O	directors and officers
DB	defined benefit
DBA	1) Davis-Bacon Act; 2) doing business as
DBPP	defined benefit pension plan
DC	defined contribution
DCA	dollar cost averaging
DCAA	Defense Contract Audit Agency
DCAP	Dependent Care Assistance Program
DCF	discounted cash flow
DCPP	defined contribution pension plan
DEFRA	Deficit Reduction Act
DFA	Department of Finance and Administration
DFEH	Department of Fair Employment and Housing
DINKS	dual income no kids
DJIA	Dow Jones Industrial Average
DMADV	Define, Measure, Analyze, Design, Verify
DMAIC	Define, Measure, Analyze, Improve, Control
DOB	date of birth
DOC	United States Department of Commerce
DOD	United States Department of Defense
DOH	date of hire

DOI	date of injury
DOJ	United States Department of Justice
DOL	United States Department of Labor
DOLETA	Department of Labor Employment and Training Administration
DOT	1) Dictionary of Occupational Titles; 2) United States Department of Transportation
DRIP	dividend reinvestment plan
DRP	disaster recovery plan
DSI	discretionary salary increase
DSPP	direct stock purchase plan
DTI	Department of Trade and Industry
DVOP	Disabled Veterans Outreach Program
DW	dislocated worker
DWC	Division of Workers' Compensation
EAC	employee advisory committee/council
EAP	employee assistance program
EAPA	Employee Assistance Professionals Association
EB	extended benefits
EBO	employee buyout
EBRI	Employee Benefits Research Institute
EBS	Employee Benefits Security
EBSA	Employee Benefit Security Administration
EBT	earnings before tax
ECI	Employment Cost Index
ECOA	Equal Credit Opportunity Act
ECPA	Electronic Communications Privacy Act
EDA	economically depressed area
EDI	electronic data interchange
EDP	1) electronic data processing; 2) employee development plan
EE	employee
EEO	equal employment opportunity
EEO-1/EEO-4	EEO-1 or EEO-4 Report/Standard Form 100 Report
EEOC	Equal Employment Opportunity Commission
EEOICPA	Energy Employee Occupational Illness Compensation Program Act
EFT	electronic funds transfer
EFTA	European Free Trade Area
EGTRRA	Economic Growth and Tax Relief Reconciliation Act
EI or EQ	emotional intelligence
EIC	earned income tax credit
EIN	employer identification number
EMT	1) executive management team; 2) emergency medical technician

EO	executive order
EOB	explanation of benefits
EOD	end of day
EOI	evidence of insurability
EOY	end of year
EPA	1) Equal Pay Act; 2) Environmental Protection Agency
EPLI	employment practices liability insurance
EPPA	Employee Polygraph Protection Act
EPS	earnings per share
ER	employer
ERISA	Employee Retirement Income Security Act
ERTA	Economic Recovery Tax Act
ESA	Employment Standards Administration
ESL	English as a second language
ESO	employee stock option
ESOP	employee stock option plan
ESOT	employee stock ownership and trust
ESP	exchange stock portfolio
ESS	employee self-service
ETA	1) Employment and Training Administration; 2) estimated time of arrival
EU	European Union
EV	enterprise value
EVA	economic value added
E-VERIFY	United States Department of Labor New Hire Screening System
EVM	earned value management
EX	exempt
FAAS	Financial Assurance and Accountability Standards
FACT	Fair and Accurate Credit Transactions Act
FAQ	frequently asked questions
FAS	Financial Accounting Standards
FASAB	Financial Accounting Standards Advisory Board
FASAC	Financial Accounting Standards Advisory Committee
FASB	Financial Accounting Standards Board
FCC	Federal Communications Commission
FCCPA	Federal Consumer Credit Protection Act
FCPA	Foreign Corrupt Practices Act
FCRA	Fair Credit Reporting Act
FDA	Food and Drug Administration
FDCPA	Fair Debt Collection Practices Act
FDIC	Federal Deposit Insurance Corporation

FEA	Fair Employment Act
FECA	Federal Employees' Compensation Act
FEIN	federal employment identification number
FELA	Federal Employment Liability Act
FEMA	Federal Emergency Management Agency
FEP	Fair Employment Practice
FERS	Federal Employees Retirement System
FES	factor evaluation system
FFY	federal fiscal year
FHA	Federal Housing Administration
FICA	Federal Insurance Contributions Act
FICO	Fair Isaac Credit Organization
FIE	foreign invested enterprise
FIFO	first in, first out
FLC	Foreign Labor Certification
FLRA	Federal Labor Relations Authority
FLSA	Fair Labor Standards Act
FMLA	Family Medical Leave Act
FMSHA	Federal Mine and Safety Health Act
FMV	fair market value
FOIA	Freedom of Information Act
FOM	Field Operations Manual
FOREX	Foreign Exchange
FR	Federal Register
FRA	Federal Reserve Act
FRB	Federal Reserve Board
FROI	first report of injury
FRS	Financial Reporting Standards
FSA	flexible spending account
FSB	Fortune Small Business
FSET	Federal/State Employment Tax
FSLMRA	Federal Service Labor-Management Relations Act
FT	full time
FTA	free trade agreement
FTC	Federal Trade Commission
FTD	federal tax deposit
FTE	full-time equivalent
FTP	File Transfer Protocol
FUA	Federal Unemployment Account
FUTA	Federal Unemployment Tax Act
FY	fiscal year

GAAC	Government Accounting and Auditing Committee
GAAFR	Governmental Accounting, Auditing, and Financial Reporting
GAAP	Generally Accepted Accounting Principles
GAAS	Generally Accepted Auditing Standards
GAGAS	Generally Accepted Government Accounting Standards
GAO	General Accounting Office
GAS	Governmental Accounting Standards
GASB	Governmental Accounting Standards Board
GATB	General Aptitude Test Battery
GATT	General Agreement on Tariffs and Trade
GDP	gross domestic product
GED	General Equivalency Diploma
GIC	guaranteed investment contract
GICS	Global Industry Classification Standards
GIF	guaranteed investment fund
GINA	Genetic Information Nondiscrimination Act
GIPS	Global Investment Policy Standard
GIS	geographic information system
GL	1) general ledger; 2) general liability
GLB	Gramm-Leach-Bliley Act
GLSO	Group Legal Services Organization
GM	gross margin
GNP	gross national product
GPHR	Global Professional in Human Resources Certification
GPROI	gross profit return on investment
GPS	global positioning system
GR	general revenue
GS	general schedule
GSI	general salary increase
GTL	group term life insurance
HAS	highest average salary
HAZMAT	hazardous material
HB	House Bill
HC	human capital
HCE	highly compensated employee
HCFA	Health Care Financing Administration
HCM	human capital management
HCN	home-country nationals
HCO	health care organization
HCSA	Health Care Spending Account
HCTC	Health Coverage Tax Credit

HHS	Department of Health and Human Services
HICP	Harmonized Index of Consumer Prices
HIPAA	Health Insurance Portability and Accountability Act
HIPC	health insurance purchasing cooperatives
HITECH	Health Information Technology for Economic and Clinical Health Act
HIV	human immunodeficiency virus
HMO	health maintenance organization
HR	human resources
HRA	Health Reimbursement Account
HRCI	Human Resource Certification Institute
HRCS	Human Resource Competency Study
HRD	1) human resources development; 2) human resources department
HRIS	human resources information system
HRLY	hourly
HRM	human resources management
HRMS	human resources management system
HROD	human resources and organizational development
HSA	health savings account
HTML	Hypertext Markup Language
HUD	United States Department of Housing and Urban Development
I-9	United States Immigration Form I-9
IAG	International Auditing Guidelines
IAS	International Accounting Standards
IASC	International Accounting Standards Committee
ICC	International Chamber of Commerce
ICE	United States Immigration and Customs Enforcement
IFEBP	International Foundation of Employee Benefit Plans
IHRIM	International Association of Human Resource Information Management
IIPP	injury and illness prevention programs/plans
ILAB	International Labor Affairs Bureau
ILO	International Labor Organization
IME	independent medical examination
INA	Immigration and Naturalization Act
INS	Immigration and Naturalization Service
IOS	International Organization for Standards
IPA	inflation protected annuity
IPI	Industrial Protection Index
IPMA	International Personnel Management Association
IPO	initial public offering
IPS	1) inflation protected security; 2) investment policy statement

IRA	individual retirement account
IRB	Internal Revenue Bulletin
IRC	Internal Revenue Code
IRCA	Immigration Reform and Control Act
IRR	internal rate of return
IRS	Internal Revenue Service
ISO	1) International Standards Organization; 2) incentive stock option
ISP	Internet service provider
ISSA	International Securities Services Association
IT	information technology
ITA	United States International Trade Administration
ITIN	Individual Taxpayer Identification Number
IUR	insured unemployment rates
IVR	interactive voice response
J&S	joint and survivorship
JAN	Job Accommodation Network
JD	1) job description; 2) Juris Doctorate; 3) job date
JEEP	Joint Ethics Enforcement Plan
JGTRRA	Jobs and Growth Tax Relief Reconciliation Act
JIT	just in time
JOA	joint operating agreement
JPAC	Joint Public Advisory Committee
JPEG	Joint Photographic Experts Group
JSSA	Jury Selection and Service Act
JTPA	Job Training Partnership Act (replaced by WIA)
JV	joint venture
JVA	Jobs for Veterans Act
KM	knowledge management
KPI	key performance indicator
KSA	knowledge, skills, and abilities
KSOP	401(k) employee stock option plan
LA	labor area
LAN	local area network
LAR	Legislative Appropriations Request
LAUS	Local Area Unemployment Statistics
LBB	Legislative Budget Board
LBO	leveraged buyout
LCA	Labor Condition Application
LCD	labor cost distribution
LDI	liability-driven investment
LDP	last day paid

LDW	last day worked
LEI	leading economic indicators
LEO	long-term equity options
LEPO	low exercise price option
LF	labor force
LFPR	labor force participation rate
LFY	last fiscal year
LHWCA	Longshore and Harbor Workers' Compensation Act
LIFO	last in, first out
LLC	limited liability company
LLP	limited liability partnership
LMA	labor market area
LMI	labor market information
LMRA	Labor Management Relations Act
LMRDA	Labor-Management Reporting and Disclosure Act
LMS	learning management system
LO	learning objectives
LOA	leave of absence
LOC	letter of commitment
LOI	letter of intent
LOR	letter of response
LOS	length of stay
LOW	lack of work
LP	limited partnership
LR	labor relations
LRO	labor relations officer
LT	lost time
LTC	long-term care
LTCM	long-term capital management
LTD	long-term disability
LTFP	long-term financial plan
LTIP	long-term incentive plan
LTO	long-term option
LTV	loan-to-value ratio
LWDI	lost workday injury rate
LWO	leave without pay
LWP	leave with pay
M&A	merger and acquisition
MBO	management by objectives
MBTI	Myers-Briggs type indicator
MER	management expense ratio

PART III

MEWA	Multiple Employer Welfare Arrangement
MHAEA	Mental Health and Addiction Equity Act
MHPA	Mental Health Parity Act
MHPAEA	Mental Health Parity and Addiction Equity Act
MIRR	modified internal rate of return
MIS	management information system
MLA	minimum liquid assets
MLM	multilevel marketing
MLP	master limited partnership
MLR	*Monthly Labor Review*
MLS	mass layoff statistics
MNC	multinational corporation
MOC	market on close
MOF	Ministry of Finance
MOU	memorandum of understanding
MPPAA	Multiemployer Pension Plan Amendments Act
MRD	minimum required distribution
MSA	1) medical savings account; 2) metropolitan statistical area; 3) merit salary adjustment
MSDS	material safety data sheet
MSFW	migrant and seasonal farm worker
MSHA	Mine Safety and Health Act
MSP	managed service provider
MSPA	Migrant and Seasonal Agriculture Worker Protection Act
MSPB	Merit Systems Protection Board
MSPR	Medicare secondary payer rules
MST	marketable securities tax
MTD	month to date
MTHLY	monthly
NAAEC	North American Agreement on Environmental Cooperation
NAALC	North American Agreement on Labor Cooperation
NAB	nonaccrual basis
NAFTA	North American Free Trade Agreement
NAFTA-TAA	NAFTA Transitional Adjustment Assistance
NAICS	North American Industry Classification System
NASDAQ	National Association of Securities Dealers Automated Quotations
NASDR	National Association of Securities Dealers Regulation
NATO	North Atlantic Treaty Organization
NAV	net asset value
NAVPS	net asset value per share
NAWW	national average weekly wage

NCCI	National Council on Compensation Insurance
NDNH	National Directory of New Hires
NEO	new and emerging occupations
NEX	nonexempt
NFA	net financial asset
NFE	net financial expense
NFI	net financial income
NFO	net financial obligation
NHCE	non-highly compensated employee
NI	net income
NIH	National Institutes of Health
NIOSH	National Institute of Occupational Safety and Health
NL	no load
NLRA	National Labor Relations Act
NLRB	National Labor Relations Board
NMB	National Mediation Board
NMHPA	Newborns' and Mothers' Health Protection Act
NMS	normal market size
NOA	net operating assets
NOI	net operating income
NOL	net operating loss
NOPAT	net operating profit after taxes
NPV	net present value
NRA	nonresident alien
NRET	nonresident withholding tax
NSC	National Security Council
NSTA	National Securities Trade Association
NSX	National Stock Exchange
NT	near term
NVI	Negative Volume Index
NYSE	New York Stock Exchange
O*Net	Occupational Information Network
OA	operating assets
OAS	option-adjusted spread
OASDHI	Old Age, Survivors, Disability, and Health Insurance
OASDI	Old Age and Survivors Disability Insurance
OASI	Old Age Survivors Insurance
OBRA	Omnibus Budget Reconciliation Act
OCF	operating cash flow
OD	organizational development
ODDS	online data delivery system

PART III

OE	operating expense
OEBS	Office of Employee Benefits Security (replaced by PWBP)
OER	operation expense ratio
OES	Occupational Employment Statistics
OFCCP	Office of Federal Contract Compliance Programs
OHCA	organized health care arrangement
OI	operating income
OIS	occupations information system
OJT	on-the-job training
OL	operating liabilities
OM	options market
OMB	Office of Management and Budget
OOB	out of business
OOH	Occupational Outlook Handbook
OPM	Office of Personnel Management
OR	operating revenue
OSHA	Occupational Safety and Health Administration
OT	overtime
OTC	over the counter
OTI	OSHA Training Institute
OTS	Office of Thrift Supervision
OWBPA	Older Workers Benefit Protection Act
P&L	profit and loss
PAR	Public Accounting Report
PBGC	Pension Benefit Guaranty Corporation
PBO	projected benefit obligation
PBSI	performance-based salary increase
PBT	profit before tax
PC	1) personal computer; 2) politically correct
PCAOB	Public Company Accounting Oversight Board
PCE	1) preexisting condition exclusion; 2) private commercial enterprise
PCI	per-capita income
PCN	parent-country nationals
PD	position description
PDA	1) Pregnancy Discrimination Act; 2) personal data assistant; 3) public display of affection; 4) payday advance loan
PDF	Portable Document Format
PDQ	position description questionnaire
PE	price-to-earnings ratio
PEG	price-to-earnings growth
PEO	professional employer organization

PEPPRA	Public Employee Pension Plan Reporting and Accountability Act
PERT	project evaluation and review techniques
PEST	political, economic, social, and technological
PFK	pay for knowledge
PHI	protected health information
PHR	Professional in Human Resources Certification
PHRca	Professional in Human Resources Certification – California
PIK	payment in kind
PIP	performance improvement plan
PL	public law
PM	1) profit margin; 2) performance management
PMSA	primary metropolitan statistical area
PMV	private market value
PNG	Portable Network Graphics
POA	power of attorney
POB	Public Oversights Board
POD	1) payable on death; 2) professional and organizational development
POP	1) premium-only plan; 2) public offering price
POS	point of service plan
PPA	Pension Protection Act of 1987
PPACA	Patient Protection and Affordable Care Act
PPE	personal protective equipment
PPI	Producer Price Index
PPO	preferred provider organization
PR	public relations
PRC	peer review committee
PSI	performance salary increase
PT	part time
PTO	paid time off
PTSD	post-traumatic stress syndrome
PV	present value
PW	present worth
PWBA	Pension and Welfare Benefits Administration
PWBP	Pension and Welfare Benefit Program
PWC	Public Works Commission
PWD	prevailing wage determination
PY	program year
QA	quality assurance
QAIP	quality assurance and improvement plan
QBU	qualified business unit
QC	quality control

QCEW	Quarterly Census of Employment and Wages
QCR	quarterly contributions report
QDRO	qualified domestic relations order
QMAC	qualified matching contributions
QMCSO	qualified medical child support order
QME	qualified medical examiner
QNEC	qualified non-elective contributions
QPAM	qualified professional asset manager
QR	1) quarterly report; 2) quality review
QREC	Quality Review Executive Committee
QTD	1) qualified total distribution; 2) quarter to date
QWI	quarterly workforce indicators
R&C	reasonable and customary
R&D	research and development
RA	resident alien
RAP	Regulatory Accounting Principles
RCR	recruiting cost ratio
RE	residual earnings
REA	Retirement Equity Act
RFB	request for bid
RFI	request for information
RFID	radio frequency identification
RFP	request for proposal
RFQ	request for quote
RIC	regulated investment company
RICO	Racketeer Influenced and Corrupt Organizations Act
RIF	reduction in force
RIPA	Retirement Income Policy Act
RMP	risk management plan
RNFA	return on net financial assets
ROA	return on assets
ROC	return on capital
ROI	return on investment
ROIC	return on invested capital
ROM	range of motion
RONA	return on net assets
ROOA	return on operating assets
ROR	return on revenue
ROS	return on sales
ROTA	return on total assets
ROTC	Reserve Officer Training Corps

RPI	Retail Price Index
RR	retention rate
RRSP	registered retirement savings plan
RSU	restricted stock unit
RTO	reverse takeover
RTW	1) return to work; 2) right to work
RWA	risk weighted asset
RYR	recruitment yield ratio
S&P	Standard and Poor's
SAAR	seasonally adjusted annual rate
SAR	1) summary annual report; 2) stock appreciation right
SARSEP	Salary Reduction Simplified Employee Pension
SAS	Statement of Accounting Standards
SAT	Scholastic Aptitude Test
SB	Senate Bill
SBA	Small Business Administration
SBAP	Small Business Assistance Program
SBBA	sales and buy-back agreement
SBJPA	Small Business Job Protection Act
SBLC	standby letter of credit
SBO	Small Business Ombudsman
SC	Securities Commission
SCA	McNamara-O'Hara Service Contract Act
SCM	supply chain management
SDB	small disadvantaged business
SDI	state disability insurance
SE	1) salaried exempt; 2) self-employed
SEA	Securities Exchange Act
SEC	Securities and Exchange Commission
SEP	Simplified Employee Pension
SEPPAA	Single Employer Pension Plan Amendments Act
SERP	supplemental executive retirement plan
SESA	State Employment Security Agency
SFAS	Statements of Financial Accounting Standards
SHRM	Society for Human Resource Management
SHRM-CP	SHRM Certified Professional
SHRM-SCP	SHRM Senior Certified Professional
SIA	Securities Industry Act
SIB	Securities and Investment Board
SIC	Standard Industrial Classification
SIPA	Securities Investment Protection Act

SITC	Standard International Trade Classification
SLA	service level agreement
SLOB	separate lines of business
SMART	Specific, Measurable, Achievable, Relevant, Timed
SMI	supplemental medical insurance
SMM	summary of material modifications
SMSA	standard metropolitan statistical area
SMT	senior management team
SNAP	Supplemental Nutrition Assistance Program
SNE	salaried nonexempt
SOC	Standard Occupational Classification
SOL	statute of limitations
SOP	statement of position
SOX	Sarbanes-Oxley Act
SPD	summary plan description
SPHR	Senior Professional in Human Resources Certification
SPX	Standard and Poor's Index
SRA	supplemental retirement annuity
SRO	self-regulatory organization
SROI	subsequent report of injury
SS	Social Security
SSA	Social Security Administration
SSB	Securities Supervisory Board
SSD	Social Security Disability
SSDI	Social Security Disability Indemnity
SSI	supplemental security income
SSN	Social Security number
STD	short-term disability insurance
STEEPLED	social, technological, environmental, economic, political, legal, ethics, and demographics
STF	Summary Tape File
STIP	short-term industry projections
STW	school-to-work
SUB	supplemental unemployment benefit
SUTA	State Unemployment Tax Act
SWOT	strengths, weaknesses, opportunities, and threats
T&D	training and development
TAMRA	Technical and Miscellaneous Revenue Act of 1988
TANF	Temporary Assistance to Needy Families
TBD	to be determined
TCN	third country national

TDA	tax-deferred annuity
TDB	temporary disability benefits
TEA	Transportation Efficiency Act
TEFRA	Tax Equity and Fiscal Responsibility Act
TER	total expense ratio
TESSA	tax-exempt special savings account
TEUC	Temporary Extended Unemployment Compensation
TEV	total enterprise value
TIL	truth in lending
TIP	Transportation Improvement Program
TL	time and labor
TN	temporary visitor visa
TOC	theory of constraints
TOM	traded options market
TPA	third-party administrator
TPD	temporary partial disability
TPL	third-party liability
TQM	total quality management
TRA	Tax Reform Act
TRASOP	Tax Reduction Act ESOP
TSA	tax-sheltered annuity
TSB	targeted small business
TSP	thrift savings plan
TTD	temporary total disability
TUR	total unemployment rates
TVI	trade value index
TWA	time weighted average
U&C	usual and customary
UAW	United Auto Workers
UBTI	Unrelated Business Taxable Income
UCA	Unemployment Compensation Amendments Act
UCC	Uniform Commercial Code
UCI	unemployment compensation insurance
UCR	usual, customary, and reasonable
UFW	United Farm Workers
UGESP	Uniform Guidelines on Employee Selection Procedures
UGMA	Uniform Gifts to Minors Act
UI	unemployment insurance
UIC	Unemployment Insurance Commission
ULP	unfair labor practice
UN	United Nations

UNCITRAL	United Nations Commission on International Trade Law
UR	1) utilization review; 2) unemployment rate
URL	Uniform Resource Locator (website address)
URO	utilization review organization
US DOJ	United States Department of Justice
US DOL	United States Department of Labor
USC	United States Code
USCIS	United States Citizenship and Immigration Services
USDA	United States Department of Agriculture
USERRA	Uniform Services Employment and Reemployment Rights Act
USITC	United States International Trade Commission
USM	Unlisted Securities Market
USTC	United States Tax Court
UTMA	Uniform Transfers to Minors Act
VA	Veterans Administration/Affairs
VBIA	Veterans Benefits Improvement Act
VEBA	Voluntary Employees' Beneficiary Association
VETS	Veterans Employment and Training Service
VETS-4212	VETS-4212 Report (replaced VETS-100)
VEVRA	Vietnam-Era Veterans Readjustment Act
VOC-ED	vocational education
VOC-REHAB	vocational rehabilitation
VPN	virtual private network
VPT	volume price trend
VWAP	value-weighted average price
VWPT	value-weighted price trading
VWPX	volume-weighted price uncrossing
WACC	weighted average cost of capital
WAI	Wealth Added Index
WARN	Worker Adjustment and Retraining Notification Act
WC	workers' compensation
WCB	Workers' Compensation Board
WDC	Workforce Development Center
WHCRA	Women's Health and Cancer Rights Act
WIA	Workforce Investment Act
WIP	work in progress
WKLY	weekly
WOTC	Workforce Opportunity Tax Credit
WPA	Wagner-Peyser Act
WPE	workforce planning and employment

WPI	Wholesale Price Index
WPPDA	Welfare and Pension Plan Disclosure Act (repealed by ERISA)
WRA	weighted risk assets
WRAEA	Workforce Reinvestment and Adult Education Act
WTO	World Trade Organization
WTW	Welfare to Work
XML	Extended Markup Language
XRA	expected retirement age
YTD	year to date
YTM	yield to maturity
ZBB	zero-based budgeting

PART III

Case Laws by Chapter

Generally speaking, there are three types of federal laws. First are the acts taken by Congress to legislate mandates. Congressional actions, when completed, become the "law of the land." Second are the implementing regulations publicized by the federal agencies and departments that specify in detail how the laws passed by Congress will be administered. Third are the court interpretations of those congressional actions and regulatory rules. When the U.S. Supreme Court or an agency such as the National Labor Relations Board (NLRB) issues a ruling about how the laws should be applied and interpreted, the ruling becomes "case law." It establishes a precedent that must be followed by everyone within the court's jurisdiction.

This appendix lists the cases that interpret important issues that have influence on human resource (HR) management. We provide a brief summary of key case law decisions. We recommend you review each case in its entirety by going to the link listed under each case and searching by citation title. HR professionals at all career levels should have a working knowledge of these cases and their impact in the workplace. This information may appear on the certification exam in one way or another.

Chapter 3: Talent Acquisition

Year	Citation	Decision
1971	*Griggs v. Duke Power Co.* (401 U.S. 424) www.law.cornell.edu/supct/html/historics/USSC_CR_0401_0424_ZS.html	When an employer uses a neutral test or other selection device and then discovers it has a disproportionate impact on minorities or women, the test must be discarded unless it can be shown that it was required as a business necessity.
1978	*Regents of University of California v. Bakke* (438 U.S. 265) http://caselaw.lp.findlaw.com/cgi-bin/getcase.pl?court=us&vol=438&invol=265	Medical school admission set-asides (16 of 100 seats) are illegal if they discriminate against whites and there is no previous discrimination against minorities established.

Year	Citation	Decision
1979	*United Steelworkers v. Weber* (443 U.S. 193) http://supreme.justia.com/cases/federal/us/443/193/case.html	Affirmative action plans are permissible if they are temporary and intended to "eliminate a manifest racial imbalance."
1982	*Connecticut v. Teal* (457 U.S. 440) http://caselaw.lp.findlaw.com/cgi-bin/getcase.pl?court=us&vol=457&invol=440	An employer is liable for racial discrimination when any part of its selection process, such as an unvalidated examination or test, has a disparate impact even if the final result of the hiring process is racially balanced. In effect, the court rejects the "bottom-line defense" and makes clear that the fair employment laws protect the individual. Fair treatment to a group is not a defense to an individual claim of discrimination.
1987	*Johnson v. Santa Clara County Transportation Agency* (480 U.S. 616) https://supreme.justia.com/cases/federal/us/480/616/	The employer was justified in hiring a woman who scored two points less than a man because it had an affirmative action plan that was temporary, flexible, and designed to correct an imbalance of white males in the workforce.
1988	*Watson v. Fort Worth Bank & Trust* (487 U.S. 977) http://supreme.justia.com/cases/federal/us/487/977/case.html	In a unanimous opinion, the Supreme Court declared that disparate impact analysis can be applied to subjective or discretionary selection practices.
1989	*City of Richmond v. J. A. Croson Company* (488 U.S. 469) http://supreme.justia.com/cases/federal/us/488/469/	Affirmative action programs can be maintained only by showing that the programs aim to eliminate the effects of past discrimination.
1989	*Price Waterhouse v. Hopkins* (490 U.S. 288) http://caselaw.lp.findlaw.com/cgi-bin/getcase.pl?court=us&vol=490&invol=228	This decision established how to analyze an employer's actions when the employer had mixed motives for an employment decision. If an employee shows that discrimination played a motivating part in an employment decision, the employer can attempt to prove as a defense that it would have made the same employment decision even if discrimination were not a factor.
1989	*Wards Cove Packing Co. v. Atonio* (490 U.S. 642) www.law.cornell.edu/supct/html/historics/USSC_CR_0490_0642_ZS.html	An employee is required to show disparate impact violation of Title VII in specific employment practices, not the cumulative effect of the employer's selection practices. When a showing of disparate impact is made, the employer only has to produce evidence of a business justification for the practice, and the burden of proof always remains with the employee.

Year	Citation	Decision
2001	*Circuit City Stores v. Adams* (532 U.S. 105) www.law.cornell.edu/supct/html/99-1379.ZS.html	The court ruled that a pre-hire employment application requiring that all employment disputes be settled by arbitration was enforceable under the Federal Arbitration Act.
2003	*Grutter v. Bollinger* (539 U.S. 306) http://supreme.justia.com/cases/federal/us/539/306/case.html *Gratz v. Bollinger* (539 U.S. 244) http://supreme.justia.com/cases/federal/us/539/244/case.html	The diversity of a student body is a compelling state interest that can justify the use of race in university admissions as long as the admissions policy is "narrowly tailored" to achieve this goal. The University of Michigan did not do so for its undergraduate program, but the law school admissions program satisfied the standard.
2009	*Ricci v. DeStefano* (No. 07-1428) www.supremecourt.gov/opinions/08pdf/07-1428.pdf	"...under Title VII, before an employer can engage in intentional discrimination for the asserted purpose of avoiding or remedying an unintentional disparate impact, the employer must have a strong basis in evidence to believe it will be subject to disparate-impact liability if it fails to take the race-conscious, discriminatory action."
2015	*EEOC v. Abercrombie & Fitch Stores, Inc.* (No. 14–86) https://www.supremecourt.gov/opinions/14pdf/14-86_p86b.pdf	In this case, a Muslim applicant was rejected for a job because she wore a head scarf. This ruling underscored the employer obligation to accommodate the religious practices of applicants as long as they do not create "undue hardship."

Chapter 4: Learning and Development

There are no case laws that directly relate to this HRCI functional area.

Chapter 5: Compensation and Benefits

Year	Citation	Decision
1974	*Corning Glass Works v. Brennan* (417 U.S. 188) http://supreme.justia.com/cases/federal/us/417/188/	Pay discrimination cases under the Equal Pay Act require the employee to prove that there is unequal pay based on sex for substantially equal work.
1987	*Leggett v. First Interstate Bank of Oregon* (739 P.2d 1083) https://law.justia.com/cases/oregon/court-of-appeals/1987/739-p-2d-1083.html	The employer invaded the privacy of the employee when a company representative contacted the employee's psychologist (to whom the employee had been referred by an employee assistance program [EAP]), inquiring about the employee's condition.

PART III

Year	Citation	Decision
2000	*Erie County Retirees Association v. County of Erie Pennsylvania* (2000 U.S. App. LEXIS 18317 3rd Cir. August 1, 2000) https://caselaw.findlaw.com/us-3rd-circuit/1210474.html	If an employee provides retiree health benefits, the health insurance benefits received by Medicare-eligible retirees cost the same as the health insurance benefits received by younger retirees.
2005	*IBP, Inc. v. Alvarez* (546 U.S. 21) www.law.cornell.edu/supct/html/03-1238.ZS.html	Time spent donning or doffing unique safety gear is compensable, and the Fair Labor Standards Act (FLSA) requires payment of affected employees for all the time spent walking between changing and production areas.
2008	*LaRue v. DeWolff* (No. 06-856, 450 F. 3d 570) www.law.cornell.edu/supct/cert/06-856	When retirement plan administrators breach their fiduciary duty to act as a prudent person would act in investment of retirement funds, the employee whose retirement account lost money can sue the plan administrators.
2009	*Kennedy v. Plan Administrators for Dupont Savings and Investment Plan* (No. 07-636) www.supremecourt.gov/opinions/08pdf/07-636.pdf	This ruling awarded retirement benefits to an ex-spouse even though she had agreed to disclaim such benefits, because the retiree had never changed the beneficiary designation on the retirement plan. This decision pointed out the need for retirement plan administrators to pay attention to divorce decrees and qualified domestic relations orders.
2014	*Burwell v. Hobby Lobby Stores, Inc.* (S.Ct. No. 13-354) https://www.law.cornell.edu/supremecourt/text/13-354	A closely held private corporation cannot be forced to pay for contraceptives as part of the Affordable Care Act if there is an objection based on religious beliefs of the business owners.
2015	*Tibble et al. v. Edison International et al.* (No. 13–550) https://www.supremecourt.gov/opinions/14pdf/13-550_97be.pdf	The Supreme Court ruled that plan administrators of 401k plans must continue "to monitor trust investments and remove imprudent ones" to protect employees who participate in the plan.
2017	*Advocate Health Care Network v. Stapleton* (No. 16-74) https://www.supremecourt.gov/opinions/16pdf/16-74_5i36.pdf	The Supreme Court ruled that "church plan" exemption under ERISA applies to pension plans maintained by church-affiliated organizations such as healthcare facilities, even if the plans were not established by a church.

Chapter 6: Employee Relations

Year	Citation	Decision
1971	*Phillips v. Martin Marietta Corp.* (400 U.S. 542) https://supreme.justia.com/cases/federal/us/400/542/case.html	Sex discrimination means employers may not have different policies for men and women with small children of similar age.
1973	*McDonnell Douglas Corp. v. Green* (411 U.S. 792) http://caselaw.lp.findlaw.com/cgi-bin/getcase.pl?court=us&vol=411&invol=792	In a hiring case, the charging party has only to show 1) the charging party is a member of a Title VII protected group, 2) they have applied and were qualified for the position sought, 3) the job was not offered to them, and 4) the employer continued to seek applicants with similar qualifications. Then the employer must show a legitimate business reason why the complaining party was not hired. The employee has a final chance to prove the employer's business reason was really pretext for discrimination.
1974	*Espinoza v. Farah Manufacturing Co.* (414 U.S. 86) https://supreme.justia.com/cases/federal/us/414/86/case.html	Noncitizens are entitled to Title VII protection. Employers who require citizenship may violate Title VII if it results in discrimination based on national origin.
1975	*Albemarle Paper v. Moody* (422 U.S. 405) http://supreme.justia.com/cases/federal/us/422/405/	This decision requires an employer to establish evidence that an employment test is related to the job content. Job analysis could be used to show that relationship, but performance evaluations of incumbents are specifically excluded.
1976	*Washington v. Davis* (426 U.S. 229) www.law.cornell.edu/supct/html/historics/USSC_CR_0426_0229_ZS.html	When an employment test is challenged under constitutional law, an intent to discriminate must be established. Under Title VII there is no need to show intent, just the impact of test results.
1976	*McDonald v. Santa Fe Trail Transportation Co.* (427 U.S. 273) http://supreme.justia.com/cases/federal/us/427/273/case.html	Title VII prohibits racial discrimination against White as well as Black employees.
1977	*Hazelwood School District v. U.S.* (433 U.S. 299) http://caselaw.lp.findlaw.com/cgi-bin/getcase.pl?court=us&vol=433&invol=299	An employee can establish a prima facie case of class hiring discrimination through the presentation of statistical evidence by comparing the racial composition of an employer's workforce with the racial composition of the relevant labor market.

Year	Citation	Decision
1977	*Trans World Airlines, Inc. v. Hardison* (432 U.S. 63) http://supreme.justia.com/cases/federal/us/432/63/	Under Title VII, employers must reasonably accommodate an employee's religious needs unless doing so would create an undue hardship for the employer. The Court defines hardship as anything more than de minimis cost.
1984	*EEOC v. Shell Oil Co.* (466 U.S. 54) http://supreme.justia.com/cases/federal/us/466/54/	The Supreme Court affirmed authority of Equal Employment Opportunity Commission (EEOC) commissioners to initiate charges of discrimination through "Commissioner Charges."
1986	*Meritor Savings Bank v. Vinson* (477 U.S. 57) www.law.cornell.edu/supct/html/historics/USSC_CR_0477_0057_ZS.html	This defined "hostile environment sexual harassment" as a form of sex discrimination under Title VII. The decision further defined it as "unwelcome" advances of a sexual nature. A victim's failure to use an employer's complaint process does not insulate the employer from liability.
1987	*School Board of Nassau County v. Arline* (480 U.S. 273) http://supreme.justia.com/cases/federal/us/480/273/case.html	A person with a contagious disease is covered by the Rehabilitation Act if they otherwise meet the definitions of "handicapped individual."
1988	*DeBartolo Corp. v. Florida Gulf Coast Building and Construction Trades Council* (known as DeBartolo II) (485 U.S. 568) https://www.law.cornell.edu/supremecourt/text/485/568	The Supreme Court ruled that bannering, hand billing, and attention-getting actions outside an employer's property were permissible.
1992	*Electromation, Inc. v. NLRB* (Nos. 92-4129, 93-1169 7th Cir.) www.leagle.com/decision/1994118335F3d1148_11017	The NLRB held that action committees at Electromation were illegal "labor organizations" because management created and controlled the groups and used them to deal with employees on working conditions in violation of the National Labor Relations Act (NLRA).
1993	*E. I. DuPont & Company v. NLRB* (311 NLRB 893) http://scholarship.law.georgetown.edu/cgi/viewcontent.cgi?article=1013&context=legal	The board concluded that DuPont's six safety committees and fitness committee were employer-dominated labor organizations and that DuPont dominated the formation and administration of one of them in violation of the NLRA.
1993	*Harris v. Forklift Systems, Inc.* (510 U.S. 17) www.law.cornell.edu/supct/html/92-1168.ZO.html	In a sexual harassment complaint, the employee does not have to prove concrete psychological harm to establish a Title VII violation.

Year	Citation	Decision
1993	*St. Mary's Honor Center v. Hicks* (509 U.S. 502) www.law.cornell.edu/supct/html/92-602.ZS.html	Title VII complaints require the employee to show that discrimination was the reason for a negative employment action.
1993	*Taxman v. Board of Education of Township of Piscataway* (91 F.3d 1547, 3rd Cir.) https://caselaw.findlaw.com/us-3rd-circuit/1210629.html	Race in an affirmative action plan cannot be used to hinder the rights of people of other races.
1995	*McKennon v. Nashville Banner Publishing Co.* (513 U.S. 352) www.law.cornell.edu/supct/html/93-1543.ZS.html	"After-acquired" evidence collected following a negative employment action cannot protect an employer from liability under Title VII or the Age Discrimination in Employment Act (ADEA), even if the conduct would have justified terminating the employee.
1995	*NLRB v. Town & Country Electric, Inc.* (516 U.S. 85) www.law.cornell.edu/supct/html/94-947.ZS.html	This Supreme Court decision related to salting held that a worker may be a company's "employee," within the terms of the National Labor Relations Act, even if, at the same time, a union pays that worker to help the union organize the company.
1995	*PepsiCo, Inc. v. Redmond* (No. 94-3942 7th Cir.) http://caselaw.findlaw.com/us-7th-circuit/1337323.html	In this case, the district court applied the inevitable disclosure doctrine even though there was no non-compete agreement in place. An employee who had left his position in marketing PepsiCo's All Sport sports drink to work for Quaker Oats Company and market Gatorade and Snapple drinks was enjoined from working for Quaker because he had detailed knowledge of PepsiCo's trade secrets pertaining to pricing, market strategy, and selling/delivery systems.
1996	*O'Connor v. Consolidated Coin Caterers Corp.* (517 U.S. 308) www.law.cornell.edu/supct/html/95-354.ZS.html	To show unlawful discrimination under the ADEA, a discharged employee does not have to show that they were replaced by someone outside the protected age group (that is, younger than 40).
1997	*Robinson v. Shell Oil Co.* (519 U.S. 337) www.law.cornell.edu/supct/html/95-1376.ZS.html	Title VII prohibition against retaliation protects former as well as current employees.

Year	Citation	Decision
1998	*Faragher v. City of Boca Raton* (524 U.S. 775) www.law.cornell.edu/supct/html/97-282.ZO.html *Burlington Industries, Inc. v. Ellerth* (524 U.S. 742) www.law.cornell.edu/supct/html/97-569.ZS.html	These decisions distinguished between supervisor harassment that results in tangible employment action and that which does not. When harassment results in tangible employment action, the employer is liable. Employers may avoid liability if they have a legitimate written complaint policy, it is clearly communicated to employees, and it offers alternatives to the immediate supervisor as the point of contact for making a complaint.
1998	*Oncale v. Sundowner Offshore Service, Inc.* (523 U.S. 75) www.law.cornell.edu/supct/html/96-568.ZO.html	Same-gender harassment is actionable under Title VII.
1998	*Wright v. Universal Maritime Service Corp.* (525 U.S. 70) http://supreme.justia.com/cases/federal/us/525/70/	Collective bargaining agreements must contain a clear and unmistakable waiver if they are to bar an individual's right to sue after an arbitration requirement.
1999	*Kolstad v. American Dental Association* (527 U.S. 526) www.law.cornell.edu/supct/html/98-208.ZO.html	Title VII punitive damages are limited to cases in which the employer has engaged in intentional discrimination and has done so "with malice or with reckless indifference...."
1999	*West v. Gibson* (527 U.S. 212) http://caselaw.lp.findlaw.com/scripts/getcase.pl?court=us&vol=527&invol=212	This decision endorsed the EEOC's position that it has the legal authority to require federal agencies to pay compensatory damages when the EEOC has ruled during the administrative process that the federal agency has unlawfully discriminated in violation of Title VII.
2001	*Ronald Lesch v. Crown Cork & Seal Co.* (334 NLRB 699) https://caselaw.findlaw.com/us-7th-circuit/1443465.html	This NLRB decision lifted some restrictions on the employer's use of employee participation committees.
2002	*EEOC v. Waffle House, Inc.* (534 U.S. 279) www.law.cornell.edu/supct/html/99-1823.ZS.html	In this case, the Supreme Court ruled that even if there is a mandatory arbitration agreement in place, the relevant civil rights agency can still sue on behalf of the employee.

Year	Citation	Decision
2002	*Phoenix Transit System v. NLRB* (337 NLRB 510) https://www.nlrb.gov/case/28-CA-016039	This NLRB ruling struck down an employer rule prohibiting employees from discussing among themselves an employment complaint—in this instance, a complaint of sexual harassment—on the grounds that the prohibition was not limited in time and scope and interfered with a protected concerted activity.
2004	*General Dynamics Land Systems, Inc. v. Cline* (540 U.S. 581) www.law.cornell.edu/supct/html/02-1080 .ZS.html	ADEA does not protect younger workers, even those older than 40, from workplace decisions that favor older workers.
2004	*Pennsylvania State Police v. Suders* (542 U.S. 129) www.law.cornell.edu/supct/html/03-95 .ZS.html	In the absence of a tangible employment action, employers may use the Ellerth/ Faragher defense in a constructive discharge claim when supervisors are charged with harassment.
2004	*NLRB v. Weingarten, Inc.* (420 U.S. 251, 254 1975) https://supreme.justia.com/cases/federal/ us/420/251/ Overturned by *IBM Corp. v. NLRB* (341 NLRB 148 June 9, 2004) http://www.lawmemo.com/nlrb/ vol/341/148.htm	On June 9, 2004, the NLRB ruled by a 3–2 vote that employees who work in a nonunionized workplace are not entitled to have a coworker accompany them to an interview with their employer, even if the affected employee reasonably believes that the interview might result in discipline. This decision effectively reversed the July 2000 decision of the Clinton board, which had extended Weingarten rights to nonunion employees.
2005	*Smith v. City of Jackson, Mississippi* (544 U.S. 228) www.law.cornell.edu/supct/html/03-1160 .ZS.html	ADEA, like Title VII, offers recovery on a disparate impact theory.
2007	*Toering Electric Company v. NLRB* (351 NLRB 225) https://www.lawmemo.com/nlrb/ vol/351/18.htm	This NLRB ruling says that an applicant for employment must be genuinely interested in seeking to establish an employment relationship with the employer in order to be protected against hiring discrimination based on union affiliation or activity; this creates greater obstacles for unions attempting salting campaigns.
2007	*Oil Capitol Sheet Metal, Inc. v. NLRB* (349 NLRB 1348) https://casetext.com/admin-law/oil-capitol- sheet-metal-inc-2	This NLRB decision provides employers relief in salting cases by announcing a new evidentiary standard for determining the period of back pay; it requires the union to provide evidence that supports the period of time it claims the salt would have been employed.

PART III

Year	Citation	Decision
2007 and 2011	*Dana Corporation/ Metaldyne Corporation v. NLRB* (351 NLRB 434) https://www.jacksonlewis.com/resources-publication/nlrb-reconsider-decertification-bar-rule	This NLRB ruling says that a recognition bar, which precludes a decertification election for 12 months after an employer recognizes a union, does not apply when the recognition is voluntary, based on a card check. This was overruled in 2011 in Lamons Gasket, which restored the recognition bar for voluntary recognition but revised the prohibited time period from 1 year to a minimum of 6 months up to a year.
2007	*Syracuse University v. NLRB* (350 NLRB 755) https://www.jacksonlewis.com/resources-publication/nlrb-upholds-employers-promulgation-complaint-panel	The NLRB found that an employee grievance panel did not violate the NLRA because the purpose of the panel was not to deal with management but to improve group decisions.
2007	*Ledbetter v. Goodyear Tire & Rubber Co., Inc.* (550 U.S. 618) www.law.cornell.edu/supct/pdf/05-1074P.ZS	A claim of discrimination must be filed within 180 days of the first discriminatory employment act, and the clock does not restart after each subsequent act (for example, issuance of a paycheck with lower pay than coworkers if based on sex). Congress overruled this decision with the passage of the Lilly Ledbetter Fair Pay Act of 2009, which says the clock will restart each time another incident of discrimination occurs.
2010	*KenMor Electric Co., Inc. v. NLRB* (355 NLRB 173) https://casetext.com/admin-law/kenmor-electric-co-1	The NLRB ruled that a system developed and operated by an association of electrical contractors violated the NLRA because it discriminated against individuals who were salts. The board held that an individual's right to be a salt is protected under the NLRA.
2011	*Staub v. Proctor Hospital* (562 U.S. 411) http://supreme.justia.com/cases/federal/us/562/09-400/	The Supreme Court applied the "cat's paw" principle to a wrongful discharge case, finding that an employer was culpable because the HR manager did not adequately investigate supervisors' charges against the fired employee.
2011	*AT&T Mobility LLC v. Concepcion* (S.Ct. No. 09-893) www.supremecourt.gov/opinions/10pdf/09-893.pdf	The Supreme Court ruled that some state statutes restricting the enforceability of arbitration agreements in a commercial context may be preempted by the Federal Arbitration Act.
2011	*Kepas v. eBay* (131 S.Ct. 2160) https://law.justia.com/cases/federal/appellate-courts/ca10/09-4200/09-4200-2011-05-05.html	The Supreme Court refused to review a lower court decision that held in an employment case that a cost provision was severable from the balance of an arbitration agreement. The cost provision was unenforceable, but the agreement to arbitrate was enforceable.

Year	Citation	Decision
2011	*Specialty Healthcare and Rehabilitation Center of Mobile v. NLRB* (15-RC-008773) https://www.laborrelationsupdate.com/wp-content/uploads/sites/20/2017/12/Specialty-Healthcare-and-Rehabilitation-Center-of-Mobile.pdf	The NLRB indicated that in nonacute healthcare facilities, it will certify smaller units for bargaining unless the employer provides overwhelming proof of a community of interest.
2011	*UGL-UNICCO Service Company v. NLRB* (01-RC-022447) https://casetext.com/admin-law/ugl-unicco-service-company-3	The NLRB reestablished the successor bar doctrine, allowing unions a window of 6 months to 1 year of presumed majority support after the transfer of ownership of a business.
2012	*D. R. Horton, Inc. v. NLRB* (12-CA-25764) https://casetext.com/case/dr-horton-inc-v-natl-labor-relations-bd	The NLRB ruled that requiring employees to agree to a class action waiver as a term and condition of employment violates Section 7 of the National Labor Relations Act.
2013	*Vance v. Ball State Univ.* (No. 11-556) www.supremecourt.gov/opinions/12pdf/11-556_11o2.pdf	This decision determined that an employee is a "supervisor" of another employee for the purposes of liability under Title VII of the Civil Rights Act of 1964 only if they are empowered by the employer to take tangible employment actions against the other employee.
2013	*University of Texas Southwestern Medical Center v. Nassar* (No. 12-484) www.law.cornell.edu/supremecourt/text/12-484	Retaliation claims brought under Title VII of the Civil Rights Act of 1964 must be proved according to principles of "but-for-causation," not the lesser causation test applicable to bias claims.
2018	*Epic Systems Corp. v. Lewis* (No. 16–285) https://www.supremecourt.gov/opinions/17pdf/16-285_q8l1.pdf	U.S. Supreme Court held that arbitration agreements with class action waivers do not violate the NLRA, meaning that employers can include such waivers in arbitration agreements to avoid class and collective actions.
2018	*Janus v. American Federation of State, County, and Municipal Employees, Council 31, et al.* (No. 16–1466) https://www.supremecourt.gov/opinions/17pdf/16-1466_2b3j.pdf	Decided that the State's extraction of agency fees for the union from nonconsenting public-sector employees violates the First Amendment.
2018	*Mount Lemmon Fire District v. Guido et al.* (No. 17–587) https://www.supremecourt.gov/opinions/18pdf/17-587_n7ip.pdf	The Age Discrimination in Employment Act of 1967 applies to all public sector governments regardless of employee headcount. The 20-employee threshold does not apply to government entities.

PART III

Year	Citation	Decision
2020	*Bostock v. Clayton County* (No. 17–1618) https://www.law.cornell.edu/supremecourt/text/17-1618	Expanded the interpretation of Title VII by ruling that workplace discrimination because of an individual's sexual orientation or gender identity—including being transgender—is unlawful discrimination "because of sex."

Chapter 7: Compliance and Risk Management

Year	Citation	Decision
1991	*United Auto Workers v. Johnson Controls* (499 U.S. 187) www.law.cornell.edu/supct/html/89-1215.ZO.html	The Supreme Court held that decisions about the welfare of future children must be left to the parents who conceive, bear, support, and raise them rather than to the employers who hire their parents.
1998	*Bragdon v. Abbott* (524 U.S. 624) www.law.cornell.edu/supct/html/97-156.ZS.html	An individual with asymptomatic HIV is an individual with a disability and therefore is protected by the Americans with Disabilities Act (ADA). Reproduction is a major life activity under the statute.
2005	*Leonel v. American Airlines, Inc.* (400 F.3d 702, 9th Cir.) https://caselaw.findlaw.com/us-9th-circuit/1224462.html	To make a legitimate job offer under the ADA, an employer must have completed all nonmedical components of the application process or be able to demonstrate that it could not reasonably have done so before issuing the offer.
2021	*John Does v. Janet T. Mills, Governor of Maine* (No. 21A90) https://www.supremecourt.gov/opinions/21pdf/21a90_6j37.pdf	Ruled in favor of a COVID-19 vaccine mandate for healthcare workers in Maine that did not allow for a religious exemption from vaccine requirements.

Chapter 8: Early HR Career–Level Tasks

There are no case laws that directly relate to this HRCI functional area.

For Additional Study

This appendix lists additional resources that can be helpful in your study for the Associate Professional in Human Resources (aPHR) exam and for future reference as a human resource (HR) professional.

Badgi, Satish. *Practical Guide to Human Resource Information Systems.* Delhi: Phi Learning Pvt. Ltd., 2012.

Becker, Brian E., Mark A. Huselid, and David Ulrich. *The HR Scorecard: Linking People, Strategy, and Performance.* Boston: Harvard Business School Press, 2001.

Benjamin, Steve. "A Closer Look at Needs Analysis and Needs Assessment: Whatever Happened to the Systems Approach?" *Performance Improvement* 28, no. 9, 12–16, Wiley Periodicals, Inc., 1989.

Bennett-Alexander, Dawn D., and Laura P. Hartman. *Employment Law for Business, Ninth Edition.* New York: McGraw Hill, 2019.

Bliss, Wendy (Series Advisor). *The Essentials of Finance and Budgeting.* Boston: Harvard Business School Press; Alexandria, Virginia: Society for Human Resource Management, 2005.

Blosser, Fred. *Primer on Occupational Safety and Health.* Washington, D.C.: The Bureau of National Affairs, 1992.

Cherrington, David J. *The Management of Human Resources, Fourth Edition.* Englewood Cliffs, New Jersey: Prentice Hall, 1995.

DeLuca, Matthew J. *Handbook of Compensation Management.* Englewood Cliffs, New Jersey: Prentice-Hall, 1997.

DeNisi, Angelo S., and Ricky W. Griffin. *HR.* Boston: Cengage Learning, 2019.

Dessler, Gary. *Human Resource Management.* New York: Pearson Education, 2016.

Doherty, Neil. *Integrated Risk Management: Techniques and Strategies for Managing Corporate Risk.* New York: McGraw Hill, 2000.

Feldacker, Bruce, and Michael Hayes. *Labor Guide to Labor Law*. Ithaca, New York: ILR Press, 2014.

Fitz-Enz, Jac, and Barbara Davidson. *How to Measure Human Resource Management, Third Edition*. New York: McGraw Hill, 2002.

Grant, Phillip. *Multiple-Use Job Descriptions: A Guide to Analysis, Preparation, and Applications for Human Resources Managers*. New York: Quorum Books, 1989.

Harvard Business Review. *HBR's 10 Must Reads on Diversity*. Boston: Harvard Business Review Press, 2020.

Hayes, John. *The Theory and Practice of Change Management*. London: Bloomsbury Academic, 2018.

Herzberg, Frederick. *The Motivation to Work*. New Brunswick, New Jersey: Transaction Publishers, 1993.

Kavanaugh, Michael, Mohan Thite, and Richard D. Johnson (Eds.). *Human Resource Information Systems: Basics, Applications, and Future Directions*. Thousand Oaks, California: Sage Publications, 2012.

Kirkpatrick, Donald L. *How to Manage Change Effectively*. San Francisco: Jossey-Bass, 1985.

Knowles, Malcolm. *The Adult Learner: The Definitive Classic in Adult Education and Human Resource Development*. Oxford: Butterworth-Heinemann, 2005.

Lewis, Jackson. *Employer's Guide to Union Organizing Campaigns*. New York: Aspen Publishers, 2007.

Maslow, Abraham H. *A Theory of Human Motivation*. Mansfield Center, Connecticut: Martino Fine Books, 2013.

Mathis, Robert L., John H. Jackson, and Sean R. Valentine. *Human Resource Management: Essential Perspectives*. Boston: Cengage Learning, 2016.

McGregor, Douglas. *The Human Side of Enterprise* (annotated edition). New York: McGraw Hill, 2006.

Michaud, Patrick A. *Accident Prevention and OSHA Compliance*. Boca Raton, Florida: Lewis Publishers, 1995.

Milkovich, George, Jerry Newman, and Barry Gerhart. *Compensation*. New York: McGraw Hill, 2019.

Noe, Raymond, John Hollenbeck, Barry Gerhart, and Patrick Wright. *Human Resource Management*. New York: McGraw Hill/Irwin, 2018.

Richardson, Blake. *Records Management for Dummies*. Hoboken, New Jersey: John Wiley & Sons, 2012.

Rothwell, William, Cho Hyun Park, Cavil S. Anderson, Cynthia M. Corn, and Catherine Haynes. *Organization Development Fundamentals: Managing Strategic Change.* Alexandria, Virginia: ATD Press, 2015.

Senge, Peter. *The Fifth Discipline: The Art and Practice of the Learning Organization.* New York: Doubleday/Currency, 2006.

Smith, Shawn, and Rebecca Mazin. *The HR Answer Book: An Indispensable Guide for Managers and Human Resources Professional.* New York: AMACOM, 2011.

Tolbert, Pamela, and Richard Hall. *Organizations: Structures, Processes, and Outcomes.* Routledge, 2008.

Truesdell, William H. *Secrets of Affirmative Action Complianc*e. Walnut Creek, California: The Management Advantage, Inc., 2016.

Truesdell, William H., Christina Nishiyama, and Dory Willer. *PHR/SPHR Professional in Human Resources Certification Exam Guide.* New York: McGraw Hill, 2019.

Tullos, Deborah. *The Art of Employee Relations: Overcoming Your Fear of Addressing Employee Issues.* Independent, 2020.

Ulrich, David. *Delivering Results: A New Mandate for Human Resource Professionals.* Boston: Harvard Business Review, 1998.

Waddill, Deborah, and Michael Marquardt. *The e-HR Advantage: The Complete Handbook for Technology-Enabled Human Resources.* Boston: Nicholas Brealey America, 2011.

PART III

About the Online Content

This book comes complete with TotalTester Online customizable practice exam software with 250 practice exam questions.

System Requirements

The current and previous major versions of the following desktop browsers are recommended and supported: Chrome, Microsoft Edge, Firefox, and Safari. These browsers update frequently, and sometimes an update may cause compatibility issues with the TotalTester Online or other content hosted on the Training Hub. If you run into a problem using one of these browsers, please try using another until the problem is resolved.

Your Total Seminars Training Hub Account

To get access to the online content, you will need to create an account on the Total Seminars Training Hub. Registration is free, and you will be able to track all your online content using your account. You may also opt in if you wish to receive marketing information from McGraw Hill or Total Seminars, but this is not required for you to gain access to the online content.

Privacy Notice

McGraw Hill values your privacy. Please be sure to read the Privacy Notice available during registration to see how the information you have provided will be used. You may view our Corporate Customer Privacy Policy by visiting the McGraw Hill Privacy Center. Visit the **mheducation.com** site and click **Privacy** at the bottom of the page.

Single User License Terms and Conditions

Online access to the digital content included with this book is governed by the McGraw Hill License Agreement outlined next. By using this digital content, you agree to the terms of that license.

Access To register and activate your Total Seminars Training Hub account, simply follow these easy steps.

1. Go to this URL: **hub.totalsem.com/mheclaim**

2. To register and create a new Training Hub account, enter your e-mail address, name, and password on the **Register** tab. No further personal information (such as credit card number) is required to create an account.

    If you already have a Total Seminars Training Hub account, enter your e-mail address and password on the **Log in** tab.

3. Enter your Product Key: **3h74-7bph-b06d**

4. Click to accept the user license terms.

5. For new users, click the **Register and Claim** button to create your account. For existing users, click the **Log in and Claim** button.

    You will be taken to the Training Hub and have access to the content for this book.

Duration of License Access to your online content through the Total Seminars Training Hub will expire one year from the date the publisher declares the book out of print.

   Your purchase of this McGraw Hill product, including its access code, through a retail store is subject to the refund policy of that store.

   The Content is a copyrighted work of McGraw Hill, and McGraw Hill reserves all rights in and to the Content. The Work is © 2022 by McGraw Hill.

Restrictions on Transfer The user is receiving only a limited right to use the Content for the user's own internal and personal use, dependent on purchase and continued ownership of this book. The user may not reproduce, forward, modify, create derivative works based upon, transmit, distribute, disseminate, sell, publish, or sublicense the Content or in any way commingle the Content with other third-party content without McGraw Hill's consent.

Limited Warranty The McGraw Hill Content is provided on an "as is" basis. Neither McGraw Hill nor its licensors make any guarantees or warranties of any kind, either express or implied, including, but not limited to, implied warranties of merchantability or fitness for a particular purpose or use as to any McGraw Hill Content or the information therein or any warranties as to the accuracy, completeness, correctness, or results to be obtained from, accessing or using the McGraw Hill Content, or any material referenced in such Content or any information entered into licensee's product by users or other persons and/or any material available on or that can be accessed through the licensee's product (including via any hyperlink or otherwise) or as to non-infringement of third-party rights. Any warranties of any kind, whether express or implied, are disclaimed. Any material or data obtained through use of the McGraw Hill Content is at your own discretion and risk and user understands that it will be solely responsible for any resulting damage to its computer system or loss of data.

Neither McGraw Hill nor its licensors shall be liable to any subscriber or to any user or anyone else for any inaccuracy, delay, interruption in service, error or omission, regardless of cause, or for any damage resulting therefrom.

In no event will McGraw Hill or its licensors be liable for any indirect, special or consequential damages, including but not limited to, lost time, lost money, lost profits or good will, whether in contract, tort, strict liability or otherwise, and whether or not such damages are foreseen or unforeseen with respect to any use of the McGraw Hill Content.

TotalTester Online

TotalTester Online provides you with a simulation of the aPHR exam. Exams can be taken in Practice Mode or Exam Mode. Practice Mode provides an assistance window with hints, references to the book, explanations of the correct and incorrect answers, and the option to check your answer as you take the test. Exam Mode provides a simulation of the actual exam. The number of questions, the types of questions, and the time allowed are intended to be an accurate representation of the exam environment. The option to customize your quiz allows you to create custom exams from selected domains or chapters, and you can further customize the number of questions and time allowed.

To take a test, follow the instructions provided in the previous section to register and activate your Total Seminars Training Hub account. When you register, you will be taken to the Total Seminars Training Hub. From the Training Hub Home page, select your certification from the Study drop-down menu at the top of the page to drill down to the TotalTester for your book. You can also scroll to it from the list of Your Topics on the Home page, and then click on the TotalTester link to launch the TotalTester. Once you've launched your TotalTester, you can select the option to customize your quiz and begin testing yourself in Practice Mode or Exam Mode. All exams provide an overall grade and a grade broken down by domain.

Technical Support

For questions regarding the TotalTester or operation of the Training Hub, visit **www.totalsem.com** or e-mail **support@totalsem.com**.

For questions regarding book content, visit **www.mheducation.com/customerservice**.

This glossary is composed of terms you will likely encounter as you move through your career in human resources. Many of the terms you may already know. Some of them, like *andragogy, Delphi technique, histogram,* or *pedagogy,* may be new to you. Yet, each of the terms here can be important to HR professionals.

Here is a suggestion: as you work through the book and discover a term that is new to you, pause long enough to flip to the glossary and look it up. Knowing how a word or phrase is used can be helpful in understanding its meaning. It won't be long before you are using these terms in your everyday encounters.

401(k) plan   A salary reduction retirement plan for employees. Contributions reduce one's taxable income, and investment income accumulates tax-free until the money is withdrawn.

80% rule   The measurement known as a "rule of thumb" used to test for disparity in treatment during any type of employment selection decisions; also identified as *adverse impact.*

ADDIE   A five-step instructional design process consisting of analysis, design, development, implementation, and evaluation.

administrative exemption   Exemption from overtime payment based on several qualifying factors, including minimum pay requirement as well as exercise of discretion and independent judgment in performing work directly related to the management of general business operations.

administrative services–only plan   Health insurance programs in which all the risk is assumed by the employer.

adult learning   The process of learning associated with people who are older than 18 to 25 and generally referred to as nontraditional learners; also identified as *andragogy.*

adverse impact   A legal category of illegal employment discrimination involving groups of workers and statistical proofs.

adverse selection   When bad-risk employees choose a benefit and good-risk employees do not under a flexible benefits plan.

adverse treatment   A legal category of illegal employment discrimination involving individual treatment or "pattern and practice" treatment of groups of workers.

affirmative action   Use of special outreach and recruiting programs to ensure participation of qualified job candidates, vendors, or students in employment, employer purchasing programs, or college admissions.

aggregate stop-loss coverage   The health plan is protected against the risk of large total claims from all participants during the plan year.

aging   A technique used to make outdated data current.

alternative dispute resolution (ADR)   A variety of processes that help parties resolve disputes without a trial. Processes include mediation, arbitration, neutral evaluation, and collaborative law.

analytics   The discovery and communication of meaningful patterns in data.

andragogy   The study of how adults learn.

applicant tracking system   A method for retention of detailed information about job applicants, either manual or computer based.

apprenticeship   A system of teaching a person in a trade or profession with on-the-job training.

arbitration   The process of submitting a labor dispute to a third party for resolution. The third party is called an *arbitrator*. Both parties agree beforehand to accept the arbitrator's decision.

assessment centers   A method for assessing aptitude and performance applied to participants using various aptitude diagnostic processes in order to obtain information on abilities or potential. Participants are measured against a norm group of successful people in the same job category.

assets   The properties an organization owns, both tangible and intangible.

asynchronous learning   A form of educational instruction where students are not interacting in the same place, or at the same time.

at-will employment   A legal employment relationship in which an employee may quit at any time for any reason and may be dismissed at any time for any reason. No "just cause" is required. This relationship is limited by prohibitions on employer actions related to public interest.

automatic step rate   Division of the pay range into several steps that can be advanced by an employee when time-in-job has met the step requirement.

average   Arithmetic average or mean arrived at by giving equal weight to every participant's actual pay; also, a number that is arrived at by adding quantities together and dividing the total by the number of quantities.

back pay   Payment of salary or wages that should have been paid initially, usually as a form of remedy for a complaint of discrimination.

background check   Investigation of an individual's personal history, including employment, educational, criminal, and financial.

balance sheet   A statement of a business's financial position.

balanced scorecard   A big-picture view of an organization's performance as measured against goals in areas such as finance, customer base, processes, learning, human capital, and growth.

BARS   Behaviorally anchored rating scales generally employed in performance appraisal processes.

base-pay systems   Single or flat-rate systems, time-based step rate systems, performance-based merit pay systems, productivity-based systems, and person-based systems.

behavioral interview   A technique that queries job applicants to describe their specific behaviors or actions they've taken in particular past situations as a basis for determining the individual's demonstrated skill sets.

bell curve   Used to describe the mathematical concept called "normal distribution."

benefits-needs assessment or analysis   Collection and analysis of data to determine whether the employer's benefits programs actually meet their objectives.

bereavement leave   Paid or unpaid time off to attend the funeral of a relative.

bias   Prejudice in favor of or against one thing, person, or group compared with another, usually in a way considered to be unfair.

"Big Data"   Extremely large data sets that may be analyzed computationally to reveal patterns, trends, and associations, especially relating to human behavior and interactions.

bill   A proposal presented to a legislative body in the U.S. government to enact a law.

blended learning   A formal education program in which a student learns at least in part through delivery of content and instruction via digital and online media with some element of student control over time, place, path, or pace.

blue ocean strategy   The pursuit of creating a new market space where there are no competitors.

boycott   A protest action that encourages the public to withhold business from an employer that is targeted by a union.

brain drain   The departure of educated or professional people from one country, economic sector, or field for another, usually for better pay or living conditions.

branding   The process of conveying key organizational values and guiding principles.

broadbanding   The combining of several pay grades or job classifications with narrow range spreads and a single band into a wider spread.

budgeting   Forecasting income and expenses by category and subcategory.

business acumen   Knowledge and understanding of the financial, accounting, marketing, and operational functions of an organization.

business case   An argument, usually documented, that is intended to convince a decision maker to approve some kind of action.

business concept   An idea for producing goods or services that identifies the benefits that can be achieved for prospective customers or clients.

business continuity   The ability to continue conducting business following an interruption of some sort.

business ethics   Generally accepted norms and expectations for business management behavior.

business intelligence (BI)   An umbrella term that refers to a variety of software applications used to analyze an organization's raw data. BI as a discipline is made up of several related activities, including data mining, online analytical processing, querying, and reporting.

cafeteria benefit plan   A plan in which employees choose the benefits they desire subject to certain limitations and total cost constraints.

career development   The concept that individuals expand their knowledge, skills, and abilities as they progress through their careers.

career management   Planning, preparing, and implementing employee career paths.

career planning   Activities and actions that individuals follow for a specific career path.

case study   Simulation of real-world problems that calls for an application of skill or knowledge to resolve.

cash award   Reward for exceeding performance goals; a formula-based bonus calculated on a percentage of profits or other pre-established measurement.

cash flow statement   A mandatory part of a company's financial reports since 1987; records the amounts of cash and cash equivalents entering and leaving a company.

cause-and-effect diagram   Also called a *fishbone diagram* and *Ishikawa diagram*. Identifies possible causes for an effect or problem.

center of excellence (COE)   Refers to a team, a shared facility, or an entity that provides leadership, evangelization, best practices, research, support, and/or training for a focus area.

central tendency error   When managers and interviewers rate all or most of the employees or interviewees as average.

certification of a union   Formal recognition of a union as the exclusive bargaining representative of a group of employees.

chain of command   The order in which authority and power in an organization is wielded and delegated from top management to every employee at every level of the organization.

change management   Transitioning individuals, groups, teams, and institutions to a desired future state.

change program   A strategic approach to organizing and implementing specific changes (for example, policies or procedures) within an organization.

childcare services   Programs designed to help working parents deal with the ongoing needs of preschool or school-aged children.

civil law   One of the two major legal systems of the modern Western world (the other is common law).

clawback   A provision of the Dodd-Frank Act that requires executives to return bonuses received, often in response to misconduct or poor company performance.

cloud computing   An application software that is on central servers and accessed or operated using Internet-enabled devices.

code of conduct   An employment policy listing personal behaviors that are acceptable and required in the workplace.

code of ethics   Principles of conduct that guide behavior expectations and decisions.

cognitive learning   The refining of knowledge by adding new information and thereby expanding prior knowledge.

collective bargaining   A formal process of negotiating working conditions with an employer for a workgroup represented by a union.

collective bargaining agreement   A union contract for a represented group of employees and designated employers. This is a term usually used in the private sector.

combination step-rate and performance   Employees receive step-rate increases up to the established job rate. Above this level, increases are granted only for superior job performance.

common law   Law developed over time from the rulings of judges as opposed to law embodied in statutes passed by legislatures (statutory law) or law embodied in a written constitution (constitutional law).

communication skills   Verbal and written abilities that enable an individual to transmit and receive messages.

commuter assistance   Employee assistance programs designed to help reduce public transportation costs associated with going to and from work.

comparable worth   A pay discrimination theory where workers in a job classification dominated by one sex are paid less than workers in a classification dominated by the opposite sex, where both job classifications are of equal value or worth to the employer or the underpaid classification is of greater value to the employer.

compa-ratio   An indicator of how wages match, lead, or lag the midpoint of a given pay range computed by dividing the worker's pay rate by the midpoint of the pay range.

compensatory damages   A monetary equivalent awarded for pain, suffering, and emotional distress as a result of a legal proceeding.

competencies   Measurable or observable knowledge, skills, abilities, and behaviors critical to successful job performance.

competency-based interview   An interview where the style of question forces candidates to give situational examples of times in the past when they have performed particular tasks or achieved particular outcomes using certain skills.

competency-based system   Pay is linked to the level at which an employee can perform in a recognized competency.

compliance evaluation   Formal audit by the Office of Federal Contract Compliance Programs (OFCCP) of a federal contractor subject to OFCCP oversight.

compliance program   Systematic procedures instituted by an organization to ensure that the provisions of the regulations imposed by a government agency are being met.

computer employee exemption   Exemption from overtime payment based on several qualifying factors, including minimum pay requirement as well as job duties involving computer programming, software analysis, or software engineering.

computer-based testing (CBT)   Testing delivery method via computer, in person, at a testing center.

conciliation   A binding written agreement between an employer and the EEOC or the OFCCP that details specific employer commitments to resolve the alleged violations set forth in the agreement.

conflict of interest   A situation that has the potential to undermine the impartiality of a person because of the possibility of a clash between the person's self-interest and professional or public interest.

construct validity   The degree to which a test measures what it claims to measure.

constructive discipline   Discipline that imposes increasingly severe consequences and penalties. This is also called *progressive discipline*.

consumer price index   The average of prices paid by consumers for goods and services.

content validity   The extent a test measures all aspects of a given job.

contingency plan   A coordinated set of steps to be taken in an emergency or disaster.

contingent worker   A worker who does not have an ongoing expectation of full-time employment, such as a part-time worker, independent contractor, temporary worker, consultant, leased employee, or subcontractor.

contract labor   Work performed under the terms of a legally enforceable contract.

contract negotiation   The process of give and take related generally to content details and provisions of an employment contract such as a union agreement or memorandum of understanding (MOU).

contrast effect   An error made in interviewing when strong candidates are interviewed after weak candidates, causing them to appear overly qualified because of the contrast.

contrast error   In an interview or performance appraisal process, an error caused by the effect of previously interviewed or appraised applicants on the interviewer.

control chart   A chart that illustrates variation from normal in a situation over time.

controlling   A management function involving monitoring the workplace and making adjustments to activities as required.

cooperative learning   A strategy in which a small group of people work on solving a problem or completing a task in a way that each person's success is dependent on the group's success. Also known as *collaborative learning*.

copyright   A legal form of protection for authors of original works.

core competency   A unique capability that is essential or fundamental to a particular job.

corporate citizenship   A self-regulatory mechanism where an organization monitors and ensures its active compliance with the spirit of the law, ethical standards, and international norms.

corporate governance   The mechanisms, processes, and relations by which corporations are controlled and directed.

corporate responsibility (CR)   Strategic goals achieved through local community relationships around social needs and issues.

cost-benefit analysis (CBA)   A business practice in which the costs and benefits of a particular situation are analyzed as part of the decision process.

cost containment   Efforts or activities designed to reduce or slow down the cost expenses and increases.

cost of living adjustment   Pay increase given to all employees on the basis of market pressure, usually measured against the consumer price index (CPI).

cost per hire   The measurement of dollar expense required to hire each new employee.

credit report   Report obtained from one of the major credit reporting agencies that explains the individual's personal rating based on financial history.

criterion-related validity   Empirical studies producing data that shows the selection procedure(s) are predictive or significantly related with important elements of job performance.

critical path math (CPM)   A sequence of activities in a project plan that must be completed on time for the project to be completed by the due date.

cross-functional work team   A group of people from different functions working together to generate a work product or resolve a problem.

cultural blending   The blending of different cultural influences in the workforce.

cultural noise   In an interview or performance appraisal process, an error caused by the effect of previously interviewed or appraised applicants on the interviewer. It results in a conscious or subconscious comparison of one applicant with another and tends to exaggerate the differences between the two.

cultural relativism   The principle that an individual human's beliefs and activities should be understood by others in terms of that individual's own culture.

culture   Societal forces affecting the values, beliefs, and actions of a group of people.

dashboard   A data visualization tool that displays the current status of metrics and key performance indicators (KPIs).

database   Systematically organized or structured repository of indexed information (usually as a group of linked data files) that allows for the easy retrieval, updating, analysis, and output of data.

database management system (DBMS)   Computer program that catalogs, indexes, locates, retrieves, and stores data; maintains the data's integrity; and outputs it in the form desired by a user.

deauthorization of a union   Removal of "union security" from the contract. The union remains as the exclusive bargaining representative, and the collective bargaining agreement remains in effect, but employees are not forced to be members of or pay dues to the union.

decertification of a union   Removal of a union as the exclusive bargaining representative of the employees.

defamation   Publication of something about an individual that the writer knows is untrue.

defined benefit plan   A pension plan that provides retirement income to retirees based on a formula that usually combines years of service and an average annual income for a set number of years.

defined contribution plan   An individual pension fund created for each employee into which the company invests a specified amount of money each year until the employee retires.

Delphi technique   A systematic forecasting method that involves structured interaction among a group of experts on a subject. The Delphi technique typically includes at least two rounds of experts answering questions and giving justifications for their answers.

demand analysis   Estimation of what customers, clients, or patrons will want in the future.

demonstration   Showing students how something is done.

dental plan   Medical insurance program that covers some or all of the cost of dental services for subscribers.

departmentalization   Manner or practice in which related individual tasks and their allocation to workgroups are combined to form a specialized functional area that is distinct from other functional areas in an organization.

developmental activities   The part of human resource management that specifically deals with training and development of employees.

differential pay   An addition to base pay that results from special job circumstances such as shift assignment, commute distance required, temporary responsibility assignments, and similar "extras."

differential piece rate system   A system in which an employee receives one rate of pay up to the production standard and a higher rate of pay when the standard is exceeded.

dilemma reconciliation   Process of seeking solutions to issues involving cultural differences.

direct compensation   Base pay, commissions, bonuses, merit pay, piece rate, differential pay, cash award, profit sharing, or gainsharing.

directing   Managing or controlling people to willingly do what is wanted or needed.

disability   Medically determinable impairment of body or mind that restricts, or causes loss of, a person's functional ability to carry on their normal activities.

disaster recovery plan   A set of procedures used to protect and recover a business from a natural or other disaster that has impacted the organization or employer.

discipline   Forms of punishment to ensure obedience with policies.

disparate impact   Adverse effect of a practice or standard that is neutral and nondiscriminatory in its intention but, nonetheless, disproportionately affects individuals having a disability or belonging to a particular group based on their age, ethnicity, race, sex, or other protected class.

disparate treatment   A discrimination theory that holds an individual is treated differently from others, based on protected group membership, who are similarly situated under similar circumstances.

distance learning   Learning that uses television, audio/video tapes, computers, the Internet, and so on instead of physical attendance at classes in a centralized facility.

diversity and inclusion   The practice of embracing differences of race, culture, and background, ensuring that everyone is a participant in workplace processes.

diversity council   Task force of various levels of employees created to work on diversity and inclusion initiatives in an organization.

diversity dimensions   Framework for diversity, including personality, internal dimensions, external dimensions, and organizational dimensions.

diversity of thought   Different types of cognitive processes.

diversity programs   Methods for recognizing and honoring various types of employee backgrounds.

divestiture   The sale of an asset.

domestic partners   Two adults who have chosen to share one another's lives in an intimate and committed relationship of mutual caring.

dual-ladder   A system that enables a person to advance up either the management or technical career development ladder in an organization.

due diligence   The first step in mergers and acquisitions involving a broad scope of research and investigation.

due process   Conduct of legal proceedings strictly according to established principles and procedures, laid down to ensure a fair trial for every accused.

duty of care   The responsibility or the legal obligation of a person or organization to avoid acts or omissions (which can be reasonably foreseen) to be likely to cause harm to others.

elder care   Programs to help employees deal with responsibilities for care of family elders.

e-learning   Internet-based training programs that can be instructor led or self-paced.

emotional intelligence (EQ or EI)   The ability of an individual to have understanding and sensitivity for another's emotions and control over their own.

employee   A person in the service of another under any contract of hire, express or implied, oral or written, where the employer has the power or right to control and direct the employee in the material details of how the work is to be performed.

employee assistance programs   Employer-sponsored benefits that provide a number of services that help promote the physical, mental, and emotional wellness of individual employees who otherwise would be negatively impacted by health-related crises.

employee complaint   A written or verbal statement of dissatisfaction from an employee that can involve charges of discrimination, lack of fairness, or other upset.

employee engagement   Where employees are fully absorbed by and enthusiastic about their work and take positive action to further the organization's reputation and interests.

employee leasing   Contracting with a vendor that provides qualified workers for a specific period of time at a specific pay rate.

employee life cycle   A human resources model that identifies stages in employees' careers to help guide their management and optimize associated processes.

employee relations programs   Methods for the management of the employer-employee relationship.

employee resource group (ERG)   A group of employees who share a diversity dimension, also called an *affinity group*.

employee stock ownership plan   A retirement plan in which the company contributes its stock, or money to buy its stock, to the plan for the benefit of the company's employees.

employee stock purchase plan   A program allowing employees to purchase company stock at a discounted price.

employee survey   A tool used to gather opinions of employees about their employment experiences.

employee-management committee   A problem-solving group of management and non-management employees focused on specific issues within the workplace.

employer sick leave   Paid leave for a specified number of hours or days absent from work because of a medical condition.

employment affirmative action   A requirement by federal regulations for some federal contractors to implement outreach and recruiting programs when the incumbent workforce is significantly less representative of certain populations than the computed availability.

employment-at-will   A legal doctrine that describes an employment relationship without a contract where either party can end the relationship at any time for any reason.

employment branding   A targeted strategy to manage the awareness and perceptions of employees, potential employees, and related stakeholders with regard to an organization.

employment policies   Rules by which the workplace will be managed.

employment reference check   Verification of references, both personal and professional, provided by a job candidate on an application form or résumé.

employment testing   Any tool or step used in the employment selection process, such as written tests, interviews, résumé reviews, or skill demonstration.

encryption   Scrambling sensitive information so that it becomes unreadable to everyone except the intended recipient.

enterprise resource planning (ERP)   Accounting-oriented, relational database–based, multimodule-but-integrated software system for identifying and planning the resource needs of an enterprise.

environmental footprint   The effect that a person, company, activity, and so on has on the environment.

environmental scanning   A process of studying the environment to pinpoint potential threats and opportunities.

e-procurement   An electronic web application for transacting and purchasing supplies and services.

equal pay   Providing equal compensation to jobs that have the same requirements, responsibilities, and working conditions regardless of the incumbent's gender.

equity   The difference between income and liabilities in a for-profit organization.

essential functions   The fundamental, crucial job duties performed in a position.

ethical universalism   A concept that implies there are fundamental ethical principles applying across cultures.

ethics   Principles and values that set expectations for behaviors in an organization.

ethnocentric   A policy calling for key management positions to be filled by expatriates.

evacuation plan   A written procedure for moving employees out of the work location to a safer location in case of fire or natural disaster.

evaluation   A constructive process to discuss strengths and weaknesses in performance.

E-Verify   A government database that employers access to confirm a match between a new employee's name and Social Security number.

executive coaching   Coaching senior- and executive-level management by a third party.

executive exemption   Exemption from overtime payment based on several qualifying factors, including supervision and minimum pay requirements.

executive incentives   Variable compensation additives for executive employees that may include company stock and use of company facilities such as vacation timeshares. These are usually variable based on the profitability of the company.

exempt employee   An employee exempt from overtime compensation by federal wage and hour guidelines.

exempt job   A job with content that is exempt from the Fair Labor Standards Act (FLSA) requirement to pay overtime for work exceeding 40 hours per week. Exemption can be based on several designated factors.

exit interview   A discussion with a departing employee to explore how they feel about their experience as an employee and what recommendations they might have for the employer.

expatriate   An employee working in a country other than that of their origin.

external coaching   Coaching that is provided by a third party via a certified coach.

external equity   Employees' perception of the conditions and rewards of their employment compared with those of the employees of other firms.

extraterritoriality   Being outside the territory of the country where you are living and therefore not subject to its laws.

extrinsic reward   A reward such as pay, benefits, incentive bonuses, promotions, time off, and so on.

factor-comparison job evaluation   A process that involves ranking each job by each compensable factor and then identifying dollar values for each level of each factor to develop an actual pay rate for the evaluated job.

fast-track program   A career development program that identifies high-potential leaders for rapid career growth and organizational knowledge.

fee-for-service plan   Allows health plan members to go to any qualified physician or other healthcare provider, hospital, or medical clinic and submit claims to the insurance company.

fiduciary responsibility   A legal and ethical relationship between two or more parties.

final warning   The last step in the disciplinary process progression prior to removing the employee from the payroll.

first impression error   Occurs when a manager or interviewer bases their entire assessment of an employee or applicant on the first impression that the employee or applicant made.

PART III

flat-rate or single system   Each worker in the same job has the same rate of pay regardless of seniority or job performance.

flexible spending account   Allows employees to set aside a pre-established amount of money on a pre-tax basis per plan year for use in paying authorized medical expenses.

floating holidays   Designated paid time off that can be used at any time during the year with the employer's approval.

flow analysis   How processes operate and how flows of products, data, or other items go through these processes.

focus group   A group of people brought together with a moderator where they share their point of view on a specific topic or problem. Focus groups aim at a discussion instead of on individual responses to formal questions and produce qualitative data (preferences and beliefs) that may or may not be representative of the general population.

force-field analysis   Technique for identifying and analyzing the positive factors of a situation that help ("driving forces") and negative factors that hinder ("restraining forces") an entity in attaining its objectives.

forced choice   An evaluation method in which the evaluator selects two of four statements that represents "most like" and "least like."

formalization   The extent to which work roles are structured in an organization and the activities of the employees are governed by rules and procedures.

frequency distribution   Listing of grouped pay data from lowest to highest.

frequency tables   Indicate the number of workers in a particular job classification and their pay data.

front pay   Payment of salary or wages that could have been earned had the individual continued to work on the job in question or had the person been employed for a future period of time.

full-time   Employees who work a designated number of hours per week, usually 30 to 40 hours.

fully funded plan   Health insurance program paid for entirely by the employer.

functional HR   A structure where HR generalists are located within business units as HR business partners and implement the policies and interact with management and employees in the unit and where headquarters HR staff create policies and strategy.

functional structure   A common type of organizational structure in which the organization is divided into smaller groups based on specialized functional areas, such as IT, finance, HR, and marketing.

functional work team   A group of people from the same function working together to generate production or resolve problems.

gainsharing plan   Extra pay provided to individual or groups of employees based on the gain in performance results in one measurement period over another period.

gamification   Elements of game playing (for example, point scoring, competition with others, rules of play) used in other areas of activity that encourage employee engagement.

Gantt chart   A project planning tool that scopes and monitors the activities of a project, the timeline, and accountability.

gap analysis   Measurement of the difference between where you are and where you want to be.

gender   Culturally and socially constructed difference between men and women.

general duty clause   A provision in OSHA regulations that imposes a duty on all subject employers to ensure a safe and healthy working environment for their employees.

general pay increases   A pay increase given to all employees regardless of their job performance and not linked to market pressures.

geocentric   A staffing policy wanting to place the best person in the job regardless of their country of origin.

geographic structure   An organizational structure used by organizations that have locations in different geographic areas that define their regions.

geographic-based differential pay   Adjustment to base-pay programs based on cost-of-living requirements in various geographic locations where employees work.

geography   Adjustments to survey numbers based on geographic differences with original survey content.

gig worker   An independent worker employed for a particular performance or for a defined short-term engagement.

giganomics   The creation of employment through the piecing together of several projects, or "gigs."

glass ceiling   A discriminatory practice that has prevented women and other protected class members from advancing to executive-level jobs.

global integration (GI) strategy   A term used to denote an organization that fashions its strategy, its management, and its operations in pursuit of a new goal: the integration of production and value delivery worldwide.

global mindset   An openness to and awareness of diversity across cultures and markets.

GPHR   Global Professional in Human Resources credential that is global competency based, validating the skills and knowledge of an HR professional who operates in a global marketplace.

global remittances   A transfer of money from migrant workers to their home country.

globalization   The worldwide movement toward economic, financial, trade, and communications integration.

golden parachute   A provision in executive employment contracts that provides special payments or benefits to the executives under certain adverse conditions such as the loss of their position or otherwise adversely impacted actions by organizational changes.

governance   Establishment of policies, and continuous monitoring of their proper implementation, by the members of the governing body of an organization.

graphic organizers   Diagrams, maps, and drawings/webs as illustrations of learning materials.

green circle rate   Pay at a rate lower than the minimum rate for the assigned pay range.

green initiatives   Relationships around community and social issues.

grievance   A formal employee complaint handled by a structured resolution process, usually found in a union-represented workgroup.

grievance procedure   A step-by-step process an employee must follow to get their complaint addressed satisfactorily. This is typically included in union (collective bargaining) agreements.

gross domestic product (GDP)   The total value of goods and services produced in a country.

group incentive program   Pay to all individuals in a workgroup for achievement by the entire workgroup.

group term life insurance   Provides lump-sum benefit to beneficiaries on the death of the insured.

halo effect   This occurs when an evaluator scores an employee high on all job categories because of performance in one area.

harassment   Persecution, intimidation, pressure, or force applied to employees by supervisors, coworkers, or external individuals that interferes with the employee's ability to perform the job assignment.

Hay method   A widely used job evaluation method that addresses three compensable factors (knowledge, problem solving, and accountability) to determine how many points should be assigned to different jobs in determining compensation categories.

hazard   Situation that may lead to a danger, emergency, or disaster.

hazard pay   Additional pay for working under adverse conditions caused by environmental or other specific circumstances.

head count   Number of individuals carried on a firm's payroll.

health insurance purchasing cooperative   Purchasing agent for large groups of employers.

health maintenance organization   Healthcare program where the insurer is paid on a per-person (capitated) basis and offers healthcare services and staff at its facilities.

health reimbursement account   Employer-funded medical reimbursement plan.

health savings account   A tax-advantaged medical savings account available to taxpayers in the United States who are enrolled in a high-deductible health plan.

high-context culture   A culture of people that emphasizes interpersonal relationships and close connections over a long period of time.

high deductible health plan   A program that helps an employer lower their costs and allows employees to pay for out-of-pocket medical and medical-related expenses using set-aside money.

histogram   A graphic representation of the distribution of a single type of measurement using rectangles.

horn effect   This effect occurs when an employee receives a low rating in all areas because the evaluator is influenced by one weakness.

host-country national (HCN)   An employee originating from the country where a remote work location is being established.

hostile environment harassment   Occurs when an employee is subject to unwelcome advances, sexual innuendos, or offensive gender-related language that is sufficiently severe or pervasive from the perspective of a reasonable person of the same gender as the offended employee.

HR audit   An objective look at the company's HR policies, practices, procedures, and strategies to protect the company, establish best practices, and identify opportunities for improvement.

HR business partner   HR staff that acts as an internal consultant to senior management.

HR Certification Institute (HRCI)   A nonprofit professional certifying organization for the human resources profession.

HR professional certification   Status awarded to HR professionals by a recognized certifying agency after satisfying qualifying requirements.

HRCI Body of Knowledge (BOK)   The description of a set of concepts, tasks, responsibilities, and knowledge associated with HRCI credentialing.

HRIS   Human resources information system. This is usually a computer-based collection of personal data for each employee.

human capital The value of the capabilities, knowledge, skills, experiences, and motivation of a workforce in an organization.

Human Resource Business Professional (HRBP) A global, competency-based credential designed to validate generally accepted professional-level core HR knowledge and skills.

Human Resource Management Professional (HRMP) A global, competency-based credential designed to validate generally accepted HR principles in strategy, policy development, and service delivery.

human resource management (HRM) The direction of organizational systems to ensure that human talent is used effectively and efficiently to accomplish organizational goals.

human resources development Systematically planned activities that help the organization's workforce meet current and future job and skills needs.

hybrid structure An approach to designing the internal operating structure of a company or other entity in a manner that makes use of several different organizational patterns rather than relying on one particular model.

identity alignment The extent to which diversity is accepted and embraced in an organization.

IIPP Injury and illness prevention program.

incentive Inducement or supplemental reward that serves as a motivational device for a desired action or behavior.

incentive pay Pay designed to promote a higher level of job performance than otherwise included in the basic design of the job.

incentive stock options Awards of rights to purchase company stock in the future at a price determined at the time of the grant.

inclusion The state of including or of being included within a group or structure.

income statement A summary of management's performance as reflected in the profitability (or lack of it) of an organization over a certain period.

independent contractor One who, in the independent exercise of their business affairs, contracts to do a piece of work according to their own methods and is subject to their principal's control only as to the end product or final result of their work.

indirect compensation Social Security, unemployment insurance, disability insurance, pension, 401(k), and other similar programs as well as healthcare, vacation, sick leave, and paid time off such as holidays.

individual incentive program An offer to individual employees in a workgroup to receive extra pay based on achievement of clearly defined objectives.

information management (IM)   Application of management techniques to collect information, communicate it within and outside the organization, and process it to enable managers to make quicker and better decisions.

inpatriate   An employee working at corporate headquarters who originated from a different country.

insourcing   Delegating a job to someone within a company, as opposed to someone outside of the company (outsourcing).

instructional method   An approach to training that is either teacher centered or learner centered.

intellectual property (IP)   Knowledge, creative ideas, or expressions of the human mind that have commercial value and are protectable under copyright, patent, service mark, trademark, or trade secret laws from imitation, infringement, and dilution.

intercultural wisdom   The awareness of what you do not know about the values, behavior, and communication styles of people from other cultures.

internal coaching   A training or developmental process whereby organizational leaders support the achievement of a personal or professional goal.

internal equity   Employees' perception of their responsibilities, rewards, and work conditions as compared with those of other employees in similar positions in the same organization.

internal investigation   Gathering verbal and written information dealing with an issue that needs to be clarified.

intrinsic motivation   Stimulation that drives an individual to adopt or change a behavior for their own internal satisfaction or fulfillment.

intrinsic reward   A reward such as meaningful and fulfilling work, autonomy, and positive feedback that leads to a high level of job satisfaction.

investigation   A detailed search for facts involving records, witnesses, and other inputs.

investigation file   A collection of documents related to complaints or charges of discrimination, policy violation, or criminal behavior assembled by an employer about an employee or event.

involuntary separation   An individual leaving the payroll for involuntary reasons, such as a performance deficiency, policy violation, or unauthorized absence.

ISO 9000 standards   Standards and guidelines on quality management and quality assurance developed by the International Organization for Standardization (ISO).

item response theory (IRT)   Method used to calibrate the difficulty level of questions on an exam to properly score individuals on the behaviors or abilities being measured.

job analysis   A process to identify and determine the particular job duties and requirements for a given job.

job application   A form used to gather information significant to the employer about an individual candidate for employment.

job classification   A system for objectively and accurately defining the duties, responsibilities, tasks, and authority level of a job.

job content–based job evaluation   A job evaluation method in which the relative worth and pay of different jobs are based on their content and relationship to other jobs within the same organization.

job description   A document that contains a summary of duties and responsibilities of a given job assignment and a description of the physical and mental requirements of the job.

job enlargement   Broadening the scope of a job by expanding the number of tasks.

job enrichment   Increasing the depth of a job by adding responsibilities.

job evaluation   A systematic determination of the relative worth of jobs in an organization.

job evaluation method   Quantitative or nonquantitative program allowing the sorting or categorizing of jobs based on their relative worth to the organization.

job ranking   Comparison of jobs based on each job's measurable factors.

job rotation   The process of shifting a person from job to job.

job sharing   Two or more employees who work part-time in the same job to create one full-time equivalent person.

job specification   A statement of employee characteristics and qualifications required for satisfactory performance of defined duties and tasks comprising a specific job or function.

judgmental forecast   A projection based on subjective inputs.

judgment-based forecasting   Simple estimates, the Delphi technique, focus group or panel estimates, or historically based estimates used in human resource management.

jurisdiction   Power or right of a legal or political agency to exercise its authority over a person, subject matter, or territory.

key performance indicators (KPIs)   Key business statistics, such as number of new orders, cash collection efficiency, and return on investment (ROI), used to measure a firm's performance in critical areas.

key risk indicators (KRIs)   A measure used in management to indicate how risky an activity is.

knowledge   Facts and information gathered by an individual.

knowledge management   The way an organization identifies knowledge in order to be competitive and for the design of succession plans.

knowledge-based system   Pay is based on the level of knowledge an employee has in a particular field.

KSAs   Knowledge, skills, and abilities needed to perform a job.

K-W-L table   Display of what students know (K), what they want to know (W), and what they actually learned (L).

labor cost differential   Adjustment to pay structures based on local competitive comparisons.

labor union   A group of people who represent workers in different occupations and work to protect the rights of the workers, such as working conditions and wages.

lagging indicator   Measures the results of a process of a change, such as sales, profits, and customer service levels; a metric commonly used in the balanced scorecard.

layoff   Suspension or termination of employment (with or without notice) by the employer.

leadership   1) The individuals who are the leaders in an organization, regarded collectively. 2) The activity of leading a group of people or an organization or the ability to do this.

leadership concepts   The study of leadership styles and techniques.

leadership development   Teaching of leadership qualities, including communication, the ability to motivate others, and management, to an individual.

leading indicator   A measure that precedes, anticipates, or predicts future performance; a measure commonly used in the balanced scorecard.

learning management system (LMS)   A comprehensive system that tracks training content, employee skill sets, training histories, and career development planning.

learning objects (LOs)   Defined learning elements that may be used in other contexts in the organization (for example, animated graphics and training aids).

learning organization   An organization that quickly responds and adapts to changes.

lecture   An oral presentation intended to teach or present information.

leniency error   Occurs when ratings of all employees fall at the high end of the range.

leveling   Adjustments to survey numbers by an appropriate percentage needed to achieve a match with specific jobs.

liabilities   An organization's debts and other financial obligations.

local responsiveness (LR) strategy   A strategy that adapts to the needs of local markets, allowing an organization's units to meet the needs of their unique market.

location-based differential   An adjustment-to-base-pay program based on work location remoteness, lack of amenities, climatic conditions, and other adverse conditions.

lockout   Employer action that prevents workers from entering the workplace to do their normal jobs.

long-term care insurance   Covers cost of long-term care at home, in an assisted living facility, in a nursing home, or as an inpatient in a hospice facility.

long-term disability   Begins where short-term disability ends. Covers some or all of an employee's income for up to a specified period, usually from 6 months to age 65 or an alternative number of years.

long-term incentive   A reward for attaining results over a long measurement period.

low-context culture   A communication style that relies heavily on explicit and direct language.

lump-sum increase   Either a stand-alone performance bonus or part of an annual pay increase.

managed care plan   Insurance that provides plan subscribers with managed healthcare for the purpose of reducing costs and improving the quality of care.

management by objectives (MBO)   A method of performance appraisal that specifics the performance goals that the employee and manager identify.

management skills   The abilities required to succeed at a management job. They include such skills as leadership, communication, decision making, behavior flexibility, organization, and planning.

managerial estimate   A projection based on managerial experience alone.

mandatory bargaining issues   Issues that must be discussed by the employer and union when negotiating a contract of representation.

market-based job evaluation   Key jobs are measured and valued against the market, and the remaining jobs are inserted into a hierarchy based on their whole-job comparison to the benchmark jobs.

marketing   The process of encouraging people to purchase the organization's products or services.

mathematically based forecasting   Staffing ratios, sales ratios, or regression analysis used in human resource management analysis of data elements.

matrix structure   A command-and-control structure in which some employees have dual responsibilities and dual bosses.

maturity curve   Measures salaries based on years of directly related experience in the profession, such as research or teaching.

mean (average)   Arithmetic average arrived at by giving equal weight to every participant's actual pay.

measuring   Collecting and tabulating data.

median   The middle number in a range.

mediation   Use of an independent, impartial, and respected third party in the settlement of a dispute instead of opting for arbitration or litigation.

medical file   A collection of documents related to medical evaluations or status of an employee.

memorandum of understanding   Union contract for a represented group of employees and designated employers. A term usually used in the public sector.

mentoring   A career relationship between an experienced individual and another individual who has less experience.

mergers and acquisitions (M&A)   The joining together of two separate organizations (merger) or the acquiring of another organization (acquisition).

merit pay   Basing an employee's salary on their performance over a predetermined period and according to an agreed-upon criteria.

metric   A standard of measurement by which efficiency, performance progress, or quality of a plan, process, or product can be assessed.

minimum premium plan   A health insurance program paid for in part by the employer and in part by the employee.

mission statement   A statement describing what an organization does, who its customer/client base is, and how it will do its work.

mobile learning   Learning across multiple contexts, through social and content interactions, using personal electronic devices.

mode   The most frequently appearing number in a range.

modified duty   Temporary alteration of job duties that can be performed by an employee who is medically restricted for a designated period of time.

moral hazard   Lack of incentive to guard against risk where one is protected from its consequences.

motivation concepts   Notions about what motivates individuals that have come about as a result of scientific studies. Examples of researchers involved with such studies include Herzberg, Maslow, and McGregor.

multicriteria decision analysis (MCDA)   A subdiscipline of operations research that explicitly considers multiple criteria in decision-making environments.

multinational enterprise (MNE)   An enterprise operating in several countries but managed from one (home) country.

multiple linear regression   A statistical technique based on an assumed linear relationship between a dependent variable and a variety of explanatory or independent variables.

national origin   Nation of origin. This usually means national heritage and is a protected category within Title VII of the Civil Rights Act of 1964.

needs analysis   See *needs assessment.*

needs assessment   Determining through analysis what gaps exist between a standard or an objective and existing capabilities.

negative emphasis   The rejection of a candidate based on a small amount of negative information.

negligent hiring   A legal tort claim against an employer for injury to someone inside or outside the organization in a way that should have been predicted by the employer if a proper background check had been completed.

negligent retention   A legal tort claim against an employer for keeping someone on the payroll who is known to be a danger to others inside or outside the organization.

net assets   The difference between income and liabilities in a nonprofit organization.

new employee orientation   The process of welcoming new workers into the organization, which may include completing payroll or benefits documents and a tour of the workplace.

nominal group technique   Development of forecasts based on input from several groups of people.

noncash award   A prize, gift, or award presented in recognition of service or production or other designated achievement.

nonexempt job   A job with content that requires payment of overtime for work in excess of 40 hours per week under the Fair Labor Standards Act (FLSA).

objective measurement   Impartial assessment of a result.

objectives   End-result intentions.

occupational categories   Groupings of job titles with similar levels of responsibility or skill requirements.

occupational illness   A physical or mental malady caused by job-related conditions.

occupational injury   A physical or mental injury caused by job-related conditions.

offboarding   Moving employees out of the organization and off the payroll.

offshoring   The relocation of functions or work to another country.

on-the-job training (OJT)   Training that takes place while the employee is performing a job. This usually involves a coworker or supervisor providing the coaching or training while job content is being learned.

onboarding   Transitioning new employees into the organization; organizational socialization.

oral employment contract   Verbal agreement involving promises of duration or conditions in the employment relationship.

oral warning   Verbal notice that a rule or policy has been violated and further discipline will result if the behavior is repeated.

organization exit   Final formal meeting between the management and an employee leaving the firm; usually called an *exit interview*.

organizational culture   The way an organization treats its employees, customers, and others.

organizational development   The process of structured analysis and planning for strategic organizational accomplishment.

organizational learning   Organization-wide continuous process that enhances its collective ability to accept, make sense of, and respond to internal and external change.

organizational restructuring   A process by which an organization radically changes its internal structure or operations and processes.

organizational values   The operating philosophies or principles that guide an organization's internal conduct as well as its relationship with its customers, partners, and shareholders. These are core values.

organizing   1) The process of bringing order out of chaos. 2) Union efforts to convince employees to support a union as the designated bargaining agent for a workgroup.

orientation   A process or program for introducing new employees to their jobs, organization, and facility.

OSHA   The Occupational Safety and Health Administration as well as the Occupational Safety and Health Act.

outplacement   A program that assists employees in finding a job when their job is eliminated.

outside sales exemption   Exemption from overtime payment based on several qualifying factors, including the primary duty being making sales or obtaining orders for products or services. Work must be customarily and regularly engaged in away from the employer's place of business.

outsourcing   Contracting for services with a third party rather than having them performed in the organization.

overtime pay   An additional amount of money paid in accordance with federal law to hourly employees who work more than 40 hours in a workweek.

paid holidays   Designated days each year that are awarded to employees as paid time off.

paid leave   Paid time off for a specific designated reason.

paid sick leave   Accrued paid time off for medical reasons and usually based on length of service.

paid time off (PTO)   A bank of hours in which an employer pools sick days, vacation days, and personal days that employees can use as the need arises.

paid vacation   Accrued paid time off, usually based on length of service.

paired comparison   Method of evaluation in which each employee and job is compared with each other employee and job.

parent-country national (PCN)   An employee sent from the home country to a remote country for a work assignment.

Pareto chart   One of the seven tools of quality control, it is a bar graph that displays variances by the number of their occurrences.

partially self-funded plan   Health insurance program where the employer purchases one or two types of stop-loss insurance coverage.

part-time   Employees who work fewer than the number of hours required to be considered full-time.

pass rate   The number of people, shown as a percent, who were successful in passing an exam.

pay compression   Pay inequities that arise when new employees demand and get wages higher than those being paid to the current employees.

pay differential   Additional compensation paid to an employee as an incentive to accept what would normally be considered adverse working conditions, usually based on time, location, or working conditions.

pay equity   Degree to which the actual pay of an employee matches what they think they deserve. High pay equity means high employee satisfaction with their job; low pay equity increases the potential for absenteeism, grievances, strikes, and turnover. This is often called *pay satisfaction*.

pay for performance (P4P, PfP)   The notion that employees are compensated based on the results they achieve on their job.

pay grades   The way an organization organizes jobs of a similar value into job groups as a result of the job evaluation process.

pay ranges   Pay amounts constrained by the upper and lower boundaries of each pay grade.

pay survey   Collections of data on prevailing market pay rates and information on starting wage rates, base pay, pay ranges, overtime pay, shift differentials, and incentive pay plans.

payroll   The function of recordkeeping and computation of compensation for each employee that results in the issuance of a check or electronic deposit and the collection and deposit of payroll taxes and other withholdings.

payroll administration   The act of managing the payroll function.

payroll system   A usually computerized software program designed to accept work time data and generate paychecks or electronic deposits.

pedagogy   The method and practice of teaching, especially as an academic subject or theoretical concept.

Pension Benefit Guaranty Corporation   A federal corporation established under ERISA that insures the vested benefits of pension plan participants.

percentiles   Distribution of data into percentage ranges, such as top 10 percent and so on.

performance appraisal   A process of evaluating how employees perform their jobs.

performance bonus   Compensation in excess of base pay that is paid in recognition for exceeding performance/results objectives.

performance grant   Stock-based compensation that is linked to organizational performance.

performance improvement program (PIP)   A written plan a supervisor provides to an underperforming employee that specifies performance results required by a certain date.

performance management   The process used to identify, measure, communicate, develop, and reward employee performance.

performance measures   Methods for identifying quantities and qualities for job performance.

performance standards   Indicators of what a job is to accomplish and how it is to be performed.

performance-based merit pay system   A system with pay determined based on individual job performance.

PART III

permissible bargaining issue   An issue that may be discussed by the employer and union during contract negotiations. It is neither required nor prohibited.

perquisites (better known as perks)   Special privileges for executives, including club memberships, company cars, reserved parking, use of the company airplane, and other such benefits.

personal protective equipment (PPE)   Equipment worn by employees for protection against injury or illness hazards on the job.

person-based system   A system that considers an employee's capabilities rather than how the job is performed to determine the employee's pay.

personnel file   One or more sets of documents held by an employer that contain information about the employee's employment status, performance evaluations, disability accommodations, and so forth, collectively considered one personnel file.

PESTEL analysis   Used in SWOT analysis, a framework or tool used to analyze and monitor the external environment factors that have an impact on an organization.

phantom stock plan   Employee benefit program giving selected senior management employees pretend stock rather than actual stock, with the same financial benefits over time.

phased retirement   Partial retirement while continuing to work a reduced schedule.

PHR   Professional in Human Resources is a credential that demonstrates mastery of the technical and operational aspects of HR practices and U.S. laws and regulations.

PHRca   Professional in Human Resources – California. A credential for experts in employment regulations and legal mandates specific to the state of California. The PHRca combines the former PHR-CA and SPHR-CA credentials effective April 1, 2016.

PHRi   Professional in Human Resources – International. A credential for internationally based HR practitioners, validating professional-level competency, knowledge, and skills in a single international setting.

picketing   Technique used by unions to announce to the public a problem with an employer over issues involving working conditions or benefits.

pilot program   A small-scale, short-term experiment that helps an organization learn how a large-scale project might work in practice. This is also called a *feasibility study* or *experimental trial.*

plateau curve   A type of learning curve in which learning is fast at first but then flattens out.

pluralism   A work environment in which differing groups have their own agendas and conflict is overcome via negotiations as in a labor environment.

point-factor job evaluation An approach using specific compensable factors as reference points to measure relative job worth.

point-of-service plan A type of managed care plan that is a hybrid of HMO and PPO plans.

policies Statements describing how an organization is to be managed.

polycentric A condition that occurs when jobs at headquarters are filled with people from other countries and positions in remote countries are filled with people from the headquarters' country.

portal to portal From door to door. This is usually applied to employees traveling from home to work or from home to a remote job site.

preferred provider organization Healthcare program including an in-network and an out-of-network option for services.

premium Excess over apparent worth.

premium-only plan Authorized under the IRS Code, Section 125. Allows employer-sponsored premium payments to be paid by the employee on a pre-tax basis instead of after-tax. This is sometimes called a *POP plan*.

premium pay Payment at a rate greater than straight pay for working overtime or another agreed-upon condition.

prepaid legal insurance Employer financial support for the cost of routine legal services such as wills, real estate matters, divorces, and other services.

prescription drug plan Medical insurance program that covers some or all of the cost of prescription drugs for subscribers.

primacy error Tendency of an employee performance evaluator or an interviewer to rely on early cues for their first impression.

principal agent problem A conflict arising when people entrusted to look after the interests of others use the authority or power for their own benefit instead.

procedure The method to be used in fulfilling organizational responsibilities and policies.

process alignment The linking of an organization's structure and resources with its strategy and business environment.

process-flow analysis A diagram of the steps involved in a process.

product structure A representation of the way in which the parts of a product fit together and interact, organized in levels of detail based on structure.

productivity-based system A system in which pay is determined by the employee's production output.

professional employer organization   A vendor that, as a co-employer, provides qualified workers to a client organization.

professional exemption   Exemption from overtime payment based on several qualifying factors, including minimum pay requirement, advanced knowledge or education, and use of professional discretion and judgment.

profit-and-loss (P&L) statement   A financial statement that summarizes the revenues, costs, and expenses incurred during a specific period of time.

profit-sharing plan   A plan in which direct or indirect payments are made to employees, depending on the employer's profitability.

program evaluation and review technique (PERT)   A project management tool used to organize, coordinate, and schedule tasks and people.

progressive discipline   A system of progressive penalties involving increasing sanctions that can be taken if unwanted behaviors recur.

prohibited bargaining issues   Issues that may not be discussed by the employer and union during contract negotiations. These are illegal issues under the NLRA.

project hire   An employee who is hired for the duration of a project. Once the project is completed, the employee is dismissed or laid off. See *term employee*.

project management   Guiding the implementation of a program from beginning to end.

project management concepts   The study of project management styles and techniques.

project team   A group of people with specific talents or experiences brought together to resolve a problem or accomplish some other organizational goal.

promotion   Usually considered to be an increase in responsibility or compensation, or both.

proof of identity   A document such as a passport or driver's license that contains a photo of the individual that proves that person is who they claim to be.

proof of work authorization   A document such as a Social Security card or alien work registration authorization that proves the individual is authorized to work in the United States.

protected class   Any group of people designated as protected by the Department of Housing and Urban Development (HUD) in consideration of federal and state civil rights legislation.

prudent person rule   Basic principle for investment decisions by institutional investors and professional money managers.

punitive damages   Damages intended to deter a defendant from engaging in conduct similar to that which was the basis of a lawsuit.

qualified domestic relations order (QDRO)   A court-issued order that instructs a plan administrator to pay all or a portion of a pension plan benefit to a divorced spouse or child.

qualitative analysis   Research that explores the reasoning behind human behavior; often uses open-ended interviewing.

quantitative analysis   Research based on quantifiable data.

quartiles   Distribution of data into four quadrants: bottom quarter, lower-middle quarter, upper-middle quarter, and top quarter.

quid pro quo harassment   Insisting on sexual favors in exchange for some job benefit, be it promotion, compensation, or just retaining employment. This normally occurs between supervisor and subordinate. Literally, *quid pro quo* means "this for that."

range spreads   Dispersion of pay from the lowest boundary to the highest boundary of a pay range.

ratio analysis   Comparison of current results or historic results at a specific point in time.

realistic job preview (RJP)   A recruiting approach used by an organization to communicate the important aspects of the job prior to the offer of a position.

reasonable accommodation   Adjustment to a job condition or workplace that will allow an employee to perform the essential job duties.

reasonable cause   One possible determination from a state or federal enforcement agency concerning an investigation of a charge of illegal discrimination.

recency error   Occurs when an evaluator gives greater weight to recent events of performance.

recognition   Acknowledgment of accomplishments by individual employees.

recordkeeping   Documentation involving any aspect of employee management from discussions to personal employee information.

recruitment   Process of seeking out qualified job candidates for open positions.

red circle rate   Pay at a rate higher than the maximum for the assigned pay range.

redeployment   Assignment to a new job, often at a remote work location.

regiocentric   Orientation to culture in a specific region or collection of countries such as Asian, South American, or European.

regression analysis A statistical process of estimating the relationships among variables.

rehire A former employee who is hired back onto the payroll.

reliability Consistency and validity of test results determined through statistical methods after repeated trials.

remuneration survey A survey that collects information on compensation and benefit practices in the prevailing market.

repatriate An employee who returns to their home country following a work assignment in a different country.

replacement planning Succession planning using a snapshot assessment of existing qualified talent for key positions.

request for proposal A written document asking for vendor input and suggestions along with cost estimates for any given work to be performed in the establishment.

residual risk Exposure to loss remaining after other known risks have been countered, factored in, or eliminated.

responsibility A required part of a job or organizational obligation.

restructuring Redesigning the organizational structure and altering reporting relationships and responsibility assignments.

results measurement Method for monitoring the amount of progress that has been accomplished toward a stated goal or objective.

retention Measurement of the quantity of new employees remaining with the employer over a given period of time.

retiree An ex-employee who met the qualification requirements for retirement under the organization's definition or plan.

return on investment (ROI) The calculation showing the value of expenditures versus the investment.

return to work Clearance to return to active employment activities following an illness, injury, or other absence.

reverse innovation Also known as *trickle-up innovation*. A term referring to an innovation seen first, or likely to be used first, in the developing world before spreading to the industrialized world.

risk A probability or threat of damage, injury, liability, loss, or any other negative occurrence that is caused by external or internal vulnerabilities and that may be avoided through preemptive action.

risk appetite   The level of risk a person or corporation is willing to take in order to execute a strategy.

risk control   The probability of loss arising from the tendency of internal control systems to lose their effectiveness over time and thus expose (or fail to prevent exposure of) the assets they were instituted to protect.

risk management   Identifies and manages potential liabilities that come from operating a business.

risk position   The extent of exposure to a particular risk, expressed usually in monetary terms.

risk scorecard   The gathering of individual characteristics of risk and keeping track.

risk tolerance   Capacity to accept or absorb risk.

role-play   Technique for simulating individual participation in real-life roles involving performance or action involved with solving a problem.

Rucker plan   A company-wide incentive plan in which compensation is based on a ratio of income to value added by employees engaged in the production process.

rule of law   Absolute predominance or supremacy of ordinary law of the land over all citizens, no matter how powerful.

safety audit   The process of evaluating the workplace for safety hazards and determining any needed corrective action.

sales personnel incentive programs   Bonuses or commissions based on predetermined formulas involving performance and time.

scaffolding   Teacher modeling skills and thinking for students, allowing students to take over those expressions based on the initial structure provided by the teacher.

Scanlon plan   Cost-saving productivity-incentive plan in which any savings (computed per unit of output) compared with an agreed-upon standard labor cost are shared equally between the workers and the firm.

scatter diagram   A graphical tool that depicts the relationship among variables.

scenario "what if" analysis   The process of determining the effects on outcomes with altering details to determine a likely outcome.

seasonal employee   A worker hired for a specific seasonal surge in work levels; common in the retail industry and also agriculture and other food processing businesses.

Section 125 cafeteria plan   Allows employees to pay certain qualified expenses on a pre-tax basis. See *premium-only plan.*

selection   The ultimate choice in a field of multiple choices. This is usually applied to job candidate selection.

selection screening   The process of sorting out job candidates based on specified criteria of job requirements. This is accomplished through the use of interviews, tests, and demonstrations.

self-directed team   A group of people with a specific assignment permitted to select its own leadership and direction to take toward the problem or task.

self-directed work team   Assignment of employee group with multiple knowledge and skill specialties represented from multiple disciplines.

self-funded plan   Health insurance program where the employer assumes all the risk as a self-insured entity.

seniority   The length of service in a job, employer organization, industry, or union.

seniority pay increase   A pay increase given based solely on the length of service.

service level agreement (SLA)   A contract between a service provider and a customer that details the nature, quality, and scope of the service to be provided. This is also called a *service level contract*.

severance package   Voluntary payment by some employers to laid-off employees. It may include pay for a designated number of work days, job retraining, outplacement services, and paid benefits premium assistance.

shared services HR model   An HR organizational structure where specific functions of HR expertise develop HR policies, and units of HR can determine what it needs for the menu of services.

short-term disability   Begins where sick leave ends. This covers some or all of an employee's income for up to a specified period, usually 6 months.

SHRM-CP   A certification from the Society for Human Resource Management denoting "certified professionals."

SHRM-SCP   A certification from the Society for Human Resource Management denoting "senior certified professionals."

simple linear regression   A technique in which a straight line is fitted to a set of data points to measure the effect of a single independent variable. The slope of the line is the measured impact of that variable.

simulation   Imitation of a real-world system or process. A learning exercise designed to be as realistic as possible without the risk of a real-life circumstance.

single or flat-rate system   A system in which each worker in the same job has the same rate of pay regardless of seniority or job performance.

situational judgment test (SJT)   A type of psychological test that presents the test-taker with realistic, hypothetical scenarios and asks the individual to identify the most appropriate response or to rank the responses in the order they feel is most effective.

Six Sigma   A data-driven approach and method for eliminating defects.

skill-based system   When pay is based on the number and depth of skills that an employee has applicable to their job.

SMART goal model   Model for creating goals that are specific, measurable, achievable, relevant, and time bound.

social media   Contemporary methods of communicating with other individuals or groups. A term applied to Internet services such as Facebook, Pinterest, LinkedIn, and Twitter as examples.

social movement unionism   A type of union activity devoted to topics associated with social issues.

Society of Human Resource Professionals (SHRM)   The world's largest HR membership organization devoted to human resource management, representing more than 285,000 members in over 160 countries.

software as a service (SaaS)   Software rental from a centralized location, described as the "cloud," as opposed to having software installed on a desktop computer.

solution analysis   Statistical comparison of various potential solutions.

sourcing   The process of finding applicants and suppliers of goods or services.

span of control   The number of subordinates reporting to a supervisor or manager.

specific stop-loss coverage   The health plan is protected against the risk of a major illness for one participant, or one family unit, covered by the plan.

SPHR   Senior Professional in Human Resources credential for those who have mastered the strategic and policy-making aspects of HR management in the United States.

SPHR-CA   Senior Professional in Human Resources credential for experts in employment regulations and legal mandates specific to the state of California (no longer recognized effective April 1, 2016; see *PHR-ca*).

SPHRi   Senior Professional in Human Resources – International. A credential for internationally based HR leaders validating senior-level HR mastery and global competency in a single international setting.

staff units   Specialized services provided to workgroups.

staffing   Filling job openings with qualified applicants.

stakeholder   An individual with an interest in an organization's success or outcomes.

PART III

stakeholder concept   A conceptual framework of business ethics and organizational management that addresses moral and ethical values in the management of a business or other organization.

standard   The yardstick by which the amount and quality of output are measured.

standard deviation   Scores in a set of data that spread out around an average.

state employment service   The agency responsible for assisting citizens with job placement and unemployment benefits in each state.

statistical forecasting   The use of mathematical formulas to identify patterns and trends.

step rate with performance considerations   A system allowing performance to influence the size or timing of a pay increase along the step system.

stereotyping   Broadly classifying people into groups based on characteristics that may not be accurate ("all blonds are dumb," for example).

storytelling   The use of multimedia technology such as PowerPoint to present interactive opportunities involving any subject.

straight piece rate system   A system in which the employee receives a base rate of pay and is awarded additional compensation for the amount of output produced.

strategic business management   That which formulates and produces HR objectives, programs, practices, and policies.

strategic fit   A situation that occurs when a specific project, target company, or product is seen as appropriate with respect to an organization's overall objectives.

strategic planning   Identifying organizational objectives and determining what actions are required to reach those objectives.

strategy   1) A method or plan chosen to bring about a desired future, such as achievement of a goal or solution to a problem. 2) The art and science of planning and marshalling resources for their most efficient and effective use.

stress interview   Emotionally charged interview setting where the interviewee is put under psychological stress to evaluate how they perform under pressure.

strictness   An error in which a manager is too strict in evaluating the performance of employees, leading to decreases in motivation and performance.

strike   Work stoppage resulting from a failed negotiation between employer and union.

structured interview   Fixed-format interview in which all questions are prepared beforehand and are put in the same order to each interviewee.

subject matter expert   A person who is well-versed in the content of a specific knowledge area.

subjective measurement   Assessment of a result using opinion or perception.

substance abuse   Personal use of alcohol or drugs in excess of amounts prescribed by a medical professional, or any use of illegal substances. Abuse generally results in an impairment of the individual's physical or mental capacities.

succession planning   A process of identifying a plan for the replacement of key employees.

supplemental unemployment benefits   An unemployment benefit in addition to government benefits offered by some employers.

supply analysis   Strategic evaluation of job candidate sources, plant locations, and other factors.

supply chain   An entire network of entities, directly or indirectly interlinked and interdependent in serving the same consumer or customer.

suspension   Temporary hiatus of active employment, usually as a disciplinary step, that can be paid or unpaid.

sustainability   Ability to maintain or support an activity or process over the long term.

SWOT analysis   A process in strategic planning that looks at an organization's strengths, weaknesses, opportunities, and threats.

synchronous learning   A form of instruction where students are learning or engaging with learning materials at the same time.

talent management   The management and integration of all HR activities and processes that aligns with the organization's goals and needs.

talent retention   The retention of those employees who are considered key talent because they are the strongest performers, have high potential, or are in critical jobs.

taskforce   A group of people assembled to address major organizational issues.

teacher exemption   Exemption from overtime payment based on several qualifying factors, including the primary duty of teaching in an educational establishment.

team   A group of people focused on specific organizational issues.

temp-to-lease   Conversion of an employee provided by a temporary agency to regular employee status in the client organization.

term employee   An employee who is hired for the duration of a project. Once the project is completed, the employee is dismissed or laid off. See *project hire.*

termination   End of the employment relationship.

theory of constraints (TOC)   Concepts and methodology aimed mainly at achieving the most efficient flow of material in a plant through continuous process improvement.

third-country national (TCN)   An employee who is moved from one remote location to another remote location for a work assignment.

third party   Someone other than the two primary parties involved in an interaction.

third-party administrator plan   Health insurance programs in which the employer assumes all the risk but hires an independent claims department.

time-based differential pay   Shift pay that is generally time-based rewards for employees who work what are considered undesirable shifts like night shifts.

time-based step rate system   Determining pay rate based on the length of time in the job.

total quality management (TQM)   A management system for achieving customer satisfaction using quantitative methods to improve processes.

total rewards   Financial inducements and rewards, as well as nonfinancial inducements and rewards, such as the value of good job content and a good working environment.

total rewards strategy   An integrated reward system encompassing three key elements that employees value from their employment: compensation, benefits, and work experience that attracts and retains talent.

totalization agreement   An agreement between several nations that avoid double taxation of income for workers who divide their working career between two or more countries.

trade union   An organization whose membership consists of workers and union leaders, united to protect and promote their common interests.

trainability   The readiness and motivation to learn.

training   The process whereby people acquire skills, knowledge, or capabilities to perform jobs.

training effectiveness   Measurement of what students are expected to be able to do at the end of the training course or module.

training technique   An approach to training using virtual, classroom, on-the-job, or one-on-one tutoring.

transactional leadership   A leadership style that focuses on rewards, or threat of discipline, in an effort to motivate employees.

transfer   Movement of a current employee to a different job in a different part of the organization.

transfer of learning The ability of a trainee to apply the behavior, knowledge, and skills acquired in one learning situation to another.

transformational leadership A form of socialized leadership that motivates employees by inspiring them. It is concerned with the collective good transcending one's own interests for the sake of others.

travel pay Extra pay provided for travel time, either under legal requirement or by other agreement.

trend analysis Comparison of historical results with current results to determine a trend.

triple bottom line Financial, social, and environmental effects of a firm's policies and actions that determine its viability as a sustainable organization.

tuition reimbursement Employer financial support for employee continuing education efforts.

turnover analysis Comparison of the reasons for employees leaving the workforce and the organizational problems that may be causing it.

unfair labor practice (ULP) Legally prohibited action by an employer or trade union, such as refusal to bargain in good faith.

uniform guidelines Federal regulations that specify how job selection tools must be validated.

unpaid sick leave Accrued unpaid time off, usually based on length of service.

unweighted average Raw average of data that gives equal weight to all factors, with no regard to individual factors.

validity The extent to which a test measures what it says it measures.

value Resulting benefits created when an organization meets its strategic goals.

value chain Interlinked value-adding activities that convert inputs into outputs, which, in turn, add to the bottom line and help create a competitive advantage.

value driver An entity that increases the value of a product or service by improving the perception of the item and essentially provides a competitive advantage.

values The principles or standards of behavior that are most important to either an individual or entity.

variable pay Performance-based pay that includes individual performance bonuses, executive bonuses, profit sharing, gainsharing, group incentives, and other incentives tied to productivity as opposed to base pay.

PART III

variance analysis   Process aimed at computing variance between actual and budgeted or targeted levels of performance and identification of their causes.

veteran   A former member of the U.S. military service in any branch.

veto   The action of canceling or postponing a decision or bill in the U.S. legislature.

vicarious liability   Obligation that arises from the relationship of one party with another.

vision care plan   Medical insurance program that covers some or all of the cost of vision care (exams and corrective lenses) for subscribers.

vision statement   A statement that describes the desired future of an organization.

voluntary separation   An individual leaving the payroll for voluntary reasons, such as retirement, obtaining a different job, returning to full-time education, or personal reasons.

wage compression   A reduction in the relative wage differentials between high- and low-paying jobs resulting in insufficient incentives required for higher-level job responsibilities and skills.

weighted average   An average result taking into account the number of participants and each participant's pay.

Weingarten rights   A term that refers to a union employee's right to have a union representative or coworker present during an investigatory interview.

well-being   A good or satisfactory condition of existence; a state characterized by health, happiness, and prosperity; welfare.

work council   An organization that represents employees on a local level. A work council often provides a useful collective bargaining tool for employees who require an organization that is more familiar with their particular situation than a national labor union, for example.

work-life balance (WLB)   A comfortable state of equilibrium achieved between an employee's primary priorities of their employment position and their personal lifestyle.

workers' compensation   A program that provides medical care and compensates employees for part of lost earnings as a result of a work-related disability.

workforce analysis   Assessment of the workforce and the items that are influencing it.

workforce management   Managing employees' work activities, responsibilities, and work hours as well as planning, scheduling, and tracking the results of the work effort.

workforce planning and employment   The process of recruiting, interviewing, staffing, ensuring equal employment opportunity and affirmative action, providing new employee orientation, and managing retention, termination, and employee records, all performed by the employer.

workplace violence   Personal behavior that ranges from shouting to hitting or worse taking place on an employer's premises.

workweek   A period of 7 days that always begins at the same hour of the same day each week.

written employment contract   A written agreement involving promises of duration or conditions in the employment relationship.

written warning   A written notice that a rule or policy has been violated and further discipline will result if the behavior is repeated.

zero-based budgeting   A model of budgeting that is based on expenditures being justified for each budget year.

zero-sum   Whatever is gained by one side is lost by the other.

INDEX

A

absenteeism, 227–228
ACA. *See* Affordable Care Act (ACA)
accident reporting for OSHA compliance, 272–274
acclimation in orientation, 124
achievement awards, 214
acronyms, 307–327
actual damages penalties in Civil Rights Act, 49
ADA. *See* Americans with Disabilities Act (ADA)
ADAAA (Americans with Disabilities Act Amendments Act), 44–48
ADDIE model for learning objectives, 127–128
ADEA (Age Discrimination in Employment Act)
    description, 53
    Learning and Development area, 122
    payroll records, 175
administrative paperwork in onboarding, 109–111
ADR (alternative dispute resolution), 260
affective-based learning, 125–126
affirmative action
    Executive Order 11246, 54–55
    job analysis, 83
Affordable Care Act (ACA)
    description, 57
    eligibility, 179
    marketplace plans, 180
    provisions, 158
after-action reviews for training program evaluation, 138–139
Age Discrimination in Employment Act (ADEA)
    description, 53
    Learning and Development area, 122
    payroll records, 175
age harassment, 233
agricultural workers, visas for, 62
Airline Flight Crew Technical Corrections Act, 55
aliens
    Immigration and Nationality Act, 27
    Immigration Reform and Control Act, 28
    visas, 63–64
alternative dispute resolution (ADR), 260
alternative staffing practices, 85
alternative work arrangements, 215–216
American Arbitration Association, 260
American Health Benefit Exchanges, 57
American Recovery and Reinvestment Act (ARRA), 27, 53
Americans with Disabilities Act (ADA)
    enforcement, 47–48
    "essential job function" provisions, 46

"job accommodation" provisions, 46–47
job analysis, 82
Learning and Development area, 122
"major life activities" conditions, 45–46
medical examinations, 108
overview, 44
policies, 212
provisions and protections, 44
recordkeeping requirements, 47
"substantially limits" conditions, 45
Supreme Court interpretation, 45
Americans with Disabilities Act Amendments Act (ADAAA), 44–48
analysis phase in ADDIE model, 127
annual accident summaries for OSHA compliance, 274
aPHR (Associate Professional in Human Resources), 4
aPHR exam
    body of knowledge, 11–14
    preparing for, 16–17
    readiness for, 17
    registration process, 15
    test development process, 14–15
aPHRi (Associate Professional in Human Resources – International), 4, 6
applicant databases
    description, 94–95
    managing, 294
applicant tracking systems (ATSs), 94–95
applicants
    interviewing, 296
    question handling, 295
    screening, 294–295
    tests and assessments, 296–297
appraisal methods
    comparative, 225
    narrative, 225–226
    overview, 223–224
    performance improvement plans, 227
    self-assessment, 226
    shortcomings, 226–227
apprenticeships, 135
arbitration, 260
ARRA (American Recovery and Reinvestment Act), 27, 53
assessments
    applicants, 296–297
    self-assessment, 226
Associate Professional in Human Resources (aPHR), 4
Associate Professional in Human Resources – International (aPHRi), 4, 6

associations for external recruitment, 93
ATSs (applicant tracking systems), 94–95
attendance issues, 227–228
audits for risk minimization, 291–292
automatic step rate pay systems, 169
awards, 214

B

background checks, 107
base pay systems, 168–170
behavior measures for training program evaluation, 138–139
behavioral interviews, 102
behaviorally anchored rating methods (BARS), 226
behaviors
    ethical, 289–290
    workplace. *See* workplace behavior
benefits
    communicating, 194–195
    functional area. *See* Compensation and Benefits functional area
    government-mandated, 177–178
    off-boarding, 241
benefits programs
    enrollment in, 109
    supporting, 298–299
bereavement leave, 189
biases
    appraisal methods, 226
    interviewing, 105–106
    unconscious, 219
blended training, 134–135
blending in mergers and acquisitions, 265
Bloom, Benjamin, 125
Bloom's Taxonomy, 125–126
Body of Competency and Knowledge (BoCK) in SHRM, 8
Body of Knowledge (BoK)
    aPHR exam, 11–14
    Compensation and Benefits area, 155–156
    Compliance and Risk Management area, 251–252
    Employee Relations area, 203–204
    HRCI, 4
    Learning and Development area, 121
    Talent Acquisition area, 79–80
branding and marketing in external recruitment, 90
broadbanding, 167
buddy pairings in onboarding, 111
Bureau of Apprenticeship and Training (BAT), 135
business continuity, 264

C

callback pay, 173
candidate pipelines for external recruitment, 93
career development practices
    career counseling, 144
    career pathing, 143
    dual-ladder careers, 143–144

overview, 140–141
succession planning, 141–142
career-level tasks
    applicant database management, 294
    applicant interviews, 296
    applicant question handling, 295
    applicant screening, 294–295
    applicant tests and assessments, 296–297
    claims processing, 300
    compensation and benefits communication, 298
    compensation and benefits issue resolution, 300
    decision support, 283–284
    document preparation, 286–287
    employee benefits program activities, 298–299
    employee data maintenance, 285
    employee relations program coordination, 303
    employment offer coordination, 297
    endnotes, 304
    external provider coordination, 285
    form processing, 286
    internal customer service, 287–288
    interview coordination, 296
    job functions documentation, 292–293
    job listing posting, 293
    laws and regulations compliance, 284
    organization core values communication, 289–290
    orientation and onboarding, 300–301
    overview, 281
    payroll-related information coordination, 299–300
    performance reviews and development plans, 303–304
    personal experience, 281–283
    policies and procedures communication, 288
    post-offer employment activities, 298
    review, 304
    risk identification, 290–291
    risk minimization, 291–292
    training coordination, 301
    training process, 302
case laws
    Compensation and Benefits area, 331–332
    Compliance and Risk Management area, 340
    Employee Relations area, 333–340
    Talent Acquisition area, 329–331
catastrophes in OSHA reports, 33
catch-up contributions, 187
category ratings in performance management, 224–225
CBAs (collective bargaining agreements), 258
CDHPs (consumer-driven health plans), 182
celebrations
    cultural, 219–221
    holiday, 215–216
central errors in appraisal methods, 226
certification organizations, 3–4
    HRCI, 4–8
    IPMA-HR, 9
    SHRM, 8–9
change management, 145–147
charges of illegal discrimination, 48
checklists for appraisal methods, 225

child labor provisions in FLSA, 25–26, 157
childcare services, 191
chunking, 129
Civil Rights Act (Title VII) (1964)
    description, 48–49
    Learning and Development area, 122
Civil Rights Act (1991), 49
Civil Service Reform Act, 59
claims processing, 300
classification, job, 162–163
classrooms, 132–133
Clayton Act, 20
co-worker introductions in onboarding, 111
COBRA (Consolidated Omnibus Budget
  Reconciliation Act)
    description, 53
    provisions, 158
code of conduct violations, 228–230
Codes of Fair Competition, 30
COLAs (cost-of-living adjustments), 169
collective bargaining, 257
collective bargaining agreements (CBAs), 258
college recruiting, 93
communication
    compensation and benefits, 194–195, 298
    e-mail, 209–210
    external providers, 285
    legal requirements, 193–194
    organization core values, 289–290
    organizational, 209–210
    policies and procedures, 288
commuter assistance, 191
compa-ratios, 167–168
company parties, 215
comparative methods for performance management, 225
compensation and benefits
    communicating, 298
    issue resolution, 300
    policies, 212
Compensation and Benefits functional area
    aPHR exam weights, 12–13
    base pay systems, 168–170
    benefits communication, 194–195
    case laws, 331–332
    common benefits, 185–189
    endnotes, 202
    financial incentives, 171–173
    government-mandated benefits, 177–178
    healthcare benefits, 179–184
    job evaluations, 160–165
    knowledge, 155–156
    laws and regulations, 156–158
    legal compliance, 192–194
    organization-based pay, 174
    overview, 155
    payroll, 174–176
    person-based systems, 171
    pricing and pay rates, 165–168
    productivity-based systems, 170–171
    questions, 196–201

review, 195–196
    supplemental benefits, 190–192
    total rewards programs, 159–160
compensatory damages penalties in Civil Rights Act, 49
competency-based pay systems, 171
complaints
    diversity and inclusion programs, 222
    investigation methods, 233–235
    labor unions, 259
    OSHA reports, 33
Compliance and Risk Management functional area
    aPHR exam weights, 14
    case laws, 340
    Department of Labor, 255–256
    EEOC, 255
    employment-at-will, 255
    endnotes, 280
    knowledge, 251–252
    labor unions, 256–260
    laws and regulations, 252–255
    OSHA compliance, 272–274
    overview, 251
    questions, 274–279
    review, 274
    risk mitigation. See risk mitigation
    workers' compensation, 270–272
computer-based surveys, 217–218
computers and technology, policies for, 213
confidentiality in onboarding, 109
conflict-of-interest statements policies, 212
conflicts, employee, 230
Congressional Accountability Act, 59–60
Consolidated Omnibus Budget Reconciliation
  Act (COBRA)
    description, 53
    provisions, 158
Consumer Credit Protection Act, 20
consumer-driven health plans (CDHPs), 182
content chunking, 129
contract labor, 86
contractor payrolling, 87
contracts
    employment, 106
    labor unions, administering, 258
    labor unions, costs, 257–258
    labor unions, negotiating, 257
contrast errors
    appraisal methods, 226
    interviewing bias, 105
coordination
    employee relations programs, 303
    employment offers, 297
    external providers, 285
    interview scheduling, 296
    payroll-related information, 299–300
    training, 301
Copeland "Anti-Kickback" Act, 20
Copyright Act
    description, 20
    Learning and Development area, 122

core values, communicating, 289–290
corporate universities, 133
cost-of-living adjustments (COLAs), 169
cost per hire metric, 112–113
costs
    healthcare benefits, 184
    labor union contracts, 257–258
    turnover, 112
counseling, career, 144
counteroffers, 106
courtesy in interviews, 104
credential verification, 107
critical incidents method
    appraisals, 225
    training program evaluation, 138–139
cross-training, 136
cultural celebrations, 219–221
cultural noise as interviewing bias, 105
cultural sensitivity and acceptance, 219
culture
    communicating, 289–290
    mergers and acquisitions, 265
    onboarding discussions, 111
customer service tasks, 287–288
customer theft, 269
cyber-crimes, 267–268

D

D&I programs. *See* diversity and inclusion
    (D&I) programs
data security, 267–268
databases
    applicant, 94–95, 294
    candidates, 142
    employee skills, 88–89
    résumés, 91
Davis-Bacon Act, 20–21
death, terminations from, 239
decreasing returns learning curves, 130–131
deferred profit-sharing plans, 174
defined benefit plans, 186
defined contribution plans, 187
delayering organizational structure, 208–209
delivery systems healthcare costs, 184
dental plans, 184
Department of Labor (DOL)
    compensation requirements, 38
    description, 255–256
    medical leave, 56
dependent care flexible spending accounts, 183
design phase in ADDIE model, 127
determinations for complaints and grievances, 234
development phase in ADDIE model, 127
development plans, monitoring, 303–304
differential pay, 172
differential piece-rate pay systems, 171
direct compensation, 160
directive interviews, 102

disabilities
    employer benefit plans, 185
    harassment, 232–233
    Rehabilitation Act, 35
    terminations from, 240
disabled status in self-identification, 100–101
discipline
    policies, 213
    progressive. *See* progressive discipline
diversity and inclusion (D&I) programs
    cultural sensitivity and acceptance, 219
    measurements, 222
    overview, 218–219
    social responsibility, 219–220
diversity groups for external recruitment, 93
divestitures, 264–266
divisional organizational structure, 209
document preparation, 286–287
documenting
    job functions, 292–293
    progressive discipline, 237–238
    terminations, 241
Dodd-Frank Wall Street Reform and
    Consumer Protection Act, 21
DOL (Department of Labor)
    compensation requirements, 38
    description, 255–256
    medical leave, 56
downsizing, 266
Drug-Free Workplace Act, 49–50
drug testing, 108
dual-ladder careers, 143–144
Due Process Protocol, 260
duplicate workforces in mergers and acquisitions, 265
duties and responsibilities in job descriptions, 84

E

e-learning, 133–135
e-mail communication, 209–210
E Nonimmigrant Visas, 61–62
E-Verify system, 60, 110–111
EAPs (employee assistance programs), 186
EB employment-based visas, 64
Economic Growth and Tax Relief Reconciliation Act
    (EGTRRA), 21
ECPA (Electronic Communications Privacy Act), 21
educational references for background checks, 107
EEOA (Equal Employment Opportunity Act)
    description, 51
    policies, 212
EEOC (Equal Employment Opportunity Commission)
    Compliance and Risk Management area, 255
    self-identification, 100
EGTRRA (Economic Growth and Tax Relief
    Reconciliation Act), 21
elder care, 191
Electronic Communications Privacy Act (ECPA), 21
emergencies, handling, 264

emergency evacuation in IIPPs, 262
emergency exits item in onboarding, 111
emergency medical care in IIPPs, 263
emergency temporary standards in OSHA, 34
employee affinity groups for external recruitment, 93
employee assistance programs (EAPs), 186
employee behavior in code of conduct violations, 229
employee benefits
    government-mandated, 177–178
    programs support, 298–299
employee conflicts, 230
employee cyber-theft, 268
employee data, maintaining, 285
employee engagement programs, 213–216
employee feedback, 216
    processes, 217–218
    surveys, 216–218
employee handbooks
    onboarding, 109
    topics in, 211–213
employee leasing, 87
employee lifecycle information, 213
employee-of-the-month awards, 214
Employee Polygraph Protection Act, 22
employee recognition programs, 190
employee referrals for external recruitment, 92
Employee Relations functional area
    aPHR exam weights, 13–14
    case laws, 333–340
    complaints and grievances, 233–235
    diversity and inclusion programs, 218–222
    employee engagement programs, 213–216
    employee feedback, 216–218
    endnotes, 249
    human resource policies, 211–213
    knowledge, 203–204
    laws and regulations, 204–205
    off-boarding, 240–241
    organizational strategy, 206–211
    overview, 203
    performance management, 222–227
    progressive discipline, 235–240
    questions, 242–249
    review, 242
    rights and responsibilities, 205–206
    workplace behavior, 227–233
employee relations program coordination, 303
employee resource groups, 218
employee retention metric, 112
Employee Retirement Income Security Act (ERISA)
    Compensation and Benefits area, 157
    description, 22
    health benefits eligibility, 179
    retirement plans, 186–187
employee rights and responsibilities, 206
employee self-service (ESS) technologies
    communication through, 193–194
    payroll systems, 176

employee skills databases, 88–89
employee suggestion awards, 214
employee theft, 269
employment agencies for external recruitment, 92
employment-at-will, 255
employment authorization – Form I-9, 110
employment contracts, 106
employment offer coordination, 297
employment references in background checks, 107
employment services for external recruitment, 92
employment visas, 61–64
enforcement
    ADA, 47–48
    Drug-Free Workplace Act, 50
    FLSA, 26
    Mine Safety and Health Act, 29
    OSHA, 33
    SOX, 37
engagement surveys, 216
Equal Employment Opportunity Act (EEOA)
    description, 51
    policies, 212
Equal Employment Opportunity Commission (EEOC)
    Compliance and Risk Management area, 255
    self-identification, 100
Equal Pay Act (an Amendment to the FLSA), 22
equipment damage, preventing, 269
equipment security, 268
ERISA. See Employee Retirement Income Security Act (ERISA)
escalation in progressive discipline, 238–239
ESS (employee self-service) technologies
    communication through, 193–194
    payroll systems, 176
essay format for appraisals, 225
essential health benefits, 180
ethical behaviors, communicating, 289–290
ethics in code of conduct violations, 229–230
evaluation phase in ADDIE model, 127–128
evaluations
    job, 160–165
    training programs, 136–140
executive involvement in diversity and
    inclusion programs, 222
Executive Order 11246, 54–55
Executive Order 13706, 57
executives, visas for, 63
exit interviews, 241
expectations in orientation, 124
external providers, 285
external recruitment, 89–94

F

FAA Modernization and Reform Act, 22
factor comparison job evaluation method, 161, 164
factor evaluation system (FES), 163
Fair and Accurate Credit Transactions Act (FACT), 23

Fair Credit Reporting Act (FCRA), 23
Fair Labor Standards Act (FLSA)
    Compensation and Benefits area, 157
    description, 23
    enforcement, 26
    job analysis, 83
    overtime computation, 26
    payroll records, 175
    provisions and protections, 23–24
    recordkeeping requirements, 24–26
False Claims Act, 60
Family and Medical Leave Act (FMLA)
    description, 55–56
    provisions, 158
fashion models, visas for, 62
fatalities in OSHA reports, 33
FCPA (Foreign Corrupt Practices Act), 26–27
FCRA (Fair Credit Reporting Act), 23
federal government employees, laws and regulations for,
    59–61
Federal Insurance Contributions Act (FICA), 39
Federal Labor Relations Authority (FLRA), 59
federal laws and regulations. *See* U.S. laws and regulations
Federal Unemployment Tax Act, 178
fee-for-service (FFS) plans, 181
feedback, 216
    complaints and grievances, 234
    processes, 217–218
    surveys, 216–218
FES (factor evaluation system), 163
FFS (fee-for-service) plans, 181
FICA (Federal Insurance Contributions Act), 39
final paychecks in off-boarding, 240–241
financial incentives, 171–173
financial references in background checks, 107
first-impression interviewing errors, 105
fishbowl interviews, 103
flat organizational structure, 208–209
flat-rate pay systems, 169
flexible spending accounts (FSAs), 183
floater employees, 86
floating days, 189
FLRA (Federal Labor Relations Authority), 59
FLSA. *See* Fair Labor Standards Act (FLSA)
FMLA (Family and Medical Leave Act)
    description, 55–56
    provisions, 158
focus groups for employee feedback, 218
followups in OSHA reports, 33
forced choice appraisal methods, 225
forecasting staffing needs, 81–82
Foreign Corrupt Practices Act (FCPA), 26–27
foreign nationals, employment visas for, 61–64
Form I-9
    Immigration Reform and Control Act, 28
    onboarding, 110
Form W-4, 109
formative evaluation in ADDIE model, 127–128
former employees for internal recruitment, 89

FSAs (flexible spending accounts), 183
full-time employees, 85
functional organizational structure, 209
furloughs, 266–267
gainsharing, 174
gender in self-identification, 99–100

G

General Duty Clause, 32
General Schedule (GS) classification system, 162
Genetic Information Nondiscrimination Act (GINA), 51
geographic differentials, 173
gig assignments, 136
gig employees, 86
GINA (Genetic Information Nondiscrimination Act), 51
Global Professional in Human Resources (GPHR), 4–6
glossary of terms, 349–389
goals in organizational strategy, 206
government approval for mergers and acquisitions, 265
government-mandated benefits, 177–178
GPHR (Global Professional in Human Resources), 4–6
graphic scales appraisal methods, 224
green circle rates, 168
grievances
    investigating, 233–235
    labor unions, 259
group incentives, 173
group interviews, 103
group life insurance plans, 186
group lunches in orientation, 125
GS (General Schedule) classification system, 162
guidelines on discrimination because of sex, 51
gym memberships, 192

H

H visas, 62–63
hacker theft, 267–268
halo errors
    appraisal methods, 226
    interviewing bias, 105
handbooks
    onboarding, 109
    topics in, 211–213
harassment
    policies, 212
    workplace, 230–233
hard-copy records for résumés and job applications, 99
hardship withdrawals in defined contribution plans, 187
Hay plan for job evaluations, 163–165
hazard pay, 172
HDHPs (high-deductible health plans), 182
heading information in job descriptions, 84
Health Information Technology for Economic and
    Clinical Health (HITECH) Act, 27
Health Insurance Portability and Accountability Act
    (HIPAA)
    description, 27
    provisions, 157

health insurance purchasing cooperatives
  (HIPCs), 182
Health Maintenance Organization (HMO)
  plans, 181
health monitoring, 263
health reimbursement accounts (HRAs), 182–183
health savings accounts (HSAs), 183
healthcare benefits
  costs, 184
  dental plans, 184
  eligibility, 179
  enrollment, 179–180
  overview, 179
  plan designs, 180–183
  prescription drug plans, 183
  vision care plans, 184
high-deductible health plans (HDHPs), 182
HIPAA (Health Insurance Portability and
  Accountability Act)
  description, 27
  provisions, 157
HIPCs (health insurance purchasing cooperatives), 182
hiring halls, 258
hiring management systems (HMSs), 94–95
HITECH (Health Information Technology for Economic
  and Clinical Health) Act, 27
HMO (Health Maintenance Organization) plans, 181
HMSs (hiring management systems), 94–95
holiday celebrations, 215–216
holiday pay, 173, 188
Homeland Security Act, 60
honesty in interviews, 104
horizontal organizational structure, 208–209
horn errors
  appraisal methods, 226
  interviewing bias, 105
hours worked provisions in FLSA, 157
housing assistance, 192
HR Certification Institute (HRCI), 4–8
HR documents, preparing, 286–287
HR forms, tasks, 286
HRAs (health reimbursement accounts), 182–183
HRCI (HR Certification Institute), 4–8
HRISs. See human resource information systems (HRISs)
HSAs (health savings accounts), 183
human resource certification
  aPHR exam, 11–17
  benefits, 10–11
  certification organizations, 3–9
  endnotes, 18
  professional certifications, 3
  review, 17
human resource information systems (HRISs)
  applicant databases, 94–95
  data maintenance, 285–286
  overview, 210–211
  payroll systems, 176
  security, 267
human resource policies, 211–213

I

IIPPs (injury and illness prevention plans), 260–263
illness and terminations, 240
Immigration and Nationality Act (INA), 27
Immigration Reform and Control Act (IRCA)
  description, 28
  employment authorization, 110
imminent danger incidents in OSHA reports, 33
implementation phase in ADDIE model, 127
Implicit Association Test, 219
improvement programs for workplace behavior, 228
INA (Immigration and Nationality Act), 27
incident reports for OSHA compliance, 33, 274
inconsistency in interview questioning, 105
increasing returns learning curves, 130–131
independent medical exams for workers' compensation,
  271–272
indirect compensation, 160
individual achievement awards, 214
injuries, terminations from, 240
injury and illness prevention plans (IIPPs), 260–263
inquisitiveness in interviews, 104
inspections
  OSHA, 33
  workplace safety, 261–263, 272
instructional design
  learning objectives, 125–127
  overview, 125
internal customer service tasks, 287–288
internal investigators for complaints and grievances, 234
internal recruitment, 88–89
International Public Management Association
  for Human Resources (IPMA-HR), 9
Internet for external recruitment, 91
internships, 136
interviewing techniques, 101
  bias, 105–106
  guidelines, 103–105
  types, 101–103
interviews
  applicants, 296
  complaints and grievances, 234
  coordinating, 296
  exit, 241
  stay, 217
intracompany transferees, visas for, 63
inventory security, 268
investigations
  complaints and grievances, 233–235
  OSHA reports, 33
investors, visas for, 62
involuntary terminations, 240
IPMA-HR (International Public Management Association
  for Human Resources), 9
IRCA (Immigration Reform and Control Act)
  description, 28
  employment authorization, 110
IRS Intermediate Sanctions, 28
issue resolution for compensation and benefits, 300

J

Job Accommodation Network (JAN), 47
job analysis, 82–83
job descriptions and job specifications, 83–84
job evaluations
    factor comparison method, 164
    job classification method, 162–163
    job-ranking method, 161–162
    overview, 160–161
    point-factor method, 163–164
job fairs for external recruitment, 94
job functions, documenting, 292–293
job offers, 106
job postings
    career-level task, 293
    internal recruitment, 89
job rotation in on-the-job training, 136
job sharing, 85
job-to-predetermined-standard comparisons, 162
Jobs for Veterans Act, 41
jury duty leave, 189

K

Kirkpatrick, Donald, 136
Kirkpatrick's model, 136–137
knowledge and qualifications in job descriptions, 84
knowledge-based learning, 125–126
knowledge-based pay systems, 171
Kotter's theory, 146–147

L

L-1 visas, 63
Labor-Management Relations Act
    (LMRA; Taft-Hartley Act), 28
Labor-Management Reporting and Disclosure Act
    (Landrum-Griffin Act), 28–29
labor unions, 256
    collective bargaining, 257
    complaint handling, 259
    contract administration, 258
    contract costs, 257–258
    contract negotiation, 257
    external recruitment, 94
    mediation and arbitration, 260
    recognition procedures, 256–257
    unfair labor practices, 258–259
Landrum-Griffin Act, 28–29
Lanham (Trademark) Act, 40
laws and regulations. See U.S. laws and regulations
layoffs, 240
learner-centered approaches, 128–129
Learning and Development functional area
    aPHR exam weights, 12
    career development practices, 140–144
    change management, 145–147
    endnotes, 153–154
    knowledge, 121
    laws and regulations, 122

    overview, 121
    questions, 147–153
    review, 147
    training and development. See training
        and development
learning curves, 129–131
learning objectives
    ADDIE model, 127–128
    chunking, 129
    instructional design, 125–127
    learner-centered approaches, 128–129
    learning curves, 129–131
    teacher-centered approaches, 128
leasing, employee, 87
leaves, paid, 187–189
legal compliance in Compensation and Benefits area,
    192–194
legal insurance, 191–192
legal issues
    background checks, 108
    job analysis, 82
    medical examinations, 109
leniency errors in appraisals, 226
Lewin, Kurt, 145
Lewin's change management model, 145–146
life insurance benefits, 185–186
Light Duty Assignments in FMLA, 56
Lilly Ledbetter Fair Pay Act, 51
Lincoln Law, 60
LinkedIn for external recruitment, 91
listening technique in interviews, 104
LMRA (Labor-Management Relations Act), 28
long-term care (LTC) insurance, 186
long-term disability (LTD) benefits, 185
longevity in diversity and inclusion programs, 222
loss prevention, 269
LTC (long-term care) insurance, 186
LTD (long-term disability) benefits, 185

M

M&As (mergers and acquisitions), 264–265
male vs. female harassment, 232
managed healthcare plans, 181
managed service providers (MSPs), 87
management involvement in diversity and
    inclusion programs, 222
managers, visas for, 63
marketing in external recruitment, 90
marketplace plans in ACA, 180
matrix organizational structure, 209
McKinsey 7-S model, 146
McNamara-O'Hara Service Contract Act, 38
measurements for diversity, 222
mediation for labor unions, 260
medical care in IIPPs, 263
Medical Certification Process in FMLA, 56
medical examinations
    talent acquisition, 108–109
    workers' compensation, 271–272

Medicare benefits, 178
memoranda of understandings (MOUs), 258
Mental Health Parity Act (MHPA), 56
Mental Health Parity and Addiction Equity Act
    (MHPAEA), 56
mentor pairings in onboarding, 111
mergers and acquisitions (M&As), 264–265
Merit Guidelines, 170
merit pay systems, 170
Merit Systems Protection Board (MSPB), 59
MHPA (Mental Health Parity Act), 56
MHPAEA (Mental Health Parity and
    Addiction Equity Act), 56
Military Caregiver Leave in FMLA, 55
Miller, George A., 129
Mine Safety and Health Act, 29
minimum wage in FLSA, 157
mission
    communicating, 289–290
    organizational strategy, 206
mitigating circumstances in ADA, 45
modified-duty assignments, 271
monitoring
    health and safety, 263
    performance reviews and development plans,
        303–304
MOUs (memoranda of understandings), 258
MSPB (Merit Systems Protection Board), 59
MSPs (managed service providers), 87

N

narrative appraisal methods, 225–226
National Commission for Certifying Agencies
    (NCCA), 4
National Defense Authorization Act, 56
National Guard and Military Reserve Family
    Leave in FMLA, 55
National Industrial Recovery Act, 30
National Institute of Occupational Safety and Health
    (NIOSH), 31
National Labor Relations Act (NLRA; Wagner Act), 30
National Labor Relations Board (NLRB), 256–257, 259
National Mediation Board, 35
national origin harassment, 232
NCCA (National Commission for Certifying Agencies), 4
NDAs (non-disclosure agreements)
    onboarding, 109
    policies, 212
Needlestick Safety and Prevention Act, 30–31
needs analysis in ADDIE model, 127
negative emphasis as interviewing bias, 105
NIOSH (National Institute of Occupational Safety and
    Health), 31
NLRA (National Labor Relations Act), 30
NLRA (Norris-LaGuardia Act), 31
NLRB (National Labor Relations Board), 256–257, 259
non-disclosure agreements (NDAs)
    onboarding, 109
    policies, 212

nondirective interviews, 102
nonqualified retirement plans, 187
nonquantitative job evaluation methods, 161
nontaxable benefits legal issues, 192–193
nonverbal behavior in interviews, 104
nonverbal interviewing bias, 105
normal standards in OSHA, 33–34
Norris-LaGuardia Act (NLRA), 31
note-taking in interviews, 104

O

O-1 visas, 63
Obamacare
    description, 57
    eligibility, 179
    marketplace plans, 180
    provisions, 158
objectives in organizational strategy, 206
OBRA (Omnibus Budget Reconciliation Act), 34
observations in training program evaluation, 139
Occupational Safety and Health Act (OSHA), 31
    compliance, 272–274
    enforcement, 33
    provisions and protections, 31–32
    recordkeeping requirements, 32
    standards, 33–34
off-boarding, 240–241
Office of Federal Contract Compliance Programs
    (OFCCP)
    affirmative action, 55
    drug-free workplace, 50
    job analysis, 83
    self-identification, 100
Office of Personnel Management (OPM), 59
offshoring, 264–265
Older Workers Benefit Protection Act (OWBPA), 54
Omnibus Budget Reconciliation Act (OBRA), 34
on-call pay, 173
on-site visits by OSHA, 33
on-the-job training (OJT), 135–136
onboarding, 109
    administrative paperwork, 109–111
    conducting, 300–301
    for retention, 111
online content, 345–347
online records for résumés and job applications, 99
open houses for external recruitment, 94
OPM (Office of Personnel Management), 59
organization-based pay, 174
organization core values, communicating, 289–290
organizational communication, 209–210
organizational strategy, 206–211
organizational structure, 208–209
organizational values in training and development, 123
organizations for the disabled for external recruitment, 92
orientation
    conducting, 300–301
    expectations in, 124–125
    onboarding, 111

OSHA. *See* Occupational Safety and Health Act (OSHA)
outside investigators for complaints and grievances, 234–235
outsourcing, 87
overtime pay
    description, 172
    FLSA, 26, 157
OWBPA (Older Workers Benefit Protection Act), 54

P

P visas, 63
paid holidays, 188
paid leaves, 187–189
paid sick leave for federal contractors, 57
paid time off (PTO), 188
paid volunteer time, 190
panel interviews, 103
paper surveys, 217
part-time employees, 85
participant surveys for training program evaluation, 138
parties, company, 215
passwords, 270
Patient Protection and Affordable Care Act (PPACA)
    description, 57
    eligibility, 179
    marketplace plans, 180
    provisions, 158
patterned interviews, 102
pay-for-performance (PFP) plans, 174
pay grades and ranges, 166–168
pay stubs, 176
payroll
    administration, 175
    off-boarding, 240–241
    overview, 174–175
    systems, 176
    wage statements, 176
payroll-related information, coordinating, 299–300
PCAOB (Public Company Accounting Oversight Board), 37
peer-to-peer awards, 214
penalties in Civil Rights Act, 48–49
Pension Protection Act (PPA), 34
PEOs (professional employer organizations), 87
performance-based merit pay systems, 170
performance improvement plans (PIPs), 227
performance management
    appraisal methods, 223–227
    category ratings, 224–225
    overview, 222–223
    standards, 223
performance reviews, monitoring, 303–304
performance tests for training program evaluation, 138
person-based pay systems, 171
personal conflicts, 230
personal days, 189
personal information in onboarding, 109
Personal Responsibility and Work Opportunity Reconciliation Act, 34

PFP (pay-for-performance) plans, 174
phased retirement, 86
PHR (Professional in Human Resources), 4–5
PHRca (Professional in Human Resources – California), 4, 6
PHRi (Professional in Human Resources – International), 4, 6–7
picnics, company, 215
PIPs (performance improvement plans), 227
plateau learning curves, 130–131
point-factor job evaluation method, 161, 163–164
point of service (POS) plans, 181–182
policies
    communicating, 288
    employee manuals, 211–213
    mergers and acquisitions, 265
    workers' compensation, 271–272
Portal-to-Portal Act, 35
POS (point of service) plans, 181–182
post-interview activities, 106
    background checks, 107–108
    job offers, 106
    medical examinations, 108–109
post-offer employment activities, 298
post-testing for training program evaluation, 138
posting job listings, 293
PPA (Pension Protection Act), 34
PPACA. *See* Patient Protection and Affordable Care Act (PPACA)
PPO (Preferred Provider Organization) plans, 181
pre-employment skill testing, 101
pre-testing for training program evaluation, 138
Preferred Provider Organization (PPO) plans, 181
Pregnancy Discrimination Act, 52
prepaid legal insurance, 191–192
prescreening interviews, 102
prescription drug plans, 183
prevention and wellness programs, 184
pricing and pay rates
    overview, 165
    pay grades and ranges, 166–168
    variations, 168
primacy errors in appraisals, 226
Privacy Act, 60–61
privacy issues
    background checks, 108
    credit, 23
    ECPA, 21
    health, 27, 53
    medical examinations, 109
    Privacy Act, 60–61
procedures, communicating, 288
productivity-based pay systems, 170–171
professional associations for external recruitment, 93
professional certifications, 3
professional employer organizations (PEOs), 87
Professional in Human Resources (PHR), 4–5
Professional in Human Resources – California (PHRca), 4, 6

Professional in Human Resources – International (PHRi), 4, 6–7
profile job evaluation method, 164–165
profit-sharing plans, 174
progressive discipline, 235
    documenting, 237–238
    escalating, 238–239
    policies, 213
    steps, 236–237
    terminations, 239–240
project hires, 86
proof of identity, 110
proof of work authorization, 110
Public Company Accounting Oversight Board (PCAOB), 37
Public Contracts Act (Walsh-Healey Act), 42
public employment services for external recruitment, 92
public records for background checks, 107
punitive damage penalties in Civil Rights Act, 49

Q

qualifying events for healthcare benefits, 180
quality of hire metric, 112
quantitative job evaluation methods, 161
questionnaires for training program evaluation, 138
questions
    from employees, 287
    interviewing bias, 105

R

race in self-identification, 99–100
racial harassment, 232
Railway Labor Act, 35
ranges, pay, 166–168
ranking method in job evaluations, 161–162
rapport in interviews, 104
REA (Retirement Equity Act), 36
realism in interviews, 104
reasonable accommodation in workers' compensation, 271
recency errors in appraisals, 226
recertification process, 7–9
recognition programs, 190, 213–214
recordkeeping requirements
    ADA, 47
    Drug-Free Workplace Act, 50
    FLSA, 24–26, 157
    Mine Safety and Health Act, 29
    OSHA, 32
    SOX, 37
records retention requirements, 95–97
red circle rates, 168
references for background checks, 107
referrals
    external recruitment, 92
    OSHA reports, 33
regular rate of pay, 172
Rehabilitation Act, 35, 44
rehires, 88

relationships in training and development, 124–125
religious harassment, 232
relocation assistance, 192
reporting
    OSHA compliance, 272–274
    training program evaluation, 140
    workers' compensation requirements, 270
reporting time pay, 172
resignations, 239
resources for additional study, 341–343
restructuring workforces, 264–267
résumé mining for external recruitment, 91
résumés vs. job applications, 97–99
retention
    onboarding for, 111
    stay interviews, 217
    talent sourcing metric, 112
retiree annuitants, 86
retirement
    phased, 86
    terminations, 240
Retirement Equity Act (REA), 36
retirement plans, 186–187
return on investment (ROI)
    talent sourcing, 112–113
    training program evaluation, 139–140
return-to-work policies for workers' compensation, 271–272
Revenue Act, 36
rights and responsibilities, 205–206
risk mitigation, 260
    audits for, 291–292
    business continuity, 264
    emergencies, 264
    health and safety monitoring, 263
    IIPPs, 260–263
    risk identification, 290–291
    security, 267–270
    workforce restructuring, 264–267
ROI (return on investment)
    talent sourcing, 112–113
    training program evaluation, 139–140

S

S-shaped learning curves, 130–131
sabbaticals, 188–189
safety and security
    monitoring, 263
    policies, 213
safety equipment item in onboarding, 111
safety inspections
    forms, 261–262
    workplace, 263, 272
sales achievement awards, 214
Sarbanes-Oxley Act (SOX), 36
    enforcement, 37
    provisions and protections, 36–37
    recordkeeping requirements, 37

SARs (summary annual reports), 193
schedules
    employee handbooks, 212
    time-based step rate pay systems, 169
secrecy for total rewards programs, 160
Securities and Exchange Act, 37
security policies, 213
security risk, 267
    data security, 267–268
    equipment damage, 269
    equipment security, 268
    inventory and supply security, 268
    passwords, 270
    terrorism, 270
    theft prevention, 269
self-assessment appraisal methods, 226
self-identification, 99–101
Senior Professional in Human Resources (SPHR), 4–5
Senior Professional in Human
    Resources – International (SPHRi), 4, 7
service anniversary awards, 214
Service Contract Act, 38
severance packages, 189
sex in self-identification, 99–100
sexual harassment, 231
sharps, 30–31
Sherman Anti-Trust Act, 38
shift pay, 172
SHOP (Small Business Health Options Program), 57
shoplifting, 269
short-term disability (STD) benefits, 185
SHRM (Society for Human Resource Management),
    4, 8–9
SHRM Certified Professional (SHRM-CP), 8
SHRM-CP (SHRM Certified Professional), 8
SHRM-SCP (SHRM Senior Certified Professional)
    certifications, 8–9
SIC (Standard Industrial Classification) Code, 32
sick leave, 188
similar-to-me interviewing bias, 105
simulations for training program evaluation, 139
single-rate pay systems, 169
situational interviews, 103
skilled workers, visas for, 64
skills
    databases, 88–89
    on-the-job training, 135
    pre-employment testing, 101
skills-based learning, 125–126
skills-based pay systems, 171
Small Business Health Options Program (SHOP), 57
Small Business Job Protection Act, 38–39
SMART outline for learning objectives, 125–126
SMMs (summary of material modifications), 193
social media
    background checks, 108
    external recruitment, 91
social responsibility in diversity and inclusion programs,
    219–220

Social Security Act
    description, 39
    provisions, 158
Social Security benefits, 177–178
Society for Human Resource Management (SHRM),
    4, 8–9
SOX (Sarbanes-Oxley Act), 36
    enforcement, 37
    provisions and protections, 36–37
    recordkeeping requirements, 37
SPDs (summary plan descriptions), 193
special demands in job descriptions, 84
special events, 215–216
special occupations, visas for, 62
SPHR (Senior Professional in Human Resources), 4–5
SPHRi (Senior Professional in Human
    Resources – International), 4, 7
staffing needs, forecasting, 81–82
Standard Industrial Classification (SIC) Code, 32
standards
    OSHA, 33–34
    performance management, 223
standards of conduct, 212
state employment services for external recruitment, 92
state laws. See U.S. laws and regulations
stay interviews, 217
STD (short-term disability) benefits, 185
step rate with performance considerations
    pay systems, 169
stereotypes
    interviewing bias, 105
    unconscious, 219
straight piece-rate pay system, 171
strategic planning, 206–207
stress interviews, 102–103
strictness errors in appraisals, 226
structure, organizational, 208–209
structured interviews, 102
SUBs (supplemental unemployment benefits), 187
succession planning, 141–142
suggestion awards, 214
summary annual reports (SARs), 193
summary objective of the job in job descriptions, 84
summary of material modifications (SMMs), 193
summary plan descriptions (SPDs), 193
summative evaluation in ADDIE model, 128
supervisors
    onboarding introductions, 111
    in orientation, 125
    termination documentation, 241
supplemental benefits, 190–192
supplemental unemployment benefits (SUBs), 187
suppliers for external recruitment, 93
supply security, 268
surveys
    employee, 216–218
    training program evaluation, 138
suspensions in progressive discipline, 236–237
SWOT analysis, 206–207

T

Taft-Hartley Act, 28
Talent Acquisition functional area
    aPHR exam weights, 11–12
    case laws, 329–331
    knowledge, 79–80
    laws and regulations, 80–81
    overview, 79
    talent sourcing. *See* talent sourcing
    workforce planning, 81–88
talent sourcing
    applicant databases, 94–95
    endnotes, 119–120
    external recruitment, 89–90
    internal recruitment, 88–89
    interviewing techniques, 101–106
    onboarding, 109–111
    post-interview activities, 106–109
    pre-employment skill testing, 101
    questions, 113–119
    records retention, 95–97
    résumés vs. job applications, 97–99
    return on investment, 112–113
    review, 113
    self-identification, 99–101
Tax Reform Act, 39–40
taxable benefits legal issues, 192–193
Taxpayer Relief Act, 40
teacher-centered approaches to learning, 128
team achievement awards, 214
team incentives, 173
team interviews, 103
temp-to-lease programs, 87–88
temporary employees, 85
temporary workers, visas for, 62
terminations
    involuntary, 240
    progressive discipline, 237
    voluntary, 239–240
terrorism, 270
tests and testing
    applicants, 296–297
    drug, 108
    pre-employment skills, 101
    training program evaluation, 138
theft prevention, 269
360-degree appraisals for training program evaluation, 139
360/180 degree surveys, 216–217
time-based step rate pay systems, 169
time to fill metric in talent sourcing, 112
total rewards programs, 159–160
total rewards statements, 194
Total Seminars Training Hub, 345
TotalTester Online, 347
tour of employee common areas in onboarding, 111
tracking in training program evaluation, 140
trade associations for external recruitment, 93

Trademark Act
    description, 40
    Learning and Development area, 122
traders, visas for, 61
traditional media for external recruitment, 90–91
trained compliance officers for OSHA, 33
trainees, visas for, 63
training and development
    conducting, 302
    coordinating, 301
    delivery format, 131–136
    instructional design, 125–131
    organizational values, 123
    orientation expectations, 124
    overview, 123
    program evaluation, 136–140
training delivery format
    classrooms, 132–133
    considerations, 131–132
    e-learning, 133–135
    on-the-job training, 135–136
transfers, 88
transgender harassment, 231–232
transparency in total rewards programs, 160
travel stipends, 192
treaty investors, visas for, 62
treaty traders, visas for, 61
tuition reimbursement, 190
turnover cost metric, 112
turnover rates in diversity and inclusion programs, 222

U

U.S. laws and regulations
    Compensation and Benefits area, 156–158
    compliance, 284
    Compliance and Risk Management area, 252–255
    Employee Relations area, 204–205
    employment visas for foreign nationals, 61–64
    endnotes, 75–76
    federal government employees, 59–61
    fifteen or more employees, 44–52
    fifty or more employees, 54–57
    Learning and Development area, 122
    minimum wage, 157
    one hundred or more employees, 57–58
    one or more employees, 19–44
    overview, 19
    questions, 65–74
    review, 64–65
    Talent Acquisition area, 80–81
    twenty or more employees, 52–54
U.S. Patent Act, 122
unconscious biases and stereotypes, 219
Unemployment Compensation Amendments (UCA), 40
unemployment insurance, 178

unfair labor practices, 258–259
Uniform Electronic Transactions Act, 99
Uniform Guidelines on Employee Selection Procedures
    description, 52
    Learning and Development area, 122
Uniformed Services Employment and Reemployment
   Rights Act (USERRA)
    description, 40–41
    Learning and Development area, 122
    provisions, 158
unions. *See* labor unions
universities, corporate, 133
university recruiting, 93
unusual circumstances in progressive discipline, 239
updating job functions, 292–293
USA PATRIOT Act, 61
USERRA (Uniformed Services Employment and
   Reemployment Rights Act)
    description, 40–41
    Learning and Development area, 122
    provisions, 158

V

vacation pay, 188
values in organizational strategy, 206
vendors for external recruitment, 93
verbal warnings in progressive discipline, 236
vested defined contribution plan contributions, 187
veteran status
    harassment, 233
    self-identification, 100–101
veterans' organizations for external recruitment, 92
Vietnam Era Veterans Readjustment Assistance Act, 41
violations of workplace standards, 228
violence, workplace, 263
virtual classrooms, 133
visas, 61–64
vision
    communicating, 289–290
    organizational strategy, 206
vision care plans, 184
voluntary terminations, 239–240
volunteer time, paid, 190

W

wage statements, 176
Wagner Act, 30
Wagner-Peyser Act, 41–42
walk-ins for external recruitment, 94
Walsh-Healey Act (Public Contracts Act), 42

WARN (Worker Adjustment and
   Retraining Notification) Act
    description, 57–58
    downsizing, 266
    terminations, 241
warnings in progressive discipline, 236
weekend pay, 173
welcoming step in onboarding, 111
whistleblower laws, 43–44
whole-job comparisons for job evaluations, 161–162
work assignment conflicts, 230
work/life balance, 214–215
Work Opportunity Tax Credit (WOTC), 42–43
work schedule policies, 212
Worker Adjustment and Retraining Notification
   (WARN) Act
    description, 57–58
    downsizing, 266
    terminations, 241
workers' compensation
    compliance, 270–272
    description, 178
    policies, 212
Workforce Innovation and Opportunity Act, 41–42
Workforce Investment Act, 42
workforce planning, 81
    alternative staffing practices, 85–86
    contractor payrolling, 87
    employee leasing and professional employer
      organizations, 87
    job analysis, 82–83
    job descriptions and job specifications, 83–84
    outsourcing and managed service providers, 87
    phased retirement, 86
    rehires and transfers, 88
    staffing needs forecasts, 81–82
    temp-to-lease programs, 87–88
workforce representation in diversity and
   inclusion programs, 222
workforce restructuring, 264–267
workplace amenities, 190
workplace behavior, 227
    attendance and absenteeism, 227–228
    code of conduct violations, 228–230
    employee conflicts, 230
    workplace harassment, 230–233
workplace harassment, 230–233
workplace safety inspections, 272
workplace violence, 263
WOTC (Work Opportunity Tax Credit), 42–43
written complaints, 234
written warnings in progressive discipline, 236